GARDENING AND HOME LANDSCAPING

GARDENING AND HOME LANDSCAPING

A Complete Illustrated Guide

by Jack Kramer

1817

HARPER & ROW, PUBLISHERS

New York, Evanston, San Francisco, London

Chapters 11, 12, 13, 18, 19 and 20 have appeared in different form in *The Complete Book of Patio Gardening* (G. P. Putnam & Sons) and *Container Gardening, Indoors and Out* (Doubleday & Co.), both by Jack Kramer.

Contents

Tables

Acknowledgments

Gardening books are never the product of an author's sole efforts; there are always nurseries, mail-order suppliers, product manfacturers and horticulturists, and many times the guy-next-door, who give freely of their time and information about gardening and garden products. To these people grateful acknowledgment is made for their assistance.

George Ball Seed Company
George W. Park Seed Company
Burpee Seed Company
Pan American Seed Company
Wayside Gardens
Merry Gardens Nursery
Armstrong Nurseries
Star Roses
Northrup King and Company
True Temper
Kemp Shredder Company
Pennsylvania Lawn Products
American Plywood Association
National Concrete Masonry Association
Buckingham Virginia Slate Company
Pella Wood Products
Westinghouse Electric Company
General Electric Company
California Redwood Association
Architectural Pottery Company
Aluminum Greenhouses of Cleveland, Ohio

Plasto Pool Incorporated
Featherock Incorporated
Tube Craft Incorporated
Tile Council of America
California Association of Nurserymen
Potted Plant Information Center
Window Shade Association
United States Department of Agriculture
Lee L. Woodward Furniture Company
Brown Jordan Furniture Company
Molla Furniture Company
Eldon Danhausen, Sculpture
Theodore Brickman, Landscape Architect
Phil Hutchison, Horticulturist
California Tomorrow

I also wish to thank Roger Scharmer, Landscape Architect, and Andrew Roy Addkison, Environmental Designer, for their help with the landscape and design sections of this book.

Special gratitude goes to my artists: Adrián Martínez, who labored many weekends to produce the fine how-to drawings, and Charles Hoeppner, whose lovely botanical drawings are included in this volume. Also my sincere thanks to Lolita Werner for reading and rereading the manuscript and for her suggestions; and, finally, thanks to Marion Kelley, my typist, who always happily put up with my endless revisions.

Introduction

The purpose of this book is to actually show and tell you how to create a beautiful garden and outdoor area, starting with the bare site to the finished picture. We have included suggestions for planning, layout, and design of your place to get you started, and information on the basic things we believe extremely important, such as climate and plants, tools and conveniences, and the physiology of the plants themselves, so that you will understand why you are doing what you are doing. The essentials of the garden setting—vital to the whole composition—are fully covered: patios and terraces; fences and screens; overhangs and canopies; pools and fountains; garden structures, sculpture, and furniture; lighting; and swimming pools. Many construction drawings show you how these things really work.

We have concentrated on lawns and ground covers, trees and shrubs, annuals and perennials and bulbs, for *these are the garden*. And we have shown you how to protect your plants from pests and diseases. There is a chapter on vegetables, fruits, and herbs for those with special tastes, and a chapter on special gardens for those with a favorite flower. For the city gardener, we have tried to include information on rooftop and penthouse greeneries, doorway gardens and container gardens, and, finally, there are chapters on greenhouse growing and a special list of over one hundred indoor plants.

We have employed no hocus-pocus, no absolute do's and don'ts in our landscaping details and plant-and-planting instructions. We have provided numerous line drawings to guide you every step of the way, clear, concise exposition to inform you, and lovely photographs to keep the ultimate dream in mind.

This, we hope, is a total guide for gardeners just getting their outdoor settings started, or for those with a garden who want to keep it handsome. We hope this book is all you will need in your hand to acquire the proverbial green thumb and to preserve and enjoy natural beauty in a small piece of land of your own.

JACK KRAMER

GARDENING AND HOME LANDSCAPING

CHAPTER 1

Design of the Garden

A garden is a piece of nature, refined, cultivated, and put to its owner's use. Although a garden can be many things, there are basic principles that underlie all garden planning. Following these principles will bring about a high standard of design than relying on personal tastes.

To some people a garden is a place for beauty and relaxation, to others it is a colorful show of flowers that change with the seasons, and to still other homeowners, a garden should be a living green frame that suits the architecture of the house. In some cases, it is a combination of all these things, not easily attained but certainly worth striving for. The garden can be formal or informal in character with variations on these themes.

Whatever theme your garden takes depends on many things: (1) natural conditions like the site, trees, and shrubs, existing boundaries, (2) man-made projects such as fences, screens, terraces, and paths, and (3) fixed conditions such as climate and soil. To a degree we can manipulate the site to our own desires and we can select appropriate plant material and even, if necessary, alter the boundaries. We can also build the structures and terraces necessary. But we cannot control the climate—rainfall and temperature.

Today, a successful garden plan unifies the house and grounds into an attractive picture and at the same time provides important additional living space. Strive for a uniform and harmonious scene—house, garden, pavings, natural background and plant material. Each element depends on the other. Proportion, unity, scale, line, and form are all involved, and are discussed later.

No matter what the site is—level, upslope, or downslope—creating its design results from an arrangement of forms and objects into a harmonious composition. The plan evolves from the imagination of the designer to the practical solution to the problem, using the landscape advantageously.

The most interesting and practical plan is if the garden can become an outgrowth of natural conditions. As the organic house that seems to spring from the ground and "belong" is successful, so is the garden plan that takes advantage of natural conditions and becomes part of the total setting. A garden out of place with its background is difficult to care for and requires constant attention.

AN OVERALL PLAN

Creating your own plan is an exciting challenge. It is fashioning a workable and æsthetically pleasing setting for you and your family. The arrangement you select, the plants you put into the ground, the entire picture is your very own. But unlike pictures on walls and furniture in a room this plan has the advantage of changing with the seasons and of growing into a lasting piece of nature. It is a little like playing God. Indeed, you do have to work with the elements of nature to achieve your goal. This can be a completely satisfying experience.

If you have a large place you might want to consult a landscape architect. He will ask you all the right questions and develop an overall plan for you, possibly a three- to five-year project. If you do not want professional help, you can meet with a garden consultant or landscape man at your local nursery. Whether you develop your own plan or have help, the ultimate arrangement of the landscape is your own. It must be because it works for you and your family and your family's needs.

Landscaping your property is not something to do in a month or even a year. It takes several years to achieve the desired setting. And, too, there will be changes along the way. Do not rush. Take your time; start right.

TYPES OF GARDENS

Gardens are universal. Man has through the centuries continually tried to beautify his surroundings. The Hanging Gardens of Babylon flourished around 600 B.C. The Persians and Egyptians had houses built around open courtyards, and the Greeks combined magnificent architecture with intensive landscape design. There were flower beds, pools, stately trees, and even pot plants; and symmetry was the keynote. The Romans, who followed the Greeks, were skillful gardeners too. And the garden pavilions of Rome are still known today. Even in the Dark Ages, gardens persisted.

But it was in the great villas and palaces of Italy and France and the country manors of England that gardening and landscaping blossomed. These were vast formal gardens, symmetrical in design and utterly beautiful—but totally impractical. It was left to the British to restyle and produce the more natural garden. Formality was over, houses were smaller, grounds were smaller, and a new type of garden design was initiated.

In early America, the garden was considered a place to grow flowers, nothing more. Now it is a way of life—the extra living space. Today, the average property is even smaller than it was ten years ago, and housing complexes, although never totally neglecting the outdoor living idea, have reduced (because of land costs) the garden to a small area.

The contemporary garden demands something different from what we have known in the past. New structural materials, synthetic materials, new plants and new ways of growing them make today's gardening an exciting adventure.

Gardens have a particular feeling or style about them. You have probably noticed that they tend to follow a theme because it is easier to achieve a pleasant picture when we have a specific idea in mind. Some people admire the stark beauty of the Oriental garden with sand and stone and a few plants. Other homeowners are enthralled with the formal garden of past eras, while still other people prefer the natural or informal kind of garden plan.

The formal and the informal garden have been with us for many years and while neither one can be accomplished in an average lot, they offer us a starting place. The fallacy of the formal garden lies in the vast areas needed for it—no longer possible now. In the formal arrangement there is a strong separation like a line cutting the middle of the design. One side mirrors the scene on the other side. This creates symmetry. Generally, the garden becomes a geometrical pattern, and as such can be pleasing when it suits the

house. But one needs a broad canvas to paint the formal plan.

The informal landscape is an easier arrangement for the small lot, but it, too, has fallacies. It assumes that old trees and shrubs are there. Often they are not. The informal or natural theme depends on asymmetrical balance. There are no pairs of trees, no straight lines or borders; it is a continuous flow of plant material.

The majority of today's garden plans take a little from each scheme—some formal ideas, other informal qualities. Climate too plays a part in what kind of landscape to select. And of course, the nature of the site must be considered.

THE SITE

The shape of your property dictates what kind of landscape plan to have. There are advantages and disadvantages to every piece of land, and knowing something about these limitations before you start helps to determine an intelligent plan.

Long, narrow lot. At first glance this may seem like a limited area for a successful plan. But on the contrary, it has advantages because it is easily sectioned into individual areas. Each part of the plan can be pulled together to form a harmonious landscape. Geometrical shapes work well for this type of lot, and a charming plan can be created. Avoid very large trees and shrubs and masses of flowers.

Rectangular lot. This is a common type of lot and one of the easiest to work with. Generally, intelligent screening (fences and hedges) is necessary to achieve a private setting. Because the space is somewhat confining and monotonous, plan areas with paving and stepping-stones to give line and form. Use bushy plants to give mass and grace to the area.

Wedge-shaped lot. If the narrow end is toward the street, this is a desirable situation because it leaves most of the property behind the house where all kinds of garden structures can be set up. This site allows a large varied garden plan of many interests.

Corner lot. These are considered choice sites, and yet they present a difficult landscaping challenge. Both the side and the front are open to the public, and private space is lost. Here, court entries and interesting galleries can be used to compensate for lost space.

LAYING OUT THE GARDEN

Laying out the garden involves shapes and dimensions of the house and site, the functions and uses desired by the owners, and the plants and structural materials to be used. A lot is a given space that will consist of several small spaces separated and yet

This house is intelligently landscaped; space, house, and plantings are
well coordinated to create a pleasing picture that is a total scene.
(Molly Adams)

Here, a hilly site was used for a luxuriant carpet of grass, certainly
a pleasant sight to welcome a guest.
(Molly Adams)

The frame for this simple house
is a lovely garden and lawn area,
completely in keeping with the
character of the house.
(Molly Adams)

joined by walks and paths. Divide the lot into individual areas for easy planning.

Generally, there is the approach to the house or public area; it is here the guest receives the first impression of what is to come. There is an outdoor living area which generally includes a patio, perhaps a barbecue or a swimming pool. Even where summers are short, paved areas are vital. This is where most of the family will spend most of its time. Plan it carefully so that it will be convenient for cooking or cocktails, sitting or walking. Allow a functional service area to make things convenient for you. Consider that there will be garbage cans, places for cars, driveways, and easy access to the house for hauling groceries. The fourth area is the play space for children or an area for adult games.

First, whether this is a new plan for a bare site or for an old house and garden, consider which way the land faces. Get directions in mind and remember exposures. In southern states the sun will strike the garden differently from the way it will in northern latitudes.

Observe where the boundaries are; you want to use as much of the property as possible. Visualize where the walls, fences, and hedges will be. Inspect the soil. Take advantage of what natural conditions are offered such as a rolling hill, a backdrop of stately trees or, on the other hand, a close-by neighbor or an unsightly view that will have to be screened. Note existing trees and shrubs; decide whether they will stay.

If it is a new house, leave access somewhere in the rear or at the sides for trucks to deliver lumber and soil, necessary landscaping materials. All deliveries today are tailgate (left at your door), and hauling material from the front of the house to the garden takes time, labor, and money.

Try to develop the landscape plan in a style to harmonize with the architecture of the house. The Colonial house needs a somewhat formal design; the Cape Cod cottage needs intimacy and charm; and the contemporary house—sometimes somewhat sterile—dictates a natural garden. The Georgian house requires more symmetrical planning, whereas the ranch-type home is perhaps best landscaped with a combination of informal and formal designs.

When you start to lay out the garden consider all aspects of the situation before you start. Use your feet as well as your head. Walk the property several times; look at the house from the grounds, and then view the property from the inside of the house.

HOW TO PLAN ON PAPER

Planning on paper may seem silly at first, but it is much easier to erase a pencil mark than to pull out a fence or demolish a tree. Planning on paper is basically putting mass and form, line and volume to work. You are deciding between asymmetrical and symmetrical balance.

A general ground plan for the property does not have to be drawn to scale. It can be a sketch. Try to obtain a plot plan showing the dimensions of the site. Your builder can give you one. Using this as a guide, transpose the location of the house and the boundary lines onto graph paper. Let each square represent one foot. Draw the outline of the house. Include steps, walks, and driveways. Show existing trees and shrubs.

Determine the ground slope; this can make a difference in a plan. Stretch a string crossways across the plot. Use a mason's level on the string and measure the distance between the ground and the string to determine just how much of a grade there is. Note the high and low areas and how much the grade drops and mark it on the graph paper. Now put in designations to show where there is sun, shade, and the north point. Study the composition. If all existing features are present, you can start to plan the garden now.

Over the graph paper, lay a sheet of tracing paper. Keep a list of what you want in the garden and a list of space requirements—patio, play area, service area—close at hand. Sketch traffic patterns first on the tracing paper. Then draw rough sizes and shapes of objects you want outdoors such as terrace, garden beds, raised beds, new trees and shrubs, pools or fountains or barbecue built-ins, and whatever else is necessary to your overall plan. The irregular shapes you have drawn should start to relate to each other. If you are not pleased with the layout, start over again on a new piece of tracing paper. First arrangements are rarely satisfactory. Consider all things carefully and make several plans so that all members of the family have a chance to agree.

Once you have a rough sketch that is agreeable to all and solves most of the problems, a detailed design is necessary. Exactness counts now, so be sure to have proper measurements of the house and lot, objects, and existing plant material. This is the time to decide how much construction will be necessary in the garden—fences, terraces, pools, walls—and how much planting will be needed.

Here are some ideas to help you plan.

Rectangular or square patterns are simple and most natural to use. They are usually projections of the house form. Working with a uniform module (that is, a space repeated again and again) simplifies a plan. The module can be 3 by 4 feet or 5 by 5 feet, or almost any block size that fits your needs. The patio can be paved with 3 by 4 blocks, stepping-stones can be the same size, and planting islands and beds can also relate to the same module. In this way, every design line in the plan is in proportion and pleasing to the eye. There will be simplicity, and yet there will be concise organization of space.

Acute or obtuse angles or triangles reflect the angular form of the house and site and they lead the eye to a focal point and give a sense of space and direction.

Circular forms add interest to the pattern, and in proper balance with straight lines can give a pleasing composition.

Free curves are curving lines with a constantly changing radius. These are sweeping natural lines of nature and, skillfully used with geometric forms, produce richness in motion.

The simple basic forms we have mentioned are responsible for all linear patterns that develop in the garden. From these, any number of combinations of patterns can be drawn.

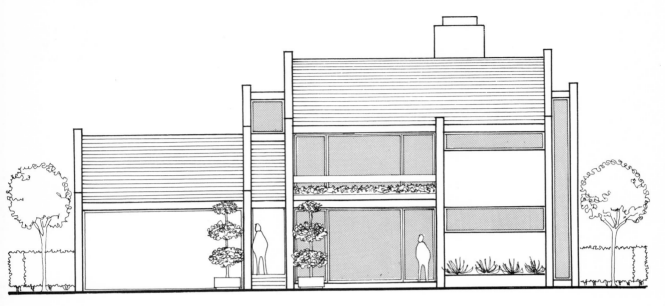

FORMAL

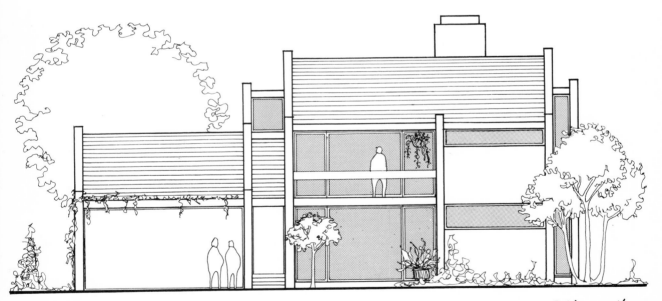

INFORMAL

design: adrián martínez

Formal & Informal Planting

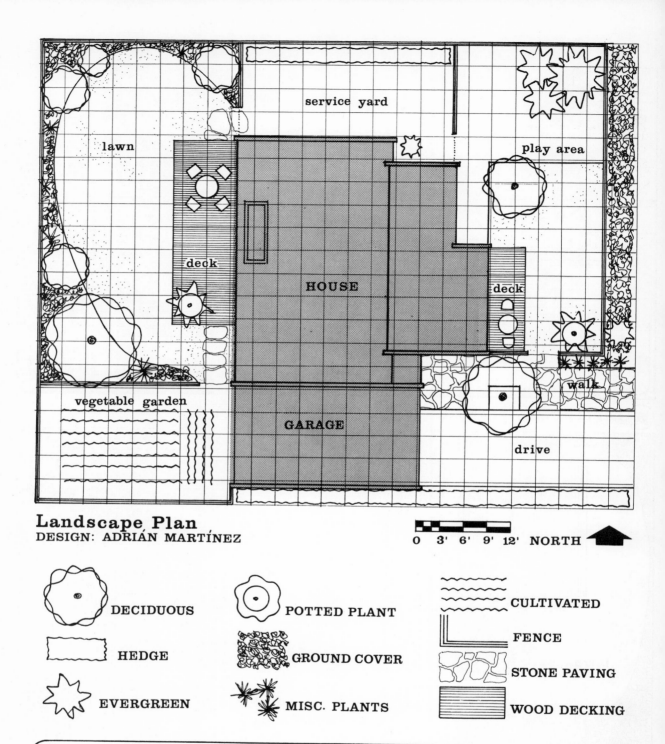

Landscape Plan
DESIGN: ADRIÁN MARTÍNEZ

0   3'   6'   9'   12'   NORTH

Labels within plan: service yard, lawn, play area, deck, HOUSE, deck, vegetable garden, GARAGE, walk, drive

⬭ DECIDUOUS   ⬭ POTTED PLANT   〜 CULTIVATED

▭ HEDGE   ▦ GROUND COVER   ⌐ FENCE

✳ EVERGREEN   ✲ MISC. PLANTS   ▱ STONE PAVING

▭ WOOD DECKING

Landscape Symbols

This plan shows the definition of separate areas—service area, play area, deck, lawn, vegetable garden. Yet each one ties into the other. There is harmony and scale. There is ample use of plants and yet plenty of paved area for outdoor uses.

Hedges and walks are well planned; the sweep of greenery around the lawn is a handsome border for privacy and visual appeal. A fence frames the property, although it is quite possible it would not be needed for the garden is obscured from view by the plantings on almost all sides.

The paved areas may be concrete block, brick, tile. Only the lawn is mandatory, as it is an essential balance for texture and color within the whole framework.

Plotted on graph paper with a three-foot scale, the plan also shows landscape symbols and how to use them to plot your property.

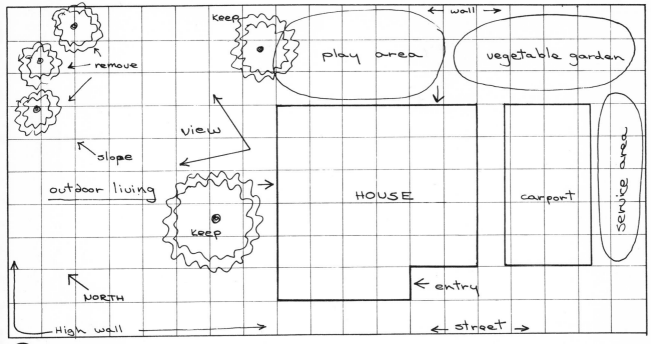

(a) PRELIMINARY PLAN site conditions, existing & proposed areas

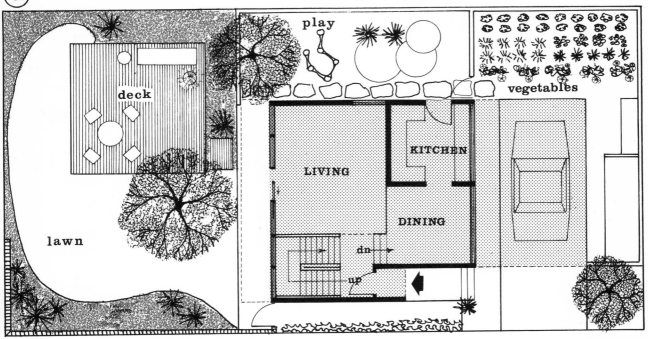

(b) FINISHED PLAN area development, planting

Making a Landscape Plan

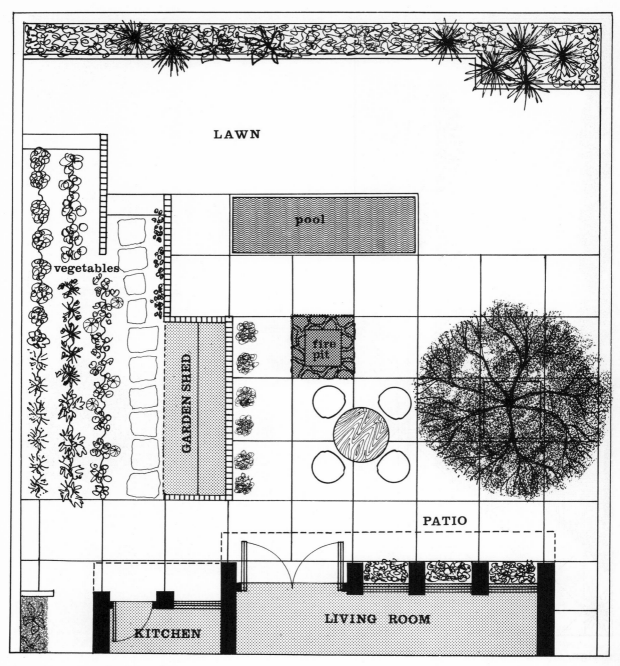

LAWN

pool

vegetables

GARDEN SHED

fire pit

PATIO

LIVING ROOM

KITCHEN

design: adrián martínez

Form in the Garden: Rectangular

Using a small lot, this rectangular plan offers a lot of usable area in a small space. There is a vegetable garden, a seating area, a fire pit, a garden shed, and a lovely lily pool. The patio of concrete blocks is indeed serviceable and convenient to the kitchen and living room.

Planting is kept to a minimum with only one large shade tree and planters at the rear of the property. The lush green lawn is a perfect foil for the concrete patio.

Random shaped stepping-stones give access to the vegetable garden and at the same time provide eye interest in an otherwise rectangular plan. The brick facing of the vegetable garden and along the shed repeats the rectangular design and adds a needed note of texture to the design.

Planter boxes at the living-room window walls balance the rear plantings. There is perfect scale and good proportion in this garden plan.

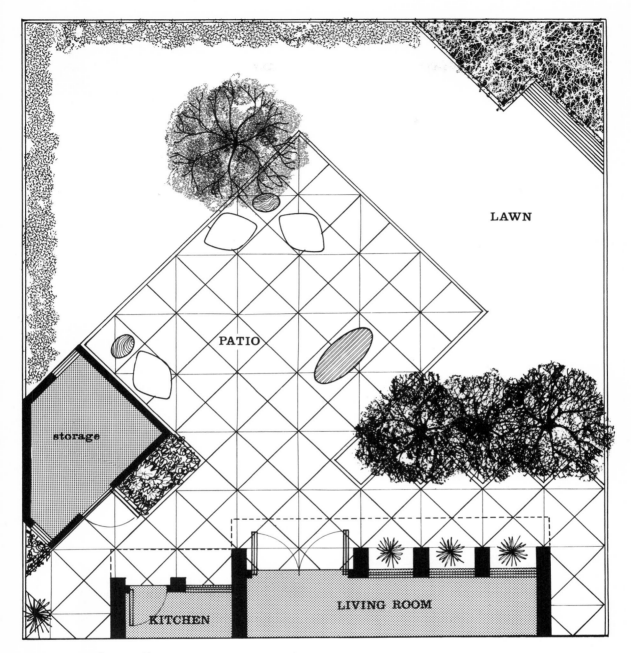

LAWN

PATIO

storage

KITCHEN

LIVING ROOM

design: adrián martínez

Form in the Garden : Triangular

This rectangular site employs triangular design to give it dimension and appeal. The patio is spacious and juts into the garden, its corner a design relief in the plan. The lawn envelops the patio on three sides and by design is never monotonous but rather almost an undulating sea of green around the patio area.

Planter boxes at the rear are angled as is the patio, and balance is achieved in the plan. Even the lawn design in the left rear is triangular, further enhancing the arrangement.

Four large trees are the dominant feature of the garden, one near the patio for shade, the others a necessary line of green bordering the patio. Planter boxes of greenery border the storage area to further soften the effect of the concrete expanse.

An uninteresting site has been made attractive by the use of triangular design throughout, and what could have been a mundane garden now holds infinite interest.

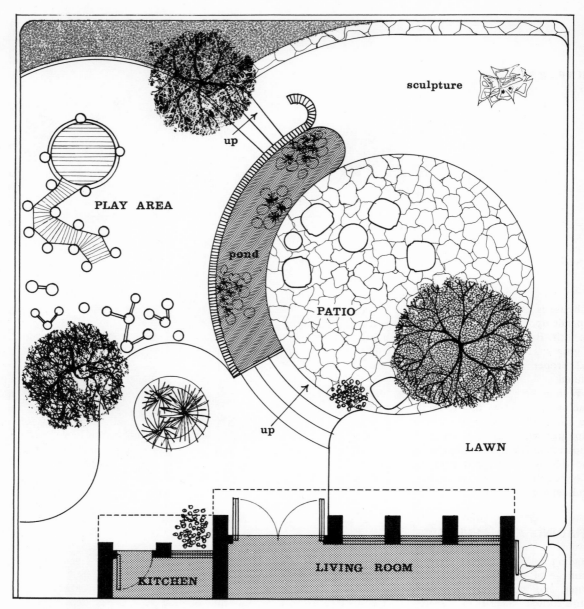

design: adrián martínez

Form in the Garden: Circular

This contemporary designed garden in circular form complements the steel-and-glass home. Within the garden plan there is infinite grace and rhythm; not a sharp line is present to disturb this fanciful arrangement. The areas are well defined—play area, lawn, sculpture area, patio, pool—and different levels provide constant eye interest.

The dominant patio area away from the house is flagstone shaded by a large tree and framed with a brick-walled lily pool. Flagstone is repeated in the wall at the rear of the property as a cohesive note to the design. A lawn frames the circular patio and each is an island in itself. Color, texture, and design have been well thought out here. The vertical sculpture in the right rear is a

necessary design element that complements the patio area. (A tree could be used in place of the sculpture.)

The sweeping patio area outside the kitchen is concrete and decorated with container plants. A children's play area far enough from the house not to be a bother and near enough for convenience occupies the other segment of this plan.

Note that the patio areas are handsomely separated by slightly curved concrete steps at each proper juncture between kitchen patio and center patio, play area and sculpture area. This is a multileveled outdoor area that affords interest and great appeal.

Planting was kept to a bare minimum—only three trees and a lawn—so maintenance is never a problem.

CHAPTER 2

Preparing the Property

A house is as good as its foundation. A garden too depends upon the soil. Every plant will live, grow, or die in it. But before the soil is brought in for plants to grow in, rough grading and leveling must be done and proper runoff of excess water must be considered.

With a new house, all too often, the subject of grading is forgotten in the excitement of furnishing the home. But now is the time to observe and determine just what has to be done to assure trouble-free landscaping. Many new homes have a naked feeling, and the owner is faced with compacted land from heavy equipment. The grounds are hardly ready for landscaping.

GRADING AND LEVELING

Grading is done to control erosion, to assure proper drainage of water, to make level areas for outdoor living, and to provide planting areas that will not cause trouble later. It may seem like a costly procedure, but it is absolutely necessary. Give grading careful consideration before anything else is done.

Many times when the contractor leaves the site, the subsoil is several inches below the house; this must be filled in so that the slope of the land will carry off excess water. Often, earth has been pushed against tree trunks, and it must be removed if you want the trees to live.

With most new homes the topsoil has been removed or pushed aside in a gigantic hill. If you had a considerate contractor who supervised his subcontractors (a rare occurrence), the moved topsoil will be left on the site. If the topsoil is gone, you will have to replenish it, an expensive undertaking. An average site of a half acre can require as much as 80 yards of topsoil.

However, before you do anything about topsoil, the lot must be graded and leveled. A large area will require the help of a rented bulldozer or front-end loader. On a level lot not much grading will be needed before you start unless there is to be a pool or a terrace. On a sloping or hillside lot, more grading is needed.

On a small lot, grading can be done with a rake and shovel. It is a time-consuming chore, but not impossible. Break up stones, remove all trash. Then smooth and level all mounds and hollows. Additional help may be needed if you are going to have a lawn. Here, a perfectly flat surface without interruption is the ideal terrain.

The rough grading refers to the moving and shaping of the contour of the lot. If the existing level is high, it must be sheared off; if it is low, it must be filled in. Once the fence is up and the shrubbery in place at the boundaries, it is impossible to get equipment in to grade the areas. Determine now where you want the terrace; decide now where a flat surface for a lawn is needed.

After grading, be sure that the subsoil or earth layer left by the contractor is not excessively hard. Modern earth-moving equipment is heavy and often compacts the soil and creates an impervious layer. Before spreading the topsoil, be sure the subsoil is rototilled or broken up so that both strata of soil will mingle to permit the free passage of air and water. Water travels both up and down in the soil.

Leveling is done when the grading is finished. It is the process of smoothing and leveling the ground so there are no hollows or hills.

When you buy a newly built home you are looking at a lot that is not ready for planting. But it is ready for planning, and now is the time to do it, provided you can afford it. You will never have a better chance.

If you buy an old house, grading, leveling, and drainage have withstood the test of time. You can assume that there will be no more investment aside from secondary projects. Perhaps you will have to

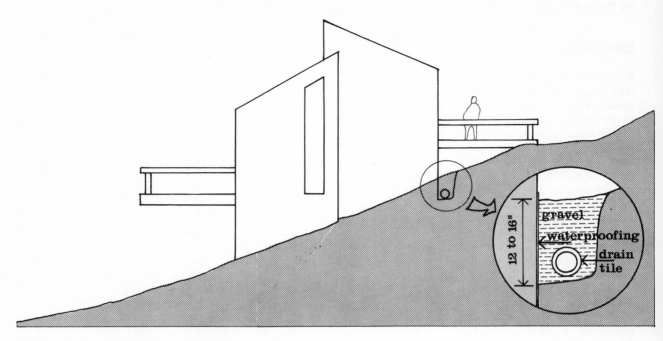

12 to 16"

gravel
waterproofing
drain
tile

SLOPE – drain around and away from the house

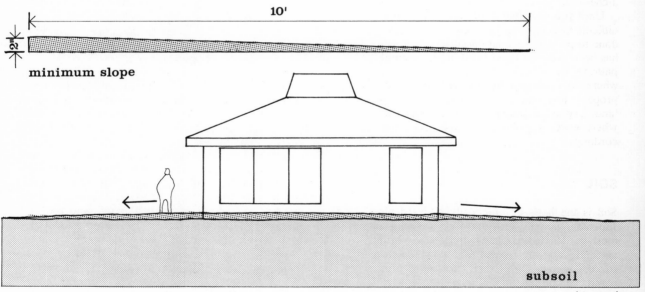

10'

2"

minimum slope

subsoil

ADRIÁN MARTÍNEZ

LEVEL – grade and slope away from the house

Drainage: Preparing for Planting

bring in some topsoil or make a few changes, but in cost it will be nothing like the investment in preparing the new lot for planting.

DRAINAGE

Rainwater must drain off your property. Hollows create bogs, and rises are unsightly. The land must be graded to slope away from the house to carry water to the nearest street, storm drain, or watercourse. The finished surface should be flat, without rises or hollows. Be sure the slope is in one direction, either toward the street or toward the rear. Where the water runoff is more than the ground can handle without causing erosion, ditches can be dug at the edge of the property in inconspicuous places to collect the water and channel it to a lower area where it can seep away.

Instead of a ditch, a line of drain tile may be used to carry water off the ground if your soil is extremely heavy. Drain tiles do not need a deep ditch, but they should be placed in a straight line in a bed of gravel, then covered with gravel.

Surface water must be kept moving, but if it moves too fast, it will create a gully; if it goes slowly, it will create a bog. Provide a gradual slope with the earth slightly pitched away from the house. Allow 2 inches to every 10 feet.

Until you have had some rain or a spring thaw it is difficult to determine just how much work has to be done to provide adequate drainage. In a new site that has been excavated and filled in, the natural drainage patterns have been interrupted. You do not know where the water will go and where it will run off your property to perhaps cause problems on a neighbor's land. Try to determine the natural slope of the land where water would run off and grade the land accordingly.

SOIL

Soil is the basis of practically all gardening. While Japanese gardens may have only rocks and sand, most gardens have plants, trees, and shrubs. Light, air, and water are needed too, but these elements are for the taking. Only when the soil is properly prepared can you start to landscape.

Earth or soil has two layers: topsoil and subsoil. The subsoil is beneath the surface layer; it has been there for hundreds of years, and it can be a few inches below the surface or as much as 20 inches deep. The subsoil varies greatly in composition and can be sandy or claylike. A very sandy subsoil that retains little moisture is useless to plants. If it is very claylike it holds water so long that plants literally drown in it. It should be broken up, or in severe cases, a drainage system may have to be installed to carry off water.

Topsoil is composed of small particles of disintegrated rock, minerals, and decomposing organic matter. In addition, it has living organisms such as bacteria and fungi and water which hold the dissolved mineral salts and air. Most soils over the years lose their mineral content, and the soil must be reworked and revitalized. Topsoil may be a few inches deep or several inches deep. It is generally a darker color than the deeper subsoil because of organic content.

There are three kinds of soil: clay, which is heavy; a sandy soil, which is light; and a loamy soil, which is porous. A heavy clay soil is difficult to work with. It is slow in drying out in the spring, does not absorb the sun's rays as readily as a lighter soil and thus does not warm up as quickly in the spring as eager new plants demand. Frequently, a clay soil forms a crust that makes it impossible for air or water to reach the roots of plants. You must add humus and sand to it to improve its structure. How much of each you use depends on the density of the particular soil.

Sandy soil is easy to work with, and warms up quickly in spring, but it does not retain moisture nor provide good drainage. And many of the soluble plant foods will be lost through leaching. Adding liberal quantities of organic matter will improve a sandy soil.

A fertile soil that is a mixture of clay, sand, and humus is porous in texture and provides good drainage. It is spongy, so it retains moisture; it has humus, so it provides good conditions for the growth of soil bacteria, which is essential for plant nutrition. This is the kind of soil we want in our garden But in most cases, it must be built by a program of soil conditioning.

Humus—animal manure, compost, leafmold, peat moss—is decayed organic matter. This refers to living organisms, or their remains which have decayed. Humus adds body to light soils and provides aeration for clay soils. It dissolves in the soil and provides nourishment for plants and microorganisms. It is constantly used and depleted and must be replaced. Maintenance of the proper proportion of humus in the soil is vital to good plant growth.

A convenient source of humus is peat moss, which is available at nurseries. While there are differences between the various types of peat available, I have through the years used many kinds and they all proved satisfactory. A second source of humus is leafmold; it is exactly what it says—decayed leaves and grass clippings. It is easy to make and usually free. Simply rake leaves into a pile and let them decompose. Another excellent source of humus is

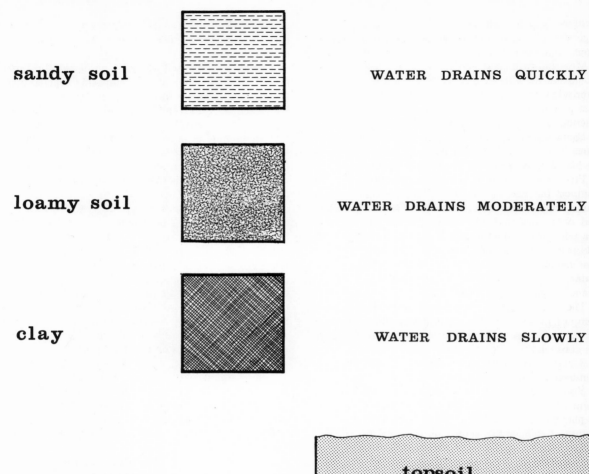

sandy soil — WATER DRAINS QUICKLY

loamy soil — WATER DRAINS MODERATELY

clay — WATER DRAINS SLOWLY

SUBSOIL SHOULD BE
MIXED WITH TOPSOIL
BEFORE PLANTING

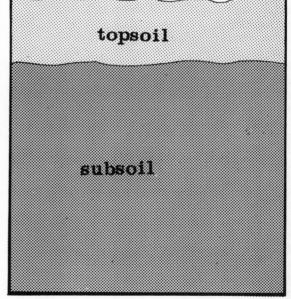

topsoil

subsoil

Soil Structure Chart

compost, and this too is free. It is basically decayed vegetable matter of many kinds. (Leaves, grass clippings, dead flowers and twigs can also be added.)

Most old-fashioned gardens have compost piles. I would not be without one. It is an easy way to keep improving soil without much trouble. For the compost pile, select a small (about 6 feet square) inconspicuous place near the garden. Put boards around it to about 4 feet high and leave an opening for a gate. I use 2- by 12-inch boards one on top of the other, anchored in the ground with wooden stakes.

First, throw a few inches of manure into the compost bin and then as you garden add grass clippings, leaves, and twigs. Vegetable matter, eggshells, and other similar kitchen garbage can be added to the pile too. When the pile is about 18 inches high, add some more manure and a dusting of lime. Keep the materials moist, never saturated; sprinkle with water occasionally. After a few months, turn the heap, bringing the sides to the top.

There is a more sophisticated way of making a compost heap. Materials are put through a shredder (from garden suppliers), which speeds up the process considerably. Or you might want to try chemicals that hasten the decaying process. They are available at nurseries under different trade names.

You must be your own judge about how much humus to add to soil. It depends on the soil, the kind of plants being grown, and the existing content of the humus. I mix about 1 inch of compost to about 6 inches of soil; this has proven satisfactory through the years for my garden.

Even though you add humus to the soil, you also have to use fertilizers to supplement it. Fertilizers contain nitrogen, phosphorus, and potassium (potash). But fertilizers are not substitutes for humus, nor can decayed organic matter completely do the work of fertilizers. Soil will need both.

A good soil has excellent water absorption, so moisture can be transported through pores quickly to the roots of the plant where it is stored for future use. The pores also carry away excess water, so that the topsoil does not become soggy. Once soil is waterlogged, air is prevented from circulating freely —a necessary factor for good plant growth.

Good drainage is essential to prevent a waterlogged situation that can kill plants. Plants develop shallow roots in this condition and perish from a lack of moisture because they cannot reach down for the stored water below. Poor drainage is a common fault of most soils and is generally caused by a layer of hard earth.

Plant roots need oxygen, so soil must be porous. It should be crumbly and have an open texture so that provisions for air and water are perfect. Air comes in with water that drains through the soil.

Improve the physical structure of the soil by turning it, keeping it porous, and using composts and mulches throughout the year. Porosity is the key to good soil. Only when these little air tubes are in the soil is it worthwhile to fertilize and work your garden. Fertility alone will not give good plant growth. The physical condition or tilth of the soil is just as important in the overall working of the soil.

As soon as you are in your new home, dig up some soil and crumble it in your hand. If it is lumpy and claylike, you will need to add the necessary sand and humus. If it is sandy and falls apart in your hand, you will need to add some organic matter. A good soil crumbles between the fingers. It feels like a well-done baked potato—porous with good texture.

pH SYMBOL

The pH scale is like a thermometer but instead of measuring heat, it measures the acidity or alkalinity of soil. Soil with a pH of 7 is neutral; below 7 the soil is acid; and above 7 it is alkaline.

It is important to know what kind of soil you have so that maximum use of all fertilizers supplied to it can be used. To determine the pH of your garden soil you can have it tested by the state agricultural authorities or you can make your own test with one of the kits available from suppliers.

Most of our commonly grown trees and shrubs prefer a neutral soil; some grow better in an acid condition, and several types prefer an alkaline soil. But generally, a soil reaction as nearly neutral as possible (between 6 and 7) allows you to grow the most plants successfully.

In alkaline soils, potash becomes less and less effective and eventually becomes locked in. In very acid soils, the element aluminum becomes so active that it becomes toxic to plants. Acidity in soil controls many functions. It governs the availability of the food in the soil and determines which bacteria thrive in it. It also, to some extent, affects the rate at which roots can take up moisture and leaves can manufacture food.

To lower the pH of soil (increase the acidity), apply ground sulfur at the rate of one pound to 100 square feet. This lowers the pH symbol of loam soil about one point. Spread the sulfur on top of the soil and then apply water.

To raise the pH of soil (sweeten it) add ground limestone at the rate of 10 pounds per 150 square feet. Scatter the limestone on the soil or mix it well with the top few inches of soil and water. It is best to add ground limestone or hydrated lime in several applications at 6- or 8-week intervals instead of using a lot of it at one time.

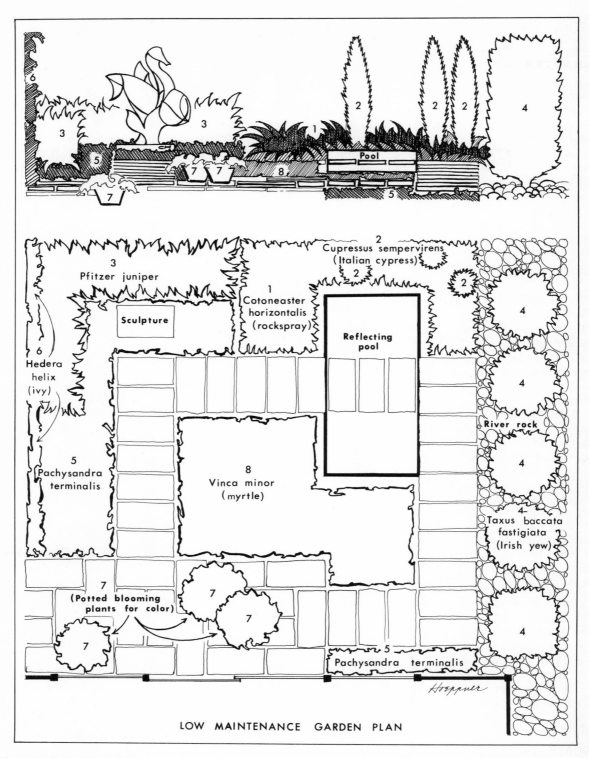

3
Pfitzer juniper

2
Cupressus sempervirens
(Italian cypress)

Sculpture

1
Cotoneaster
horizontalis
(rockspray)

2

Reflecting
pool

6
Hedera
helix
(ivy)

4

5
Pachysandra
terminalis

8
Vinca minor
(myrtle)

4

River rock

4

4
Taxus baccata
fastigiata
(Irish yew)

7
(Potted blooming
plants for color)

7

7

7

4

5
Pachysandra terminalis

Hoeppner

LOW MAINTENANCE GARDEN PLAN

This appealing garden plan relies on evergreens and ground cover for all-year beauty and low maintenance. Container plants are used for seasonal color, instant and portable, and a reflecting pool and sculpture are the features of the garden.

River rock surrounds the Irish yews *(Taxus baccata 'Fastigiata')* so weeding is never needed; concrete blocks or stepping-stones are used throughout, providing access to the garden and at the same time eliminating direct ground planting. A quick hosing cleans this entire area in a few minutes.

Shapes and forms of plants are carefully considered in this plan; there is a union of vertical and horizontal beautifully combined with the spreading *Cotoneaster* and Pfitzer junipers. *Vinca minor* (myrtle) occupies the center of the garden, the dark-green color a perfect foil for the concrete pavings. Leaf texture and size of leaves are also given careful thought; there is indeed a variety that blends the entire scene into a lush green painting.

For all its beauty the garden requires little work but offers a great deal of viewing pleasure: a handsome place for a leisurely stroll, a delightful picture from the house.

CHAPTER 3

Fundamentals of Landscape Planning

Landscaping with a definite plan in mind increases the value of your property. But a good garden plan, like the plants it contains, must mature to show its beauty; allow three to five years. Do one area at a time—patio or terrace, play area—and follow a master plan. Slight changes and alterations can certainly be made (and should be made) as you go along.

Achieving an æsthetically pleasing and functional garden requires the meshing of many elements— natural and man-made materials. The texture of leaves and the color of flowers, the appearance of wood or stone, paving and lawn—all play a part in the total plan. It also involves proportion, scale, harmony, and balance. Creating a landscape is blending many things together. It is much more than just prettying up a house. It is a total setting to give you maximum use of your property.

While there are no set rules in planning a garden, there are some general simple and sound fundamentals:

- Suit the design to the site and to the style of the house.
- Keep all parts of the plan in scale.
- Create accent areas.
- Have a definite overall plan.
- Select appropriate plant materials for conditions you can offer.
- Lay out property with minimum maintenance.

SCALE, PROPORTION, AND UNITY

Plants have definite forms. They are spreading or horizontal, round or globular, weeping or trailing, or vertical in appearance such as pyramidal or columnar in shape. Dogwood, pin oak, hawthorn have strong horizontal lines and carry the eye from one plant to another. For low, flat houses, these are good

selections. Beech, flowering cherry, or weeping willow are delicate and fragile in appearance and create softer lines. They are good in front of stiffer subjects.

The form of a plant is vitally important in landscaping. Unless you know what the plant will look like when it is mature, it is somewhat like a guessing game. When you make selections, try to visualize the plant fully grown. Some species lose their symmetrical form with age. Others, like pines and some of the firs, lose their lower branches as they get older. Scale and proportion must be carefully considered in landscaping. They are, perhaps, the keys to an attractive setting.

Scale is the visual relationship of each form to every other form and to the design as a whole. It can be called a relationship of size. A large house looks incongruous with a small entrance; a cottage with an elaborate court and garden is unpleasing. We must establish an appealing scale relationship between the garden and the house. The starting point can be a tree. A large tree will link the house and the garden together. It is part of the joining process. With a small house the usual procedure is to have a small tree, but here the principle can be altered. Use a very large tree; this makes the house seem charming. Creating an illusion of space with plant materials is an exciting kind of landscaping.

Proportion is the harmonious relationship of one part of a total picture to another and to the whole. A large paved terrace and a small lawn can be in proportion, while in another site, the patio should be small and the lawn large. But to make both areas the same size would be a mistake. Then there is no interest, and one element does not complement the other. Vertical forms should be balanced with several horizontal elements.

Unity in a composition is the putting-together of materials so that it is a whole. You do not want a hodgepodge of unrelated masses insulting the eye. Plants of related forms, colors, and textures, well-

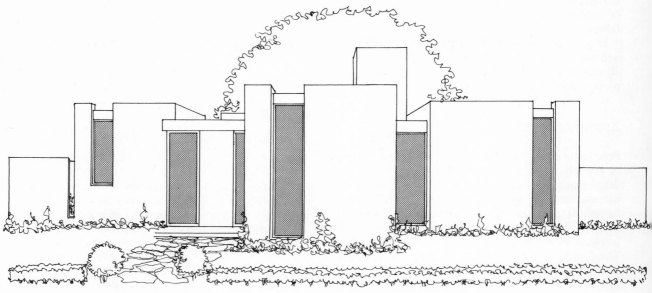

poor scale, proportion & unity

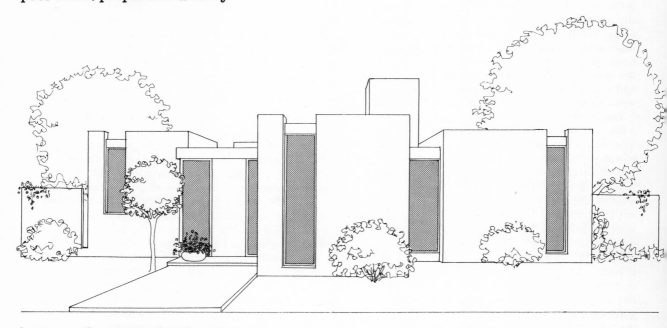

better scale, proportion & unity

designs: adrián martínez

Landscaping a Modern House

chosen, achieve the unity every attractive garden needs.

Other elements to consider are rhythm in the composition—this involves repeating the same group of plants or the same plant to give a sense of movement; and balance—this means having elements of similar size and form and emphasis for use as one feature.

If you study each of these terms individually you will see that one depends on the other and they are all interrelated. Generally, if you get the scale and proportion right, the other elements fall in line.

APPROACH TO THE HOUSE

Practically every property can be separated into three or possibly four distinct parts, each of which serves a definite purpose. And each one is treated in a different manner, just as a living room requires certain furnishings, and a bedroom other decor. The divisions of the landscape plan are the approach to the house, the outdoor living area, and the service area. The fourth division would be the play area for children, or game area for adults.

Most homeowners immediately launch a program to make the outdoor living area in the rear of the property usable and completely forget the front of the home. Yet, this area serves as a setting for the entire picture. It is here the guest first receives an impression of what is to come. Good taste and simplicity are necessary. Too many times the front of the house is a hodgepodge of flowers and steps, pools and rocks. These things, if they are to be in the plan at all, should be in the rear of the property.

Do not treat the front of the house as a flower garden. It destroys the spaciousness of the property. The exceptions are a rustic or cottage-type home where it is permissible to use borders and flower beds in keeping with the architecture.

Paths or walks for people, and driveways for cars, are the first consideration of this area. A path should not be cramped but broad enough for two people to walk abreast, and its width should bear some relationship to its length. Usually the distance from the street to the house is short, and a straight direct path is best. Curves have their place, but space is needed to make them appealing. Where an entrance walk is not a necessity, stepping-stones may be used with great effectiveness. They help to accent the front of the house and they eliminate the decisive break of a straight path.

Driveways besides being straight to be easy to use should also be wide enough to accommodate a car, and preferably have space enough for a car to pass another parked car. Otherwise, one car at the entrance to the house leading from the drive to the steps blocks the drive in both directions.

Many homes have garages adjacent to the building. Wherever possible, put in a turn court, or if there is not enough space, a "Y" turn may be the answer. The location of the house on the site, the lot lines, and the necessary walks and paths will determine the exact positioning of the driveway.

In the front of the house use plantings that give a simple and restrained picture. There are several ways to accomplish a handsome setting. Foundation plantings, lawns, groups of trees and shrubs, and combinations of several of these elements are used. Most properties remain unfenced and unclosed, but this is not mandatory. Entrance courts and patio courts are permissible, depending upon the site. Where an enclosure is necessary it can be a fence, wall, lattice, hedge, or a shrub border.

Street trees are necessary for shade and appearance, and generally these are on the property. Other trees in front of the house are desirable for accent or for shade and to help frame the house. Trees here should be chosen with respect to their habits. Those that drop flowers, fruit, or litter should be avoided. Select trees with a root system that will not interfere with the lawn and whose growth habit is compact while pleasing in color and texture. There are large trees and small ones, compact growers and branching types. Choose accordingly. (See Chapter 11.)

Many homeowners select plants and groups of shrubs for the front corners of the house or on either side of the entrance walls and drives. These shrubs can become traffic hazards as they mature. Choose low-growing species, simple and neat. Often, the front planting arrangement is balanced, but it does not have to be. A large group of shrubs at one end of a house need not be balanced by the same arrangement on the other side. Use a medium-size tree here, perhaps.

Narrow flower beds bordering walks and flower beds in general are not necessary. Do your gardening in the back of the house; there is no sense accenting strictly utilitarian features. Doorway gardens are an exception; these are more often created with pot plants rather than with plants in the ground.

Foundation plantings close to a building are disappearing. And well they should. They do not serve any true purpose with today's architecture, and often are a mass of tangled shrubs, hardly pleasant to see. Many years ago, when houses were on high foundations, the plantings disguised construction features. Most contemporary homes have underground foundations, so masses of shrubs are not needed.

Try to avoid using large conifers and other plants in the front of the house. As seedlings they are certainly appealing, but in a few years they soon become completely out of scale with the house. Select plants with a natural growth habit and ultimate height that are in scale and proportion to the building. Of course, larger plants can be kept trained

A herringbone brick path unites the patio with the house in this picture.
Note the selection of plant material . . . for scale and for texture,
a completely total scene in all.
(Landscape Architect Nelvo Weber; Molly Adams photo)

An impressive entrance beautifully landscaped with tree standards,
espaliers, and a well-trimmed hedge. The small tree at the right
is perfect for the spot and in proportion to the scene.
(Hube Henry, Hedrich·Blessing)

and within bounds, but then they appear rigid and unattractive.

Today, houses are on low foundations or on a concrete pad; the style of architecture is generally a mass of verticals and horizontals.

Here are some general rules for planning the front of the house:

- Accentuate vertical and horizontal lines of the building with appropriate-type plantings.
- Use well-designed plant groups at the corners of the building to soften the rather long strong architectural lines and to give more width to the house if necessary.
- Well-groomed, handsome specimen plants are assets near the front entrance.
- Make the planting area in the front of the house pleasing in shape. Straight single rows of plants are tiresome to the eye. Use flowing curves and free-form patterns.
- Keep annuals and perennials in the garden; they are too striking in bloom for the front of the house; besides, in winter the area will be bare.
- Use ground cover and edging material where necessary.
- Low-growing evergreens, like yews and junipers, hollies and barberries, are excellent in front of the home.

OUTDOOR LIVING AREA

For most families, the outdoor living area is the most important space in the garden. Even where summers are short, outdoor living is desirable. It is designed for family relaxation and entertainment. Terraces or patios, lawns and flower beds are all incorporated in this area. Just how to designate the use of each piece of land depends upon individual needs and the size of the lot.

The first and most important thing to consider concerning the terrace or patio is that it be within easy access from the living portion of the house. The entrance may be from the dining room or living room or, more often, through sliding glass doors from the family or recreation room

The paved area for the patio or terrace can have a soft surface—pebbles, gravel, grass—or a hard surface—brick, concrete, or tile. It can be wood, too, or a combination of masonry and wood, soft surface, and hard surface. While the shape is generally rectangular or square, it can also be of a free-form design. It can be large or small, depending on its use. For instance, if you are fond of outdoor cookery, the patio must be of good size to accommodate barbecue units and accessories. There should also be space for furniture.

The patio area should be sheltered from sun and wind. It is a place to retreat from the heat and humidity, so be sure it is shaded in the hot afternoon. Fencing or screening may be needed to buffer winds or to provide privacy.

The outdoor living area is a combination of many things. There are plants and shrubs, flower beds, a lawn, perhaps, near the patio, and often play space for children. Man-made objects like fences, raised beds, steps, and low walls are other essentials of a well-planned garden. Generally, planting is kept to the sides of the site and the center is open; play areas are to the side, and large trees and shrubs in the background. This is an easy, effective way of planning; but it is by no means mandatory. However, no matter how the area is divided, it must be unified. One part should logically lead to another.

The theme of the garden—woodland, Oriental—must be considered as well as the style of the garden—formal or informal. And these considerations must be correlated with the style of architecture of the house to make a unified scheme.

The woodland type of garden incorporates well in a small area and makes the terrace or patio more charming. Here there would be masses of shrubs, several trees, and twisting paths. This is a walk-around garden, shaded and inviting, cool and refreshing.

The Japanese garden theme with sparse planting is another kind of plan. The few same plants are repeated throughout the area. Strategically placed statues and stones are used, and water is often a part of the setting. This is not a colorful garden or a walk-through area. It is a scene to be viewed from house or terrace.

Plants in raised beds are pleasant to look at and practical to have. They are on display, and tending them is easy because you don't have to stoop so much. Planting boxes can be used in the same way in the patio or terrace. Different heights and shapes can be put together in interesting combinations.

Steps in the plan make for interesting arrangements, and the possibilities are unlimited. They can be irregular with turns and angles, of many materials, and in many different designs.

SERVICE AREA

Service areas were part of the garden plan years ago, and today they deserve more attention than we give them. Garbage cans and space for trash, a convenient walkway to carry groceries from the garage to the house, and a place for gardening must be considered. And it is wise to include vegetable gardens and compost piles in the service area too.

This brick patio is an important part of the outdoor living area.
Because it is somewhat large, a center pattern has been used so
there will not be a monotonous effect.
(Friede Stege, Landscape Architect; Molly Adams photo)

Here, an area of grass borders a raised terrace. Geraniums in a
half circle embellish the scene.
(Molly Adams)

The approach to this house is landscaped informally to create a cozy, charming entrance. Note tall accent planting at left of doorway and the side of the house left in natural state. *(Molly Adams)*

The service area of this plan includes a handsome fence, a curved driveway, and a striking tree. *(Molly Adams)*

Wheelbarrows, spraying equipment, and hoses all have to be stored. Too often they are put in the garage. This is not the place for them.

Designers, seeing the need for storage areas for tools, now include small tool sheds and work centers on the property close to the garage and yet still within the service area. These structures are generally at the back of the garage or to one side of the site where they are convenient and yet within easy access to the garden. They should be screened from the neighbors and from the garden by shrub borders or fences.

The service area is the behind-the-scenes workshop of the garden. It can be a convenient no-fuss, no-muss way of getting things to the patio and of keeping tools and the hundred little necessities that make a good garden successful.

Some rules to follow when planning the service area:

- Place garbage cans far enough from the house so that odors are not objectionable within the house.
- Even when there is an electric dryer, clotheslines are sometimes necessary; allow space for them.
- The tool shed or work structure must be accessible for trucks to deliver and unload materials.
- Continuous paving should connect the service area to the outdoor living area.
- If there is fencing, provide wide gates for truck deliveries.

PLAY AND GAME AREA

Play space for children is a convenience of a well-planned garden. Select pavings carefully. Brick can be slippery after a rain, and bruised knees are to be expected if you have a concrete floor. Soft surfaces like gravel or pebbles are a better choice.

The area should be close to the house to enable you to keep an eye on the children. At the same time it must be far enough away so that it is the children's own place. Play equipment, sandboxes, and what-have-you are all good possibilities. And it is wise to provide some overhead shelter, so that on rainy days the kids can still play outdoors.

LANDSCAPE PLANS: COUNTRY HOUSE, SMALL HOUSE, COTTAGE

Whether the house is small or large, country or formal in appearance, it is always more attractive with clever landscaping. A small house becomes larger with strategically placed trees and shrubs; and the country house with an extension of its woodland setting becomes a totally attractive composition. The cottage, informal in character, needs an intimate landscape design, a frame of greenery that appears as though it has always been there.

Although every house is different in design and every lot is different, some general ideas can be applied to all of them. The following landscape plans of the small house, the country house, and the cottage offer some suggestions.

The Country House

Because of the large land area, lawns are purposely separated from the informal meadow and rough turf areas. A large pin oak shades the patio, but still allows a view of the surrounding meadow. The maples are strategically placed to assure privacy on the one open side of the house, and to balance the wooded scene at the other end. A flowering dogwood accents the long patio, and pachysandra softens the edges of the paving and also provides a frame for the three trees.

The entrance of the house is exquisitely landscaped with low maintenance vinca, flowering dogwoods for accent, and a row of pyracantha for horizontal interest. Witch hazel is used off the living room for golden fall color and helps to relate natural plantings to other plantings in the landscape. Japanese yews form a barrier along the garage entrance complemented by a pair of Norway spruce.

Planting Materials

Acer platanoides (Norway maple)
Acer saccharum (sugar maple)
Malus floribunda (flowering crab apple)
Quercus palustris (pin oak)
Thuja occidentalis (American arborvitae)
Picea abies (Norway spruce)
Cornus florida (flowering dogwood)
Tsuga canadensis (Canadian hemlock)
Taxus cuspidata capitata (Japanese yew)
Pyracantha (firethorn)
Hamamelis vernalis (witch hazel)
Vinca
Pachysandra terminalis

The Small House

The intent of the plan for the small house is to create an outdoor living area in conjunction with indoor activity areas. The patio off the living room in a diamond shape encompasses a major portion of the house, making it appear larger than it really is. The paving can be rough aggregate squares with redwood grids, or it might be brick. The flowering dogwoods at one corner of the patio provide spring color, fall and winter decorative fruit. The large plane tree shades the house from hot summer sun, and the forsythia along the property line gives spring color.

Corner arborvitae tie taller boundary plantings to low plantings. Low ground cover mats of vinca are below the crab apple trees behind the carport. The low yews at the other property line form an enclosure, but it is possible to see over them. Cotoneaster off the dining-room area provide evergreen foliage and red berries in winter, and do not interfere with the view. A solitary viburnum is an accent on another wall.

Planting Materials

Liquidambar styraciflua (sweet gum)
Quercus palustris (pin oak)
Cornus florida (flowering dogwood)
Thuja occidentalis (American arborvitae)
Acer platanoides (Norway maple)
Malus sargenti (flowering crab apple)
Platanus occidentalis (plane tree)
Taxus cuspidata (Japanese yew)
Forsythia intermedia (forsythia)
Viburnum opulus (European cranberry bush)
Cotoneaster horizontalis (spreading cotoneaster)
Vinca minor (vinca)

The Cottage

Three large trees along the rear property line provide needed big accent, and Norway spruces balance the plan. On the bedroom side of the house there is a charming intimate garden with stepping-stones, honeysuckle, and flowering crab apple; a graceful weeping willow dominates the area.

The deck forms a continuance of the living area and offers outlook to the view. Ivy is used for ground cover and there is a planter between the living room and deck for some colorful annuals. Pfitzer's juniper breaks the dining-room wall line and red-twigged dogwood is featured on the deck. Small areas of ivy frame part of the house as an extension of the deck and along garage wall. Honeysuckle is used as a horizontal line along walkway. The plan is not heavily landscaped but still affords a lush green view from almost any place in the house.

Planting Materials

Salix babylonica (weeping willow)
Liquidambar styraciflua (sweet gum)
Acer platanoides (Norway maple)
Gleditsia triacanthos (honey locust)
Malus (flowering crab apple)
Cornus florida (flowering dogwood)
Picea abies (Norway spruce)
Cornus stolonifera (red-twigged dogwood)
Lonicera tatarica (Tatarian honeysuckle)
Juniperus chinensis pfitzeriana (Pfitzer's juniper)
Taxus cuspidata capitata (Japanese yew)

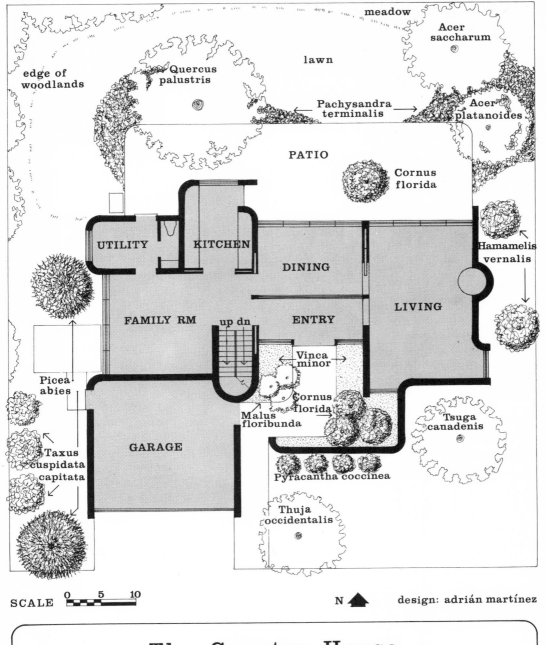

meadow

Acer saccharum

edge of woodlands

Quercus palustris

lawn

← Pachysandra terminalis →

Acer platanoides

PATIO

Cornus florida

UTILITY   KITCHEN

Hamamelis vernalis

DINING

FAMILY RM   up dn   ENTRY   LIVING

Picea abies

Vinca minor

Taxus cuspidata capitata

Malus floribunda

Cornus florida

GARAGE

Tsuga canadenis

Pyracantha coccinea

Thuja occidentalis

SCALE   0   5   10   N   design: adrián martínez

The Country House

The design of this house borrows from the natural woodlands around it. The rear and side plans of plantings are merely an extension of what one sees in the background. There are no fences, no barriers, and the house is planned to spring from the natural surroundings.

A large free-standing pin oak *(Quercus palustris)*, next to the patio, sets the scale and provides shade for the paved outdoor room. The maples *(Acer)* at the corner are smaller, less dominant, to balance the scene. *Pachysandra* is used as ground cover, a garland around the trees where lawn would be impractical.

The lawn joins the background greenery to the house, and to further assure scale a flowering dogwood *(Cornus florida)* is set into the patio. The trees are impressive and tie the house down to the ground, eliminating sharp corners.

The entry of the house has a superlative garden area to welcome the visitor. A trio of flowering dogwood *(Cornus florida)* and a showy crab apple *(Malus floribunda)* line the inner court with *Vinca* as ground cover. A *Pyracantha* hedge adds a necessary vertical accent and the arborvitae *(Thuja occidentalis)* and hemlock *(Tsuga canadensis)* provide all-year beauty.

The sides of the house continue the woodsy effect with evergreens at the garage side and witch hazel *(Hammamelis vernalis)* at the living-room window.

To complete the lovely picture, drifts of annuals and perennials border the edge of the woodlands at upper left. This is a high-maintenance garden that requires care, but is a gardener's paradise.

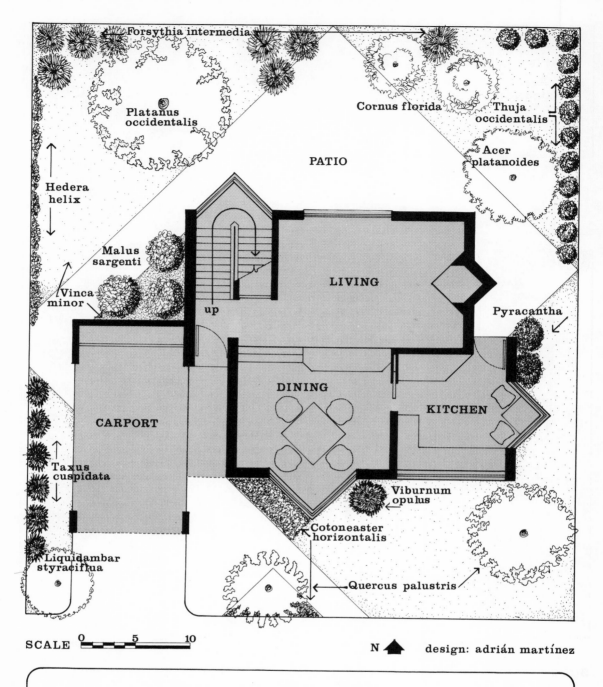

Forsythia intermedia

Platanus occidentalis

Cornus florida

Thuja occidentalis

Acer platanoides

PATIO

Hedera helix

Malus sargenti

Vinca minor

up

LIVING

Pyracantha

CARPORT

DINING

KITCHEN

Taxus cuspidata

Viburnum opulus

Cotoneaster horizontalis

Liquidambar styraciflua

Quercus palustris

SCALE 0 5 10

N   design: adrián martínez

The Small House

This small house is extensively landscaped—a gardener's garden. The overall effect of lush plantings gives the home an intimate and charming setting. The diamond-shaped patio is unique; it includes service walk to the carport and surrounds most of the home. From the living room and upstairs bedrooms a complete frame of greenery greets the viewer. The house itself is adroitly framed with plants—*Malus sargentii, Cotoneaster,* and *Pyracantha.*

The plant material is well chosen for visual effect and also to provide privacy at the rear of the grounds and at the street. The buttonwood *(Platanus occidentalis)* at the rear (left) gives some shade to the patio and is the feature of the planting area balanced with dogwoods *(Cornus florida)* and Norway maple *(Acer platanoides)* at the other end of the property. Forsythia is used at one end of the area and evergreens at the other, and ivy ground cover predominates.

The front of the house is equally well landscaped with two accent trees (pin oaks) and spreading cotoneaster along the dining-room window wall. The front lawn makes the house seem larger than it is and the service area is lined with attractive evergreens and a sweet gum *(Liquidambar styraciflua)* tree. All in all, a very handsome landscape plan.

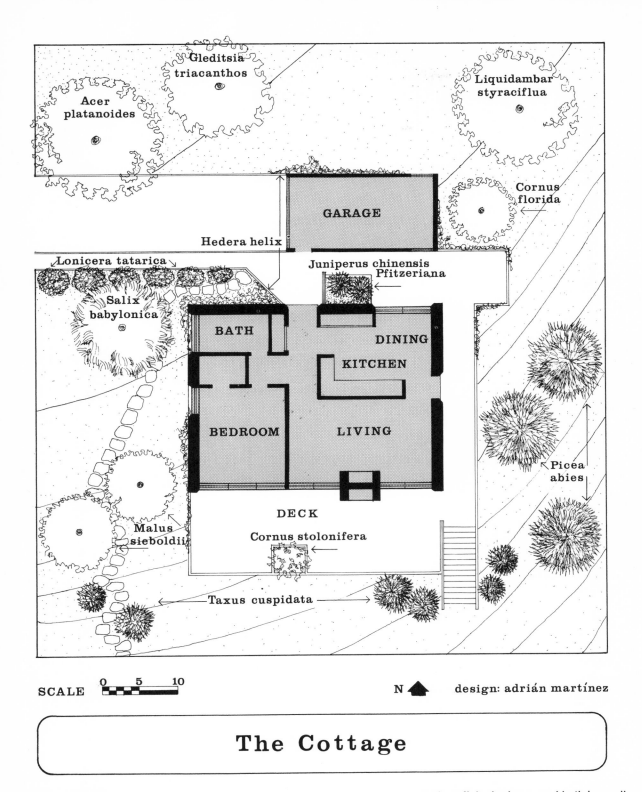

Acer
platanoides

Gleditsia
triacanthos

Liquidambar
styraciflua

Cornus
florida

GARAGE

Hedera helix

Lonicera tatarica

Juniperus chinensis
Pfitzeriana

Salix
babylonica

BATH

DINING

KITCHEN

Picea
abies

BEDROOM

LIVING

Malus
sieboldii

DECK

Cornus stolonifera

Taxus cuspidata

SCALE 0 5 10

N design: adrián martínez

The Cottage

Trees and shrubs are used generously on this sloping site to give the cottage a lush green frame. There is effective use of large trees throughout—some evergreen, some deciduous—so there is constant flow of color all year. From any room in the house the viewer is greeted with a sea of green.

The living room and dining room look out on evergreen Norway spruce trees *(Picea abies);* the rear of the house is accented with a Norway maple *(Acer platanoides),* honey locust *(Gleditschia triacanthos)* and a sweet gum tree *(Liquidambar styraciflua).*

The intimate garden off the bedroom and bath is small but charming and enhanced with a random path of stepping-stones. Weeping willow *(Salix babylonica)* and crabapple trees decorate the area along with honeysuckle *(Lonicera tatarica)* and ivy *(Hedera helix).*

The deck is another bonus of this intelligent plan; a red twig dogwood *(Cornus stolonifera)* in a planter is in this area. There is never a dull moment in the entire plan for there is constant greenery in varying shades of color and in an infinite variety of textures.

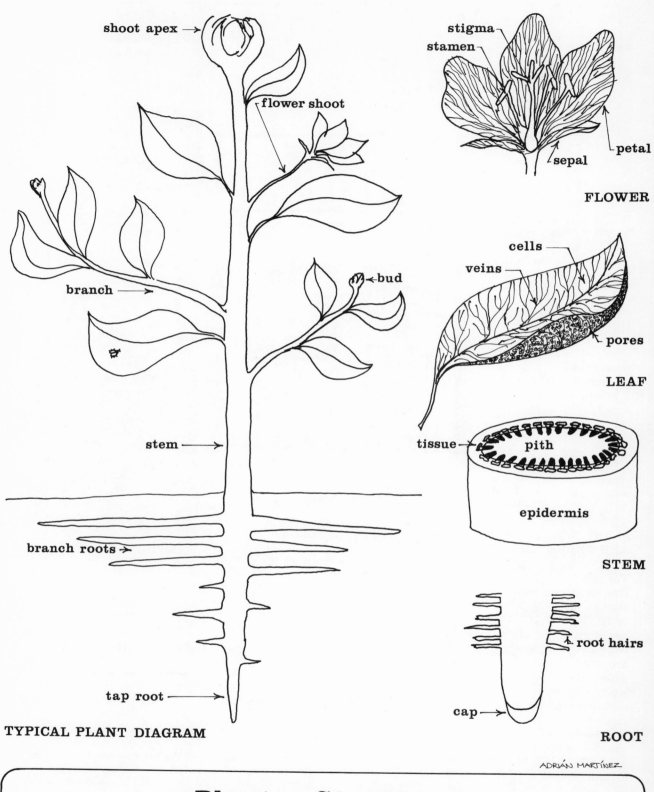

shoot apex

flower shoot

stigma
stamen

petal

sepal

FLOWER

branch

bud

cells
veins

pores

LEAF

stem

tissue

pith

epidermis

branch roots

STEM

root hairs

tap root

cap

TYPICAL PLANT DIAGRAM

ROOT

ADRIÁN MARTÍNEZ

Plant Structure

CHAPTER 4

The Plants

The plant is a living organism, a wonderful combination of various parts working together to support life and to create offspring. It is capable of making its own food from inorganic materials, and it can store energy. But unlike animals and people who can move about—if necessary—to another place if the environment does not suit them, plants are anchored in the ground and they must adapt to their environment.

Before you start gardening, it is wise to know something about how plants grow and live. You do not have to be a botanist or a horticulturist to have lovely plants, but some understanding of them will make it easier for you to keep them healthy.

In simple terms, plants have several parts: roots, stems, leaves, flower, fruit, and seeds. These organs work together to create a living plant.

PLANT PARTS—ROOTS, STEM AND TRUNK, LEAVES

The roots' first function is to hold the plant in the ground, and the root network conforms to the necessities of the plant. Some have a long taproot, like a carrot. Other plants have fat roots that store food, and stems and leaves are not tall. Corms, rhizomes, and bulbs have short feeding roots to gather moisture and food. Grass roots are shallow because they gather food just below the surface of the soil, whereas the roots of a large tree branch out into an enormous network to grip the soil and hold the tree in place.

Roots also absorb water and at the same time absorb chemical substances necessary to make plants grow. There is a relationship between the total leaf surface exposed to the sun and the total root surface in contact with the soil. If water is not available to the roots, the plant dies. Root tips are made of cells that are tough and flat and push forward from pressure in the rear. They squeeze and force their way

through the ground, surmounting obstacles, even growing into a crevice of a rock and by expansion bursting it apart. Behind the root tip or cone is the growing area of the root. These are young cells multiplying by dividing in two. As the plant develops, so do the roots. Main roots send out smaller ones, and these in turn also develop roots. The older roots become tubes that carry the water and nutrients to the plant, or sometimes act as storage reservoirs for food. Roots also develop delicate hairs; these cells do the actual absorption of water and food. These tiny hairs are sensitive to light and dryness; they shrivel and die quickly when exposed to air.

Roots cannot grow upward. Each cell has a substance that floats to rest on the bottom of the cell, and root growth is a downward curve. Although the root is a part of a plant, all of its food comes from the leaves. If leaves suffer, no new roots form, and often old roots may stop growing.

Stems and trunks store, distribute, and process the products of leaf and roots of nearly all modern plants. Each cell in a stem must have a constant supply of moisture, food, and air. It must also store food for emergencies. The sugar must be transformed into starch or other complicated proteins, oils, and waxes before it is stored. So a stem manufactures and processes as well as stores and handles distribution and transportation.

As growth begins in a plant, the central stem, or group of stems, develops and pushes up from the ground seeking light. The growth tip of the seed forms the stem. The stem carries on the functions of the roots and root hairs to transport water and nutrients to buds, leaves, and flowers, and it returns sugars manufactured in the leaves to the roots. The stem also supports the plant, and can be rigid or flexible. It is essentially the conveyor pipe that moves the sugars from the leaves to the roots, where it is stored as starch.

It is the special function of the leaves to make

organic food out of sunlight, air, water, and earth salts. In other words, most of the carbohydrates required by the plant are manufactured in the leaves by the process of photosynthesis. The energy of the sun is changed into a form that can be used in the life process of a plant. This process depends upon chlorophyll, or the green material in plants which takes carbon dioxide, water, and the energy of the sun to produce the carbohydrates and sugar.

A leaf is actually a complicated chemical factory with cell upon cell and motion and flow everywhere. The entire process of the leaf is to combine gas and liquid. In one form or another it obtains oxygen, hydrogen, carbon, and nitrogen, along with other elements. Water supplies the hydrogen and oxygen. Carbon comes through the roots as humus in earth, and nitrogen is vital to the plant, but it can only be used in liquid form. Another leaf activity is transpiration, or the loss of water as vapor.

When plants cannot get moisture, leaves wilt and shrivel and eventually the plant dies. A leaf has three surfaces: epidermis, middle of the leaf, and veins. The epidermis is usually a single layer of different kinds of cells to protect the tissue within from drying out. The middle section of the leaf has cells that mostly contain chlorophyll, and the veins have elements to conduct water, inorganic salts, and foods.

FLOWERS AND FRUIT

Plants reproduce and perpetuate themselves through the production of seeds. The flower contains the female parts that, when fertilized with pollen—male sexual cells—produce seed. One of the miracles of nature is the variety of devices used to accomplish this mating. The seed holds the life for an indefinite time until the right conditions occur to start it growing.

HOW PLANTS GROW

The growth of a plant depends on its genetic factors, and is also determined by light, temperature, and water. Soil and nutrients in the soil are other considerations. When these conditions are at optimum levels, the plant thrives; but rarely is there a precise balance of the elements, so we must help to modify the temperature for the plants, provide shade if necessary, and apply moisture when it is needed.

A plant, like a pet, becomes a responsibility and requires some care. Some get along fine with little care; others need more attention; and mature plants, like mature pets, get along with less fuss than young ones.

To make plants grow, use Nature. She is there and she is a very capable assistant. See that the plant has enough sun if it needs it, or put it in partial shade if that is its requirement. When there is little rain, water the plant so that it can continue to grow. If there is too much wind, modify it with screens or fences. Feed plants so that they have the necessary nutrients to keep them thriving.

Air, light, food, temperature, and water all play a part in the life of a plant. Each element is as important as the next one. A perfect balance is what you are striving for, for your plants; but even if the balance is far from perfect, the plants will survive. They may not grow rapidly, but they will not die.

Air. A good circulation of air is necessary to keep plants healthy. Crowded conditions rob them of light, and dusty and smoggy air hinders their growth by blocking air pores and cells. The rate of water loss from a plant is influenced by the relative humidity of the air. The drier the air, the more water lost. If water loss is too great, the plants wither. This is why house plants are difficult to grow in low humidity. Wind increases the rate of water loss and modifies the water content of plant cells. It also affects the form of growth of plants.

Light. The relationship between light and plants is complex and is often misunderstood because the effect of light upon growth involves light intensity, light quality, and the duration of light. Light affects the processes associated with photosynthesis and the synthesis of chlorophyll. It also affects the temperature of a plant. Most of the light that strikes the foliage is changed to heat and raises the temperature. The form and growth of the leaves are also controlled by light. Plants with thick leaves like sun. Those that grow in shade generally have thin leaves.

Food. The three most important elements in a plant's diet are nitrogen, phosphorus, and potassium. In addition, there are trace elements required, but these are of lesser importance. Nitrogen promotes leaf growth, phosphorus promotes root and stem development, and potash stabilizes growth and intensifies color. These elements must be in the soil to maintain proper plant health. The lack of any one of those elements halts normal growth development.

Temperature. Temperature influences every process that goes on in a plant. Photosynthesis, assimilation, digestion, respiration, water absorption, transpiration, and formation of enzymes are some of the important processes governed by one factor: temperature. Optimum or ideal temperature, for one process may differ from those of another process going on at the same time. Temperature is one of the factors (water is the other) that determine the general distribution of vegetation on earth.

Water. An adequate supply of water is necessary if plants are to do their best. When all other conditions

Untie but do not remove the burlap when planting; it eventually decomposes.
(Joyce R. Wilson)

Trees in cans ready for planting.
(Joyce R. Wilson)

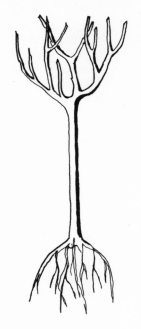

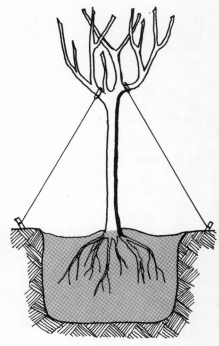

BARE ROOT

① prune to shape ② set on mound in hole ③ fill w. soil, brace & water

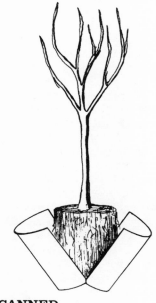

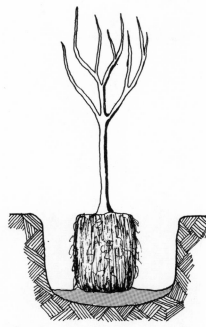

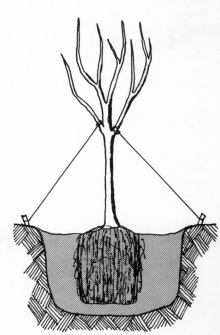

CANNED

① remove carefully ② loosen roots & set in hole ③ fill w. soil, brace & water

Planting Trees

are good, plants can consume a great deal of water. If it is lacking, they do not grow as rapidly as they will with moisture. They suffer, and if the water supply is greatly curtailed, they can die. Of course, certain plants such as succulents and cacti can tolerate very dry situations. They have adapted throughout the centuries to the conditions and require far less water than other plants.

PLANTING METHODS

Some gardeners like to start at the beginning and grow their own plants from seed. Certainly this is an exciting adventure, and there is an immense satisfaction in seeing your own plants mature. But most people buy plants already started for them at nurseries. Annuals, perennials, ground covers, and shrubs and trees are available in their season at local garden centers. Or you can buy plants from mail-order specialists throughout the country.

In Flats

A flat is a wooden or plastic shallow container with seedlings that are ready to go into the ground. Soil with adequate nutrients has been furnished for them, and now it is a matter of taking them from the container and putting them in place in your garden. With a kitchen knife or a trowel, separate the plants by cutting straight down around them, or simply tease a plant with a mass of roots away from the soil. Jiggle it gently until it comes loose. Dig holes large enough to accommodate the plant and its roots; do not push the plant into the opening or wedge it into place. Gently place it in the hole and firm the soil around its collar. Be sure that the crown of the plant is slightly higher than the soil line and the surface is somewhat concave (a water well) to allow sufficient space for water. A flat terrain does not allow the water to break through the surface; it runs off and does little good for the plant.

Seedlings in peat pots are set in the ground in the same way; do not remove the peat band from the plant.

Balled and Burlapped

Shrubs and trees are sold balled and burlapped (or they are bare root). This means exactly what it says. The tree is dug from the ground with a ball of soil around it and is wrapped in burlap and tied at the crown with string to keep it intact.

Evergreen shrubs, conifers, and some deciduous shrubs are sold balled and burlapped. When you see the plants at your nurseries, then you know the planting season has arrived.

Although balled-and-burlapped trees will take some abuse, do not handle them unnecessarily roughly. Do not use the trunk as a handle; rather, cradle the root ball in your hands if you can. And do not pull a tree across a pavement; this can harm the root system. The plant's first few weeks in new conditions are the most critical time. Once it is in the ground, it can help itself. Until then, it is at your mercy.

Make the planting hole deep: about twice the size of the diameter of the root ball and at least half again as deep as the height of the root ball. Put a mound of soil in the bottom of the hole and place the plant on it so that the crown is slightly above the soil line. Pour in some water and let the soil settle for a few moments. Then cut the twine and spread out the burlap. The material decomposes in time.

Fill the hole to the top with soil. Form the water well around the plant. Soak, fill the well a few times and allow water to penetrate into the soil. And then when you think you have given the plant enough water, add some more.

Bare Root

Deciduous fruit trees, shade trees, and shrubs are at nurseries bare root in early spring, sometimes before. Bare-root trees cost less than trees in containers the next year, and often are healthier and more vigorous than when started later in the year from a can. With bare-root planting, you put in all the soil. This can be an advantage; it assures uniform water penetration to the roots.

Be sure the roots are plump and fresh when you buy the plant. If there is any suggestion that they might be dry, soak the plant overnight in a bucket of water. Dig a hole large enough to accommodate the roots when they are spread out. Do not squeeze, bend, or cut the roots to make them fit the hole. If a training stake is necessary, put it in place now.

Place the plant next to the stake on a mound of soil and fill in and around it with soil. Work the soil around the roots with a potting stick or a blunt-edged piece of wood. Do not pack the soil tightly in place, but be sure it is firm. Tie the tree to the stake in several places with plastic or cloth ties. Dig a water well and soak the plant thoroughly. Then for the next few weeks, water it moderately. These are dormant trees that require less water than actively growing ones. When the leaves appear, you can start watering regularly.

Plants in Cans

Plants in containers are available at nurseries, at all seasons, in a variety of sizes and prices. Some have been at the nursery for months, and the soil ball is hard and claylike, making it difficult for water to

Getting ready to plant a small
tree; can being cut.
(Joyce R. Wilson)

Removing plant ball from cut can.
(Joyce R. Wilson)

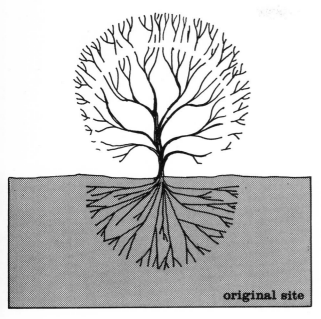

① prune ⅓ of the shrub

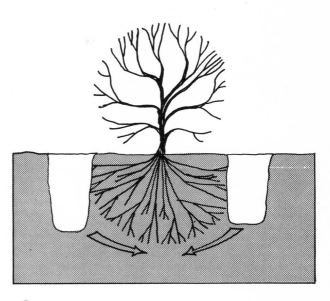

② dig trenches to remove root ball

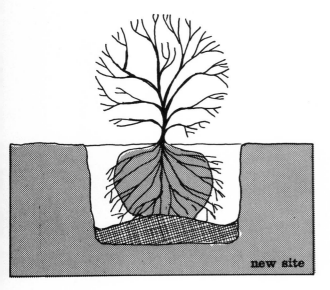

③ add 2" compost, mound soil; spread roots

④ fill w. topsoil; ridge & water

ADRIÁN MARTÍNEZ

Transplanting a Shrub

get to the roots. Avoid buying a plant if you see roots growing through the drainage hole of the container.

Many container plants at nurseries are grown in a loose soil mix to promote fast growth. Once in the ground, they will need a good portion of soil. Dig the hole for them at least twice the size of the diameter of the container and dig deep, at least 24 inches, for a plant in a 5-gallon can. If you do not have a can-cutter, have the nurseryman cut the can. Now place the cut can on its side, pry away one of the sides, then tease the plant loose. Crumble away some of the old soil from the roots and then follow the same planting procedure for balled and burlapped trees and shrubs.

If you cannot get the plant into the ground the same day, keep it cool and watered until planting time.

Depth of planting holes for different plants:

- Annuals—5 to 7 inches.
- Perennials—7 to 9 inches.
- Shrubs—18 to 24 inches.
- Trees—24 to 36 inches.

TRANSPLANTING

Transplanting is a far more important part of garden practice than is generally realized. While it is true that most plants have a reserve of food to offset a bad moving job, the plant will be healthier if the operation is done intelligently. What you are doing is moving an entire plant factory to a new location. With small plants, the job is simple. With trees and shrubs, the task is more complicated.

In general, spring blooming plants are best moved in August or early September, and later blooming ones can be moved in early spring. However, there are no hard-and-fast rules for transplanting. Individual plant requirements, climate, and growing con-ditions must be considered. The idea is to try to transplant them when they are dormant.

To dig up a tree or large shrub, start by digging a circle into the ground at the outer ends of the roots and work toward the trunk. By spading and forking the earth from the roots, most main ones and many of the fibrous ones come out intact. Do not take away the soil that clings to the roots.

A deciduous tree or large shrub or an evergreen is best moved with a ball of earth. A few days before transplanting it, soak the root ball thoroughly so that it will hold together when you lift it. Dig a trench as described above. Some plants have a dense root system which holds the root ball together. Others, like many of the junipers with loosely arranged roots, are more difficult to move because the root ball has a tendency to break apart. If the soil ball holds to-gether reasonably well, the transplanting operation is generally a success. If it crumbles, as it might in sandy soil, the chances of a successful move are less. If the root ball starts to break apart as you take the plant from the hole, try slipping some burlap around it and tie it at the crown of the plant. This is easier said than done, so do not fret if you are not success-ful the first time. Try again.

Sometimes a planting hole just won't drain. When this occurs air is shut off, and mold and rot occur in the plant. To overcome this situation, dig a hole within a hole. After the planting hole is ready, tunnel down with a post-hole digger. Fill the excavation with fine sand or ground bark. If it is impossible to dig into the soil after the planting hole is made, loosen the soil in the bottom with a spade as well as possible and mix it with backfill. Rough up the sides of the hole with the shovel edge so that the roots will grasp the sides of the soil.

Moving very large trees and shrubs is a difficult process requiring chains and ropes, pulleys, and so on. It is a job for a professional tree service.

CHAPTER 5

Climate and Plants

Plants come from all over the world, and they can be as colorful for us in our garden as they are in their native lands. While it is true that many plants come from tropical humid forests, the majority of them are found in temperate and subtropical regions. Within these regions there are different plants growing at different levels. In the tropical zone, for instance, palms and bananas grow between sea level and 3,000 feet; above them are tree ferns and figs; higher in subtropical zones are myrtles and laurels; and above them is a vast region of evergreen shrubs and trees. Deciduous and coniferous trees follow as altitude increases, and finally above 12,000 feet there is a stratum of alpine shrubs. This pattern of growth is easily seen when you drive through the mountains. *As rainfall and temperature change,* so does the plant life.

The two chief factors governing the geographical distribution of plants are the combined influences of temperature and available water in the soil. These factors are further influenced by topography—hills and valleys—and nearness to the ocean. (Soil is sometimes a determining factor in plant distribution; at other times it is a modifying agent.)

Climates vary greatly throughout the world. If you will glance at a world map of annual rainfall, you will see that there are very wet regions, moderately wet ones, arid locales, and so on. Where it is wet and warm you find the most plants growing. But we must also consider how the rain falls. Is it heavy all year? Moderate, but heavy at times? Moderate in winter? Or is the rain scanty all year?

In general, precipitation runs from almost nothing in some deserts to over 400 inches of rain in some tropical regions. Rain can be evenly distributed throughout the year or come in seasons or it can come in the form of snow. Temperature varies from extreme heat in Death Valley of California to extreme cold in areas of Siberia.

Basically, plants grow together in communities that have distinguishing characteristics. Certain plants grow in forests, other kinds—cacti and succulents—in deserts, and still other plants in grassland regions. The environment of the plant is complex and depends on a number of interacting factors such as climate, soil, other plants, and animals.

The forests of the world include conifers or softwoods, temperate hardwoods, tropical hardwoods, and mixed conifers and hardwoods. Tropical rain forests produce evergreen plants and mostly broadleaf species. Tropical regions with periodic dry spells produce other kinds of plants, depending on the amount of rainfall. Monsoon forests have heavy rains, savannah forests not so much rain, and there are regions of the tropics where precipitation is very scanty and vegetation is different again. Plants grow in all these regions.

CLIMATE AND YOUR GARDEN

With the advent of new gardening aids—fertilizers, insecticides, and other chemicals—many people have lost sight of what gardening really is. Too often these days the homeowner sprinkles granules and applies sprays and feeds and protects his plants in a marathon program. None of the new products are miracle workers. Gardening is still working with nature. Most gardeners simply do not pay enough attention to the climate of the area in which they live.

Climate in your own area has a tremendous influence on what kind of plants you can grow. Rainfall, sun, humidity, wind, and seasonal characteristics are all part of the gardening program. And in every region, climatic factors are different. Even in a 10-mile radius, climate can vary considerably especially if you are near hills, lakes, and streams.

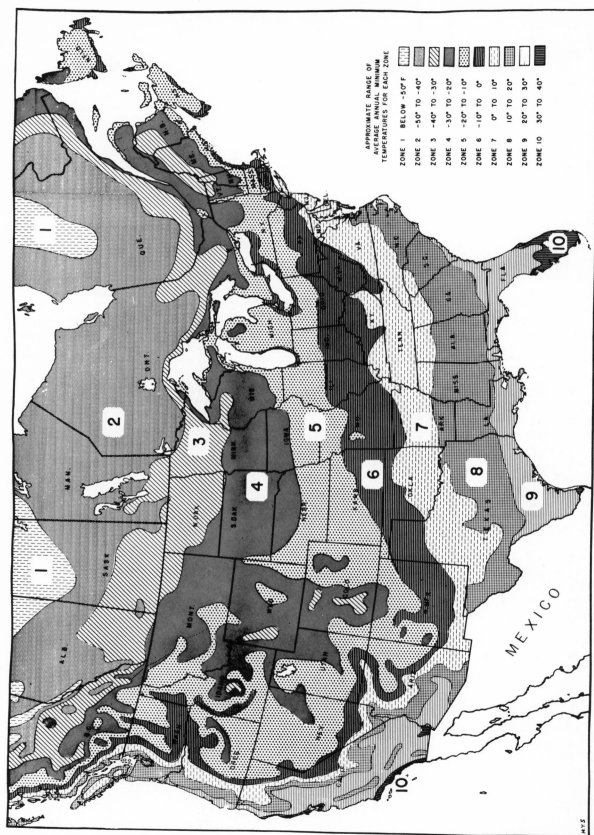

Zones of Plant Hardiness
(USDA)

For example, my house is 14 miles from San Francisco. In summer, it is 15 degrees warmer here than it is in the city. Our annual rainfall is about 38 inches. In the city it is about 17 inches. And only 14 miles separate the two areas.

The East Coast has similar climatic differences within its own regions because in some parts it is quite hilly and there are many lakes and streams. Rainfall varies considerably and so does the growing season. In the South where moderate temperatures prevail all year, we have another kind of gardening picture.

Today's intelligent gardener has to be somewhat of a weatherman and indeed should have specific maps (available from the Weather Bureau) of his state. He should pay attention to local weather forecasts, variable though they may be. Since this is not a book on climatology, but we are concerned with aspects of climate and effect on plants, the information contained is general; you will still have to temper these suggestions with knowledge of your climate.

This is not difficult to do. Any person who has lived in an area for a year knows or can know something about rain and wind, temperature and humidity. If he is new in the area, he can ask a neighbor or the local nursery. And of course, the United States weather maps will help him considerably.

Climate, of course, can be modified somewhat. You cannot stop the wind, but you can stop its harmful effects. Branch breaking can be stopped by having trees properly pruned. Fruit trees that can be harmed by wind can be grown espaliered against walls and fences, and hedges can be put in place to break the force of the wind.

If you are in a rainy area, be sure that drainage on the property is well provided for. The soil will be constantly leached, so be prepared to add fertilizer to it more often. And in dry regions with scanty rainfall consider that plants adapt to water shortage to some degree.

If your lot has too much sun, plant under trees or to the north of the building. Expect a reduction of flowering in plants. Provide a means to combat loss of moisture, which is the chief effect of excess sun. Mulching the soil helps a great deal.

There are hundreds of superlative plants that will grow in your garden but you will not see them in other parts of the country or perhaps even in other parts of your state. Even the same plant against your house wall, protected from wind, may not grow on a hill above your house.

As mentioned, know something about your climate. Know how much wind to expect, observe how and where the sun strikes the site, and inquire about types of soil and rainfall. Your area may have advantages; know what they are and take advantage of them. If there are disadvantages, know these too and combat them.

PLANT HARDINESS

The reference guide to growing plants in different areas of the United States is the hardiness zone map, which is used by nurserymen and most publications. It is somewhat like a universal guide book of what you can or cannot grow and is prepared by the Agricultural Research Service of the United States Department of Agriculture. These maps, based on average minimal night temperatures from weather stations, separate areas of the United States into zones and are very helpful in predicting the adaptability of plants to specific climates. The zone map is included in this chapter. Throughout this book, however, we refer to actual temperature rather than zone number to avoid confusion and constant reference back and forth to maps.

While the zone maps are helpful, they do not and cannot show temperature differences between hill and valley or sites along bodies of water. Thermal belts and fog belts are always at work, and each little variation cannot be cited. For example, there are some zones in northern California where specific conditions exist only in a 5- to 10-mile radius; outside this region, temperatures may be 5 to 10 degrees lower, winds stronger, and other different conditions prevailing.

The subject of plant hardiness does not have to be complicated; there are only a few things you must know to make the subject simple. Hardiness of plants influences your choice of plants, but it need not stop you from experimenting. My garden includes several plants—lilacs, bougainvillaea—that are not supposed to be able to grow in my region. But they do. True, they are strategically placed; the bougainvillaea is purposely protected by the house walls because it needs warmth in winter; the lilacs are in a more exposed place where they get the coolness they require to thrive.

A hardy plant survives without injury the climatic extremes of a given area. It has the ability to withstand freezing. A chemical reaction makes it possible for it to bind its water against low temperatures. Nonhardy plants cannot do this. Usually, the greater the chilling required, the hardier the plant is and the more resistant it is to freezing. The rest period prevents growth when it would be detrimental to the plant.

Injury to plants from freezing comes from ice forming within its tissues. When temperature drops quickly, plant tissues freeze quickly, ice crystals form, and the plant dies. When temperatures fall gradually, the plant's tissues freeze slowly and can recuperate, provided it does not happen too many times. Repeated freezings and thawings increase the possibility of injury to plants.

To protect your plants against freezing, they need to make steady growth through the growing season

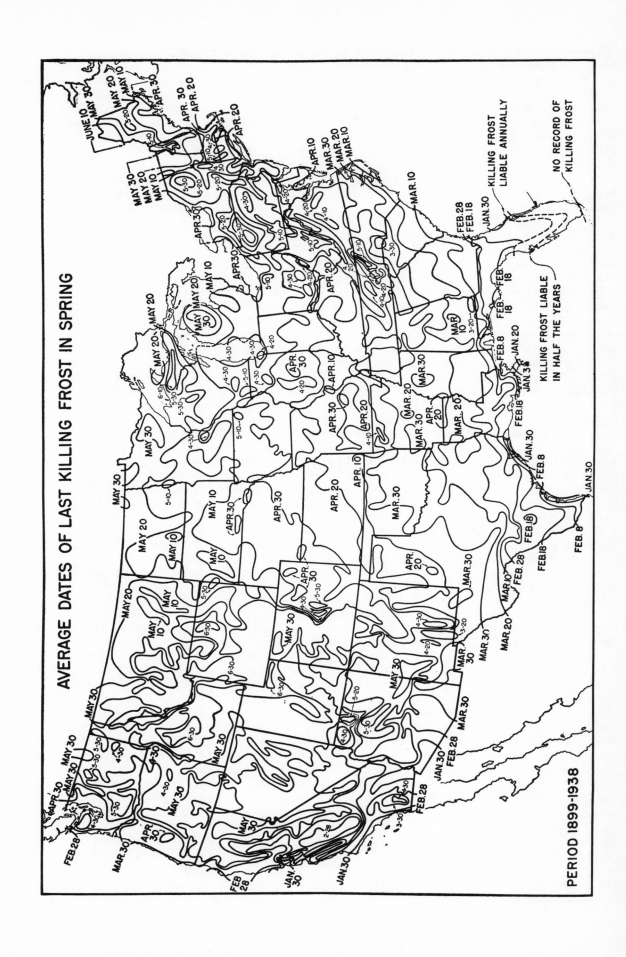

AVERAGE DATES OF LAST KILLING FROST IN SPRING

PERIOD 1899-1938

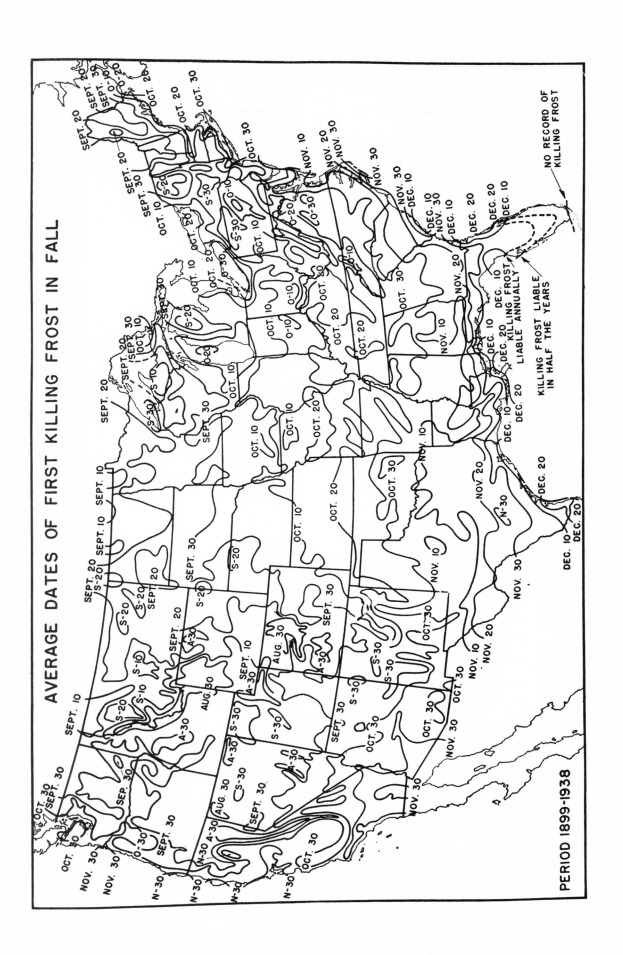

AVERAGE DATES OF FIRST KILLING FROST IN FALL

PERIOD 1899-1938

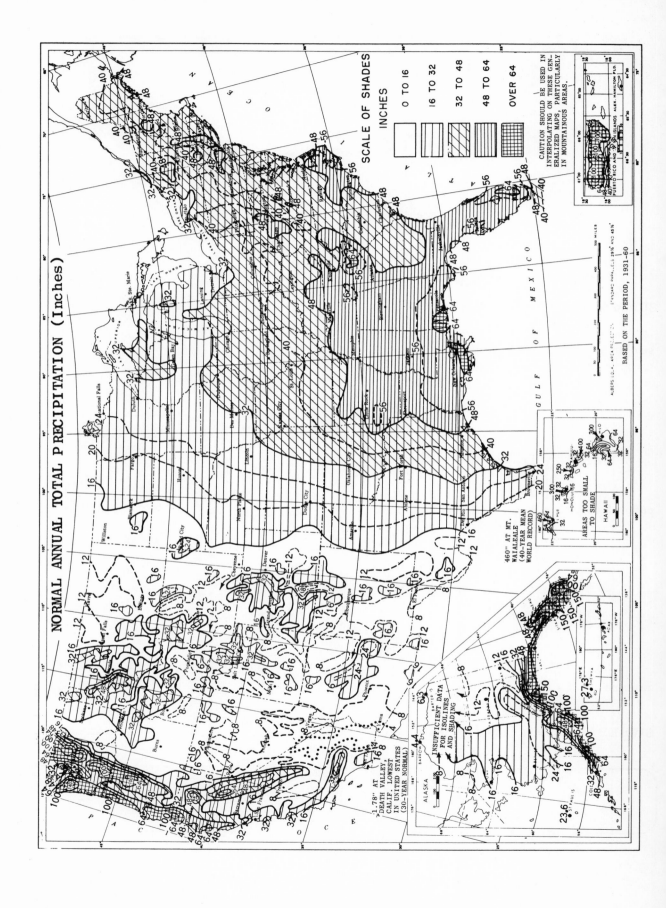

NORMAL ANNUAL TOTAL PRECIPITATION (Inches)

SCALE OF SHADES
INCHES

0 TO 16
16 TO 32
32 TO 48
48 TO 64
OVER 64

CAUTION SHOULD BE USED IN
INTERPOLATING ON THESE GEN-
ERALIZED MAPS, PARTICULARLY
IN MOUNTAINOUS AREAS.

BASED ON THE PERIOD, 1931-60

ALBERS EQUAL AREA PROJECTION, STANDARD PARALLELS 29½° AND 45½°

AREAS TOO SMALL
TO SHADE

HAWAII

460" AT MT.
WAIALEALE.
(40-YEAR MEAN
WORLD RECORD)

1.78" AT
DEATH VALLEY,
CALIF. LOWEST
IN UNITED STATES
(30-YEAR NORMAL)

ALASKA

INSUFFICIENT DATA
FOR ISOLINES
AND SHADING

PUERTO RICO AND VIRGIN ISLANDS   ALEX. HAMILTON FLD.

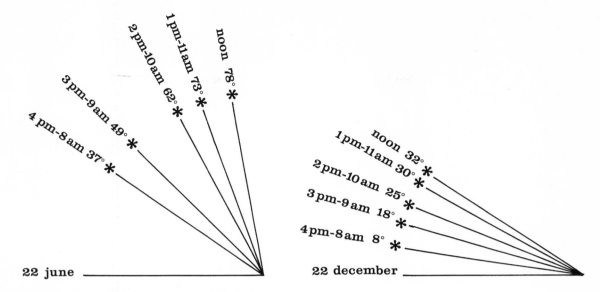

SUMMER and WINTER SUN ANGLES latitude 34°

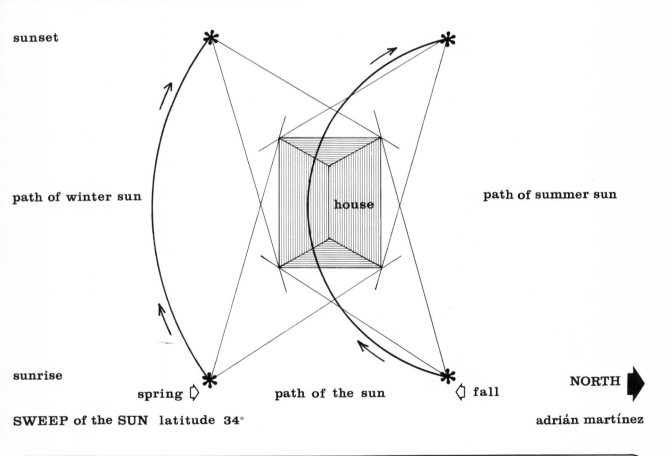

SWEEP of the SUN latitude 34°

The Sun & Orientation

with a gradual cessation from mid-August until the first killing frost. Fertilization and watering must be carefully given starting in midsummer. Fluctuations in growth of the plant should be avoided. Plants that lose their leaves because of insects or disease are especially vulnerable to premature freezing. Late growth can happen too and then the plant will be too immature to survive winter.

There are some cultural rules to help you help your plants in regard to hardiness. Late feeding with high nitrogen fertilizers can force late succulent growth and reduce hardiness of many plants like roses, perennials, and broad-leaved evergreens. Do not feed plants in late summer.

Permanent mulching, also, can reduce hardiness of plants by keeping the soil temperature warm late in the season. Mulches should be removed in fall and replaced before actual winter weather starts. Temporary mulches are invaluable and they are different from permanent kinds.

Soil moisture is important too for the hardiness of a plant. Evergreens and deciduous trees and shrubs lose water through their stems all winter. The stronger the wind, the greater the loss; and when the ground is frozen, the plant is unable to absorb water and to replenish the moisture lost. So mulches are desirable. (See Chapter 6.)

If you buy plants from a supplier in a warmer climate than your own, be sure the species is hardy in your zone. Remember, you can modify your zone somewhat and adjust locations within your zone. But if you would rather not be bothered with winter protection methods, as described above, choose plants listed in the zone hardiness map for one-half zone colder than your own.

MICROCLIMATES

Certain influences within your garden create microclimates (little areas a few feet or a few hundred feet wide) that are somewhat apart from the general climate of your region. For example, a fence facing south will accumulate heat; a hill away from the protection of the house will be cooler. Warm air rises and cold air sinks, so gardens in hilly terrains have several microclimates where temperature and humidity vary.

A plant protected from western sun will experience a gradual drop in temperature, and the same plant in full west sun will have a gradual drop in leaf temperature well above air temperature. As the sun sets, a rapid temperature drop occurs and severe damage to the plant can happen. This occurs frequently with broad-leafed evergreens or with tree trunks that get scalded by sun.

Where there are windbreaks—other houses, roofs —heat radiates from the buildings, and a mass of warmer air can temper the existing temperatures considerably. Yet these houses may be recent additions to the landscape, and plants formerly suggested for the area no longer will grow there.

Large bodies of water affect the climate within a zone considerably. They temper the overall climate of adjoining areas and raise the zone as high as one full zone from inland regions. Ponds and lakes can to an extent do the same thing. On the other hand, sites close to the shore exposed to severe wind will have a lower hardiness zone than expected.

CHAPTER 6

Keeping Plants Growing

Once plants are in the ground, keep them healthy. Trees and shrubs, like furniture in the home, are investments and are part of a total plan. Replacing them is costly.

The various factors involved in keeping a plant healthy are temperature, humidity, light, wind, soil, and of course the plant itself. We cannot do too much about the weather and we assume that the soil has been properly mixed and has adequate nutrients. So watering the plant becomes the prime concern of most gardeners (in addition to keeping them free of insects and disease).

There are many ways of watering plants—hose, sprinkler, underground watering systems—and so on. (See Chapter 9.) For now, the important thing is when to water and how much to water. While these are variable factors there are some general rules to help you help your plants make satisfactory growth.

WATERING PLANTS

It takes water more time to penetrate soil than we think. If you water for one hour under normal circumstances, the soil is penetrated to a depth of about 48 inches. So plants that get water for only five minutes are getting hardly any moisture. Water must penetrate the soil and get to the roots below the surface of the soil. Moisture moves through soil in a lateral movement. It does not spread out like a fan. If only the top of the soil is kept wet, roots will become shallow. They do not work their way into deep soil to search out moisture, and they become susceptible to damage from heat. Now, you have heard it before, but it is such sound information I must say it again here. While it is essential to water plants thoroughly, it is just as important to allow them to dry out before watering them again.

If there is too much water in the soil, the supply of oxygen to the roots is blocked, and plants start to drown. Allow enough time between waterings for total moisture absorption by the soil and roots. This is the tricky part of watering—not how much *but how much when*. And the when depends on wind, temperature, light intensity, humidity, soil, and rainfall. Clay soil holds water longer than sandy soil. The length of time that loamy soil holds water falls somewhere in between the two.

There are scientific devices to measure the amount of moisture absorption of the soil and to determine what kind of soil you have. If you do not want to bother with apparatus and soil test kits, simply dig up some soil and see if it is sandy or clayey. And know something about your climate. If you have lived in an area for about a year, you can anticipate what kind of winds, temperature, and humidity to expect from season to season.

To offer some guidance about moisture and soil: consider that to thoroughly soak a 50-square-foot area to a depth of 24 inches, about 60 gallons of water is needed by a sandy soil, about 100 gallons by a loamy soil, and almost 175 gallons by a soil that is heavy or claylike.

A hose under normal volume runs about 5 gallons a minute, so it takes about 15 minutes to soak a sandy soil, 20 minutes for loamy ground, and about 40 minutes for clay soil. The sandy soil would dry out in about 7 to 9 days, the loamy soil in about 14 days, and clay in about 20 days or longer.

METHODS OF WATERING

An array of watering devices—sprinklers, bubblers, subsoil irrigators, perforated hoses—are available. For average gardens, a hose or a sprinkling system—automatic or manual—is used. (See Chapter 9.) Sprinklers save time and work, but first you must

DEPTH	COARSE SAND	SANDY LOAM	CLAY w. LOAM
0			
6"			
12"	15 MINUTES	30 MINUTES	60 MINUTES
18"			
24"		60 MINUTES	
30"	40 MINUTES		
36"			
42"			
48"	60 MINUTES		

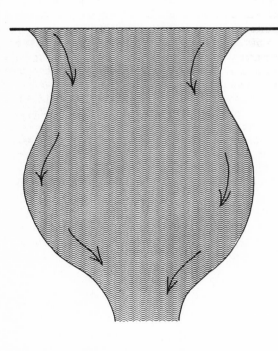

WATER MOVES LATERALLY
DOES NOT FAN OUT TO ANY DEGREE

Water Absorption Chart

know how much water they actually give. An empty coffee can will give you the answer. Set it in place on the ground and make note of the time it takes to fill it with one inch of water. Multiply this time by the number of inches you want the water to penetrate a depth and leave the sprinkler on that length of time.

Sprinkling—from a hose or a sprinkler—is the best way to apply water evenly over a large area. And, too, many plants benefit from overhead watering: leaves are washed of dust and soot, and the moisture discourages certain pests from attacking the foliage.

A thorough soaking is necessary for all plants, but more so for trees and shrubs. They really need water in growth, so soak them. Put the hose at the base of the water well and let it run moderately for a time, or use a water bubbler that breaks up the force of the flow without decreasing the volume; thus soil will not wash out of the well. Another way to get water to the roots of a large shrub or moderate-size tree is with a subsoil irrigator. This is a perforated pipe that attaches to the end of the hose and is set into the ground.

FERTILIZERS

There are about fifteen essential elements necessary to provide nutrition for plants. The three most important are nitrogen, phosphorus, and potassium (potash). These are most likely deficient in cultivated soils. In early spring, when plants most need nitrogen, it is generally at its lowest content in the soil, or heavy rains have leached it out.

Nitrogen stimulates vegetative development, and it is necessary in the growth of stems and leaves. Phosphorus is needed in all phases of plant growth, particularly in the production of fruits and seeds; it also produces good root development. Potassium promotes the general vigor of a plant, making it resistant to certain diseases and also has a balancing influence on other plant nutrients. Also important are various trace elements such as copper, iron, manganese, sulfur, and zinc.

Plants need feeding when they begin to grow in the spring and while they are making active growth in summer. Generally, woody plants and trees should not be fed after August 1 because this stimulates growth which may not survive fall frosts.

It is better to apply a weak feeding solution more frequently than one massive dose that might burn roots and foliage. Do not feed new plants; wait a few weeks until they have overcome the shock of transplanting. And do not feed ailing plants; they do not have the capacity to absorb additional food.

To feed shrubs, vines, flowers, and vegetables, simply spread fertilizer on the ground around the plant and scratch it lightly into the soil. Water thoroughly to dissolve the fertilizer. It must be in solution for roots to absorb it. Generally, trees are best fed through holes punched in the ground.

Foliar feeding is usually for small plants. Plant food is applied in a solution to the leaves and is instantly available to the plant. But while this stimulates a plant quickly, its benefits do not last long. It is also costly and cannot be relied upon for all-season feeding.

Today, there are dozens of plant foods, and selecting the right one can be confusing. Basically, most of them are composed of nitrogen, phosphorus, and potassium, with some trace elements. The contents are on the package or the bottle. The first numeral denotes the percentage of nitrogen, the second of phosphorus, and the third of potassium. These plant foods are called complete inorganic fertilizers because they are made of chemicals. However, a 100-lb. bag of plant food does not contain 100 lbs. of nutrients. The total of the three figures on the bag is what you are actually getting. A bag of 10–10–5 fertilizer has 10 lbs. of nitrogen, 10 lbs. of phosphorus, and 5 lbs. of potash. The rest is inert filler.

Fertilizers are offered in five forms:

Powdered. Good, but blows away on a windy day; may stick to foliage and if stored in a damp place, will cake.

Concentrated liquids. Used for all fertilizing.

Concentrated powders. Diluted in water and applied to foliage and plant roots.

Concentrated tablets. Used mostly for house plants. Dissolves in water and is applied in liquid or put in soil and allowed to dissolve gradually with water.

Pelleted or granular. Easy to spread; some granular fertilizers also have insecticides; others have weed killers.

In addition to the man-made fertilizers (most often used) there are nitrogen materials to help plants grow.

Quickly available nitrogen materials are water soluble, and nitrogen becomes available to the plant immediately. Results are quick, but they do not last long, and frequent light applications are necessary to obtain uniform growth over a long period of time. These materials include ammonium sulfate, ammonium nitrate, urea, nitrate of soda, ammonium phosphate, calcium nitrate, and others.

Slowly available nitrogen materials release their nitrogen over relatively long periods. These materials depend upon soil bacteria to decompose and transform the resultant compounds into the nitrogen forms which then become available to the plant. There are two groups of slowly available nitrogen materials: (1) Organic matter, which includes sewerage sludge, animal and vegetable tankage, manures, cottonseed meal, and others. (2) Ureaform

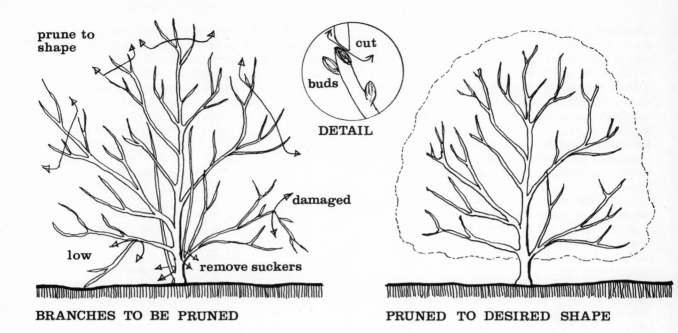

prune to shape

cut

buds

DETAIL

damaged

low

remove suckers

BRANCHES TO BE PRUNED

PRUNED TO DESIRED SHAPE

Pruning Shrubs

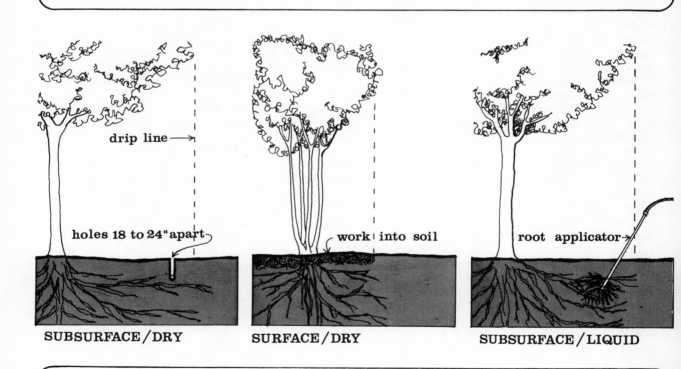

drip line →

holes 18 to 24" apart

work into soil

root applicator →

SUBSURFACE/DRY

SURFACE/DRY

SUBSURFACE/LIQUID

Fertilizing Trees

compounds, which are synthetic materials made by chemical union of urea and formaldehyde. Do not confuse urea (quickly available nitrogen) with ureaform.

There are also fertilizers for specific plants—roses, azaleas, camellias. These are especially prepared and are perhaps more valuable for certain plants than the general fertilizers. It is somewhat like which is the best dog food for your dog.

Because there are so many plant foods, know which ones will do what for your garden. For example, if you want to feed a lawn, use a high nitrogen food like 20–20–10. For flower beds and to make plants bloom, select a food with high phosphorus content like 12–12–12 or 5–10–5. If you want something to improve the soil structure and to release nutrients slowly, choose an organic food like blood meal or bone meal.

Plant food used wisely greatly aids a plant in producing better growth and flowers. Used with abandon, it can kill a plant.

MULCHES

An easy garden practice that is often ignored is called mulching. It is a process that can mean the difference between healthy plants or weak ones. Mulching decreases the amount of moisture lost through evaporation from the soil surfaces and keeps the soil cooler than when it is fully exposed to the sun.

Generally, mulches are organic materials that decay in time, contributing to soil improvement.

A mulch also helps to control weed development; under a protective coating many weeds fail to germinate or if they do, they are weak and easy to remove.

Any material spread between and around a plant to cover the soil is a mulch. Apply it in a layer 2 to 4 inches thick. No one mulch does everything, however. Some materials allow more air to enter the soil than others. Some mulches, such as oak leaves and pine needles, have acid content, a vital requirement for azaleas, rhododendrons, and other acid-preference plants. Use different mulches in different places around your garden.

Some growers keep plants mulched all year. Others apply a mulch after the soil has warmed up in spring and growth has started. If mulches are put in place too early, they stop growth because soil stays cool. In fall, apply mulches after the soil has frozen.

ORGANIC MULCHES

Leaves. Old leaves are best; oak leaves and pine needles are just right for acid-loving plants.

Hay and straw. Salt hay is best because it decomposes slowly and is weed free.

Grass clippings. Good when mixed with a coarse material so they do not mat.

Cocoa beans and pecan shells. Decompose slowly and make a satisfactory mulch, but do not use for acid-loving plants.

Ground fir bark. Several grades; extremely good material that decomposes slowly and is attractive and stays in place.

Sawdust. Usually free for the asking and quite satisfactory as a mulch. Use it alone or mix it with peat.

Conifer boughs. Used for winter mulching for flowers and shrubs. Give protection against snow and sun.

There are also inorganic mulches such as stones and gravel, roofing paper, or insulated fiber; but of course these materials will not help in improving the soil.

PRUNING

Pruning and trimming plants are part of a good garden program. Pruning shapes plants, allows free circulation of air and light, directs growth, and removes dead or injured parts. It also increases the quality or yield of fruits or flowers.

The kind of pruning needed varies at different times in the life of the plant. Many trees and shrubs must be cut back somewhat severely at planting time so that there will be strong new growth. Some ornamental trees and most fruit trees must be pruned to grow properly, and of course vines and some trees and shrubs need training to make them handsome.

Where and How to Cut

It is important to know where to make a cut when pruning. Indiscriminate butchering must be avoided. Make a cut only above a bud or a small side branch or a main branch. Do not leave a small stub; it will wither and die and is an invitation to decay and to insects to get into a plant. Cut branches in the direction you want the new growth to take. If you need vertical accent for the garden design, keep the lower branches pruned. However, remove them only after they have served their purpose in nourishing the tree or shrub. If you are trying to shape a plant to a pattern, trim away twiggy and unattractive growth so that well-placed branches can be seen.

Shade Trees

Young shade trees need pruning to help them develop strong frameworks that resist wind. Remove

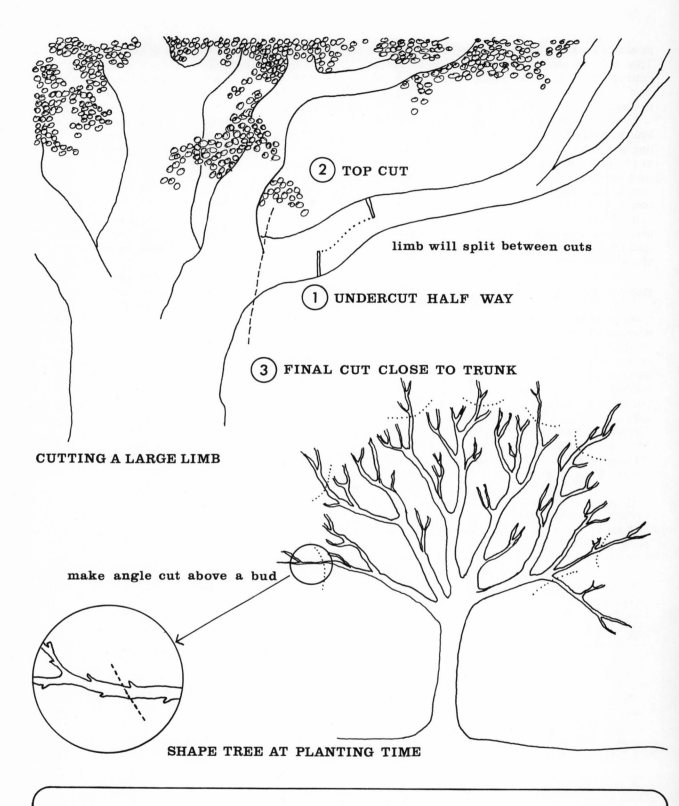

② TOP CUT

limb will split between cuts

① UNDERCUT HALF WAY

③ FINAL CUT CLOSE TO TRUNK

CUTTING A LARGE LIMB

make angle cut above a bud

SHAPE TREE AT PLANTING TIME

Pruning & Shaping

unwanted branches before they become formidable. Trim out crossed branches; these give a tree an unkempt appearance. If one branch grows faster than others, prune it when it is young to keep the tree shapely.

Large trees are best pruned by a professional. Special equipment and skill are necessary when cutting heavy limbs. It is hazardous work; and it is wiser to pay a tree service fee than a hospital bill. Shade trees are usually trimmed in summer, but if the temperature is not too low, they can be cut at any time.

In all pruning—but especially with shade trees—never leave a stub. Cut branches flush with the trunk. And cover all cuts with tree wound solution (available at nurseries).

Deciduous Flowering Shrubs and Trees

Some deciduous shrubs and trees bloom on old branches while others have flowers on current or new wood. Before pruning deciduous shrubs and trees, learn which one belongs to which class. Shrubs that bloom on previous years' wood in spring or early summer can be pruned immediately after they flower. Cut away weak shoots, unattractive branches, and old flowering stems. The idea is to allow light and air to the plant so that new flowering branches can grow. If you prune shrubs and trees in spring or winter, only thin them out; do not do any drastic cutting.

Shrubs that bloom on current wood are pruned in winter or early spring. They can be cut back drastically if you want them low. Thin out weaker shoots to make a more handsome plant.

Fruit Trees

Fruit trees should be pruned every year when they are bare to make them more attractive and to reduce the number of buds, which results in the production of bigger fruit. Vigorous growers such as peaches and nectarines need hard pruning, apricot and plum not so much cutting, and slow growers such as apple, pear, and cherry need some corrective thinning once the framework is mature.

Again, the basic principles for pruning are as follows: Cut cleanly so that water does not stand on the open wound. Use only clean tools. Apply wound paint to large cuts. Burn diseased parts of plants. Use sharp tools. (Pruning tools are described in Chapter 9.)

CHAPTER 7

Troubleshooting Plant Problems

Today's world runs on speed and convenience, and this overflows into our gardening. Yet the very nature of planting and growing things and working with nature calls for patience. When most people see an insect in the garden, they immediately purchase a barrage of chemicals. If they see withered leaves or plants not doing well, they quickly blame insects.

Not all or very many plant problems in the small garden are caused by insects or by disease. Look to culture first. Are the plants getting enough water? Are they getting enough light or, perhaps, too much sun? What about wind; is it harming a plant? In other words, is the problem caused by culture rather than insects? Determine this before you do anything else.

Once you have decided an insect is responsible for a plant's failing to grow, identify the pest before buying a preventative. There are many different insecticides and fungicides. Know what you are fighting before you do battle; and do not think that chemicals will solve all insect problems. Most gardens will still have their share of pests, good ones and bad ones, so first ask yourself if an insecticide is really needed.

The small garden will, by its very nature, present small problems. Frequently it is better to use an old-fashioned remedy to eliminate a few insects rather than hauling out a sprayer, mixing insecticides, and fussing and fuming. A strong hosing with water rids plants of aphids; beetles can, if necessary, be hand-picked, and mealybugs can be soaked off a plant.

I am not against using poisons in the garden, but I am not for them either. I use them only as a last resort. When I was away for a week and on my return found the bougainvillaea completely infested with aphids, I did use a spray. There was no other remedy if I wanted to save the plant.

BEFORE YOU SPRAY

As I have mentioned, not all plant problems are caused by insects or disease; sometimes you are the culprit. Cultural conditions have not been tended to as they should have been. Before you start the battle of the bugs, read the following paragraphs.

Plants that develop leaves with brown or crisp edges may be getting too much heat and fluctuating soil temperatures. New growth that quickly withers may be caused by the same conditions. Lower the temperature, if at all possible, and keep soil evenly moist.

If new leaves are yellow, the cause can be a lack of acidity in the soil. If leaves turn yellow and drop off, this may be a natural condition. If leaves develop brown or silvery streaks, they are getting too much sun. If they appear lifeless, they are not getting enough water.

Buds suddenly dropping off plants is a complaint of many gardeners. This is caused by fluctuating temperatures, and there simply is no remedy. If plants are not blooming as they should, they are not getting enough sun. On the other hand, if stems turn soft and leaves wilt, the plant is in too much shade with too much moisture.

Healthy plants are rarely attacked by predators or prone to disease. They are simply too strong. When you buy new plants, inspect them carefully before you put them in the garden. Be sure there is nothing wrong with them.

In conclusion, if you want to keep plants free of insects, keep the garden clean. This simple step goes a long way in assuring healthy robust plants. Throw away trash, pick faded flowers, cut and burn dead wood.

CONTROL METHODS

Know how to apply pesticides before you start to use them. There are several methods to control pests. Decide which is the best and most convenient way for you.

Spraying. This is a satisfactory method because it is possible to reach all parts of the plant. You can use a flit gun or trombone-type sprayer, a sprayer that attaches to a hose, or a portable sprayer. The equipment you choose depends on how much soil you have to cover. Before you spray, be sure the ground is wet. Do the job in early morning or late afternoon; hot sun on treated plants sometimes harms them. After spraying, clean all equipment thoroughly. Wash sprayer with soapy water, rinse with clean water, and force water through the nozzle before you use it again.

Dusting. This is a messy procedure but it is faster than spraying and eliminates the mixing process. Use a dust gun or crank-type or rotary duster. Do the job on a calm day; otherwise, your lungs will get more insecticide than the plants.

Spreading. This is the easiest way to eliminate insects. It is fast and clean, and merely requires sprinkling insecticide on the ground and watering it.

Systemic control. This is the new and most popular method of killing insects. The poison in granular form (there is also liquid) is sprinkled on the ground, and water is applied. The poison is absorbed by the plant roots, and all parts of the plant become toxic to many insects (but not all) for a period of 4 to 6 weeks. The names in this group of chemicals are Di-syston and Meta-systox-R. While these poisons are popular with gardeners because they are so easy to apply, they are not above suspicion as to their effects on humans. Use them only if absolutely necessary and then with extreme caution, according to directions on the package. In reality, systemics control only a few insects—aphids, leafhoppers, and mealybugs—and any careful gardener can surely control these without using dubious chemicals.

Biological control. This method is gaining followers. It is fighting nature with nature and involves using natural enemies of insects rather than poisons. It also includes using plants such as onions and others that naturally discourage insects. Ladybugs, praying mantises, lacewing bugs are all part of the organic gardener's weapon force. This control method also involves mulching plants and using a great deal of compost in the soil. It is gardening without poison. It involves not disturbing the balance of nature and, as such, it has much to recommend it.

INSECTS

Insects can be divided into sucking and chewing pests. The sucking type get their food by piercing plant tissue, and the chewers bite off and eat portions of the plant. The first group can be controlled with contact poisons applied to their bodies. The other group is controlled by applying poisons to the plant parts attacked, and the insects die of internal poisoning.

Some insects attack any plant; others have a preference and limit their diet to rhododendrons or azaleas, for instance. Many insects are easily seen. Others are so minute they are almost invisible; these are the most difficult to control. They include root lice, mites, and stem borers, to mention a few.

Timing is important when applying insecticides. Many insects are more vulnerable in the early stages of their life or after they have hatched from their eggs. For instance, scale insects are more susceptible to chemicals when they are right out of the egg than in later stages of their life.

Not all insects are detrimental to plants. On the contrary, many of them are necessary to maintain a balance of nature. There are many beneficial insects, so when you spray plants to kill aphids you might also be killing the larvae of the lacewing fly, which is a voracious exterminator of plant lice and other insects. Ladybugs, too, eat their weight many times over in insects, and are invaluable in keeping the insect population under control. So are the larvae of the ladybug. Tachina flies make a diet of cutworms and caterpillars. The praying mantis can devour hundreds of insects a day. Digger wasps and wheel bugs are other beneficial insects that eat larvae of various detrimental insects.

Think twice before you start killing insects. There is more involved than meets the eye; many times when you spray to kill a few attacking pests, you may be killing off hundreds of beneficial insects that are, in truth, friends of the garden.

BENEFICIAL BIRDS

The most common birds in the garden are likely to be friendly ones. However, there are some birds that eat fruit and berries, along with their basic diet of insects. But preventing occasional damage from birds is not difficult compared to the problem of checking

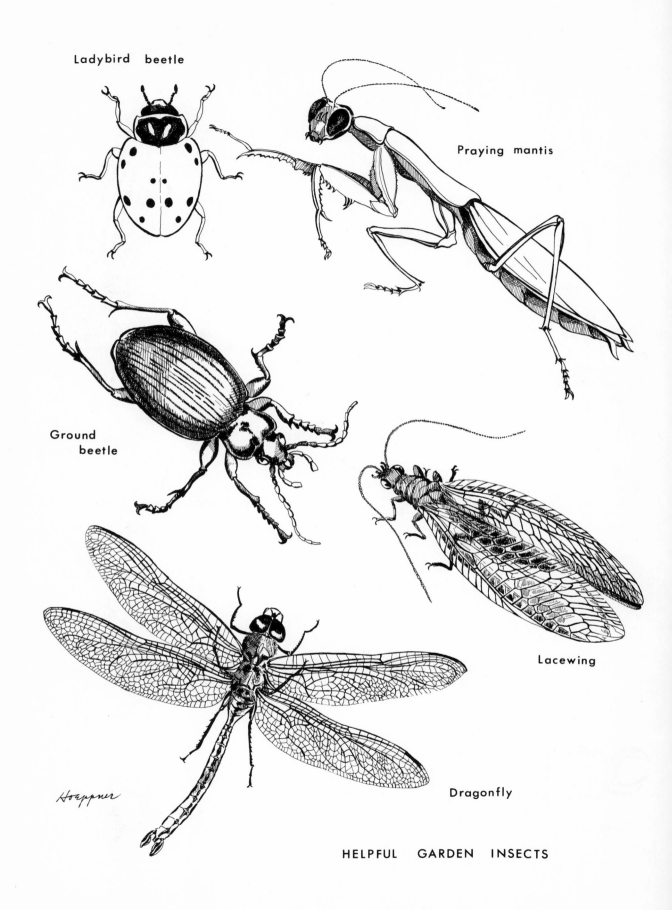

Ladybird beetle

Praying mantis

Ground beetle

Lacewing

Hoeppner

Dragonfly

HELPFUL GARDEN INSECTS

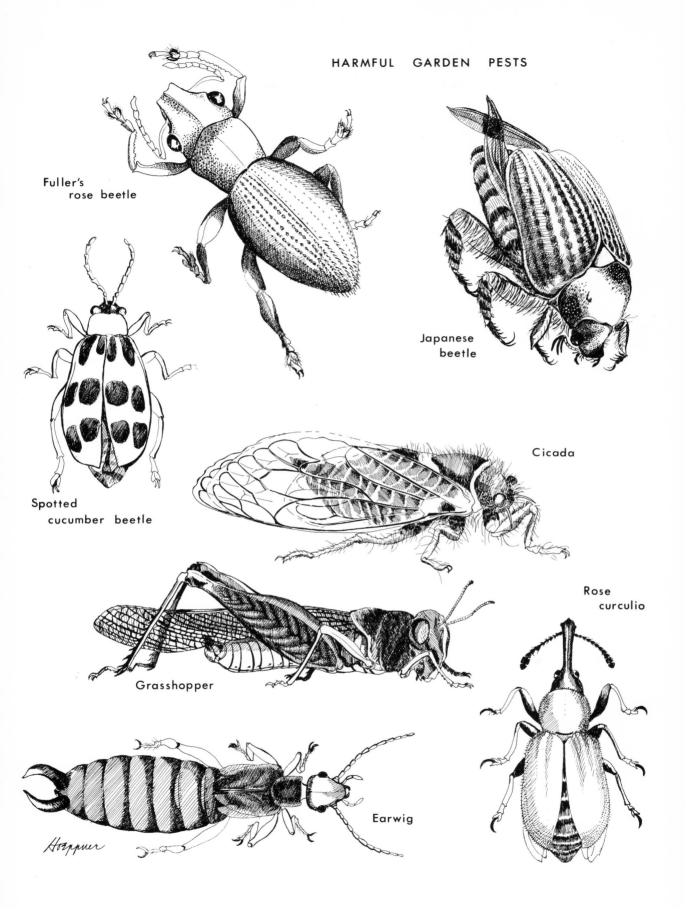

Fuller's
rose beetle

Japanese
beetle

Spotted
cucumber beetle

Cicada

Rose
curculio

Grasshopper

Earwig

Hoeppner

Table 1. Insects and How to Control Them

Insects	What They Look Like	What They Attack	What They Do	Control
aphids	Green or black, pink or yellow, or red, soft-bodied insects	Almost all plants	Plants stunted, leaves deformed	Malathion, rotenone
beetles (many kinds)	Usually brown or black, wingless	Flowers and vegetables	Eat leaves and flowers	Handpick if possible, or use sevin
borers (many kinds)	Caterpillars, grubs	Woody and herbaceous plants	Wilting; holes in stems and branches	Diazinon
caterpillars (include bagworms, cutworms, cankerworms, tent caterpillar)	Easily recognized	All kinds of plants	Defoliate plants	Rotenone, diazinon, malathion
chinch bugs	Small black-and-white insects	Mainly lawns	Brown patches	Sevin
cutworms (generally in soil)	Hairless moth caterpillars	Many plants	Eat leaves	Sevin, dibrom
grasshoppers	Familiar insect	Plants, trees	Eat leaves	Sevin
lacebugs	Small bugs with lacy wings	Azaleas, oaks, birches, hawthorn; other plants	Leaves appear mottled	Malathion
leafhoppers	Wedge-shaped insects that hop	Many plants	Leaves pale or brown; plants stunted	Malathion
leaf miners (many kinds; hollyleaf miner, boxwood miner)	Larvae of various insects	Many plants	Leaves spotted, blotched	Systemics, diazinon
leaf rollers	Small caterpillars	Deciduous plants; other plants	Leaves roll up	Sevin
mealybugs	White cottony insects	Many plants	Plants stunted, don't grow	Sevin, diazinon
mites	Minute sucking insects	Almost all plants	Discolor leaves	Systemics
nematodes	Microscopic worms	Many plants	Plants stunted, die back	Sterilize soil
scale	Tiny, hard, oval insects	Many plants	Yellowing or loss of leaves	Diazinon
snails, slugs (not insects but common pests)	Easily recognized	Many plants	Eat foliage	Metaldehyde
spittle bugs	Brown, gray, or black insects wrapped in froth	Many plants	Plants and fruit stunted	Malathion
springtails	Tiny black jumping bugs	Some plants	Leaves pitted	Malathion
squash bugs	Dark-brown insects	Few plants	Plants turn black and die	Malathion, sevin
thrips	Tiny winged insects	Few plants	Leaves become silvery	Malathion
wireworms	Hard, shiny, coiled worms	Flowers, vegetables	Kill seedlings; work underground	Diazinon

SOURCE: Much of this data was derived from "The Thoughtful Gardener's Guide," *Cry California, the Journal of California Tomorrow,* Vol. 4, No. 3 (Summer 1969).

Notes on Insecticides:
Malathion safest to humans and pets.
Sevin—a carbonate, one of the safest of synthetics
Dibrom—quite toxic
Diazinon—very toxic
Systemics—highly toxic (cumulative and persistent effects not yet proven)

Do not use metaldehyde which contains arsenicals.

Check with your local Agricultural Station (listed in the Appendix) for further information on insects in your area and suggestions for how to eliminate them.

the work of chewing, sucking, and blight pests.

Swallows are fine garden friends and perform an insect-eating scavenger service that is all to our good. You can see these birds sweeping the sky back and forth in early evening as nocturnal bugs begin to swarm. With large throats and open mouths, swallows scoop insects from the air with amazing speed. Barn swallows will nest in the eaves of your garage or other outbuildings, so don't chase them away.

The purple martin is an invaluable garden keeper and will gladly stay with you if you provide a birdhouse for him. These birds nest in a community house. They feed on wasps, flies, and other unwanted summer pests.

Another group of desirable birds is the flycatcher family, of which the kingbird is a member. His diet consists of many insects, and he will also pick off aphids and caterpillars at ground level or catch insects on the wing. Keep him around if you want to garden without poisons. Wrens, titmice, and bushtits are other friendly birds that can keep your garden almost insect free. The Baltimore oriole is another insect eater and will consume caterpillars, pupae, and adult moths.

As I have mentioned, some birds are undesirable. These include the English sparrow, the linnet, or house finch, and very often mockingbirds can be detrimental in the garden, feeding on berries and other fruits.

To attract birds to your garden, give them a supply of water; not only water in birdbaths but also sprays or mists. Many birds love a light shower. Supply them with food and birdhouses. Birds are not only lovely to watch; they, in turn, watch your garden and help keep it free from insects.

INSECTICIDE AND APPLICATION DATA

Insecticides are offered in a bewildering number, and although packages list active ingredients, they are not readily distinguishable to most people. Many times they are listed by chemical name rather than generic name and they are impossible to decipher. By all

means, question your local nurseryman about insecticides. Some are inorganic, others botanical or synthetic. Arsenic is an example of the inorganic type and is generally no longer in use. Pyrethrin and rotenone derived from plants are botanical preventatives and are coming back into use. The synthetic chemicals derived by man include chlorinated hydrocarbons, carbamates, and organophosphates. DDT is a prime example of the hydrocarbon type; chlordane, lindane, and aldrin are in the same class.

Researchers have discovered that many years after application, hydrocarbon chemicals remain in the soil, and that chlorinated hydrocarbons are found today in virtually all living organisms in all corners of the earth. This is an alarming fact, and every day data are being released to prove it a validity.

Read all instructions carefully before applying chemicals, and always use less rather than more. Handle poisons with care. Keep them out of reach of children and pets. Repeated applications may be necessary. This information is given on the package. Some products are for spraying, others in granular form for applying to the ground (then watered in), and others are dusts.

The ecologist's main concern is not how poisonous a chemical is but rather how persistent and accumulative. Since this is not a book on ecology or biology of pesticides, facts and figures will not be cited, but they exist in other works. However, to protect our own world, I feel it prudent not to apply any chemicals that include chlorinated hydrocarbons.

CONTROLLING INSECTS WITH NONPERSISTENT POISONS

Table 1 suggests controls to eliminate insects and pests that, although still toxic, are not persistent poisons.

It is better to have a few plants eaten and a few trees marred than a totally insect-free, beautiful garden with no one around to appreciate it.

PLANT DISEASES

Many destructive plant diseases are caused by bacteria, fungi, and viruses. Diseases are generally named for their dominant symptoms—blight, canker, leaf spot—or for the organism causing disease—rust, powdery mildew. Many times unfavorable conditions and poor cultural practices open the way for these agents to cause trouble. A poorly grown plant, like a human being in poor health, is more susceptible to bacteria and virus. Insects, too, add to the problem because many of them spread diseases from one plant to another.

Environment also plays a part in the development of bacterial and fungal attacks, since they are responsive to moisture and temperature. Moisture is particularly important because it is necessary for the germination of spores of the organisms of disease. Excessive moisture in the soil can lead to root rot. Frequently, plants in shade are more prone to develop disease than those in light.

Here is a simple explanation of the organisms that can cause plant disease.

Fungi. This is familiar to us because we have seen old bread and fruits and mushrooms on which fungi have developed. There are thousands of different kinds of fungi, some of which can cause serious plant damage. Rot, wilt, rust, and powdery mildew are basically due to specific fungi.

Bacteria. Microscopic organisms that survive in soil or plant parts and cause blights, rot, galls, or wilting. Human diseases are caused by bacteria, and so are several plant ailments. Bacteria is the causative agent of fire blight and iris rhizome rot.

Virus. Many of the most serious diseases of ornamental plants are from a virus. We are still trying to decipher viruses in humans, and they are as much of a mystery when they attack plants.

Listed here are some of the diseases that can occur in plants and the remedies for them. However, to be quite frank, once plants are infected, it is difficult to save them. Further, generally highly poisonous controls are necessary and while we list some here, we do not sanction using them unless as a last resort.

Rust. Leaves and stems are affected with reddish spores in powdery pustules or gelatinous lumps. Foliage turns yellow. Several different kinds of rust affect hollyhock, snapdragon. Control: Spray with Actidione or ferbam.

Powdery mildew. White or gray growth usually on the surface of leaves or branches or fruit. Leaves are powdery with blotches and sometimes curled. Plants are often stunted. Control: Hose or heavy rain will naturally control it.

Leaf Spot. Can do extensive damage to ornamental plants, resulting in defoliation. Leaves have distinct spots with brownish or white centers and dark edges. Rarely fatal, but cut off affected foliage. Control: Spray with zineb or ferbam.

Rot. Many different kinds of rot occur on plants. The disease can attack irises and calla lillies and other plants—crown rot on delphiniums, for instance. Affected spots appear watery and turn yellow or brown. (The iris borer helps to spread this disease.) Control: Destroy infected plant parts. Sterilize soil before planting again.

Blight. Many different kinds of blights caused by several kinds of organisms. Azalea petal blight, camellia flower blight, botrytis blight. Gray mold appears on plant parts. Control: For botrytis, spray with zineb or ferbam. For other blights, spray with zineb or treat soil with Terraclor.

Wilt. Due to various causal organisms, and can affect mature plants and seedlings. Usually wilt organisms live in soil. Cut away infected parts. Control: No known chemical control.

Mosaic. Virus disease; leaves show a yellow and green mottling; sometimes deformed. Plants are stunted. Many viruses distributed by aphids and leafhoppers. Control: Destroy infected plants.

Cankers. Lesions on woody stems, with fungi entering through unbroken tissue. Control: Cut away infected parts.

Dodder. A parasitic plant; a leafless vine that suckers to the stem of the host plant. Control: Cut away dodder.

Galls. Enlargements of plant tissue due to fungi, bacteria, or insect attack. Control: Destroy plant.

CHAPTER 8

Make Your Own Plants (Propagation)

Everyone likes something for nothing, and plants are generous with their offspring. You can root geraniums or fuchsia cuttings, divide bulbs, tubers and perennials, grow shrubs from cuttings, and graft fruit trees. You can also sow seed for the miracle of seeing plants grow daily.

While the propagation process may seem complicated, many methods are ridiculously simple and easily performed. And once your garden is completed and growing lavishly, I strongly urge you to try growing your own plants. There is immense satisfaction in it.

SOWING SEEDS

The miracle of life is well demonstrated by seeds. They are ready to grow and need only moisture, warmth, and air. Some seeds have exacting requirements of humidity and warmth, so propagating cases are necessary for them. Other seeds are easy to grow and can be put directly into the ground.

The time of year you put seed in the soil plays a great part in whether you get a successful crop. Annuals must be planted early so that they will bloom in hot weather. Perennials must be sown before extreme summer heat arrives. Choose the time of sowing seeds carefully; most packages have planting dates on them.

Sowing seed in the ground is an easy and sure way to propagate many annuals. Choose a place with good drainage and sun. Dig down about 6 to 8 inches and be sure the soil has been properly conditioned with adequate nutrients. Put the seed in rows about 8 inches apart if they are to be moved later to another place. If they are to stay, place them about 10 inches apart. Make furrows with a stick, and plant seed twice their own depth. Poppies, for in-

stance, go barely beneath the soil; nasturtiums, somewhat larger seeds, about 1/2 inch under the soil. Cover the seeds with a fine sprinkling of soil and firm them in place. Label plants. Spray water gently over the seed bed and keep it evenly moist until seeds germinate.

If you sow seeds in a box or a container, cover it with plastic to assure good humidity. Remove the cover occasionally for ventilation, but leave it in place at night to protect seeds from coolness. When seedlings appear, gradually remove any shading. Thin out plants as soon as they are up so that there is growing space for the stronger seedlings. When they have a second set of leaves, put plants in permanent places in the garden.

With seed growing, keep watch for a fungus disease called damping-off. If stems start to rot at the ground level, apply a fungicide.

SOWING SEEDS INDOORS

To sow seeds indoors use shallow boxes (flats) or azalea pots or pans. Be sure there are drainage holes in them and put 1 inch of tiny broken pot pieces over the holes. Fill the container almost to the top with prepared soil. The planting medium must be sterile, moisture retentive, and of a fine texture. Some popular mixes are vermiculite and perlite (available in packages at nurseries). Moisten the mix thoroughly with a fine spray.

Now scatter the seeds evenly, leaving spaces between them. Press them lightly into the surface; sift some fine soil to barely cover them. Fine seeds such as lobelia do not need a covering. Put plastic over the boxes or pots and place them in the shade. The majority of plants require a temperature of 65F to 75F to germinate. Keep the soil evenly moist and

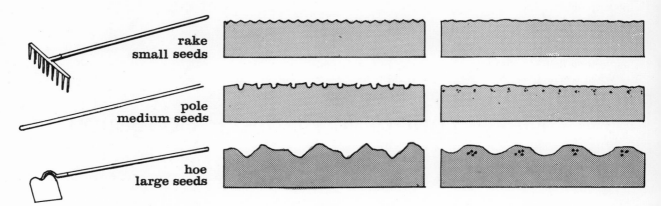

select tool for seed size; furrow soil; wet; scatter or place seeds; cover, compact soil, water

(A) SOWING IN GROUND

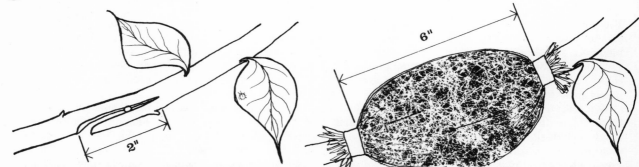

cut; hold split open w. pebble; cover w. damp sphagnum moss; seal in plastic film until roots sprout

(B) AIR LAYERING

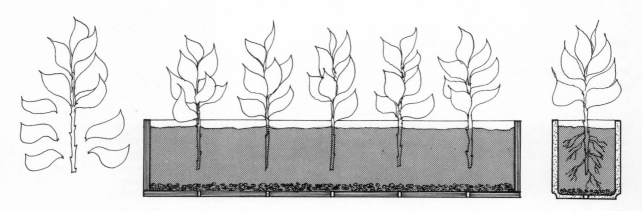

trim lower leaves; dip in root hormone; plant in flats in rooting medium; water; pot after roots sprout

(C) TAKING CUTTINGS

ADRIÁN MARTÍNEZ

Propagation of Plants

observe seeds daily. As soon as young plants are apparent, remove plastic and continue to keep the soil moist.

The average time needed for sowing seeds indoors and setting them out in the garden is about 8 weeks.

When seedlings begin to pop up, give them more light and cooler temperatures. Continue to keep soil moist, but never soggy. Transplant them when they have their second set of true leaves. Put the plants in individual peat pots, or in rows in boxes or similar containers. Leave them outdoors a few hours at a time in the shade and out of the wind before placing them in the garden permanently.

DIVISION

To keep perennials, bulbs, or any plant with a tuber or a rhizome healthy, it is necessary to divide them occasionally. This merely means separating one plant into several sections. Each division is capable of becoming a new plant that is a replica of its parent. This is an inexpensive and quick way to get many plants.

The best time to divide plants is in early spring or in the fall when they are dormant. After division, keep roots moist and plant them as soon as possible.

Bulbs that are in the garden should be left undivided until flower production falls off considerably. Then, after the foliage is ripened, dig them up and pull bulbs apart. Store until it is time to replant them.

To divide a plant, either dig it up or leave the plant in the ground and slice it with a spade or a trowel, lifting out the cut-off section.

HARDWOOD CUTTINGS

Deciduous trees and shrubs like weigela, forsythia, and deutzia can be propagated by making hardwood cuttings in late fall to early spring after leaves have fallen and plants are resting. To start cuttings, take the tip of a branch back to where wood is about 1/4 inch thick. Cut at an angle just below a leaf joint. Take a 6-inch length that includes two leaf joints. Place the cuttings in a shallow trench and cover them with about 2 inches of soil. In areas where ground freezes, provide a mulch to keep them safe from frost. Do not water them; there is enough moisture in the soil to keep the plant tissue from drying out. When warm weather starts in spring, the cuttings should have roots. Set the cuttings vertically in a trench in a shady place. Plant them in a mixture of sand and peat, or soil, and leave the top pair of leaf buds above the surface. Keep the cuttings moist through the summer. In autumn, when they have roots, cuttings are ready to plant in the garden.

SOFTWOOD CUTTINGS

Softwood cuttings are soft and succulent stems of garden perennials. Make softwood cuttings in the spring and early summer. Select a stem that is stocky, young, and brittle so that you can snap it off. It must have 3 to 5 nodes (eyes) and be at least 6 inches long. Make the cut at an angle below a node. Remove any flowers and trim away the lower leaves that would be beneath the soil, but retain a few leaves to make food for the cutting while it is rooting.

Dry out the cut end of the stem and then dust it in hormone powder. Insert the cutting in a growing medium of vermiculite or sand and peat in a shallow container with drainage holes. Set some of the nodes below the soil line. Provide high humidity for the cutting in a warm bright place. Keep soil evenly moist and transplant the cutting as soon as it is well rooted.

Some plants take a few weeks to root; others may require several months.

Plants

begonia	geranium
chrysanthemum	impatiens
coleus	sedum
fuchsia	verbena
gardenia	

SEMIHARDWOOD CUTTINGS

Semihardwood pertains to the maturity of the wood. Take cuttings in the summer or fall. The growing method is the same as for softwood cuttings.

Plants

abelia	lilac
arborvitae	mahonia
cotoneaster	pyracantha
forsythia	yew

GROUND LAYERING

Ground layering is a simple way of getting plants from branches which are simply notched into the soil to make them root while they are still in contact with the parent plant.

You need low-growing branches close to the ground. Make a partial cut about a foot from the end of the branch. Mark the ground with a stake underneath the cut branch. Dig a hole about 4 inches deep and fill it with planting mix. Bend the branch into the hole with the partial cut in the center of the hole. Secure the branch in place with a wire loop, fill the hole with soil, and anchor the branch with a stone or a brick.

Provide a protective mulch for winter. In about a year or sooner, dig down to see if roots have developed. If the layering has been successful, sever the plant and plant it. If not, put back the soil and wait. It often takes two years or more for rooting to occur.

AIR LAYERING

Air layering is a simple interesting method of increasing shrubs and trees and takes only a few minutes to perform. Choose a suitable branch, up to 1 inch in diameter, and make a slanting cut about 1/4 inch through the stem, or remove a circle of bark 1 inch wide. Scrape down to the hard core of wood at the center of the stem or branch. Now dust the cut with a rooting hormone powder and clothe the cut area with a generous amount of sphagnum moss. Wrap polyethylene around it and bind the wrapping securely at each end with string or plastic ties.

If the layering is successful you will, in a month or so, see roots forming in the moss. Wait a week or so and then separate the new plant from the parent stock. If the layering does not take, no harm done. The branch cut will eventually become callous.

GRAFTING PLANTS

The grafting process is somewhat like welding two plants together; it unites a shoot of the plant desired (scion) with the rooted stem of another plant (understock). In other words, one plant grows on another and eventually becomes part of it. Grafting saves time over most other methods of propagation; it can dwarf a plant or it can give it extra vigor.

With grafting, be sure the cambium layer (green inner bark) of one plant is firmly in contact with the cambium layer of another. Then they are bound together with cotton twine and sealed with grafting wax until they become joined.

Select vigorous understock for the grafting that is closely related to the scion. (Only closely related plants are used.) Grafting can be performed in early spring or when plants are dormant; the important thing is that both scion and understock are at the same stage of activity.

There are several types of grafts: side or whip, wedge or cleft. In side grafting, long slanted cuts are made to expose most of the cambium layer. A long tongue is shaped on one plant, a deep V cut on the other, and one plant is forced into the other and tied with string for a month or two until the union is made.

CHAPTER 9

Garden Tools and Conveniences

A garden like a home requires maintenance. Rakes, hoes, and mowers are all part of the gardener's closet. And if he wants to have a beautiful garden with thriving plants, they must be used. Gardening can be a joyful experience, or it can be drudgery. A great deal depends on whether you have the tools and equipment on hand to do the job properly. Manufacturers have given us many work-saving garden conveniences, and because there are so many it is wise to know something about them and what they can and cannot do to make garden maintenance easy. Basically, not very many or necessarily expensive tools are needed. But it is important that they are the right ones. Of course, it would be fun to have a power mower that runs by itself, but a rotary mower does the job satisfactorily too.

Trees and shrubs need pruning, weeds must be eliminated, holes must be dug, lawns must be mowed, and so on. Digging a hole for a tree or trying to cut a limb can be a frustrating experience unless you have the right tools. Specific equipment for a specific job, I assure you, is well worth the cost in the long run.

HAND TOOLS

A good pair of leather garden gloves is important. There is no sense in roughening or cutting your hands. Cloth and plastic gloves are available, but they do not wear as well nor protect your hands as well as leather ones do. And do try them on at the store. Some come in several sizes, as do dress gloves; others only in two sizes (large or small)—frustrating when you wear a medium size as I do.

A hand trowel for planting bulbs and annuals and scooping out holes is a basic tool. It has long been the symbol of gardening, and can be put to a dozen uses. Today's trowels are made from one piece of metal so that the head cannot separate from the handle. There are several shapes: scoop, spatula, and flat edge, with different type handles. You will need one scoop type and one spatula trowel. Select a well-balanced trowel that fits comfortably in your hand.

A hand weeder is a useful garden tool. There are many kinds of hand weeders; some work, and others do not. Unfortunately, it is not always possible to tell which is the best until you try it. I find the type with iron fingers shaped like a claw especially good for weeding; it can also be used to cultivate crusted soil. Another good one is the flat blade turned at a right angle to the shaft. For deep-rooted weeds (and there seem to be so many) the fishtail weeder is best. Periodically, new weeders appear, so keep an eye out for them at your local nursery. The latest one is the flame gun that eliminates stooping to get out the weeds, but I have not tried it yet.

Pruning shears and tools come in a variety of sizes and shapes. Buy the best. Keeping plants pruned is an important part of good culture. With the right tools, trimming and cutting plants can be done easily.

There are two types of pruning shears: the scissors kind with two cutting edges passing each other, and the anvil type with a cutting blade that comes down upon a flat bed. The anvil shears is more durable than the scissors type because the blades of the latter can be forced apart in cutting. Pole pruning shears to reach high places resemble hand shears except they are longer. Only the ones with levers are worth buying. The others are nuisances.

The pruning knife is overlooked, and yet it can be put to many uses. It reaches many places that are difficult to get to with shears. It has an extra-strong curved blade.

A pruning saw is straight or crescent shaped to make neat cuts of branches too large to be handled

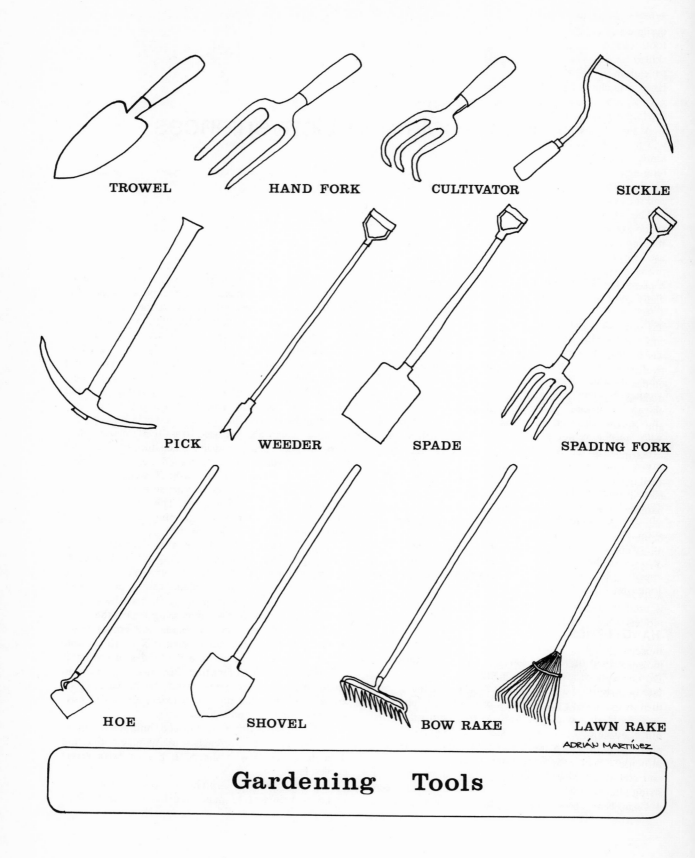

TROWEL　　HAND FORK　　CULTIVATOR　　SICKLE

PICK　　WEEDER　　SPADE　　SPADING FORK

HOE　　SHOVEL　　BOW RAKE　　LAWN RAKE

ADRIÁN MARTÍNEZ

Gardening   Tools

safely with a pair of shears. The lopping shears is also designed to cut branches too heavy for shears. These tools can be useful in the garden in the hands of skilled people. But for the average gardener it is best to call in a professional when it comes to cutting large branches. This is hard work that can be dangerous. It is fine to prune small trees and shrubs but for larger plants professional help is best.

A shovel is an essential tool in the garden. You will mix soil, dig, and lift with it. There are different kinds: round-pointed, square-blade, short-handle and long-handle shovels. I find the round-pointed, long-handle shovel the best one with which to dig, mix, and move soil.

The workhorse of the garden is the square-blade spade. It is designed for digging and turning soil, making trenches, and planting holes, and can even be used to prune roots. A long-handle spading fork with pronged teeth and a trench-type spade that comes to a point are other necessary tools. The latter is especially good for digging in narrow places.

The hoe is the oldest and simplest garden tool. It has now been modified in design, but essentially it is still used to break up crusted soils and to eliminate weeds. There is a standard hoe, a wide-blade one, a weeding hoe, and other kinds. The standard hoe comes in a lightweight or heavyweight model for making furrows in the ground and for weeding. A weeding hoe with two sides, one to dig weeds with and the other side to chop them up, is one of my most-used tools.

Caring for lawns, handling soil, and gathering debris are jobs for a rake. Many kinds of rakes are available: standard, self-cleaning, shrub rakes and a bowed type, leaf rakes and grass rakes, in steel or bamboo, to name some. For raking cut grass or leaves I prefer the fan-shaped, lightweight type with bamboo teeth. To break up spaded soil and to remove debris, an old-fashioned level-headed rake is satisfactory.

For lawn making and maintenance, a device called a spreader is a convenience; it sows seed evenly and is used to distribute fertilizers and herbicides. Many models—manual or trailer attached—are available.

A sturdy wheelbarrow saves time and aching muscles. It has a hundred uses in the garden and is indispensable for moving soil and other heavy things. Do not buy an inferior one; it will break down in a few months. Select a heavy duty model that will return its investment many times over.

Knives are not usually part of the garden tool list, but they should be. A small sharp knife for light pruning and cutting flowers is a necessity for me. I also use it to cut and open bags of soil conditioner and fertilizer that never seem to open by pulling the string attached.

Clean tools after using them. Scrape off dirt with a flat stick or putty knife, then work the tool up and down in a bucket of oiled sand to remove remaining dirt. Keep blades sharp and surfaces free of rust.

POWER TOOLS

The power revolution has brought in its wake a barrage of garden machinery. With growing grass, falling leaves, snow and insects, power tools make gardening easier than before. Many of them, however, are designed for extremely large gardens and do not belong on average grounds. What you eventually select in the way of power helpers depends on your pocketbook and the size of your property. Many people get along very well without any of them; others have several of them.

I use a rotary power mower and a lawn vacuum. If I need some soil tilled or some once-in-a-few-years project, I hire someone to do it, or I rent the necessary equipment rather than buy a piece of machinery that will stay in the garage most of its life.

Mowers. There are many kinds of mowers. Some you push; others push themselves; some you ride on; many have vacuum attachments; and so on. The choice really depends on how large the area is and what kind of turf you have. Basically, there are two types of mowers: the reel type that cuts grass like a scissors and leaves the grass neatly clipped, or the rotary mower that cuts grass in a circular motion. It is doubtful that you will need a riding mower unless you have bad feet or extensive grounds. If you are mowing with a power mower, heed these rules:

- Read the manual thoroughly.
- Fill the gas tank before starting, not while the tank is hot.
- Keep your feet clear of the mower blades.
- Be sure the lawn is free of foreign objects.
- Stop the engine before pushing the mower from one surface to another.
- Stop the engine when you leave the mower unattended.
- Do not unclog the mower while it is running.

Cleanup. This can be a backbreaking project, so I pamper myself with a lawn vacuum that cleans the grounds in a few minutes. It works like the indoor vacuum but is larger. There are air brooms and rakes too that blow or sweep clean a large area in one pass. And there is also a power lawn sweeper available.

Trimming. Electric- or battery-operated trimming tools are a convenience in the garden but somewhat of a luxury. They are lightweight and shockproof, and the hedge trimmer keeps shrubs well groomed in short order. An edger is also useful and can double as a grass trimmer.

Shredders that make compost, humus, and mulch from leaves, garden wastes, and other organic matter are also a garden aid. These are generally somewhat large machines, but if you favor organic gardening, they are indispensable.

You might also want to invest in a lightweight snow thrower. It is powered by a 2 hp electric motor that permits quick starting in cold wet weather. It is ideal for clearing snow from walks, steps, and driveways. It does not do the heavy job of snow removal but saves the time and effort it takes to shovel snow by hand.

There is a host of power machinery for gardening I have not mentioned. What you use depends on you, your property, and your pocketbook.

SPRAYING AND DUSTING EQUIPMENT

The development of bottle sprayers that screw onto the end of a garden hose and automatically dispense sprays with water has revolutionized the application of insecticides. These sprayers are available in several sizes: 4-gallon, 6-gallon, and so on. With this simple mason jar attachment the gardener with an average lot can spray to protect his plants in a few minutes. It dispenses a fine mist that covers all parts of the plant uniformly. The sprayer can also be used for applying liquid fertilizers for foliar feeding.

Dusting insecticide is preferred by some gardeners because no mixing or measuring is necessary. Unused portions of chemicals can be poured back into the containers. Several kinds of dusters are available at nurseries.

Pressure-type sprayers for applying insecticides are more for the commercial grower than the average gardener. Still, smaller models have been offered by manufacturers for the homeowner. These units have an advantage over the hose-and-bottle method because they can be carried around wherever needed, without a hose. They also give an accurate control of the exact formula to be administered. But most of them have to be pumped frequently to maintain pressure.

Old-fashioned trombone sprayers still do a good job to my way of thinking. They now come with brass parts, and are excellent for spraying small areas. Simply mix the chemical with water in the tank. The sprayers are easy to clean too.

For spot spraying in the home or greenhouse, the all-purpose pressurized aerosol cans are valuable. Select the right one for the purpose you have in mind.

WATER SPRINKLERS

Today, the method of applying water to the ground is far removed from the method used even a few years ago. Of course, a hose and a nozzle is still a satisfactory way of watering small areas, but for lawns and large gardens it is impractical, if not impossible.

An oscillating sprinkler that throws water from side to side without soaking the surface and forming puddles is one answer. The rain bird is a sprinkling device, generally used by park departments, which does a thorough job of watering. The one I have has worked well for three years. There are other watering devices; some are good, but others are not worth the metal they are made of.

The installation of an automatic or semiautomatic watering system is now within reach of most gardeners. These underground systems are a real convenience. If you are handy with tools, you can install one yourself.

The simple manual sprinkling system that you operate by hand (turning a spigot) is a low-cost method of watering. The number of sprinkler heads depends on the water pressure in the area. Generally, three or four sprinklers can be connected to the average water system.

The distribution is through underground tubing and wave or pop-up sprinklers. These are designed to moisten square or round areas from 12 to 48 feet. Parts, attachments, adapters, connectors, and pipe are available at nurseries. If you are reasonably skillful, you can install the sprinkling system in one afternoon. If you do not want to try it yourself, buy the parts and have someone else install the system. One word of caution: the plastic pipe for the system is advertised as unbreakable. From experience, I know that if you strike a sprinkler head accidentally with a mower, for instance, the pipe is likely to crack. I have several pipes in my garage to prove that the pipe does crack.

The initial time and money involved in installing an automatic watering-sprinkling system justify the expense because it gives an even distribution of moisture when it is needed and where it is needed. An electrically controlled unit turns the system on to supply water for an exact time for each system connected to it—quite a convenience. The unit can be set to apply a measured amount of water on a lawn or flower bed and at predetermined intervals. It is a boon to gardeners away from home a few days a week.

CHAPTER **10**

Lawns and Ground Covers

A good lawn is indeed a prize, but unlike some prizes that are won, you must work for this one. A lovely carpet of green just doesn't happen by itself. Good preparation and frequent maintenance are necessary. But these expenditures are worth it because a lawn, like a tree, increases in value with the years. It is the link between the house and garden, the trees and shrubs; like an indoor carpet, it becomes an integral part of the outdoor living area.

The establishment of a new lawn involves many things, but the first consideration is what kind of lawn do you want. Will it be a show area or a play area? Will it be walked on frequently? Its uses must be considered first because there are grasses for all situations. Bent grass gives a finely textured carpet; it is used for golf greens, but as a home lawn it is almost impossible to maintain. Select the kind of grass that grows well in your region and that will give you the kind of lawn you need.

The preparation of a soil bed for a lawn is vital. It is the foundation on which the grass will succeed or fail. Start with good soil to support a lawn. In most cases, this means conditioning old soil and adding new topsoil. Proper care of the lawn after it is established—mowing, feeding, weeding—will keep it green and handsome.

Some grasses need cool moist conditions; others withstand heat and drought. Many grasses need a fertile soil, but there are other kinds that succeed in a somewhat poor soil. Several grasses need sun, whereas others grow in the shade. A few lawns require constant care; others need only minimum maintenance. If there will be heavy foot traffic, only coarse grasses will be satisfactory. Fine-leaved species make a lovely lawn, but they wear poorly.

Most grasses are a mixture of many kinds rather than one pure stand. Then disease is not likely to spread from one plant to another. If infection starts, only part of the turf in a mixed planting is affected, and the other varieties take over. This is why packaged commercial grasses are mixtures.

Use the best possible seed you can afford. A lawn is a long-term investment, and inferior seed defeats the purpose. Make note of the percentage of germination stated on the container. It should not be lower than 80 percent, and preferably should be 90 percent or better.

There are two times during the year to sow a new lawn: as soon as the soil is workable in the spring, when good weather is on the way, and in the fall, when there are few variations in temperature.

PREPARATION OF THE SITE

If you have a new house, grading the area for a lawn is the first step. Mounds or depressions where water will accumulate must be leveled, and the land must slope away from the house so that there is adequate surface drainage. Frequently, the ground has been churned and compacted by heavy equipment when the house was being built. It is sometimes necessary to dig down almost 2 feet to eliminate compacted soil. Lowering or raising the grade to make a level surface is hard work. (See Chapter 2.)

After the initial grading, the subsoil must be conditioned. Work organic matter or peat moss into it. This may require rototilling the soil to break it up so that it is friable. Then add a complete fertilizer suitable to the soil in your area. (Consult your local nurseryman.) Now, some people sow grass seed directly on reconditioned soil. However, I suggest that you use a layer of at least 6 inches of topsoil.

Soil being graded and leveled in preparation for sowing seed.
(USDA)

Subsoil being dug in preparation for a new lawn. It must be workable,
not hard or tight. All debris must be removed.
(USDA)

Sloping the area for adequate drainage; leveling uneven places
with a rake before fertilizers are added to soil.
(USDA)

Here, fertilizer is being applied to the soil; then it will
be covered with a layer of topsoil.
(USDA)

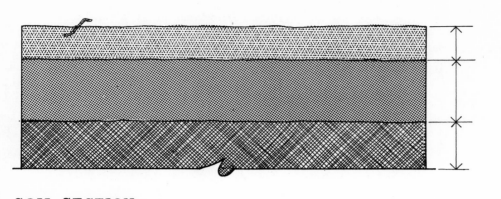

2" to 4" COMPOST

4" to 6" TOPSOIL

FILL or SUBSOIL

SOIL SECTION

① loosen and turn over soil

② add topsoil and compost; level

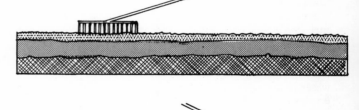

③ seed by hand or w. spreader

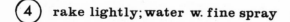

④ rake lightly; water w. fine spray

ADRIÁN MARTÍNEZ

Sowing Grass Seed

Nurseries say you can have a good lawn with 4 inches, but this is for experts and requires meticulous care. Although it is certainly possible to have a lawn on reconditioned subsoil, a layer of topsoil goes a long way in assuring a good growth of grass.

Whether you use topsoil or subsoil for your lawn, a final grading is now necessary. Strive for a level surface, but do not overrake the area. Some small lumps in the soil will help to hold the seed in place.

If trees interfere with the grading process, provide wells to protect them and keep the soil off the root area. Or an easier method is to slope the surface soil up to the trees. In other words, grade away from the trees. Avoid sharp inclines or dropoffs where it will be impossible to use a lawn mower.

SOWING GRASS SEED

Cool season grasses may be sown almost any time in mild climates and from spring through fall in cooler locations, but late summer and early fall are the best times. Fall seeding reduces the danger of heat injury, and spring sowing (as mentioned) gives grass a long season to get established. Southern grasses are best sown in spring.

Sow the seed on a calm day; if you do it by hand, mix the seed with some sand or fine topsoil. It spreads evenly then. If you use a commercial spreader, do not overlap the strips; overlapping will produce an uneven stand of grass. If the soil is dry, water it somewhat and then let it dry out before you do the sowing. When the seed is down evenly, shallowly rake it into the surface of the soil. Now whether you roll the seed after it is spread or prefer to leave it in place is your own decision. Sometimes, rolling compacts the seed into the soil, and washoff is apt to occur. Water the seed with a light mist. For best germination cover the area with a protective coating (mulch) of straw without seed heads or with a layer of grass clippings or with peat moss. This covering is not absolutely necessary, but it keeps birds from eating the seed, holds moisture in the soil, and helps to keep the soil temperature even.

Keep the seed bed moist. Do not ever let it dry out; this means watering it several times a day in hot weather. Use a fine mist of water. A heavy stream will wash away the seed or will only cover in spots. Apply water slowly so that it can be absorbed by the soil.

Germination of seed takes anywhere from 1 to 3 weeks, depending on the kinds of seed sown. With some seed—any mixture that has Windsor in it—do not expect a good stand of grass for about a year. Other grasses may be attractive in a few months. As growth progresses, water the lawn somewhat less. Generally, mulches can be left in place to decay.

SODDING, STRIPPING, AND SO FORTH

Besides the regular procedure of sowing seed for a lawn, there are other methods: sodding, stripping, plugging, and sprigging. No matter which method you choose, the soil must be thoroughly prepared before you start.

Sodding. Sodding is an easy way to have a lawn in one day. Sod is grass that is mature and ready to go into the ground. Sodding is also an expensive method. Sod comes in rectangular sheets 12 inches wide and 12 to 18 inches long and generally about 1 inch thick. The sheets of sod must be laid closely together, flush with each other on a level soil bed to create an attractive carpet of green. Tamp down or roll the sod evenly after it is in place and water it almost daily for a few weeks to start the grass growing.

Stripping. Stripping was popular once, but I have not seen it used much recently. The process is similar to sodding except that the pieces of sod are 4 to 6 inches wide and rather than piecing them together, they are spaced 3 to 6 inches apart. Eventually, the strips of soil disappear as the grass spreads. Constant weeding is necessary between the sod strips so that the grass has a chance to cover the area.

Plugging. Some warm climate grasses are not available in seed, so plugs are used. The plugs are 2 to 4 inches square and are set firmly in predug holes 12 to 16 inches apart. Soil must be constantly moistened until new growth starts; it will take about a year before the grass is established. Diligent weeding between the plugs is necessary to get this lawn started.

Sprigging. Sprigging is somewhat like plugging, and consists of starting individual stolons of grass. They are set about 12 inches apart in each direction. Do not cover the growing tips and keep the soil evenly moist to assure good growth.

TO RENOVATE AN OLD LAWN

If the lawn is spotty—filled with weeds and bare patches—it is wise to tear up the entire lawn and start fresh rather than to try to repair it. If the lawn is only poor in a few spots, renovation can be attempted.

If there is a large area to renovate, do it in early fall in the North, in late spring in the South. Small patches of lawn can be done anytime. Use a mixture rather than a single type of grass when patching a lawn; the new grass will blend in better with the old turf.

To improve a lawn, cut it closely and remove all grass clippings and other debris. Break up the soil to a depth of several inches with a spade or an aerator. Add a thin layer of topsoil and mix in some fertilizer.

BENT GRASS

soft, flat, branching

BLUEGRASS

neat, erect blades

FINE FESCUE

fine, soft, round needles

ADRIÁN MARTÍNEZ

Types of Grass

Sprinkle the grass seed and keep it moist but not soggy.

HOW TO CARE FOR A LAWN

Once the lawn is established, keep it healthy. Mowing, watering, and feeding are just as important now as good grass seed and thorough preparation were at the start. Proper care helps to keep the turf thick and the weeds down.

Mowing. Start mowing as soon as the grass starts growing. Do not let it get too tall. Cutting high grass shocks the lawn and hinders growth. Some people leave lawn clippings on the turf; they say it helps to improve the soil. Others believe—and this seems to be the trend now—that clippings left on the turf may help to encourage diseases.

Cut the grass even, but do not cut away too much of the vital green leaves. Low-cut grass has a tendency to be shaggy. Dull blades will tear grass leaves, so be sure the mower blades are sharp.

Some general rules can be given about when to cut grass and how often to cut it. The standard height for cutting Kentucky bluegrass is 1 1/2 to 2 inches. Merion Kentucky Blue is best cut 1 to 1 1/4 inches. And bent grass is usually cut 1/2 to 3/4 inch high.

If you keep the grass short, it should not be allowed to grow more than 3/4 inch before it is mowed again. If you keep the grass at 2 inches, you can let it grow about 1 inch before mowing it again. Mowing should be started in the spring and continue into fall or until growth stops. Do not let the lawn go into the winter with a thick mat; this is an invitation for disease to start.

Watering. Sun, wind, and rainfall determine the amount of water mature grass will need. The type of soil is also a factor. In general, water grass thoroughly but infrequently to encourage deep rooting. Sometimes it is better to allow grass to become slightly brown rather than to flood it with water. Too much moisture brings the roots to the surface and makes for a poor stand of grass. For details on water absorption, see Chapter 2.

Fertilizing. Complete fertilizers with lots of nitrogen are needed for lawns. The percentage of nitrogen should be about 20 percent. Some grasses—bent grass and Bermuda—need more feeding than other grasses. Apply fertilizers with a mechanical spreader to get even coverage; otherwise, there will be dark green streaks where the soil has been fertilized, and yellow areas where it has not been fed. The best time to feed lawns in the North is in autumn, with supplemental feeding in spring and early summer. In the South, feeding can start in the spring and continue through the warm months.

A lawn exhausts the supply of plant food in the soil quickly. As soon as the snow has melted, in late March or early April, it is time to feed the lawn and get it off to a good start for the year. As the soil thaws gradually, the spring rains and soil moisture will dissolve some of the nitrogen and carry it down to the grass roots.

LAWN PROGRAM

January–March:
Keep foot traffic off the turf to avoid holes and gulleys. Wait until the ground is firm before walking on it.

March–April:
Fertilize while grass is dormant and as soon as the snow thaws. Lightly rake the area, fill in low spots, and eliminate high spots. Mow the lawn as soon as the ground is free of frost.

April–June:
Aerify the lawn; feed with a complete fertilizer.

June–August:
Feed with complete fertilizer.

September:
Feed the lawn and reseed bare spots in established turf.

October–December:
Apply fungicide to combat snow mold before the first snow. Smooth out hollows and valleys.

KINDS OF GRASSES

There are several kinds of grass and grass mixtures for different parts of the country. It is best to select the grasses that do well in your region. Ask your neighbor or local nurseryman. Generally in the northern, or cool, climates a mixture with Merion bluegrass as the chief ingredient is frequently used, whereas in the South, Bermuda grass is most widely used in mixes. Zoysia is also popular in the South. In the Midwest, Kentucky bluegrass and red fescue generally make a successful combination. Between the cool climate and warm climate regions—an intermediate band that runs across the country—warm and cool grasses supplement each other, neither dominating the lawn all year. In many parts of the Great Plains states and dipping into the Southwest sectors, native dryland grasses are grown if water is not available.

Cool-Climate Grasses

Cool-climate grasses are sold either singly or in blends. Lawns of a single grass type, although handsome, could be destroyed if attacked by pests or by

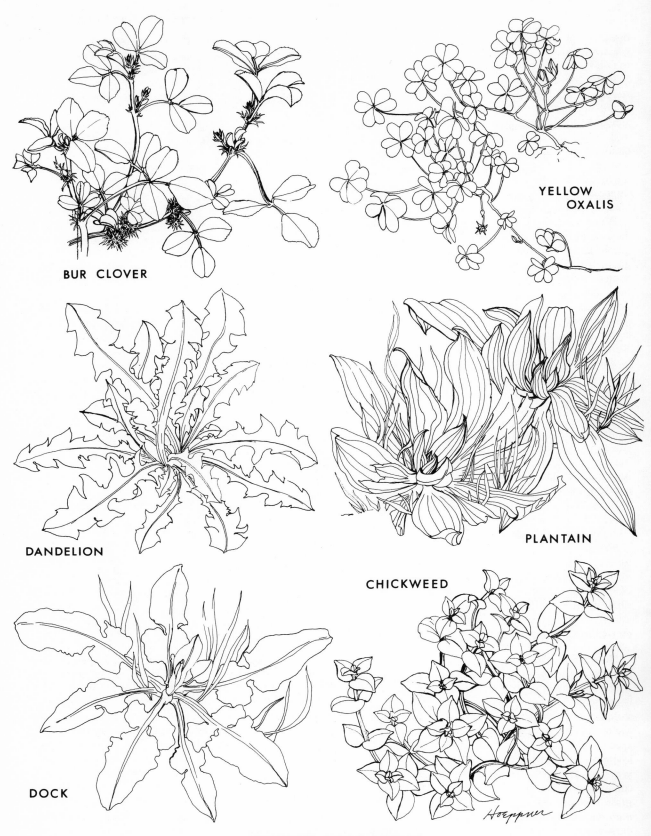

BUR CLOVER

YELLOW
OXALIS

DANDELION

PLANTAIN

CHICKWEED

DOCK

COMMON LAWN WEEDS

Hoeppner

disease or by environmental conditions. A blend of grasses is safer; even if the grass eventually dwindles to two kinds, it will still give a green carpet.

Bent grass. A fine-leaved grass that spreads by stolons. It needs close mowing, feeding, and watering but it does produce a lovely carpet of green. Takes sun or shade. Best of the Colonial bents are Astoria and Highland, which are somewhat tougher than Colonial. The creeping bent grasses include several strains—Penncross, Seaside, Toronto—with fine, flat, narrow blue-green leaves; they need meticulous care. Suggested areas for bent grass: Northeast, East Coast, Northwest Coast.

Bluegrasses. Generally considered the best of cool-climate grasses. Kentucky blue is fine-bladed, blue-green, long-lived, and produces a good stand of grass. It needs ample sun. Merion bluegrass is deeper rooted, more intense in color, and more resistant to heat. The Windsor strain is a dark vibrant green; it does well in sun or shade. Flyking Kentucky bluegrass is tough and somewhat more resistant to severe cold and standing water than others mentioned here. Rough bluegrass does well in damp, shady places; it is fine textured and apple-green in color. Suggested areas for bluegrass are Northeast, North Central, East Coast, Midwest, South Central, and parts of Southeast and Northwest coasts.

Fescues. Fescues can endure sun or shade, moist or dry soil, and generally take rough treatment and still thrive, although they cannot tolerate the summer heat of the Deep South. Red fescue, or one of its improved strains—Chewing, Pennlawn, Ranier—is good for cool climates. Tall fescue and its strains are best for play areas, producing dense leaf systems and heavy roots. Suggested areas: Northeast, North Central, Northwest Coast.

Rye grass. A perennial inexpensive part of grass mixes. It has a medium-coarse texture; it is easy to grow in a wide variety of climates, but it does not provide a lush carpet of green. Rye grass is often used as a temporary cover. It takes light shade.

Hot-Climate Grasses

Hot-climate grasses grow vigorously in summer, and are dormant in cool or cold winters. They can be overseeded with fine fescues or bluegrass to have winter color. These grasses are generally grown from stolons, plugs, sprigs, or sod, rather than from seed.

Zoysia. A popular grass for the South. Some species are used in the North. Zoysia produces a low-growing, dark-green cover. It takes about two years for Zoysia to crowd out weeds and really become established, but then it is easy to care for. This grass browns off somewhat in cold weather. *Zoysia matrella*, or Manila grass, is fine-leaved, medium dark-green. Emerald zoysia grows faster than ma-

trella; it has a richer color and is more frost resistant. *Zoysia japonica* and its improved varieties, Meyer Zoysia, are suggested for northern lawns; they prefer full sun. Suggested areas for Zoysia: Northeast, North Central, East Coast, South Central, West Coast, Southeast, and Gulf Coast.

St. Augustine grass. St. Augustine grass is effective only in frost-free areas. The variety 'Bitter Blue' makes a coarse, deep-green carpet in the shade or the sun. It is available in sod or sprig. Suggested areas: Southeast, Gulf Coast.

Bermuda grass. Most satisfactory grass for the South. It needs sun, slightly acid soil, and frequent watering in dry weather. This grass is fine-bladed and spreads well, is upright growing, and is a pale- to dark-green color. It browns out somewhat in winter, but some strains stay green longer than others. Suggested areas: Southeast, South Central, Southwest Coast.

Carpet grass. A tall, coarse, broad-leaved species; light-green color. It needs a low-moist acid situation, and grows in the sun or in part shade. Carpet grass is tough to mow. Suggested areas: Southeast, South Central, Southwest Coast.

Dichondra. A tough, ground-hugging plant that spreads by rooting surface runners. It has small bright-green, round leaves and grows best in areas with a minimum winter temperature of 25F. The amount you grow determines how quickly it will cover an area. Plant dichondra early to avoid problems with midsummer heat.

PRECAUTIONS AGAINST DEVELOPMENT OF WEEDS

An established lawn that is well cared for will deweed itself. However, we gardeners are not perfect and we are often faced with the problem of weeds. If there were only a few kinds of weeds, it would be simple to get rid of them. Unfortunately, there are many kinds of weeds; to fight them intelligently it is important to know something about them.

Broad-leaved weeds include chickweed, carpetweed, dandelion, dock, cress, purslane, pennywort, plantain, and others. Most of these can be controlled by hoeing or removing them with a hand weeder; the plants are generally recognizable as weeds and come out of the soil without too much of a struggle. The grassy weeds—crabgrass, foxtail, barnyard grass, goosegrass, and quackgrass—are more persistent because several of them spread quickly by runners that go deep underground, making it impossible to pull them out completely.

Weeds are perennial or annual; crabgrass starts from seed anew each spring (generally in April) and is at its weakest stage when it first starts to grow. With the difficult weeds, it is important to recognize them when they first appear and to undertake immediate measures to control them. Once established, they take the upper hand.

A good, dense stand of grass is the best protection against weeds developing. The next best control is to prevent annual lawn weeds from seeding; this means removing them at just the right time. Other precautions include the following:

- Use a lawn sweeper after midsummer mowings to pick up weed seeds.
- Aerate the soil as much as possible so that air and moisture get to the bottom of the soil to encourage good grass to grow. Aerate with a hand aerator or one that attaches to the tiller.
- Pull up weeds by hand; this is easy to do when soil is damp. Use a trowel or a hand weeder. Hoe weeds; this is easy to do when soil is somewhat dry. Cut through the crowns rather than try to dig up weeds.
- Cut grass at a reasonable height; low mowing gives low-growing weeds, such as crabgrass, the space to spread out and grow rapidly.
- On small areas of weeds, cover them with a heavy impervious mulch. Building paper, aluminum foil, can be used; after several weeks, roots and tops of weeds will die.

Of course, the most important precaution against weeds is to create a good soil structure with plenty of compost, humus, and leafmold so there will be a quick and vigorous growth of grass. Remember that a clay or a sandy soil will not provide good growing conditions for grass, but it can support weeds that thrive in inferior situations.

HERBICIDES FOR CONTROLLING WEEDS

With all the weeds that can invade lawns, it was inevitable that chemicals, called herbicides, to eradicate them would appear in nurseries. Herbicides, when applied to the soil, move through a plant and produce formative effects within the plant. Some are growth-regulating substances that upset the balance of growth in a plant so completely the plant is no longer able to grow. Others excite the plant into excess growth, choking it to death.

Some of the herbicides are selective, and kill certain weeds and not others; other herbicides kill almost every plant in sight. Some are for broadleaved weeds; others, for grassy weeds. The preemergent kinds (herbicides applied before weeds appear) are selective and kill weed seed before it has a chance to grow; but unless it is applied at just the right time, it is not effective.

The overall herbicide picture is indeed complex.

At this writing the most popular and widely used herbicide—2,4,5–5—has been suspended for use by the Surgeon General's report because of its fetus-deforming potential in the offspring of laboratory animals. Another long-standing herbicide—2,4–D—is under scrutiny by ecology authorities as a possible hazard to man and land.

Some other herbicides sold under various trade names also contain in part 2,4–D. I believe it makes much more sense to use natural ways of getting rid of weeds (described earlier), first, rather than messing with dubious chemicals.

The herbicides listed in Table 2 are not to be construed as an endorsement for their use. They are given here so that the careful gardener can evaluate them and know what they are and what they do. Whether these herbicides will also be investigated in the future remains to be seen, and is beyond our call here. The list includes only a few of the very many herbicides available at suppliers.

Table 2. Herbicides for Weed Control

Name	Control	Remarks
2,4–D	Broad-leaved weeds; can destroy other plants	Under scrutiny by authorities as a possible hazard to man and land
2,4,5–T	Broad-leaved weeds in established lawns; also oxalis and clover control	Suspended for use
Ammate (AMS)	Nonselective for many kinds of weeds; also poison ivy, poison oak	Reported as non-poisonous to man and land
Balan	Preemergent crabgrass control in established lawns	Wait 6 weeks before planting grass
Bandane	Preemergent crabgrass control; does not harm desirable grass	For established and seedling grass
Betasan	For crabgrass; use before weeds germinate	Sold under trade name in combination with 2,4–D (See above.)
Dachtal (DCPA)	Preemergent crabgrass control	Apply in winter or early spring
Dowpon (Dalapon)	Nonselective herbicide that kills all plants; apply after weeds come up, or for spot control	Sterilizes soil for a month

Table 2 (Continued)

Name	Control	Remarks
Pre-San	Preemergent liquid control of crab-grass	Apply in early spring
Silvex (2,4,5–TP)	For broad-leaved weeds in established lawns; also for chickweed and oxalis	Similar to 2,4,5–T, and often combined with 2,4–D (See 2,4,5–T and 2,4–D.)
Tupersan (Siduron)	Kills crabgrass, but lawn grasses are not killed	O.K. to reseed immediately
Weedone Weed-B-Gon	Kills-broad leaved weeds and stubborn lawn weeds	Comes in four different herbicides for specific uses; contains 2,4–D (See 2,4–D.)

Rules for Handling Chemicals

• Keep chemicals out of children's reach.
• Store in original container.
• Avoid spilling.
• Set aside a special set of mixing tools.
• Avoid spray or drift.
• Never smoke or eat while spraying.
• Throw away, but do not burn, empty containers.
• After spraying, wash all equipment.
• After spraying, wash hands and face with soap.
• Before mixing chemicals, read all labels carefully.

LAWN PROBLEMS

Weeds are generally the gardener's most common complaint about a lawn. However, insect infestation, fungus diseases, and small animals looking for grubs are other things—although not as prevalent as weeds —that can occur.

Lawn insects. Many kinds of insects attack grass, and you must identify the specific culprit before buying chemicals. Consult your local nurseryman.

Yellowish grass. Generally happens when there is not enough nitrogen in the soil, or if the soil has too much acidity or alkalinity.

Brown patch. A fungus disease that attacks all kinds of turf. It produces irregular-shaped brown patches. Brown patch appears during times of high humidity. Control: Fungicide.

Dollar spot. A fungus disease that mostly attacks Kentucky bluegrass, bent grass, and St. Augustine grass. It causes straw-colored red spots, forming irregular areas of damage. Most prevalent in spring and in fall, with cool nights and warm humid days. Control: Fungicide.

Burrowing animals. Moles and gophers are generally most troublesome and can cause havoc in a lawn. The ideal solution is to eliminate the grubs and other insects they are looking for. This is not always possible, so traps are occasionally used as are various old-fashioned remedies like mothballs.

GROUND COVERS

Where it is difficult to establish a lawn because of climate or hills and ravines, ground-cover substitutes are popular. Such plants offer a great deal for little cost and low maintenance. In fact, once these plants are in the ground and watered and fed regularly, that is all there is to it. Although they cannot substitute for a rich carpet of green, ground covers are attractive and useful. They bind sandy soil, check erosion on hillsides, and quickly cover an unsightly area. Many of them grow in shade; others tolerate full sun and even drought. These are tough plants. If a lawn is beyond your means, or if you do not have time to care for it, ground covers are the answer.

Evergreen ground covers are attractive in summer and winter; for mild climates there are many of them. Even for severe winter regions, there are several handsome ground covers.

In cold-weather areas, start plants in the spring. Where winters are moderate, start them in the spring or fall. In temperate, all-year climates, plant them in the fall or winter.

Plants are available in flats of 80 or 100 to a container. Put them into the ground, just like regular plants. But do not expect them to thrive in a poor, hard soil; some do, but the majority need rich soil to prosper. Most nurseries will tell you to space plants 12 to 16 inches apart. This is a matter of choice rather than a rule. The more closely the plants are spaced, the more rapidly they cover an area. With 12- to 16-inch spacing, it may take almost 2 years for complete coverage.

Shrubby ground covers once planted will continue to grow for many years. With time, they may grow out of bounds and become too high. When this happens, thin out and cut away rampant growth; it does not harm the plants.

Many ground covers become a mass of branches —a solid bed of green—and will not tolerate foot traffic. Other kinds—the flat-growing types—do take foot traffic, but generally it is best to put in stepping-stones if the area is to be walked on frequently.

Every region has its own requirements in ground-cover plants with respect to climate and soil. The plants offered at local nurseries will be those suitable for your area.

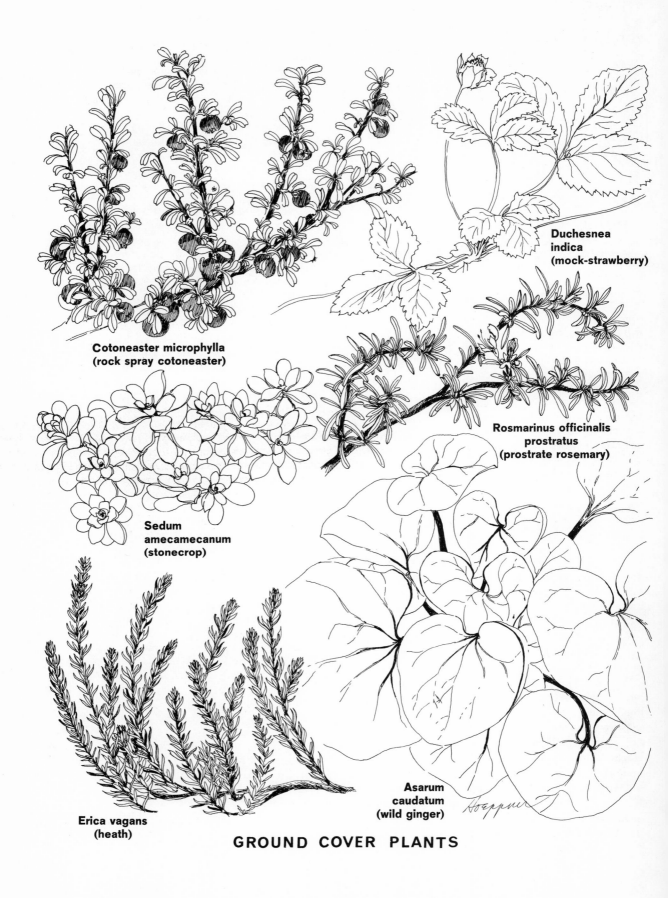

Cotoneaster microphylla
(rock spray cotoneaster)

Duchesnea
indica
(mock-strawberry)

Sedum
amecamecanum
(stonecrop)

Rosmarinus officinalis
prostratus
(prostrate rosemary)

Erica vagans
(heath)

Asarum
caudatum
(wild ginger)

GROUND COVER PLANTS

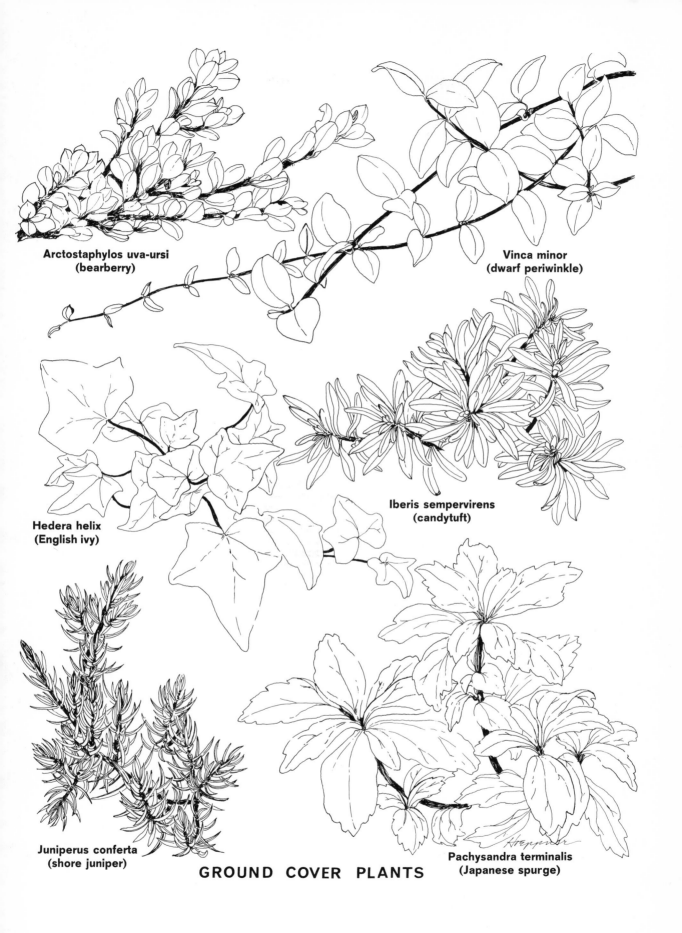

Arctostaphylos uva-ursi
(bearberry)

Vinca minor
(dwarf periwinkle)

Hedera helix
(English ivy)

Iberis sempervirens
(candytuft)

Juniperus conferta
(shore juniper)

Pachysandra terminalis
(Japanese spurge)

GROUND COVER PLANTS

This lawn is the feature of the garden and provides a pleasant vista; the edge of the lawn is accented with a garden wall.
(Roche)

A steep slope landscaped with *Vinca minor,* an excellent ground cover that provides good erosion control of a hill.
(USDA)

The following list of plants is a general selection.

List of Ground Cover Plants

Aaron's-beard (*Hypericum calycinum*). Grows to 12 inches. Sun or shade. Tolerates a sandy soil.

Ajuga. Grows to 6 inches; hardy perennial with rosettes of dark-green leaves and spikes of blue spring flowers. Sun or shade. Needs ample moisture.

Chamomile (*Anthemis nobilis*). Grows to 3 to 5 inches. An overlooked but lovely cover with light-green fernlike leaves. Needs sandy soil and full sun; even moisture.

Candytuft (*Iberis sempervirens*). Grows to 6 inches; dense little bushes with white flowers. Needs sun and rich soil.

Cotoneaster (many). Shrubby, with small leaves and decorative berries. Several good ones.

Dichondra carolinensis. Small dark-green leaves form dense mats. Needs well-drained soil and plenty of water. Tender.

Epimedium. Semievergreen; grows to 9 inches, with glossy leaves and dainty flowers. Likes moist, slightly acid soil and somewhat shady conditions.

English ivy (*Hedera helix*). One of the most popular ground covers; several handsome varieties. Some have tiny leaves; others, large foliage. Some grow quickly, whereas others take many months to become established. Sun or shade.

Heath (*Erica vagans*). Grows to 12 inches, with pointed needlelike leaves.

Honeysuckle (*Lonicera japonica* 'Halliana'). A tough rampant vine; grows to 6 inches. Sun or shade. Evergreen in the South; semievergreen in the North. Can become a pest unless kept within boundaries.

Ice plant (*Mesembryanthemum*). A large group of succulent plants; annual or perennial. Recently renamed but still are available at nurseries under the old name. Some have 1- to 2-inch stiff leaves; others grow to 8 inches. All have bright daisylike flowers. Needs sun.

Juniperus. (See Shrubs.)

Liriope muscari. Grows to 12 inches, with grassy foliage forming a dense mat. Sun or shade; any kind of soil.

Manzanita (*Arctostaphylos uva-ursi*). Grows to 12 inches; evergreen with small, nodding leaves.

Mock-strawberry (*Duchesnea indica*). Coarsely toothed leaves; good creeper.

Pachysandra terminalis. Grows to 5 to 12 inches. Evergreen for shady areas; slow growing. Has whorls of dark-green leaves. Does not do well in sun.

Periwinkle (*Vinca minor*). Excellent shade-loving evergreen creeper. Dark glossy green leaves and showy white or blue spring flowers.

Plantain lily (*Hosta*, or *Funkia*). Many varieties. Some with large leaves; others with small leaves. Likes water, but will survive a dry situation too. Prefers shade.

Rosemary (*Rosmarinus officinalis* 'Prostratus'). Evergreen; grows to 12 inches, with narrow leaves and blue flowers in spring. Needs sun; tolerates poor soil.

Stonecrop (*Sedum amecamecanum*). Low-growing, fleshy, succulent. Spreads rapidly.

Strawberry (*Fragaria chiloensis*). Small semievergreen leaves and white flowers. Grows rapidly. Sun or shade.

Thyme (*Thymus*). Low carpet plant. Tolerates hot, dry, sunny places and poor soil.

Wild ginger (*Asarum caudatum*). Handsome woodlike plant for shady moist areas. Attractive heart-shaped leaves.

In this photo, trees serve a definitive purpose; they are the link between the natural woodsy background and the small patio.
(Molly Adams)

Flowering trees make this a picture postcard scene, bright in spring and colorful in autumn.
(Molly Adams)

CHAPTER 11

Trees

Trees are desirable in the landscape; even a few of them transform an uninviting area into a picturesque spot. Indeed, if you will notice which sites sell first in a subdivision, it will invariably be the ones with trees. Such is their appeal.

If there are trees on a new site, the owner is certainly fortunate; and if there are none, he will probably want some. Some people can afford the cost of transplanting a somewhat large tree, but most people must be content with seedlings and wait for them to grow. Since all gardeners are anxious to have their property lovely, fast-growing trees are favorites. Or smaller trees are selected because it does not take them long to mature. Fortunately, there are trees for all situations. The nurseryman can direct you to the best trees for your area, but it is preferable to know something about trees yourself so that you can talk intelligently with him.

First, of course, choose a tree that will thrive in your region. When you first start landscaping, avoid experimenting; later, when the grounds are in order, you can seek unusual trees. Decide whether you are interested in year-round color or a seasonal display of flowers. Do you want tall trees to provide shade or smaller ones near a terrace? Do you want colorful foliage in the fall or an evergreen tree that stays handsome all year?

Fit the tree to the location you have for it. In both size and habit of growth, it should be in proportion to the other landscape material and to the size of the home. Consider the shape of the tree. Is it columnar, pendent, or an umbrella of green? Will the tree grow slowly and take many years to mature, or will it reach its ultimate size in a few years?

And finally, know something about the roots of the tree. Will the roots, as they grow, interfere with tile lines and water pipes?

WHERE TO PUT TREES

Once they are established, trees are virtually impossible to move. Select them carefully at the start. The best plan is to choose major shade trees first; for the average site, two or three trees will probably be all you will want. Other trees can be added later as time and money permit: to frame a doorway, to accent a lawn, and so forth. Consult Tables 3 and 4 (pages 93–97) for the ultimate height of a tree before making selections. Some trees can in years become gigantic; others might not grow as tall as you would like them to.

The front of the house needs trees too; here they are used more for accent than for shade purposes. They cannot be too large or too small in relation to the size of the house, nor should they be out of character with the architecture of the home. Some trees are stately in appearance and more suited to a formal building; other trees of spreading habit are better for an informal house.

BUYING TREES

Trees that are well started are purchased from a nursery. An economical buy is a young dormant deciduous tree that is ready to come to life when you get it. With shade trees, look for a dormant bareroot, 8- to 10-foot specimen; it is still young enough to transplant easily and old enough to be tough and add some color to the grounds.

Canned trees are popular and can be transplanted at almost any reasonable time of the year without disturbing the root system. It is merely a question of removing the tree from its container, with the root ball intact; then the tree has a much better chance of "taking" rather than when the roots are pulled or abused.

Be cautious of bargains and leftover plants that have been sitting around for months; it will be difficult to get them going again. Avoid trees with dried or wrinkled bark or limp or wilted leaves, or those that have compacted root balls.

CARE OF TREES

The first year in your garden is the most crucial time for a tree. It must survive the shock of being moved and starting new roots. Do not feed the plant immediately, but give it adequate water. Water slowly and deeply so that moisture gets to the bottom of the roots to stimulate new growth. The soil should never be dry. Remember that tree roots extend almost as far out horizontally as do the tree branches.

Basic information on pruning is given in Chapter 6. Some specific data on pruning trees follows:

Remove Y-shaped crotches by cutting away the smaller of the two branches; this stimulates the growth of the remaining branch and strengthens the wood. Shape trees as they grow rather than allowing them to grow for several years and then trying to straighten the mess with heavy pruning. If a tree is crooked but still young, it can be tied to stakes in the opposite direction to help train it. Mature trees that are overgrown should be "daylighted"; that is, all small branches and twigs removed so light can get through the framework of the tree.

If a transplanted tree dies at the top, cut it back and allow it to continue to grow. Choose a vigorous branch, and bend it into position to develop as the main trunk of the tree. Prune out other branches.

Decay will start in any open cavity of a tree, and although it takes many years for any actual harm to come to the tree, it is a simple job to avoid problems in the future. In small trees, cut away the infected parts; use a chisel and knife and get rid of all decayed matter. Shape a smooth-lined cavity and then apply a coat of shellac and tree paint.

Branches or trunks that have split can, if they are not too large, be mended rather than cut. You will have to use discretion about this. If losing the limb will make the tree seem out of shape, then by all means try to save it. Bend the branch together with tightly tied rope or put bolts through the break.

If a small tree is blown over in a storm, do not give it up as lost. Cover the roots with wet burlap. Dig another hole in the same spot where the tree previously stood and put the tree in place with guy wires. Pack soil around the roots and water thoroughly. Have professionals cut tall branches.

STAKING

Staking a tree is an important operation that most people neglect. Any young tree over 5 feet tall should, when it is transplanted, have a suitable support so that it can withstand wind. But do not drive a stake into the ground alongside a tree, as this injures the roots. Use guy wires at even distances around the tree; bend and loop each wire and thread it through a length of rubber hose that will go around the trunk at the point of attachment. Fasten the guy wires in place and attach them to 24-inch stakes set firmly in the ground. The stakes should be placed at equal distances around the tree until the wires are taut enough to hold the tree in place.

For small trees, a stake driven into the soil near the trunk, about 3 inches away, is sufficient. Tie the tree to it with strong twine. Put the stake into the ground before the tree is planted to avoid injuring roots. Leave stakes and/or guy wires in place for about a year or until the tree is strong and does not need support.

FEEDING TREES

It is best to feed trees in spring before new growth starts. Young ones, once they are in the ground, need feeding; mature trees need feeding to remain vigorous. Use a complete fertilizer. Feed balled-and-burlapped trees or container trees a few weeks after planting. Bare-root trees which do not have a functioning root system can be fed two months after they are planted. Do not mix fertilizer into the soil; instead, spread it on top and then water the soil thoroughly.

Mature trees need yearly feeding in spring. The best way to get food to the deepest roots is to drill holes at least 20 inches deep, with an auger or a drill, in a wide ring around the tree. Put the holes about 24 inches apart around the tree, and at least 3 feet from the base of the trunk for a mature tree. A general rule of thumb for other trees is to place the holes in the outer circle about 12 inches beyond the ends of the branches. A moderate rate of feeding is 1 lb. of fertilizer for each 1 inch of the trunk diameter. Fill the holes with fertilizer and then add topsoil and sand.

LISTS OF TREES

NOTE: To avoid confusion and constant reference to zone maps, plants in Tables 3 and 4 have been listed with their minimum nighttime growing temperatures so

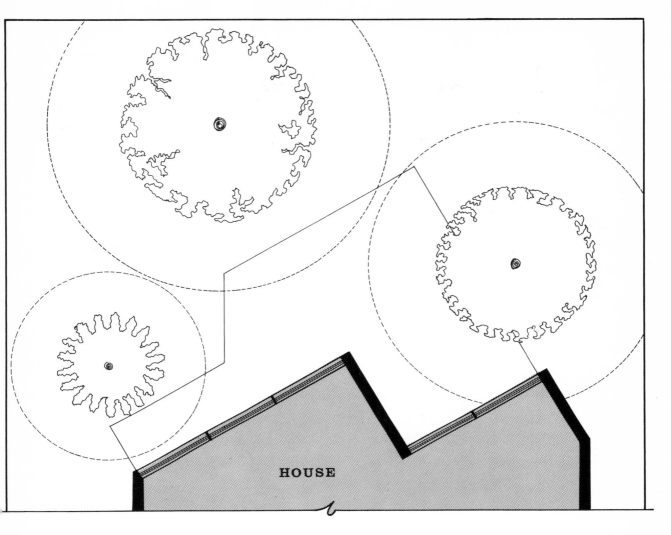

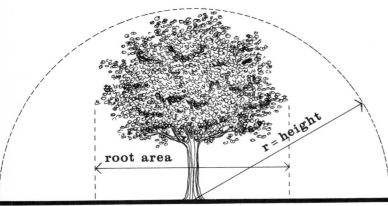

HOUSE

a tree will visually influence
the area within a half-sphere
whose radius equals the tree's
ultimate height

the root area approximates
the extent of the branches

root area

r = height

Tree Planting Plan

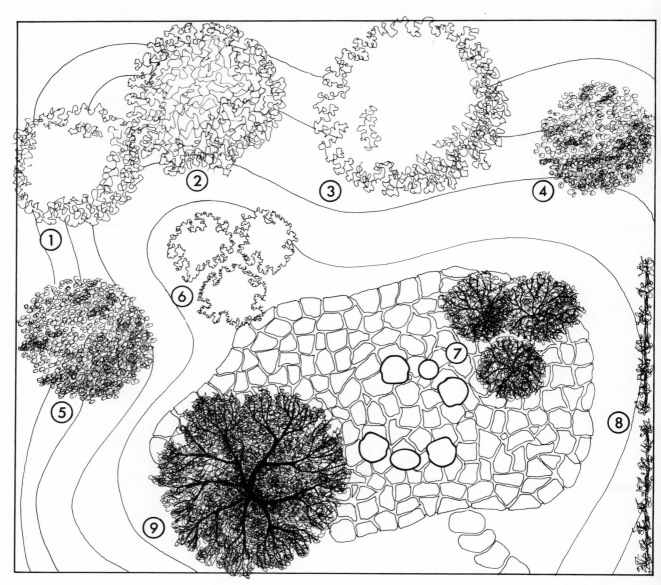

① **SORREL TREE**
white flowers & fruit,
deep-red fall leaves

② **HAWTHORN**
white to red flowers, red
berries & fall leaves

③ **JAPANESE MAPLE**
brilliant red fall leaves

④ **LOMBARDY POPLAR**
yellow fall leaves

⑤ **FLOWERING DOGWOOD**
white to pink flowers,
red berries & fall leaves

⑥ **GOLDEN CHAIN**
yellow flowers

⑦ **FLOWERING CHERRY**
white or pink flowers,
red to black fruit

⑧ **APPLE**
pink to white flowers,
red, yellow or green fruit

⑨ **PEAR** (espaliered)
white flowers, yellow or
green fruit, purple fall
leaves

ADRIÁN MARTÍNEZ

Trees for Seasonal Change

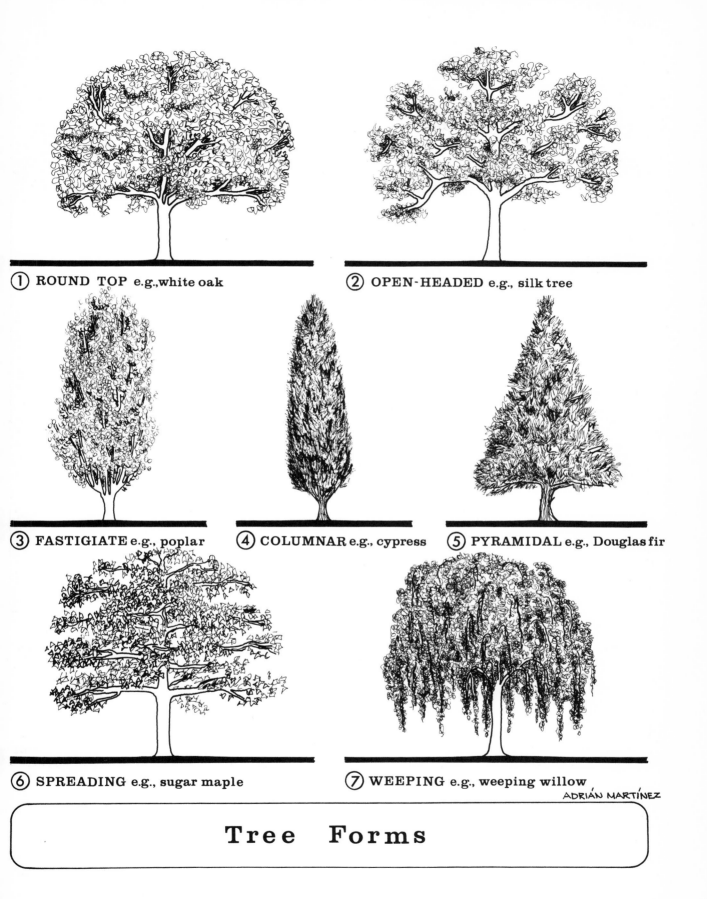

① ROUND TOP e.g., white oak

② OPEN-HEADED e.g., silk tree

③ FASTIGIATE e.g., poplar

④ COLUMNAR e.g., cypress

⑤ PYRAMIDAL e.g., Douglas fir

⑥ SPREADING e.g., sugar maple

⑦ WEEPING e.g., weeping willow

ADRIÁN MARTÍNEZ

Tree   Forms

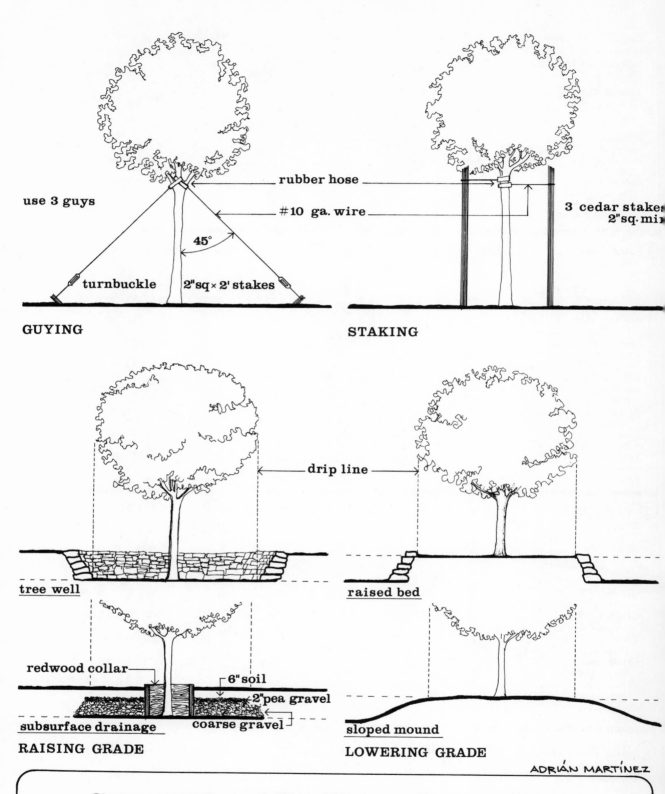

use 3 guys

rubber hose

#10 ga. wire

3 cedar stakes
2" sq. min.

45°

turnbuckle   2"sq × 2' stakes

GUYING

STAKING

drip line

tree well

raised bed

redwood collar

6" soil

2" pea gravel

subsurface drainage

coarse gravel

RAISING GRADE

sloped mound

LOWERING GRADE

ADRIÁN MARTÍNEZ

Supporting & Grading Around Trees

that you can tell at a glance whether a plant will grow in your area. These are only general guides because plant hardiness depends on many different factors. (See Chapter 5.) When in doubt, check with your local nurseryman, who is well acquainted with the plant material and weather in his specific area.

Table 3. General List of Deciduous Trees

Botanical and Common Name	Approx. Height in Ft.	Minimum Night Temp.	Remarks
Acer circinatum* (vine maple)	25	—10 to — 5F	Small, compact size
Acer ginnala (Amur maple)	20	—50 to —35F	Red fall color
Acer palmatum (Japanese maple)	20	—10 to 0F	Needs rich, well-drained soil
Acer platanoides (Norway maple)	90	—35 to —20F	Grows rapidly
Acer rubrum (red maple)	120	—35 to —20F	Best show in late spring
Acer saccharum (sugar maple)	120	—35 to —20F	Several varieties
Acer spicatum (mountain maple)	25	—50 to —35F	Grows in shade
Acer tataricum (Tatarian maple)	30	—20 to —10F	Good small tree
Aesculus carnea (red horse chestnut)	60	—35 to —20F	No autumn color
Aesculus glabra (Ohio buckeye)	30	—35 to —20F	Good autumn color
Ailanthus altissima (tree of heaven)	60	—20 to —10F	Very adaptable
Albizzia julibrissin* (silk tree)	20	5 to 10F	Very ornamental
Alnus glutinosa (black alder)	70	—35 to —20F	Tolerates wet soil
Alnus incana (common alder)	60	—50 to —35F	Round-headed habit
Betula papyrifera (canoe birch)	90	—50 to —35F	Stellar ornamental
Betula pendula (European birch)	60	—40 to —30F	Graceful, but shortlived
Betula populifolia* (gray birch)	40	—20 to —10F	Yellow color in autumn
Carya glabra* (pignut)	120	—20 to —10F	Slow grower
Carya ovata (shagbark hickory)	130	—30 to —10F	Narrow upright habit
Castanea mollissima (Chinese chestnut)	60	—20 to —10F	Round-headed, dense tree
Catalpa speciosa (western catalpa)	50	—20 to —10F	Large white flowers
Celtis occidentalis (hackberry)	75	—50 to —35F	Good shade tree
Cercis canadensis* (eastern redbud)	25	—20 to —10F	Lovely flowers
Chionanthus virginicus (fringe tree)	20	—20 to —10F	Bountiful flowers
Cornus florida* (dogwood)	25	—30 to —10F	Stellar ornamental
Cornus kousa (Japanese dogwood)	20	—10 to — 5F	Lovely flowers in June
Cotinus americanus (smoke-tree)	25	—10 to — 5F	Outstanding fall color
Crataegus mollis* (downy hawthorn)	30	—20 to —10F	Pear-shaped red fruit
Crataegus oxyacantha (English hawthorn)	20	—20 to —10F	Pink to red flowers

* See also section "Additional Comments on Trees."

Table 3 (Continued)

Botanical and Common Name	Approx. Height in Ft.	Minimum Night Temp.	Remarks
Crataegus phaenopyrum (Washington hawthorn)	30	—20 to —10F	Profuse flowers, brilliant autumn color
Diospyros virginiana (persimmon)	40	—10 to — 5F	Round-headed habit
Elaeagnus angustifolia (Russian olive)	20	—50 to —35F	Vigorous; any soil
*Fagus grandifolia** (American beech)	120	—35 to —20F	Stellar tree
Fagus sylvatica (European beech)	100	—20 to —10F	Several varieties
Franklinia alatamaha	30	—10 to 0F	Large white flowers; red foliage in autumn
*Fraxinus americana** (White ash)	120	—35 to —20F	Grows in almost any soil
Fraxinus holotricha	35	—10 to — 5F	Fast low-growing shade tree
Fraxinus ornus (flowering ash)	35	—10 to 0F	Dense foliage; pretty flowers
Gingko biloba (maidenhair tree)	120	—20 to —10F	Popular one
Gleditsia aquatica (water locust)	60	— 5 to 5F	Wants moist place
Gleditsia triacanthos (sweet honey locust)	100	—20 to —10F	Several varieties
Jacaranda acutifolia	50	30 to 40F	Blue flowers in summer
Koelreuteria paniculata (goldenrain tree)	30	—10 to — 5F	Magnificent summer bloom
Laburnum watereri (golden chain tree)	25	—10 to — 5F	Deep-yellow flowers
Liquidambar styraciflua (sweet gum)	90	—10 to — 5F	Beautiful symmetry
Liriodendron tulipifera (tulip tree)	100	—20 to —10F	Robust grower
*Magnolia soulangiana** (saucer magnolia)	25	—10 to — 5F	Many varieties; also evergreens, shrubs
Magnolia stellata (star magnolia)	20	—10 to — 5F	Very ornamental
*Malus baccata** (Siberian crab apple)	45	—50 to —35F	Lovely flowers and fruit
Malus floribunda (Japanese flowering crab apple)	30	—20 to —10F	Handsome foliage; and flowers
Phellodendron amurense (cork tree)	50	—35 to —20F	Massive branches; wide-open habit
Platanus acerifolia (plane tree)	100	—10 to — 5F	Popular street tree
Platanus occidentalis (buttonwood)	100+	—20 to —10F	Heavy frame
Populus alba (white poplar)	90	—35 to —20F	Wide-spreading tree
Populus canadensis 'Eugenei' (Carolina poplar)	100	—20 to —10F	Vagrant roots
Prunus amygdalus (almond)	25	— 5 to 5F	Handsome pink flowers
Prunus serotina (black cherry)	100	—20 to —10F	Handsome foliage; many varieties; some evergreen
Prunus serrulata (Japanese cherry)	25	—10 to 0F	Low grower; many kinds, some evergreen
Prunus triloba (flowering almond)	10	—10 to — 5F	One of the best; sometimes classed as shrub
*Quercus alba** (white oak)	80	—20 to —10F	Needs room to grow

* See also section "Additional Comments on Trees."

Table 3 (*Continued*)

Botanical and Common Name	Approx. Height in Ft.	Minimum Night Temp.	Remarks
Quercus coccinea (scarlet oak)	80	—20 to —10F	Brilliant autumn color
Quercus palustris (pin oak)	120	—20 to —10F	Beautiful pyramid
Quercus rubra (red oak)	80	—35 to —20F	Oval round-top tree
Robinia pseudoacacia (black locust)	80	—35 to —20F	Fine, late spring flowers
*Salix alba** (white willow)	40	—50 to —35F	Good upright willow
Salix babylonica (weeping willow)	40	—10 to — 5F	Fast grower
Sophora japonica (Japanese pagoda tree)	60	—20 to —10F	Good shade tree
Sorbus aucuparia (mountain ash)	45	—35 to —20F	Red autumn color
*Tilia americana** (American linden)	90	—50 to —35F	Fragrant white flowers in July
Tilia cordata (small-leaved linden)	60	—35 to —20F	Dense habit
Tilia tomentosa (silver linden)	80	—20 to —10F	Beautiful specimen tree
Ulmus americana (American elm)	100	—50 to —35F	Most popular shade tree

* See also section "Additional Comments on Trees."

Table 4. General List of Evergreen Trees

Botanical and Common Name	Approx. Height in Ft.	Minimum Night Temp.	Remarks
*Abies balsamea** (balsam fir)	70	—35 to —20F	Handsome ornamental
Abies concolor (white fir)	100	—20 to —10F	Good landscape tree
*Acacia baileyana** (Bailey acacia)	20–30	30 to 40F	Profuse yellow flowers
Bauhinia blakeana (orchid tree)	20	30 to 40F	Abundant flowers; partially deciduous
*Cedrus atlantica** (atlas cedar)	100	— 5 to 5F	Nice pyramid
*Chamaecyparis obtusa** (Hinoki false cypress)	130	—20 to —10F	Broadly pyramidal
Chamaecyparis pisifera (sawara false cypress)	100	—35 to —20F	Many varieties
Cinnamomum camphora (camphor tree)	40	20 to 30F	Dense branching habit
Cryptomeria japonica 'Lobbi'	30–50	— 5 to 5F	Pyramidal shape
Eriobotrya japonica (loquat)	20	5 to 10F	Needs well-drained soil
Eucalyptus camaldulensis (red gum)	80–100	20 to 30F	Fine landscape tree
Eucalyptus globulus (blue gum)	200	20 to 30F	Good windbreak
Eucalyptus gunnii (cider gum)	40–75	0 to 10F	Shade or screen tree
Eucalyptus polyanthemos (silver dollar gum)	20–60	10 to 20F	Fine landscape tree

* See also section "Additional Comments on Trees."

EVERGREEN TREE SHAPES

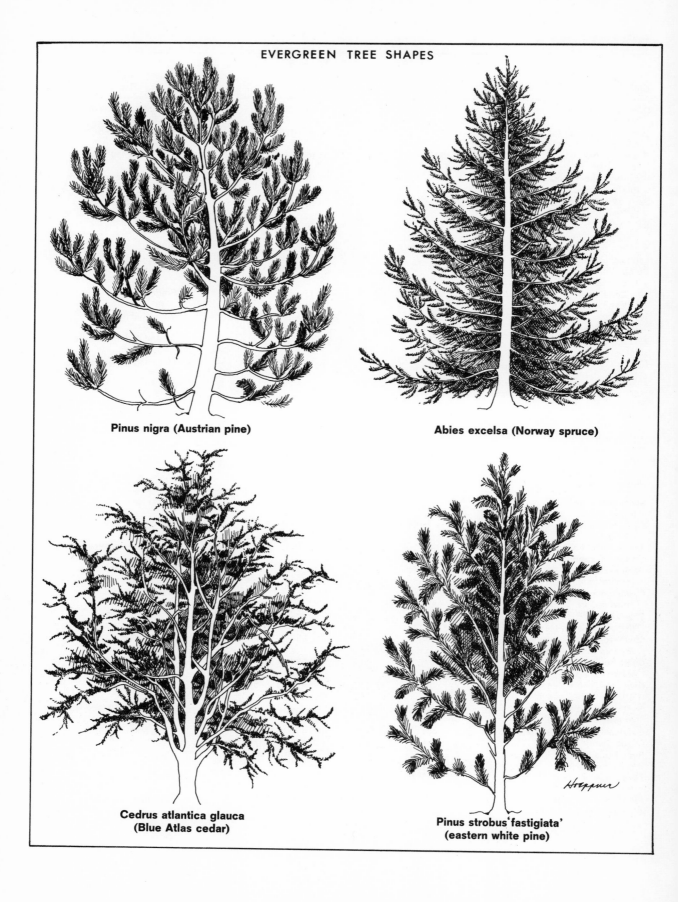

Pinus nigra (Austrian pine)

Abies excelsa (Norway spruce)

**Cedrus atlantica glauca
(Blue Atlas cedar)**

Pinus strobus 'fastigiata'
(eastern white pine)

Table 4 (Continued)

Botanical and Common Name	Approx. Height in Ft.	Minimum Night Temp.	Remarks
*Juniperus virginiana** (eastern red cedar)	30–50	—50 to —35F	Slow growing
Picea abies (excelsa)* (Norway spruce)	75	—50 to —35F	Not for small grounds
*Pinus bungeana** (lacebark pine)	75	—20 to —10F	Slow-growing tree
Pinus densiflora (Japanese red pine)	80	—20 to —10F	Flat-top habit
Pinus nigra (Austrian pine)	90	—20 to —10F	Fast-growing tree
Pinus parviflora (Japanese white pine)	90	—10 to — 5F	Handsome ornamental
Pinus ponderosa (ponderosa pine)	150	—10 to — 5F	Rapid growth
Pinus thunbergana (Japanese black pine)	90	—20 to —10F	Dense-spreading tree
Podocarpus gracilior (fern pine)	60	30 to 40F	Robust grower
Podocarpus macrophyllus (yew pine)	60	5 to 10F	Grows untended
*Taxus baccata** (English yew)	60	— 5 to 5F	Best among yews
Taxus cuspidata 'Capitata' (Japanese yew)	50	—20 to —10F	Good landscape tree
*Thuja occidentalis** (American arborvitae)	65	—50 to —35F	Sometimes needles turn brown in winter
*Tsuga canadensis** (hemlock)	75	—35 to —20F	Many uses; hedges, screens, landscape
Tsuga caroliniana (Carolina hemlock)	75	—20 to —10F	Fine all-purpose evergreen
Tsuga diversifolia (Japanese hemlock)	90	—10 to — 5F	Smaller than most hemlocks
Umbellularia californica (California laurel)	75	5 to 10F	Favorite West Coast tree

* See also section "Additional Comments on Trees."

Table 5. Trees for Windbreaks

Botanical and Common Name	Kind*
Acer ginnala (Amur maple)	D
Crataegus mollis (downy hawthorn)	D
Eucalyptus species (eucalyptus)	E
Fagus species (beech)	D
Fraxinus americana (white ash)	D
Pinus nigra (Austrian pine)	E
Pinus thunbergana (Japanese black pine)	E
Populus alba (white poplar)	D
Quercus imbricaria (shingle oak)	D
Quercus palustris (pin oak)	D
Thuja occidentalis (American arborvitae)	E
Tilia species (linden)	E
Tsuga canadensis (hemlock)	E

Table 6. Trees for Wet Soil

Botanical and Common Name	Kind*
Abies balsamea (balsam fir)	E
Acer rubrum (red maple)	D

* D = deciduous; E = evergreen.

Botanical and Common Name	Kind*
Alnus glutinosa (black alder)	D
Betula populifolia (gray birch)	D
Gleditsia aquatica (water locust)	D
Liquidambar styraciflua (sweet gum)	D
Platanus occidentalis (buttonwood)	D
Quercus palustris (pin oak)	D
Salix alba (white willow)	D
Thuja occidentalis (arborvitae)	E
Tilia americana (American linden)	D
Tsuga canadensis (hemlock)	E

Table 7. Trees for Dry Soil

Botanical and Common Name	Kind*
Acer tataricum (Tatarian maple)	D
Carya glabra (pignut)	D
Juniperus chinensis (Chinese juniper)	E
Juniperus virginiana (red cedar)	E
Picea alba (Canadian spruce)	E
Pinus sylvestris (Scots pine)	E

An old apple tree is the dominant feature of a front yard.
(Molly Adams)

Towering maples are the background for a contemporary home; a conifer and small fruit tree accent the entrance.
(Theodore Brickman, Landscape Architect; Hube Henry, Hedrich•Blessing)

Table 8. Fast-Growing Trees

Botanical and Common Name	Kind*
Acer platanoides (Norway maple)	D
Acer rubrum (red maple)	D
Betula populifolia (gray birch)	D
Catalpa speciosa (catalpa)	D
Fraxinus americana (white ash)	D
Gingko biloba (maidenhair tree)	D
Gleditsia triacanthos (honey locust)	D
Quercus palustris (pin oak)	D
Salix alba (white willow)	D
Sorbus aucuparia (European mountain ash)	D
Tilia americana (American linden)	D

* D = deciduous; E = evergreen.

Best Flowering Trees

Acacia baileyana (Bailey acacia)
Aesculus glabra (Ohio buckeye)
Albizzia julibrissin (silk tree)
Catalpa speciosa (catalpa)
Cercis canadensis (redbud)
Cornus florida (dogwood)
Cornus kousa chinensis
Franklinia alatamaha
Jacaranda acutifolia
Koelreuteria paniculata (goldenrain tree)
Magnolia grandiflora (southern magnolia)
Magnolia stellata (star magnolia)
Malus species (crab apple)
Prunus species (fruit trees)
Sophora japonica (Japanese pagoda tree)

Trees for Shade

Acer circinatum (vine maple)
Acer ginnala (Amur maple)
Acer palmatum (Japanese maple)
Acer spicatum (mountain maple)
Albizzia julibrissin (silk tree)
Alnus species (alder)
Betula papyrifera (canoe birch)
Cercis canadensis (redbud)
Cornus alba
Cornus kousa (Chinese dogwood)
Cornus mas (cornelian cherry)
Crataegus oxyacantha 'Paul's scarlet' (hawthorn)
Elaeagnus angustifolia (Russian olive)
Franklinia alatamaha (franklinia)
Fraxinus holotricha
Magnolia soulangiana (saucer magnolia)
Magnolia stellata (star magnolia)
Malus species and hybrids (flowering crab apple)
Pinus bungeana (lacebark pine)
Prunus, various (flowering cherry and others)
Sorbus, various (mountain ash)
Taxus species (yew)
Thuja species (arborvitae)
Tsuga species (hemlock)

Additional Comments on Trees

Here are some additional comments on deciduous and evergreen trees to supplement previous lists. General culture and descriptions are given to help you better select plants for your individual needs. If your favorite tree has been omitted, it was a matter of space rather than choice.

Botanical and common names are given. Species are in italics and varieties in single quotes under species names. For example:

Magnolia soulangiana (species)
('Alba') (variety)

ABIES (fir). Generally, these evergreens are pyramidal in shape and have rigid horizontal branches, making them a decisive accent in the landscape. Use them sparingly. Needles are persistent for about 5 years before they fall; cones are ornamental, but do not appear every year. The trees have few insect or disease problems, but as they mature the lower branches become unsightly and, once removed, they do not grow back so that a mature specimen lacks symmetry. Firs need a cool, moist climate to grow well or else they deteriorate rapidly. These trees are Christmas favorites.

A. concolor (white fir). Hardy to −20F; narrow, pyramidal in shape to 120 feet. Bluish-green needles; rapid grower.
A. koreana (Korean fir). Hardy to −10F. Pyramidal to 50 feet; horizontal branching habit. Dark-green needles.
A. magnifica (red fir). Hardy to −10F. Stiff pyramid to 200 feet; dense.
A. veitchii (veitch fir). Hardy to −35F. Pyramidal in shape, rather stiff, to 75 feet. Dark-green needles, whitish underneath.

ACACIA. Evergreen shrubs and trees suitable to temperate areas, these plants differ widely in foliage and growth habit. Some have feathery divided leaves, others have flattened leaves. Acacias are short lived (to about 25 years), yet they are useful and lovely in the garden especially in very early spring (February–March) when they are covered with clouds of yellow flowers.

A. armata (kangaroo thorn). Hardy to 30F; light-green, waxy leaves on thorny branches; grows to 15 feet. Single yellow flowers.
A. baileyana (Bailey acacia). Hardy to 30F; grows to 30 feet. Feathery, fine-cut, blue-gray leaves and clusters of yellow blooms.
A. decurrens (green wattle). Hardy to 30F; can grow to 50 feet. Feathery, dark-green foliage and yellow blooms.
A. longifolia floribunda (Sydney golden wattle).

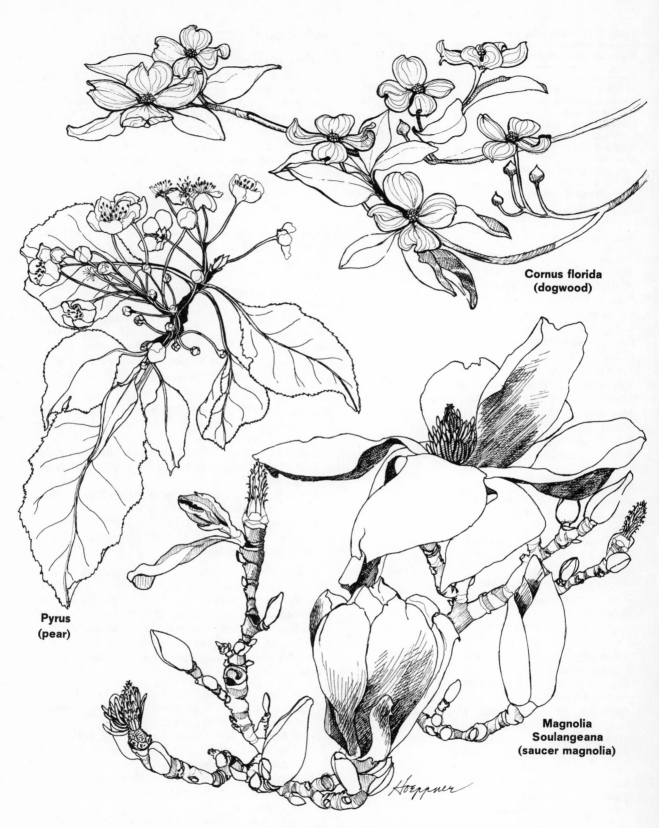

Cornus florida
(dogwood)

Pyrus
(pear)

Magnolia
Soulangeana
(saucer magnolia)

Hoeppner

FLOWERING TREES

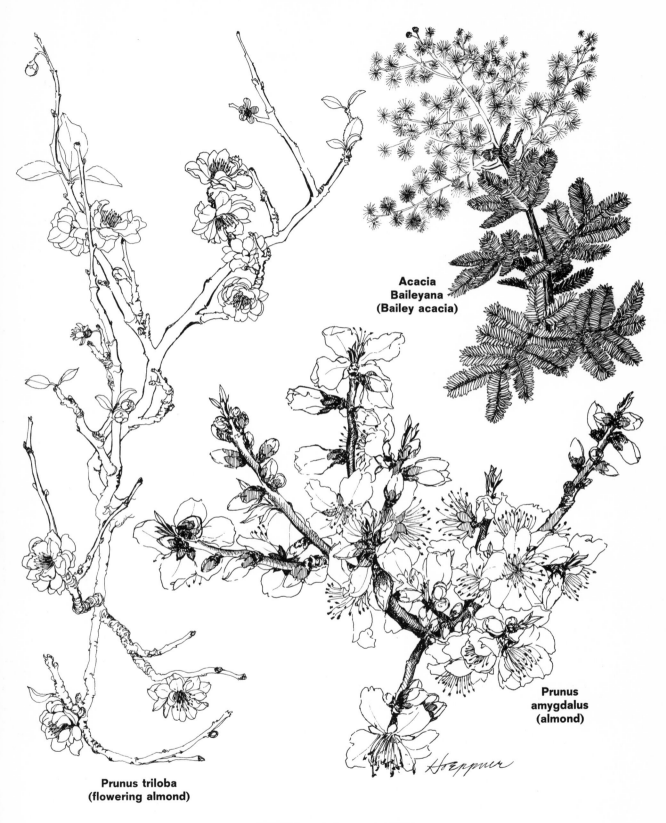

Acacia
Baileyana
(Bailey acacia)

Prunus
amygdalus
(almond)

Prunus triloba
(flowering almond)

Hoeppner

FLOWERING TREES

Hardy to 30F; spreading habit to 20 feet. Dense-leaved.

A. *pendula* (weeping acacia). Hardy to 30F; blue-gray leaves on weeping branches. Yellow flowers.

ACER (maple). Maples are popular shade trees, and there are many kinds for many uses. Varied in habit and rate of growth, size, and leaf shape, some of them (Japanese maple) are low and squatty; others (Norway maple) are round at the top and quite tall. Smaller varieties are ideal for landscaping where there is limited space. While some maples have interesting colorful bark, it is the autumn color of the foliage—brilliant red or yellow—that makes them popular. Maples grow in any good garden soil, and are generally not bothered by pests or diseases.

A. *buergerianum* (trident maple). Hardy to −5F. Rounded habit; grows to 20 feet. Foliage is brilliant red in fall. Deciduous.

A. *ginnala* (Amur maple). Hardy to −50F; grows to about 20 feet, with striking red autumn color. Deciduous.

A. *japonicum* (full-moon maple). Hardy to −10F. Can reach 30 feet, with lobed leaves. Good fall color. Deciduous.

'Aconitifolium' (fernleaf maple)—Leaves deeply lobed.

'Aureum' (golden maple)—Handsome yellow foliage.

A. *macrophyllum* (big-leaf maple). Hardy to −5F. Grows to 90 feet. Lobed leaves turn yellow in fall. Deciduous.

A. *palmatum* (Japanese maple). Hardy to −10F; rounded habit to 20 feet. Dense, handsome tree. Deciduous.

'Atropurpureum'—Bronze leaves.

'Burgundy Lace'—Finely cut leaves; red.

'Dissectum' (laceleaf maple)—Leaves cut into threadlike segments.

'Versicolor'—Leaves green with white, pink, and light-green variation.

A. *platanoides* (Norway maple). Hardy to −35F; broad-crowned to 60 feet. Leaves turn yellow in fall; greenish-yellow spring flowers. Deciduous.

'Columnare' (pyramidal Norway maple)—Slow grower.

'Faasen's Black'—Pyramidal with dark purple leaves.

A. *rubrum* (red maple). Hardy to −35F; fast-growing to 100 feet. Red twigs and buds. Deciduous.

A. *saacharum* (sugar maple). Hardy to −35F; fast grower to 100 feet. Silver-gray bark; orange and red fall color. Deciduous.

ALBIZZIA (silk tree). An overlooked good, small tree with delicate fernlike foliage and charming summer flowers. With arching stems and compact growth, it is a stellar landscape subject. It likes sun and a good garden loam somewhat on the sandy side. In the North it is likely to die down to the ground in winter; remove dead stems early in spring to encourage new growth.

A. *distachya* (plume albizzia). Hardy to 20F; fast-growing to 20 feet. Dark-green, velvety foliage and greenish-yellow flowers.

A. *julibrissin* (silk tree). Hardy to 5F; rapid grower to 40 feet. Pink fluffy flowers and ferny-leaved branches.

BETULA (birch). Birches are favorite ornamental trees, graceful in appearance; the most popular ones have handsome white bark. Somewhat short-lived, the trees are difficult to transplant unless they are balled and burlapped. Most important, move them in the spring. Once established, most birches are easy to grow and will thrive in wet or dry soil. The bright-yellow autumn color is certainly desirable in the landscape. All in all these are worthwhile garden subjects.

B. *albo-sinensis* (Chinese paper birch). Hardy to −10F; rounded habit to 90 feet. Handsome yellow color in autumn and orange-red bark. Deciduous.

B. *papyrifera* (canoe birch). Hardy to −50F; grows to 90 feet. White bark peels off in thin sheets. Deciduous.

B. *populifolia* (gray birch). Hardy to −20F; reaches 30 feet, with several trunks to a clump. Bark is white with black markings. Deciduous.

B. *verrucosa* (*pendula*) (European white birch). Hardy to −50F; pyramidal in shape. Grows to 60 feet; white bark.

'Fastigiata'—Upright grower.

'Purpurea'—Rich purple color.

'Youngii'—Pendulous branches.

CARYA (hickory). Robust trees, and once established they grow into giants. While they are free of insects and disease, they are difficult to transplant and should not be moved unless necessary. In general, hickories are excellent ornamental trees with golden autumn foliage, and make superior accents in the garden, if there is space for them. Some are broad in habit; others, narrow, upright growers.

C. *illinoinensis* (pecan). Hardy to −10F; a giant spreading tree to 150 feet. Dense-leaved, with striking yellow autumn color. Deciduous.

C. *ovata* (shagbark hickory). Hardy to −20F; upright, irregular growth to 120 feet. Golden-brown autumn color, and bark that flakes off in pieces. Deciduous.

CEDRUS (cedar). Good, big evergreen trees that need lots of space; their sculptural growth is desirable in the landscape. They need a somewhat rich soil, and are relatively trouble-free. Some species are stiff in appearance; others are more graceful, having pendent branches.

C. atlantica (atlas cedar). Hardy to −5F; widely pyramidal tree to 120 feet. Silvery to light-green needles in bunches.
  'Glauca' (blue Atlas cedar)—Silvery-blue needles.
  'Pendula'—Lovely pendent branches; graceful.
C. deodara (deodar cedar). Hardy to 0F; narrow pyramidal growth to 150 feet, with pendulous branches. Needles in dense bunches.
C. libani (cedar of Lebanon). Hardy to −10F; pyramidal growth to 120 feet, with stiff horizontal branches.

CERCIS (redbud). Small deciduous trees rarely over 25 feet with lovely heart-shaped leaves and clusters of small magenta-pink blossoms in spring. The flowers are long lasting, and foliage turns bright yellow in fall. The redbuds will grow in full sun or light shade, and are not particular about soil conditions.

C. canadensis (eastern redbud). Hardy to −20F; flat-topped tree to 35 feet. Small purplish-pink blooms and yellow leaves in fall.
C. chinensis (Chinese redbud). Hardy to −5F; often shrublike to 40 feet. Dense featherlike, rosy-purple flowers.
C. siliquastrum (Judas tree). Hardy to −5F; flat-topped tree to 30 feet. Profuse bright purplish-rose flowers.

CHAMAECYPARIS (false cypress). Favorite evergreens, with many color forms and varieties. The Japanese species withstand drier atmosphere than do others in the group. Generally dense and pyramidal in shape, these trees are free of insects and disease. They are popular additions to the garden picture, and need little care.

C. lawsoniana (Lawson false cypress). Hardy to −10F; slender tree to 120 feet. Usually with blue-green foliage; shredding bark.
  'Allumii' (scarab Lawson cypress)—Grows to 30 feet.
  'Compacta'—To 6 feet; gray-green foliage.
  'Fletcheri'—To 10 feet; blue-gray; purplish or brown winter.
  'Stewartii'—Golden-yellow foliage, usually turning green.
C. obtusa (Hinoki false cypress). Hardy to −20F; broad pyramid to 120 feet. Glossy, green scalelike leaves.
  'Aurea' (golden Hinoki cypress)—To 40 feet, dark-green leaves.

  'Filicioides' (fernspray cypress)—To 15 feet; medium-green dense foliage.
  'Nana' (dwarf Hinoki cypress)—Small form.
C. pisifera (sawara false cypress). Hardy to −35F; pyramidal to 150 feet, with horizontal branching habit. Open foliage.
  'Filifera' (thread Sawara cypress)—Dark-green foliage.
  'Plumosa Aurea'—Soft, feathery, golden-yellow foliage.
  'Squarrosa Minima'–Dwarf; several forms under this name.

CORNUS (dogwood). Dogwood trees are just about the best small deciduous trees you can find; they grow rapidly and have splendid color in bloom and are showy again in autumn with colorful foliage. There is a dogwood for almost any part of the United States. Some are wide and spreading with horizontal branches; others are narrow and upright. There are many varieties of *C. florida* offered; but not all of them are good ones, so make choices carefully.

C. alba (Tatarian dogwood). Hardy to −35F; upright growth to 10 feet. Branches densely clothed with leaves; red twigs in winter.
C. florida (flowering dogwood). Hardy to −20F; horizontal branching habit; grows to 40 feet. Red color in autumn.
  'Cherokee Chief'—Rich red leaves.
  'Pendula'—Stiff, pendulous branches.
  'Rubra'—Pink or rose flower bracts.
C. kousa (Japanese dogwood). Hardy to −10F; horizontal branching habit. Grows to 20 feet; red color in autumn.
  'Milky Way'—Profuse bloomer.
C. mas (cornelian cherry). Hardy to −20F; round, dense shrub type, to 20 feet. Red autumn color.
C. nuttallii (Pacific dogwood). Hardy to 5F; pyramidal, with dense foliage. Grows to 75 feet; large flowers, spectacular in bloom.
  'Goldspot'—Leaves splashed with yellow.

CRATAEGUS (hawthorn). A widely distributed group of deciduous trees, hawthorns are dense, twiggy, dependable, and loaded with flowers in May. Of slow growth, they are desirable because they are compact and beautiful in the landscape. Generally, it is the picturesque shapes that make them so popular and, too, the bright red fruit in fall. Hawthorns will grow in poor soil; some of them keep fruit all winter.

C. arnoldiana (Arnold hawthorn). Hardy to −20F; round habit to 30 feet. Densely branching, with red fruit in early autumn.
C. lavallei (lavalle hawthorn). Hybrid; hardy to −20F; thorny, branching to 20 feet. Dense foliage, a beautiful red in fall.

C. monogyna (single-seed hawthorn). Hardy to
−20F; round-headed, with pendulous branches.
Red color in autumn. 30 feet.
  'Stricta'—Upright grower.
C. nitida (glossy hawthorn). Hardy to −20F; round-
headed to 30 feet. White flowers; red autumn
color.
C. oxyacantha (English hawthorn). Hardy to −20F;
round-headed to 15 feet. Densely branching.
  'Paul's Scarlet'—Popular; double red-to-rose
flowers.
  'Doublewhite'—Lovely white form.
C. phaenopyrum (Washington hawthorn). Hardy to
−20F; broadly columnar. Red fall color. 30 feet.
C. pinnatifida major (large Chinese hawthorn).
Hardy to −5F; round-headed to 15 feet. Lustrous
leaves, white flowers, and brilliant red autumn
fruit.

FAGUS (beech). Elegant, the beech is deciduous and
beautiful all year, but especially in fall when it blazes
with golden color. Usually it is a large tree with a
stout trunk and smooth bark. When you plant
beeches, remember that very little can be grown
underneath them because of the shade.

F. sylvatica (European beech). Hardy to −20F;
pyramidal to 90 feet. Glossy, dark-green foliage;
dense. Bronze autumn color.
  'Atropunicea' (copper beech)—Reddish or
purple leaves.
  'Fastigiata'—Narrow form.
  'Laciniata' (cutleaf beech)—Narrow green
leaves.
  'Pendula' (weeping beech)—Spreading form,
green leaves.
  'Purpureo-pendula' (weeping copper beech)—
Purple-leaved weeping form.
  'Tricolor' (tricolor beech)—Green leaves
marked with white and pink.

FRAXINUS (ash). The ash is a rapid-growing tree;
brilliant yellow to purple color in fall. It is large;
some grow to 100 feet and need lots of space; hardly
suitable for small properties. Trees grow without
much attention in any reasonably good soil. Deciduous.

F. americana (white ash). Hardy to −35F; straight
trunk, oval-shaped crown. Grows to 100 feet, with
dense foliage.
F. excelsior (European ash). Hardy to −35F; grows
to 120 feet. Round-headed, with open branches.
  'Kimberley'—Selected male variety.
  'Nana'—Low, globe-shaped.
  'Pendula' (weeping European ash)—Spreading
umbrella-shaped tree.
F. holotricha. Hardy to −10F; upright and narrow.
Grows to 35 feet; fast grower.

F. ornus (flowering ash). Hardy to −10F; broad,
rounded crown. Grows to 40 feet; lavender-and-
yellow foliage in fall.
F. pennsylvanica (*lanceolata*) (green ash). Hardy to
−50F; dense round-headed tree to 60 feet. Yellow autumn color.
  'Marshall's seedless' ash—Selected male form.
F. velutina (Arizona ash). Hardy to −10F; round-
headed tree. Grows to 45 feet.

JUNIPERUS (juniper). These evergreens are valued
for their colorful berries in fall and winter. Both
male and female plants have to be grown near each
other to insure fruiting. The junipers are tall and
dense in habit, and prefer a somewhat alkaline soil.

J. chinensis (Chinese juniper). Hardy to −20F; pyra-
midal habit. Grows to 60 feet; scalelike leaves.
  'Columnaris'—Columnar, silvery-green foliage.
  'Keteleeri'—Stiff trunk; loose, green foliage.
  'Mountbatten'—Gray-green, narrow growth.
  'Pyramidalis'—Blue-gray needle foliage.
J. scopulorum (Rocky Mountain juniper). Hardy to
−10F; narrow and upright to 35 feet. Green to
light-blue foliage.
  'Blue Haven'—Narrow gray-blue pyramid.
  'Emerald Green'—Compact, bright-green fo-
liage.
  'Pathfinder'—Gray-blue, upright grower.
J. virginiana (red cedar juniper). Hardy to −50F;
dense pyramid to 90 feet. Foliage varies, but usu-
ally scalelike.
  'Burkii'—Steel-blue foliage.
  'Cupressifolia'—Dark-green.
  'Glauca'—Silvery-blue.

MAGNOLIA. A popular group because they have
splendid flowers; many magnolias bear bloom in
early spring before the leaves appear. In a wide range
of colors—white, pink, red, reddish-purple—the
flowers are spectacular. Many magnolias are wide-
spreading trees and tall (to 90 feet); others grow to
30 feet. Some are deciduous; others are evergreen.
Many have early flowers, and some bloom in
summer. All like a good well-drained soil and lots of
water in summer. Any pruning should be done immediately after flowering. There is a magnolia for
almost every garden; as a flowering tree, they are
tough to beat.

M. denudata (yulan magnolia). Hardy to −5F;
round habit. Grows to 35 feet. White tulip-shaped,
fragrant flowers. Deciduous.
M. grandiflora (southern magnolia). Hardy to 5F;
usually dense pyramidal form. Pure white flowers;
evergreen. 90 feet.
  'Exoniensis'—White flowers.
  'Majestic Beauty'—Immense 12-inch blooms.
  'St. Mary'—Full flowers on small tree.
  'Samuel Sommer'—Very large flowers.

M. kobus (kobus magnolia). Hardy to −5F; good, sturdy tree to 30 feet. White 4-inch flowers. Deciduous.

M. macrophylla (big-leaf magnolia). Hardy to −10F; round-headed tree to 50 feet. White, fragrant, 12-inch flowers.

M. salicifolia (anise magnolia). Hardy to −10F; pyramidal growth to 30 feet. White, fragrant flowers.

M. sargentiana robusta. Hardy to 5F; wide-spreading habit. Grows to 40 feet; large mauve-pink flowers. A spectacle in bloom. Deciduous.

M. soulangiana (saucer magnolia). Hybrid; hardy to −10F; white to pink or purplish-red flowers. Variable in size and form. Deciduous.
  'Alba'—Flowers with purple markings.
  'Alexandrina'—Deep pink-and-white blooms.
  'Brozzoni'—Huge whitish-pink flowers.
  'Burgundy'—Deep purple-and-pink blooms.
  'Lilliputian'—Small pink-and-white flowers.
  'San Jose'—Large rosy-purple flowers.

M. stellata (star magnolia)—Very early white flowers. Hardy to −10F. 20 feet.

M. veitchii. Hybrid; hardy to 5F; open habit. Grows to 40 feet; pink flowers. Deciduous.

M. virginiana (*glauca*) (sweet bay). Hardy to −10; globular shape. Creamy-white flowers. Evergreen. Grows to 40–60 feet.

MALUS (crab apple). Good ornamental, deciduous flowering trees in vivid color in May; some varieties have single blooms; others, semidouble or double flowers in color range from pure white to purple-red. Many are fragrant. The fruit of some hold color well into winter, making the trees of two-season value. Most crab apples are small, to about 30 feet, although a few reach to 50 feet. Several have pendent branches, but actually shapes run the gamut from columnar to round-headed. Crab apples need sun, and when young require some additional feeding. A regular schedule of spraying is necessary because these trees have the same problems—fire blight, scale, and borers—as the common apple.

M. arnoldiana (Arnold crab apple). Hardy to −20F; broad and spreading. Fragrant, pink flowers.

M. atrosanguinea (carmine crab apple). Hardy to −20F; upright branches. Grows to about 20 feet, with dark evergreen leaves. Fragrant crimson to rose-purple flowers.

M. baccata mandschurica. Hardy to −50F; bushy and dense to 40 feet. Dark-green foliage; fragrant white flowers.
  'Columnaris'—White, fragrant, 1-inch flowers.
  M. 'Dorothea'—Hybrid; double pink blooms.
  M. 'Hopa'—Hybrid; fragrant, single rose-red flowers.
  M. 'Katherine'—Hybrid; double pink flowers.
  M. 'Red Jade'—Hybrid; floriferous; small white flowers.
  M. 'Red Silver'—Hybrid; deep-wine-red flowers.

M. sargenti (Sargent crab apple). Hardy to −20F; rounded and low branching. Grows to 8 feet, with pure-white, fragrant flowers.

PICEA (spruce). Young spruce trees make a pretty picture in the landscape, but mature ones generally lose their lower branches and become unsightly. Because most spruces grow to about 100 feet, they are not for the small garden. Still, there are some good evergreens in the group.

P. abies (Norway spruce). Hardy to −50F; pyramidal growth to 150 feet. Dark-green needles.
  'Columnaris'—Narrow and columnar.

P. glauca (white spruce). Hardy to −50F; pyramidal and grows to 90 feet. Bluish-green needles.
  'Conica'—Compact dwarf.

P. pungens (Colorado spruce). Hardy to −50F; stiff horizontal branches. Grows to 100 feet.
  'Argentea'—Silvery-white foliage.
  'Pendens'—Bluish-white foliage.

P. sitchensis (Sitka spruce). Hardy to −5F; tall pyramidal tree to 150 feet, with wide-spreading branches. Bright-green and silvery needles.

PINUS (pine). Good evergreens; some are better than others for ornamental use. Needles vary in length on each tree, but are usually from 2 to 12 inches long. Some pines are dwarf in stature and very picturesque; others are open and shrubby in habit; and still others, rounded. Many appear graceful in the landscape; a few are quite stiff and hardly desirable. Make selection carefully.

P. aristata (bristlecone pine). Hardy to −10F; dense and bushy to 40 feet. Dark-green needles, whitish underneath.

P. banksiana (jack pine). Hardy to −50F; open and broad-headed tree, often shrubby. Bright-green needles. Grows to 70 feet.

P. bungeana (lacebark pine). Hardy to −20F; rounded to pyramidal shape, often with several trunks. Long, bright-green needles. Grows to 75 feet.

P. canariensis (Canary Island pine). Hardy to 20F; grows fast to 80 feet. Blue-green needles.

P. contorta (beach pine). Hardy to 10F; round-top, dense-headed tree to 30 feet. Dense, dark-green needles.

P. densiflora (Japanese red pine). Hardy to −20F; horizontal branching tree to 100 feet. Bright, bluish-green needles.

P. halepensis (Aleppo pine). Hardy to 20F; open rounded-top tree. Light-green needles.

P. lambertiana (sugar pine). Hardy to −5F; columnar to 200 feet. Dark bluish-green needles.

P. mugo (Swiss mountain pine). Hardy to 10F; low, pyramidal growth. Dark-green, stout needles.

P. nigra (Austrian black pine). Hardy to −20F; dense, stout pyramid to 90 feet. Very dark-green needles.

P. parviflora (Japanese white pine). Hardy to −10F; dense pyramid to 90 feet. Wide-spreading branches, with bluish-green to gray needles.

P. pinea (Italian stone pine). Hardy to 20F; broad and flat-topped to 80 feet. Gray-green, stiff needles.

P. strobus (eastern white pine). Hardy to −35F; rounded or pyramidal growth to 150 feet. Blue-green, soft needles.
  'Fastigiata'—Narrow and upright.
  'Nana'—Grows to only 7 feet.

P. sylvestris (Scotch pine). Hardy to −50F; pyramidal when young, round-topped when mature. Blue-green, stiff needles. Grows to 75 feet.

P. thunbergiana (*thunbergii*) (Japanese black pine). Hardy to −10F; dense spreading habit. Bright-green, stiff needles. Grows to 90 feet.

QUERCUS (oak). Sturdy trees valued for their autumn color; the majority of them reach large size. The wood is strong, does not easily split, and the tree is long lived. Only the North American species have autumn color; European ones do not. The oaks are fine shade trees for large properties, but they can have their problems—borers, oak gall, various leaf diseases—and must have routine spraying.

Q. agrifolia (California live oak). Hardy to 20F; round-headed to 90 feet, with spreading habit. Evergreen, hollylike leaves.

Q. alba (white oak). Hardy to −20F; broad, open-crowned tree to 90 feet. Bright-green leaves turning purple in fall. Deciduous.

Q. coccinea (scarlet oak). Hardy to −20F; open-branching habit that can reach 80 feet. Leaves turn brilliant red in autumn. Deciduous.

Q. ilex (holly oak). Hardy to 20F; round-headed habit. Dark-green foliage, yellow underneath. Evergreen. Grows to 60 feet.

Q. kelloggii (California black oak). Hardy to 5F; open habit, with spreading branches. Leaves golden-yellow in fall. Deciduous. Grows to 90 feet.

Q. laurifolia (laurel oak). Hardy to 5F; dense, round-topped oak. Grows to 60 feet with dark-green leaves. Semievergreen.

Q. palustris (pin oak). Hardy to −20F; pyramidal in shape, with drooping branches. Red leaves in autumn. Deciduous. Grows to 75 feet.

Q. robur (English oak). Hardy to −10F; broad-headed tree, with open habit. No autumn color. Deciduous. Grows to 75–150 feet.

Q. suber (cork oak). Hardy to 5F; short trunk with round top. Small leaves. Evergreen. Grows to 60 feet.

SALIX (willow). Willows like water and moist conditions. Although the weeping willow is certainly graceful and lovely, remember that in many regions willows are troubled with insects and disease and have weak wood that cracks easily. Deciduous trees.

S. alba (white willow). Hardy to −50F; spreading branches, loose and open. Yellow leaves in autumn. Grows to 80 feet.
  'Tristis' (golden weeping willow)—Graceful and lovely.

S. babylonica (weeping willow). Hardy to −5F; long, pendulous branches. Fine-textured foliage; best of the willows. Grows to 30–50 feet.

S. caprea (French pussy willow). Hardy to −20F; small tree, to 25 feet. Dark-green, broad branches.

S. matsudana (Hankow willow). Hardy to −20F; upright pyramidal growth to 50 feet. Bright-green, narrow leaves.
  'Navajo' (globe willow)—Round-topped spreading habit.
  'Tortuosa' (corkscrew willow)—Twisted branches.

TAXUS (yew). Dark-green, evergreen trees that thrive in many different kinds of soil; tough ones to kill. Some yews make excellent hedges and screens, and they bear bright-red fruit in fall. Most are slow growing.

T. baccata (English yew). Hardy to −5F; dense branching; grows to about 60 feet. Dark-green needles.
  'Aurea'—Golden-yellow leaves.
  'Erecta'—Erect and formal in appearance.
  'Repandens'—Spreading type.
  'Stricta' (Irish yew)—Dark-green columnar growth.

T. cuspidata (Japanese yew). Hardy to −20F; grows to 50 feet. Dark-green needles.
  'Capitata'—Upright pyramidal form.
  'Densiformis'—Very branched.
  'Nana'—Slow grower; small.

T. media (hybrid). Columnar or pyramidal. Hardy to −20F.
  'Hatfieldii'—Broad columnar.
  'Hicksii'—Narrow upright.
  'Hills'—Narrow upright.

THUJA (arborvitae). Generally with flat, scalelike leaves, the evergreen arborvitaes are quite shrubby and somewhat pyramidal in shape. None of them tolerates dry conditions, but rather prefers moisture at the roots and in the air too. A few of them are unsatisfactory because their leaves turn brown in winter. For the most part, this group is slow growing and has its problems.

T. occidentalis (American arborvitae). Hardy to −50F; columnar growth to 60 feet. Bright-green to yellow-green needles.

    'Douglas Pyramidal'—Vigorous green pyramid.
    'Fastigata'—Narrow, tall type to 25 feet.

T. plicata (giant arborvitae). Hardy to −10F; narrow form to 180 feet. Scalelike foliage that does not turn brown in winter.

TILIA (linden). Some stellar deciduous trees, possibly the best ones for shade, and they excel in other areas too. They have handsome heart-shaped leaves and lovely sweet-scented pendulous flowers in early summer. As a group, the lindens have much to offer, and require very little attention.

T. americana (American linden). Hardy to −50F; grows to 60 feet. Dull, dark-green leaves.

T. cordata (little-leaf linden). Hardy to −35F; densely pyramidal. Dark-green leaves, silvery underneath. Grows to 50–90 feet.

    'Greenspire'—Upright form.
    'Rancho'—Conical shape.

T. tomentosa (silver linden). Hardy to −20F; broad and dense. Light-green leaves, silvery underneath. Grows to [40–50] [90] feet.

TSUGA (hemlock). Narrow-leaved evergreens, the hemlocks are beautiful, but they need buckets of water. All of them withstand shade, but will grow better with some sun. The Japanese hemlock is possibly the best in the group. All hemlocks bear small cones, but not every year. There are many varieties offered.

T. canadensis (Canadian hemlock). Hardy to −35F; long, slender horizontal branches. Dark-green needles. Grows to 90 feet.

    'Dawsoniana'—Slow-growing, dark-green.
    'Globosa'—Dense and rounded.

T. heterophylla (western hemlock). Hardy to −5F; short, drooping branches. Fine-textured, dark-green to yellowish-green foliage. Grows to 125–200 feet.

Trees by Common Names

Aleppo pine (*Pinus halepensis*)
American arborvitae (*Thuja occidentalis*)
American ash (*Fraxinus americana*)
American beech (*Fagus grandifolia*)
American elm (*Ulmus americana*)
American linden (*Tilia americana*)
Amur maple (*Acer ginnala*)
Anise magnolia (*Magnolia salicifolia*)
Arizona ash (*Fraxinus velutina*)
Arnold crab apple (*Malus arnoldiana*)
Arnold hawthorn (*Crataegus arnoldiana*)
Atlas cedar (*Cedrus atlantica*)

Austrian black pine (*Pinus nigra*)
Austrian pine (*Pinus nigra*)

Bailey acacia (*Acacia baileyana*)
Balsam fir (*Abies balsamea*)
Big-leaf magnolia (*Magnolia macrophylla*)
Big-leaf maple (*Acer macrophyllum*)
Black alder (*Alnus glutinosa*)
Black cherry (*Prunus serotina*)
Black locust (*Robinia pseudoacacia*)
Blue gum (*Eucalyptus globulus*)
Bristlecone pine (*Pinus aristata*)
Buttonwood (*Platanus occidentalis*)

California black oak (*Quercus kelloggii*)
California laurel (*Umbellularea californica*)
California live oak (*Quercus agrifolia*)
Camphor tree (*Cinnamomum camphora*)
Canary Island pine (*Pinus canariensis*)
Canoe birch (*Betula papyrifera*)
Carmine crab apple (*Malus atrosanguinea*)
Carolina poplar (*Populus canadensis* 'Eugenei')
Carolina hemlock (*Tsuga caroliniana*)
Cedar of Lebanon (*Cedrus libani*)
Chinese chestnut (*Castanea mollissima*)
Chinese juniper (*Juniperus chinensis*)
Chinese paper birch (*Betula albo-sinensis*)
Cider gum (*Eucalyptus gunnii*)
Colorado spruce (*Picea pungens*)
Common alder (*Alnus incana*)
Cork oak (*Quercus suber*)
Cornelian cherry (*Cornus mas*)

Deodar cedar (*Cedrus deodara*)
Downy hawthorn (*Crataegus mollis*)

Eastern redbud (*Cercis canadensis*)
Eastern red cedar (*Juniperus virginiana*)
Eastern white pine (*Pinus strobus*)
English hawthorn (*Crataegus oxyacantha*)
English oak (*Quercus robur*)
English yew (*Taxus baccata*)
European ash (*Fraxinus excelsior*)
European beech (*Fagus sylvatica*)
European white birch (*Betula verrucosa* [*pendula*])

False cypress (*Chamaecyparis pisifera*)
Fern pine (*Podocarpus gracilior*)
Flowering ash (*Fraxinus ornus*)
French pussy willow (*Salix caprea*)
Fringe tree (*Chionanthus virginica*)
Full-moon maple (*Acer japonicum*)

Giant arborvitae (*Thuja plicata*)
Glossy hawthorn (*Crataegus nitida*)
Goldenchain tree (*Laburnum watereri*)
Goldenrain tree (*Koelreuteria paniculata*)
Gray birch (*Betula populifolia*)
Green ash (*Fraxinus pennsylvanica lanceolata*)
Green wattle (*Acacia decurrens*)

In winter, trees have their own beauty, too; they are handsome
silhouettes and frame the house.
(Molly Adams)

Trees by Common Names (*Continued*)

Hackberry (*Celtis occidentalis*)
Hankow willow (*Salix matsudana*)
Hinoki cypress (*Chamaecyparis obtusa*)
Holly oak (*Quercus ilex*)
Honey-locust (*Gleditsia triacanthos*)

Italian stone pine (*Pinus pinea*)

Jack pine (*Pinus banksiana*)
Japanese black pine (*Pinus thunbergii*)
Japanese dogwood (*Cornus kousa*)
Japanese flowering cherry (*Prunus serrulata*)
Japanese flowering crab apple (*Malus floribunda*)
Japanese hemlock (*Tsuga diversifolia*)
Japanese maple (*Acer palmatum*)
Japanese pagoda tree (*Sophora japonica*)
Japanese red pine (*Pinus densiflora*)
Japanese white pine (*Pinus parviflora*)
Japanese yew (*Taxus cuspidata*)
Judas tree (*Cercis siliquastrum*)

Kangaroo thorn (*Acacia armata*)
Kobus magnolia (*Magnolia kobus*)
Korean fir (*Abies koreana*)

Lacebark pine (*Pinus bungeana*)
Large Chinese hawthorn (*Crataegus pinnatifida major*)
Laurel oak (*Quercus laurifolia*)
Lavalle hawthorn (*Crataegus lavallei*)
Little-leaf linden (*Tilia cordata*)
Loquat (*Eriobotrya japonica*)

Maidenhair tree (*Gingko biloba*)
Mountain ash (*Sorbus aucuparia*)

Norway maple (*Acer platanoides*)
Norway spruce (*Picea abies*)

Ohio buckeye (*Aesculus glabra*)
Orchid tree (*Bauhinia blakeana*)

Pacific dogwood (*Cornus nuttallii*)
Pecan (*Carya illinoinensis*)
Persimmon (*Diospyros virginiana*)
Pignut (*Carya glabra*)
Pin oak (*Quercus palustris*)
Plane tree (*Plantanus acerifolia*)
Plume albizzia (*Albizzia distachya*)
Ponderosa pine (*Pinus ponderosa*)

Red cedar juniper (*Juniperus virginiana*)
Red fir (*Abies magnifica*)
Red gum (*Eucalyptus camaldulensis*)
Red horse chestnut (*Aesculus carnea*)
Red maple (*Acer rubrum*)
Red oak (*Quercus rubra*)
Rocky Mountain juniper (*Juniperus scopulorum*)
Russian olive (*Elaeagnus angustifolia*)

Sargent crab apple (*Malus sargentii*)
Saucer magnolia (*Magnolia soulangeana*)
Scarlet oak (*Quercus coccinea*)
Scotch pine (*Pinus sylvestris*)
Shagbark hickory (*Carya ovata*)
Siberian crab apple (*Malus baccata*)
Silk tree (*Albizzia julibrissin*)
Silver dollar gum (*Eucalyptus polyanthemos*)
Silver linden (*Tilia tomentosa*)
Single seed hawthorn (*Crataegus monogyna*)
Sitka spruce (*Picea sitchensis*)
Smoke tree (*Cotinus americanus*)
Southern magnolia (*Magnolia grandiflora*)
Star magnolia (*Magnolia stellata*)
Sugar maple (*Acer saccharum*)
Sugar pine (*Pinus lambertiana*)
Sweet gum (*Liquidambar styraciflua*)
Swiss mountain pine (*Pinus mugo*)
Sydney golden wattle (*Acacia longifolia floribunda*)

Tatarian dogwood (*Cornus alba*)
Tree of heaven (*Ailanthus altissima*)
Trident maple (*Acer buergerianum*)
Tulip tree (*Liriodendron tulipifera*)

Veitch fir (*Abies veitchii*)
Vine maple (*Acer circinatum*)

Washington hawthorn (*Crataegus phaeonopyrum*)
Water locust (*Gleditsia aquatica*)
Weeping acacia (*Acacia pendula*)
Weeping willow (*Salix babylonica*)
Western catalpa (*Catalpa speciosa*)
Western hemlock (*Tsuga heterophylla*)
White fir (*Abies concolor*)
White oak (*Quercus alba*)
White poplar (*Populus alba*)
White spruce (*Picea glauca*)
White willow (*Salix alba*)

Yew pine (*Podocarpus macrophylla*)
Yulan magnolia (*Magnolia denudata*)

CHAPTER 12

Shrubs

Shrubs are the backbone of a lovely garden; the deciduous ones give real splashes of color in their season, and the evergreens are for year-round beauty. And there are shrubs for all different situations. The trick is to select the ones that will grow in the soil you have and to give them a good start. Then they do not need too much attention; they grow almost free of care. Shrubs must also be selected for their character and form—spreading, round-top, low, high —and for their leaf texture.

The evergreen shrubs are the most popular where weather permits growing them; in cold climates, of course, the deciduous types are popular. The evergreens are invaluable for entrance plantings and for the front of the house or as background plants in the garden.

The main consideration with shrubs is their size; when you buy a young one—and this is the best purchase—it is difficult to imagine it at maturity. Yet you must have some idea of the full size to place it effectively in the landscape. Shrubs need room to grow, and remember that they will eventually if not immediately fill empty spaces.

HOW TO BUY SHRUBS

Shrubs are sold in containers, balled and burlapped, or bare root. The deciduous varieties that lose their leaves in winter are offered at their dormant season and are planted in early spring. At nurseries you will find them bare root. Later they are put in containers for late season sale; they are usually more expensive then.

Broadleaf and narrow-leaved evergreens are sold in containers or balled and burlapped, because they are never without foliage. Be sure to inspect the root ball; if it is very dried out, do not buy the shrub. Once roots dry out, evergreens are difficult to get growing.

If you cannot plant the shrubs immediately, keep the roots moist. Put bare-root plants in a tub of water, keep balled-and-burlapped ones sprayed with water until you can get them into the ground.

HOW TO PLANT SHRUBS

Holes for shrubs must be large and deep because the roots should be spread out when you put the plants in the ground. Break up the soil in the bottom of the hole and add some topsoil. Do not bury too much of the trunk of the plant below the ground; this is a common mistake in shrub planting. Set the bushes so that the soil level is almost the same as it was at the nursery.

Placing shrubs can create a problem for the anxious gardener who wants immediate green accents. It takes willpower to set a 2-foot shrub in a space of 12 feet, but many times that is necessary. Eventually the shrub will fill the void, but in the meantime, the garden has a spotty look.

Generally, it is not necessary to prune shrubs at planting time. Some people do trim bare-root ones; they claim that trimming makes them grow more vigorously. I have never noticed any difference in the rate of growth between an unpruned and a pruned shrub.

USING SHRUBS FOR HEDGES

Hedges used effectively are a beautiful part of a landscape design. They can be tall or low, evergreen or

Box hedge and globe shrubs
define an entryway.
(Molly Adams)

A giant rhododendron is the
feature of this charming
garden area.
(Molly Adams)

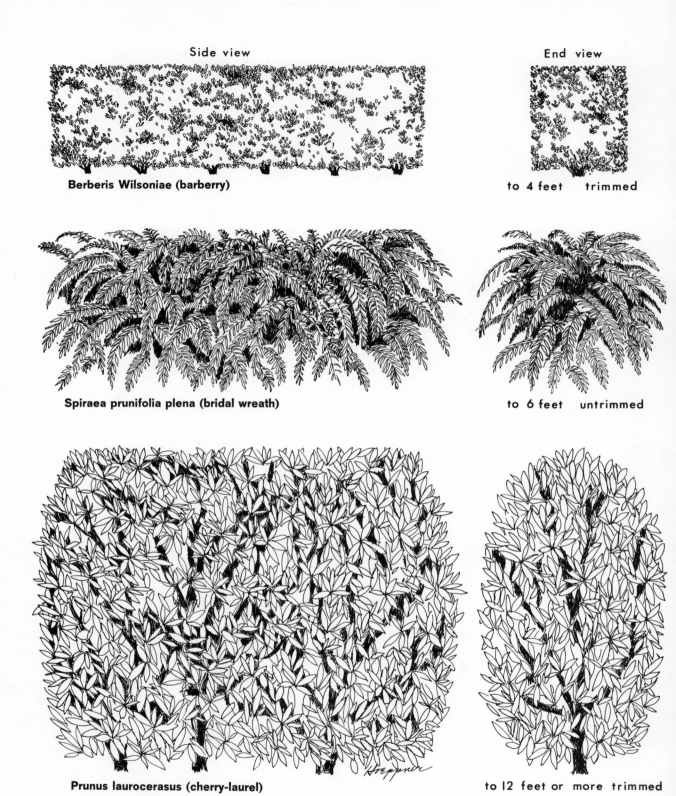

Side view   End view

Berberis Wilsoniae (barberry)   to 4 feet   trimmed

Spiraea prunifolia plena (bridal wreath)   to 6 feet   untrimmed

Prunus laurocerasus (cherry-laurel)   to 12 feet or more trimmed

HEDGES

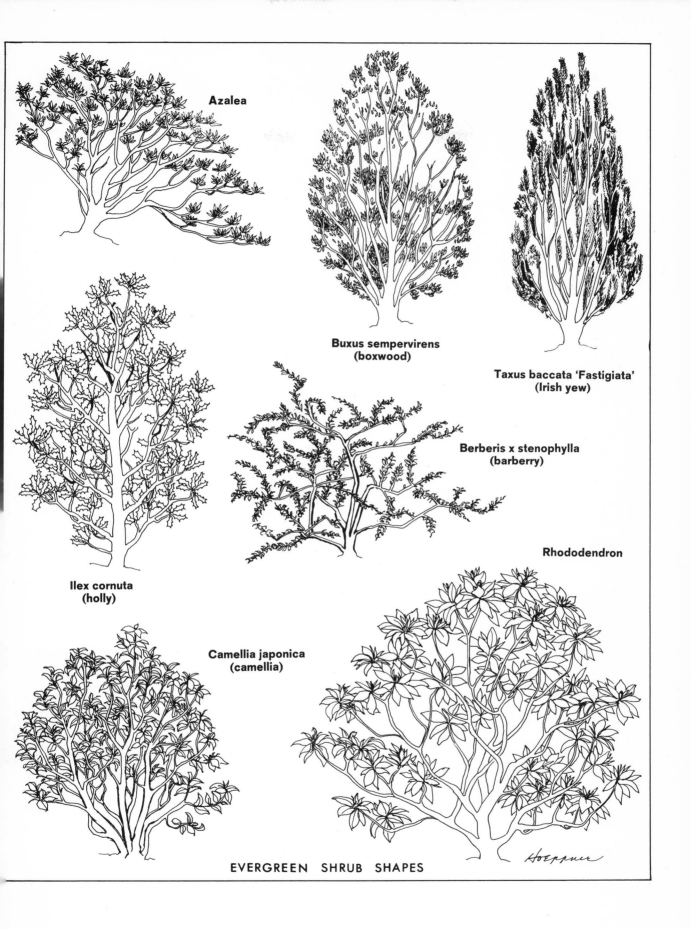

Azalea

Buxus sempervirens
(boxwood)

Taxus baccata 'Fastigiata'
(Irish yew)

Berberis x stenophylla
(barberry)

Rhododendron

Ilex cornuta
(holly)

Camellia japonica
(camellia)

EVERGREEN SHRUB SHAPES

deciduous, prostrate or rigid, clipped or left natural. They can also be used effectively for tall screenings. Some shrubs take to trimming better than others; many simply do not respond to trimming and appear shaggy. The best shrub is one of the desired height, width, and appearance that will need little pruning. Some shrubs are more suitable for hedges than others. They are naturally compact and easily pruned into desired shapes; most are inexpensive. In California, ligustrum is widely used as a hedge.

Since an attractive hedge depends upon good proportion, put it in place with care. Do not merely set plants at appointed places and expect an attractive hedge. Stretch a string along the place to be planted and mark a line on the ground. Make the first hole at the end of a furrow and decide how far apart the plants will be. Generally, privet is set 12 inches apart, barberry 12 to 16 inches, and large deciduous and evergreen shrubs about 24 to 36 inches apart; but this depends on individual size.

Evergreen hedges are usually planted in fall or spring; deciduous ones in spring.

Trim hedges wider at the base than at the top to provide for sufficient light for bottom branches. The pyramidal shape is most popular, although other shapes are frequently seen. Evergreens such as yew and arborvitae are sheared either before growth starts in spring or in very early summer, or when the new growth has had a chance to harden.

Do not fertilize hedges unless you are prepared to trim them more frequently than normal trimming.

LISTS OF SHRUBS

Table 9 gives a general list of shrubs; by no means is it meant to be a complete list. Other species and varieties will be found in garden catalogs, or your local nurseryman can help you with selections.

NOTE: To avoid confusion and constant reference to zone maps, plants in Table 9 have been listed with their minimum nighttime growing temperatures so that you can tell at a glance whether a plant will grow in your area. These are only general guides because plant hardiness depends on many different factors. (See Chapter 5.) When in doubt, check with your local nurseryman, who is well acquainted with the plant material and weather in his specific area. (For shrubs for city conditions see Chapter 20.)

Table 9. General List of Shrubs

Botanical and Common Name	SE† D E	Approx. Height in Ft.	Average Temp.	Remarks
Abelia grandiflora (glossy abelia)	SE	5	—10 to — 5F	Free flowering
Abeliophyllum distichum (Korean white forsythia)	D	3–4	—10 to — 5F	Prune after bloom
Amelanchier canadensis (shadblow service berry)	D	30	—20 to —10F	Slow grower
Amelanchier grandiflora	D	25	—20 to —10F	Large flowers
Andromeda polifolia (bog rosemary)	E	1–2	—50 to —35F	Likes moist locations
Arbutus unedo (strawberry tree)	E	10–20	10 to 20F	Does not like alkaline soil
Arctostaphylos uva-ursi (bearberry)	E	GC	—50 to —35F	Grows in any soil
Arctostaphylos manzanita	E	6–20	5 to 10F	Branching habit
Aucuba japonica (aucuba)	E	15	5 to 10F	Good for shady places
Berberis koreana (Korean barberry)	D/E	2–10	—10 to — 5F	Good outstanding colors; red berries
Berberis thunbergii (Japanese barberry) Berberis*	D/E	7	—10 to 5F	Grows in any soil
Buddleia alternifolia (fountain buddleia)	D	12	—10 to — 5F	Graceful; branching
Buddleia davidii (butterfly bush)	D/SE	15	—10 to — 5F	Many varieties
Buxus microphylla japonica (Japanese boxwood)	E	4	—10 to — 5F	Low and compact
Buxus microphylla koreana (Korean boxwood)	E	6–10	—20 to —10F	Hardiest; foliage turns brown in winter

* See also section "Additional Comments on Shrubs."
† SE = semievergreen; D = deciduous; E = evergreen.

Table 9 (Continued)

Botanical and Common Name	SE† D E	Approx. Height in Ft.	Average Temp.	Remarks
Buxus sempervirens (common boxwood)	E	20	—10 to — 5F	Many varieties
Callistemon citrinus (bottlebrush)	E	25	20 to 30F	Lovely flowers
Calluna vulgaris (heather)	E	15	—20 to —10F	Bright color and foliage
Camellia*				
Carissa grandiflora (Natal plum)	E	15	20 to 30F	Spiny, branching one
Carpenteria californica (California mock orange)	E	8	5 to 20F	Showy shrub
Ceanothus americanus (New Jersey tea)	E	3	—20 to —10F	For poor soil
Ceanothus ovatus	E	3	—20 to —10F	Upright grower
Ceanothus thyrsiflorus (blue blossom)	E	30	—20 to —10F	Grows in sandy soil
Chaenomeles speciosa (flowering quince)	D	6	—20 to —10F	Lovely flowers
Chaenomeles*				
Clethra alnifolia (summer sweet)	D	9	—35 to —20F	Fragrant summer bloom
Cornus alba 'Sibirica' (Siberian dogwood)	D	10	—50 to —35F	Spectacular autumn color
Cornus mas (cornelian cherry)	D	To 18	—20 to — 5F	Early blooming
Cotoneaster*				
Daphne odora (fragrant daphne)	D/E	4–6	5 to 10F	Fragrant
Deutzia*				
Elaeagnus angustifolia (Russian olive)	D	20	—50 to —35F	Fragrant flowers
Elaeagnus multiflorus (cherry elaeagnus)	D/E	9	—20 to —10F	Bright-red fruit
Elaeagnus pungens (silverberry)	D/E	12	5 to 10F	Vigorous grower
Enkianthus campanulatus (redvein enkianthus)	D	30	—20 to —10F	Red autumn color
Enkianthus perulatus	D	6	—10 to — 5F	Red autumn color
Erica canaliculata (heather)	E	6	20 to 30F	Pink, purple flower
Eugenia uniflora (Surinam cherry)	E	10–15	20 to 30F	White, fragrant flowers
Euonymus alata (winged euonymus)	D	9	—35 to —20F	Sturdy; easily grown
Euonymus japonica (evergreen euonymus)	E	15	10 to 20F	Splendid foliage
Euonymus latifolius	D	20	—10 to — 5F	Vigorous grower
Euonymus sanguineus	D	20	—10 to — 5F	Best deciduous one
Euonymus*				
Fatsia japonica (Japanese aralia)	E	15	5 to 10F	Handsome foliage
Forsythia intermedia (border forsythia)	D	2–9	—20 to — 5F	Deep-yellow flowers
Forsythia ovata (early forsythia)	D	8	—20 to —10F	Earliest to bloom and hardiest
Forsythia*				
Fothergilla major (large fothergilla)	D	9	—10 to — 5F	Good flowers and autumn color
Fuchsia magellanica (Magellan fuchsia)	D	3	—10 to 5F	Floriferous

* See also section "Additional Comments on Shrubs."
† SE = semievergreen; D = deciduous; E = evergreen.

Table 9 (Continued)

Botanical and Common Name	SE† D E	Approx. Height in Ft.	Average Temp.	Remarks
Gardenia jasminoides (Cape jasmine)	E	4–6	10 to 30F	Fragrant
Gaultheria shallon (salal)	E	5	—10 to — 5F	Sun or shade
Gaultheria veitchiana (veitch wintergreen)	E	3	5 to 10F	White or pink, bell-shaped flowers
Hamamelis mollis (Chinese witch hazel)	D	30	—10 to — 5F	Very fragrant flowers
Hamamelis vernalis (spring witch hazel)	D	10	—10 to — 5F	Early spring blooms
Hibiscus rosa-sinensis (Chinese hibiscus)	E	30	20 to 30F	Stellar flower
Hibiscus syriacus (shrub althaea)	D	15	—10 to — 5F	Many varieties
Hydrangea arborescens 'Grandiflora' (hills-of-snow)	D	3	—20 to —10F	Easy culture
Hypericum densiflorum	D/SE	6	—10 to — 5F	Fine-texture foliage
Hypericum prolificum	D/SE	3	—20 to —10F	Very shrubby
Ilex cornuta (Chinese holly)	E	9	5 to 10F	Bright berries; lustrous foliage
Ilex crenata (Japanese holly) Ilex*	E	20	— 5 to 5F	Another good holly
Jasminum grandiflorum (Spanish jasmine)	SE/D	10–15	20 to 30F	Blooms all summer
Jasminum nudiflorum (winter jasmine)	D	15	—10 to — 5F	Viny shrub; not fragrant
Jasminum officinale (common white jasmine)	SE/D	30	5 to 10F	Tall-growing
Juniperus chinensis 'Pfitzeriana' (Pfitzer juniper)	E	10	—20 to —10F	Popular juniper
Juniperus communis (common juniper)	E	30	—50 to —35F	Many varieties
Kalmia angustifolia (sheep laurel)	E	3	—50 to —35F	Needs acid soil
Kalmia latifolia (mountain laurel)	E	30	—20 to —10F	Amenable grower
Kerria japonica	D	4–6	—20 to —10F	Bright-yellow flowers
Kolkwitzia amabilis (beauty bush)	D	10	—20 to —10F	Has many uses
Lagerstroemia indica (crape myrtle)	D	20	5 to 10F	Popular summer bloom
Laurus nobilis (sweet bay)	E	30	— 5 to 5F	Tough plant
Leptospermum scoparium	E	6–20	20 to 30F	Ground cover and shrubs
Ligustrum amurense (Amur privet) Ligustrum*	D/E	6–30	—35 to —20F	Small spikes of white flowers
Lonicera fragrantissima (winter honeysuckle)	D/E	3–15	—10 to — 5F	Early fragrant flowers
Lonicera maackii (Amur honeysuckle)	D	15	—50 to —35F	Holds leaves late into fall
Lonicera tatarica (Tatarian honeysuckle) Lonicera* Magnolia*	D	10	—35 to —20F	Small pink flowers in late spring

* See also section "Additional Comments on Shrubs."
† SE = semievergreen; D = deciduous; E = evergreen.

Table 9 (Continued)

Botanical and Common Name	SE† D E	Approx. Height in Ft.	Average Temp.	Remarks
Mahonia aquifolium (Oregon grape)	SE/E	3–5	—10 to — 5F	Handsome foliage
Mahonia repens (creeping mahonia)	SE/E	1	—10 to — 5F	Small; good ground cover
Nandina domestica (heavenly bamboo)	SE/E	8	5 to 10F	Red berries in winter
Nerium oleander (oleander)	E	15	5 to 20F	Popular flowering shrub
Osmanthus heterophyllus (holly osmanthus)	E	18	— 5 to 5F	Sun or shade
*Philadelphus**				
Photinia serrulata (Chinese photinia)	E	36	5 to 10F	Bright-red berries
Pieris floribunda (mountain andromeda)	E	5	—20 to —10F	Does well in dry soil
Pieris japonica (Japanese andromeda)	E	9	—10 to — 5F	Splendid color
*Pinus**				
Pittosporum tobira (Japanese pittosporum)	E	10	10 to 20F	Fragrant, white flowers
Poncirus trifoliata (hardy orange)	D	30	— 5 to 5F	Dense growth; attractive foliage
Potentilla fruticosa (cinquefoil)	D	2–5	—50 to —35F	Many varieties
Pyracantha coccinea (scarlet firethorn)	E	8–10	— 5 to 5F	Many varieties; valued for bright berries
Raphiolepis umbellata (yeddo hawthorn)	E	6	5 to 10F	Sun or partial shade
*Rhododendron**				
Ribes sanguineum (flowering currant)	D	4–12	—10 to — 5F	Deep-red flowers; March to June
*Rosa**				
Salix caprea (French pussy willow)	D	25	—20 to —10F	Vigorous grower
Salix repens (creeping willow)	D	3	—20 to —10F	Good low willow for poor soil
Sarcococca ruscifolia	E	6	5 to 10F	Takes shade
Skimmia japonica (Japanese skimmia)	E	4	5 to 10F	For shade
Spiraea arguta	D	6	—20 to —10F	Free flowering
Spiraea prunifolia (bridal wreath spiraea)	D	9	—20 to —10F	Turns orange in fall
Spiraea thunbergii (thunberg spiraea)	D	5	—20 to —10F	Arching branches
Spiraea veitchii	D	12	—10 to — 5F	Good background; graceful one
*Spiraea**				
Syringa henryi 'Lutece'	D	10	—50 to —35F	Early June bloom
Syringa villosa (late lilac)	D	9	—50 to —35F	Dense, upright habit
Syringa vulgaris (common lilac)	D	20	—35 to —20F	Many varieties
*Syringa**				
Tamarix aphylla (Athel tree)	E	30–50	5 to 10F	Good wide-spread tree
Tamarix parviflora 'Pink Cascade' 'Summer Glow'	D	15	—20 to —10F	Prune immediately after bloom
Taxus canadensis (Canada yew)	E	3–6	—50 to —35F	Will tolerate shade

* See also section ''Additional Comments on Shrubs.''
† SE = semievergreen; D = deciduous; E = evergreen.

Table 9 (Continued)

Botanical and Common Name	SE† D E	Approx. Height in Ft.	Average Temp.	Remarks
Viburnum davidii	E	3	5 to 10F	Handsome leaves
Viburnum dentatum (arrowwood)	D	15	—50 to —35F	Red fall color
Viburnum dilatatum (linden viburnum)	D	9	—10 to — 5F	Colorful red fruit
Viburnum lantana (wayfaring tree)	D	15	—35 to —20F	Grows in dry soil
Viburnum lentago (nannyberry)	D	30	—50 to —35F	Good background or screen plant
Viburnum opulus (European cranberry bush)	D	12	—35 to —20F	Good many varieties
Viburnum prunifolium (black haw)	D	15	—35 to —20F	Good specimen plant
Viburnum sieboldii	D	30	—20 to —10F	Stellar performer
Viburnum trilobum (cranberry bush) Viburnum*	D	12	—50 to —35F	Effective in winter
Vitex agnus-castus (chaste tree)	D	9	— 5 to 10F	Lilac flowers
Weigela 'Bristol Ruby'	D	7	—10 to — 5F	Complex hybrid
Weigela 'Bristol Snowflake'	D	7	—10 to — 5F	Complex hybrid
Weigela florida	D	9	—10 to — 5F	Many available
Weigela middendorffiana Weigela*	D	1	—20 to —10F	Dense, broad shrubs

* See also section "Additional Comments on Shrubs."
† SE = semievergreen; D = deciduous; E = evergreen.

Kinds of Shrubs and Trees for Hedges

Shrubs (deciduous) to 5 feet

Berberis koreana (Korean barberry)
Berberis mentorensis (mentor barberry)
Berberis thunbergii 'Erecta' (Japanese barberry)
Cotoneaster lucida (hedge cotoneaster)
Euonymus alata 'Compacta' (winged euonymus)
Ligustrum vulgare 'Lodense' (privet)
Rosa species (rose)
Salix purpurea Gracilis (dwarf purple osier)

Shrubs (evergreen) to 5 feet

Berberis juliane (wintergreen barberry)
Berberis sempervirens suffruticosa (dwarf box)
Berberis verruculosa (warty barberry)
Euonymus kiautschovica
Euonymus fortunei
Ilex crenata (Japanese holly)
Ilex crenata 'Microphylla'
Picea glauca 'Conica' (white spruce) *
Pinus mugo (Swiss mugo pine) *
Taxus canadensis (Canada yew) *
Taxus cuspidata (Japanese yew) *
Thuja occidentalis varieties (American arborvitae)

Shrubs (deciduous) to 30 feet

Acer ginnala (Amur maple)
Crataegus species (hawthorn)

* Tree

Hibiscus syriacus (shrub althea)
Lonicera maackii (Amur honeysuckle)
Lonicera tatarica (Tatarian honeysuckle)
Philadelphus coronarius (sweet mock orange)
Spiraea prunifolia (bridal wreath spirea)
Spiraea thunbergii
Syringa persica (Persian lilac)
Syringa vulgaris (common lilac)
Viburnum lantana (wayfaring tree)
Viburnum sieboldii (Siebold viburnum)

Shrubs (evergreen) to 30 feet

Abelia grandiflora (glossy abelia)
Buxus sempervirens (common box)
Photinia serrulata (Chinese photinia)
Pittosporum tobira (Japanese pittosporum)
Podocarpus macrophyllus
Pyracantha coccinea (firethorn)
Tsuga canadensis (Canada hemlock) *
Tsuga caroliniana (Carolina hemlock) *

Shrubs with Fragrant Flowers

Abelia grandiflora (glossy abelia)
Ceanothus americanus (New Jersey tea)
Clethra alnifolia (summer sweet)
Daphne odora (winter daphne)
Deutzia gracilis (slender deutzia)
Fothergilla, several (fothergilla)

* Tree

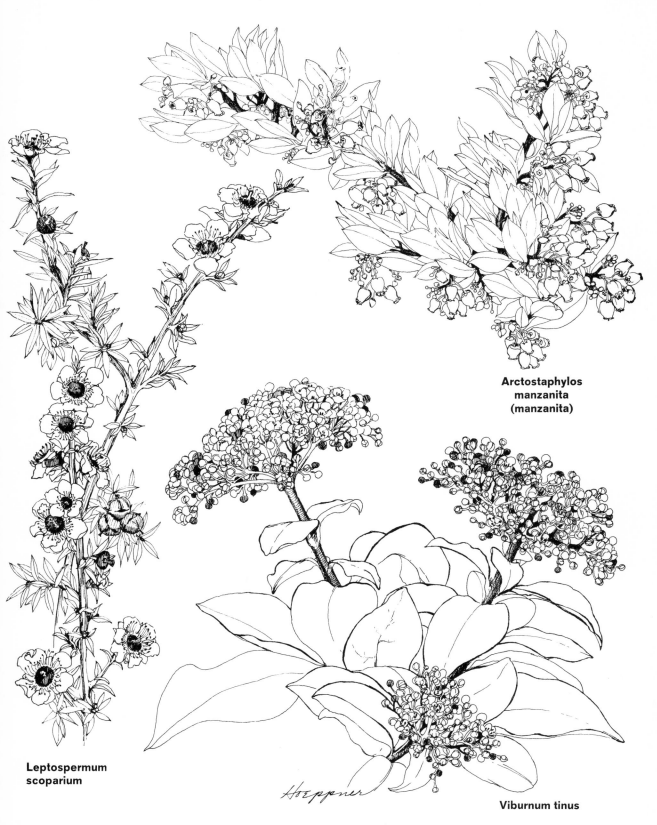

**Arctostaphylos
manzanita
(manzanita)**

**Leptospermum
scoparium**

Hoeppner

Viburnum tinus

FLOWERING SHRUBS

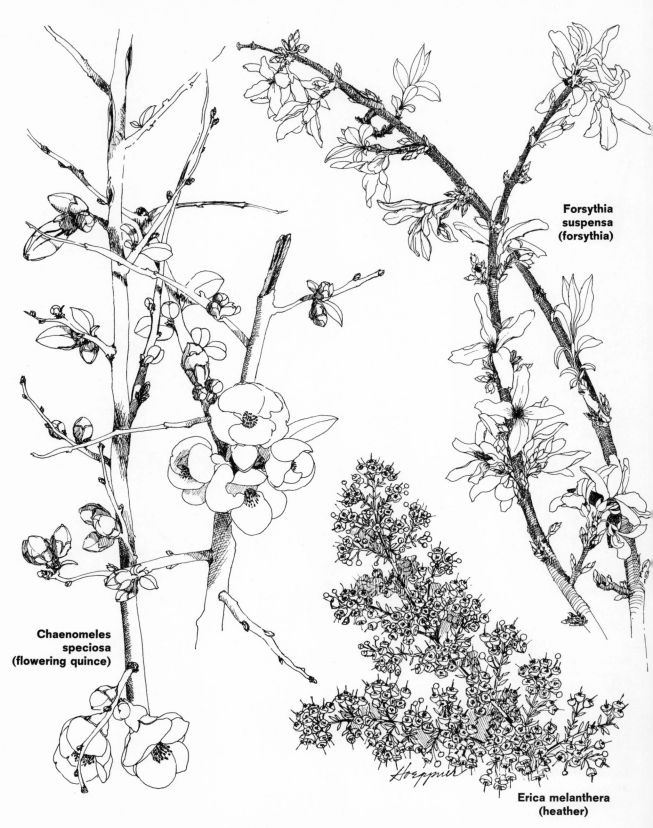

**Forsythia
suspensa
(forsythia)**

**Chaenomeles
speciosa
(flowering quince)**

**Erica melanthera
(heather)**

FLOWERING SHRUBS

Shrubs with Fragrant Flowers (*Continued*)

Gardenia jasminoides (gardenia)
Jasminum officinale (common white jasmine)
Lonicera, several (honeysuckle)
Osmanthus heterophyllus (holly olive)
Philadelphus coronarius (sweet mock orange)
Raphiolepis umbellata (yeddo hawthorn)
Rosa (rose)
Skimmia japonica

Shrubs for Screens and Windbreaks

Elaeagnus angustifolia (Russian olive)
Hamamelis vernalis (vernal witch hazel)
Lagerstroemia indica (crape myrtle)
Laurus nobilis (sweet bay)
Lonicera tatarica (Tatarian honeysuckle)
Philadelphus coronarius (mock orange)
Spiraea veitchii (Veitch spiraea)
Syringa henryi 'Lutece' (lilac)
Syringa villosa (late lilac)
Syringa vulgaris (common lilac)
Viburnum arboreum
Viburnum dentatum (arrowwood)
Viburnum opulus (European cranberry bush)
Viburnum prunifolium (black haw)

Shrubs for Wet Soil

Andromeda species (andromeda)
Calluna vulgaris (common heather)
Clethra alnifolia (summer sweet)
Cornus alba (dogwood)
Cornus sanguinea (bloodtwig dogwood)
Ilex glabra (inkberry)
Ilex verticillata (winterberry)
Kalmia angustifolia (sheep laurel)
Rhododendron (rhododendron)
Sabal minor (dwarf palmetto)
Salix caprea (goat willow)
Salix repens (creeping willow)
Spiraea menziesii (spiraea)
Spiraea tomentosa (hardhack)
Viburnum alnifolium (hobblebush)

Shrubs for Dry Soil

Arctostaphylos uva-ursi (bearberry)
Berberis, several (barberry)
Buddleia alternifolia (fountain buddleia)
Callistemon citrinus (lemon bottlebrush)
Ceanothus americanus (New Jersey tea)
Chaenomeles speciosa (flowering quince)
Cotoneaster (cotoneaster)
Cytisus (broom)
Elaeagnus angustifolia (Russian olive)
Euonymus japonica (evergreen euonymus)
Hamamelis virginiana (common witch hazel)
Juniperus communis (juniper)
Kolkwitzia amabilis (beauty bush)

Nerium oleander (oleander)
Pittosporum tobira (Japanese pittosporum)
Pyracantha coccinea (scarlet firethorn)
Raphiolepis umbellata (yeddo hawthorn)
Rosa rugosa (rose)
Tamarix species (tamarix)
Viburnum lentago (nannyberry)

Shrubs with Colorful Fruit

Arctostaphylos uva-ursi (bearberry)
Ardisia crenata (ardisia)
Berberis koreana (Korean barberry)
Berberis thunbergii (Japanese barberry)
Ceanothus ovatus (ceanothus)
Cornus mas (cornelian cherry)
Cotoneaster divaricata
Cotoneaster horizontalis (rock-spray cotoneaster)
Cotoneaster microphylla (small-leaved cotoneaster)
Elaeagnus multiflorus (cherry elaeagnus)
Euonymus alata (winged euonymus)
Euonymus japonica (evergreen euonymus)
Euonymus latifolius (broadleaf euonymus)
Euonymus sanguineus
Ilex cornuta (Chinese holly)
Ilex verticillata (winterberry)
Lonicera fragrantissima (winter honeysuckle)
Lonicera maackii (Amur honeysuckle)
Lonicera tatarica (Tatarian honeysuckle)
Magnolia stellata (star magnolia)
Malus sargentii (Sargent crab apple)
Photinia serrulata (Chinese photinia)
Pyracantha coccinea (scarlet firethorn)
Rosa, many (rose)
Sarcococca ruscifolia (fragrant sarcococca)
Skimmia japonica (Japanese skimmia)
Viburnum dilatatum (linden viburnum)
Viburnum japonicum (Japanese viburnum)
Viburnum trilobum (cranberry bush)

Blue Fruit

Fatsia japonica
Gaultheria veitchiana (Veitch wintergreen)
Ligustrum obtusifolium (border privet)
Mahonia aquifolium (holly grape)
Viburnum davidii
Viburnum dentatum (arrowwood)

Black Fruit

Mahonia repens (creeping mahonia)
Viburnum lantana (wayfaring tree)
Viburnum prunifolium (black haw)
Viburnum sieboldii

Flowering Calendar for Shrubs

Early Spring

Daphne odora (fragrant daphne)
Hamamelis mollis (Chinese witch hazel)
Hamamelis vernalis (vernal witch hazel)

Spring

Amelanchier canadensis (shadblow service berry)
Amelanchier grandiflora (apple service berry)
Andromeda polifolia (bog rosemary)
Chaenomeles japonica (Japanese quince)
Chaenomeles speciosa (flowering quince)
Cornus mas (cornelian cherry)
Cytisus decumbens
Enkianthus perulatus
Epigaea repens (trailing arbutus)
Forsythia intermedia, many (forsythia)
Forsythia ovata (early forsythia)
Jasminum nudiflorum (winter jasmine)
Lonicera fragrantissima (winter honeysuckle)
Mahonia species (holly grape)
Pieris floribunda (mountain andromeda)
Pieris japonica (Japanese andromeda)
Rhododendron (rhododendron)

Summer

Abelia grandiflora (glossy abelia)
Kalmia latifolia (mountain laurel)
Kolkwitzia amabilis (beauty bush)
Philadelphus, various (mock orange)
Potentilla fruticosa (bush cinquefoil)
Rosa (shrub type), (rose)
Spiraea, various (spiraea)

Fall

Clethra alnifolia (summer sweet)
Hamamelis virginiana (common witch hazel)
Hibiscus syriacus (althea, or hibiscus)
Hydrangea, various (hydrangea)
Prunus subhirtella
Spiraea billiardi (billiard spirea)
Tamarix, various (tamarix)

Shrubs for Background Planting

Arbutus unedo (strawberry tree)
Callistemon lanceolatus (bottlebrush)
Ceanothus thyrsiflorus (blue blossom)
Cornus mas (cornelian cherry)
Cornus officinalis
Cotoneaster frigida
Elaeagnus angustifolia (Russian olive)
Enkianthus campanulatus (bellflower)
Euonymus latifolius
Euonymus sanguinea
Euonymus yedoensis
Hamamelis mollis (Chinese witch hazel)
Hamamelis virginiana (common witch hazel)
Ilex cornuta (Chinese holly)
Ilex crenata
Ilex glabra (inkberry)
Jasminum officinale (common white jasmine)
Kalmia latifolia (mountain laurel)
Lagerstroemia indica (crape myrtle)

Ligustrum lucidum (privet)
Nerium oleander (oleander)
Osmanthus heterophyllus (holly osmanthus)
Photinia serrulata (Chinese photinia)
Poncirus trifoliata (hardy orange)
Pyracantha atlantioides
Rosa odorata
Syringa chinensis (Chinese lilac)
Syringa vulgaris (common lilac)

Additional Comments on Shrubs

Here are some additional comments on shrubs to supplement previous lists. General culture and descriptions are given to help you better select plants for your individual areas. If your favorite shrub has been omitted, it was a matter of space rather than choice.

Botanical and common names are given. Species are in italics and varieties in single quotes under species name. For example:

Deutzia scabra (species)
'Candidissima' (variety)

Nurserymen in your area may have other varieties to suggest, for new ones are introduced from time to time.

BERBERIS (barberry). A group of dense, thorny shrubs, deciduous and evergreen, with small, bright flowers. Plants are effective as barriers, and can also be used as landscape specimens, for many species have a lovely branching habit. Small bright red or purple-black berries appear in autumn; while most barberries lose their fruit quickly after it ripens, the Japanese barberry holds its color through winter. These shrubs grow in almost any kind of soil, in sun or in light shade. A very useful group of plants.

B. buxifolia (Magellan barberry). Hardy to −10F; upright growth to 6 feet, with small leathery leaves. Orange-yellow flowers and dark-purple berries. Evergreen.

B. gagnepainii (black barberry). Hardy to −10F; thorny twigs and rangy growth. Narrow leaves; blue-black berries. Evergreen.

B. koreana (Korean barberry). Hardy to −10F; grow to 6 feet. Deep-red autumn color in fall and winter, and yellow flowers in May.

B. mentorensis (mentor barberry). Hybrid; hardy to −10F; evergreen in some regions, deciduous in others. Dark-red berries and yellow flowers.

B. thunbergii (Japanese barberry). Hardy to −5F; graceful in growth, with arching stems. Deep-green foliage and fiery-red berries in fall. Deciduous. Many varieties.

B. verruculosa (warty barberry). Hardy to −10F;

Philadelphus
(mock orange)

Spiraea

Rose

Hydrangea
(hydrangea)

Hypericum
(Saint-John's-wort)

TEXTURES OF SHRUBS

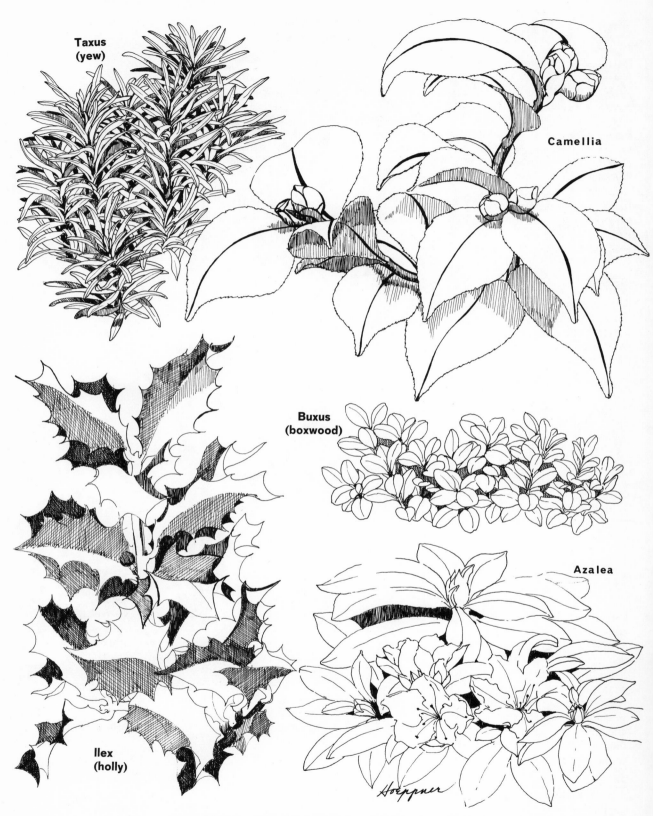

Taxus
(yew)

Camellia

Buxus
(boxwood)

Azalea

Ilex
(holly)

Hoeppner

TEXTURES OF EVERGREEN SHRUBS

neat habit, and grows to about 4 feet. Glossy, dark-green leaves and golden-yellow flowers.

CAMELLIA. Evergreen shrubs that bear handsome flowers from January to May with over 3,000 named kinds that vary in color, size, and form. The japonica hybrids are perhaps the most popular, with flowers from pure white to dark red with many shades in between. Sasanqua hybrids are desirable too; these bear smaller, generally single, flowers that bloom before the japonicas.

Both kinds of camellias need a well-drained, rich soil, and like to be cool at the roots. Never plant them with the trunk base beneath the soil line. Keep camellias moist, but never overly wet; fertilize them with a commercial acid plant food. Prune immediately after blooming or in fall. Watch for aphids, scale, and mites on plants and apply appropriate remedies if needed. (See Chapter 28.) Scorched or yellowed areas on the leaves are due to sun-scald; yellow leaves with green veins indicate the soil needs more iron. (Iron chelate is available at nurseries.) If flower buds drop, don't panic; it is probably from overwatering, or many times it is a natural tendency of the plants.

C. japonica (common camellia). Hardy to 5F; large shrub variable in growth habit and flower color.

'Adolph Audusson'	'Prince Eugene Napoleon'
'Aunt Jetty'	'Purity'
'C. M. Hovey'	'Reg Ragland'
'Finlandia'	'Tiffany'
'Herme'	'White Nun'
'Lady Clare'	

C. sasanqua (sasanqua camellia). Hardy to 5F; vary in habit from upright and dense to vinelike and spreading. Dark-green, shiny leaves; flowers produced in early autumn; very floriferous.

'Blanchette'	'Sparkling Burgundy'
'Briar Rose'	'Tanya'
'Cleopatra'	'White Frills'
'Jean May'	

CHAENOMELES (flowering quince). With bright-colored flowers that appear before the leaves, the flowering quince furnishes brilliant color in the garden for early spring. The plants have been widely hybridized; there are many stunning varieties in a wide range of flower color—white, shades of pink, red, and orange. Some have single flowers, others semidouble or double blooms; the fruits are green and turn yellow at maturity. Several varieties are thorny. The majority of quinces grow to about 6 feet, so they are ideal for small gardens.

C. japonica (Japanese quince). Hardy to −20F; grows to 3 feet. Red flowers in early May. Deciduous.

'Alpina'—Seldom grows over 1 foot tall. Dense growth, with orange flowers.

C. speciosa (flowering quince). Hardy to −20F; grows to 6 feet. Dark-green, glossy leaves, and red, pink, or white flowers.

'Nivalis'—White.
'Cameo'—Pink.
'Crimson Beauty'—Red.

COTONEASTER (cotoneaster). These shrubs grow under untoward conditions (but do not tolerate full shade) and still produce good growth. The bright-red berries are handsome, and the white or pink flowers a charming asset to the garden. Many species have interesting growth habits, making them good landscape subjects. Some cotoneasters are deciduous; others, semideciduous; and still others, evergreen. Many are native to the cool regions of China. In dry, hot weather the plants are susceptible to red spider or lace bug attacks which must be kept under control or the shrubs may die.

C. apiculata (cranberry cotoneaster). Hardy to −20F; grows to 4 feet. Bright-green leaves, pink-white flowers, and red fruit. Deciduous.

C. conspicua (wintergreen cotoneaster). Hardy to −5F; arching branches; grows to 6 feet. Narrow, oval, dark-green leaves and white flowers. Bright-red fruit. Evergreen.

C. dammeri (bearberry cotoneaster). Hardy to −10F; prostrate trailing habit. Oval, bright-green leaves, white flowers, and red fruit. Beautiful cascading plant; evergreen.

C. divaricata (spreading cotoneaster). Hardy to −10F; stiff branches. Grows to 6 feet, with dark-green leaves, pink flowers followed by red fruit. Good hedge or screen. Deciduous.

C. horizontalis (rock-spray cotoneaster). Hardy to −10F; low-growing to 3 feet, but spreading, with stiff branches. Small, glossy, bright-green leaves, white flowers, and red fruit. Good bank cover or espalier subject. Deciduous.

C. microphylla (small-leaf cotoneaster). Hardy to −10F; somewhat of a trailer, to 3 feet tall. Small green leaves and white flowers followed by large red fruit. Good ground cover. Evergreen.

C. pannosa (silverleaf cotoneaster). Hardy to 5F; erect shrub to 10 feet. Oval gray-green leaves and white flowers; red fruit. Good screen plant. Evergreen; half-evergreen in coldest weather.

C. rotundifolia (redbox cotoneaster). Hardy to −5F; erect growth to 10 feet. Dark-green, glossy leaves, white flowers, and large red fruit. Another good screening plant. Evergreen or semideciduous.

DEUTZIA (deutzia). Most species are from parts of China. They are dense-growing shrubs, growing from 3 to 8 feet. It is their spring flowers that make them so desirable. Prune the plants annually in spring to keep them handsome. Select species for bloom time; some flower in May, others later. Deutzias grow in any soil; prefer full sun but will withstand light shade. Many kinds are very floriferous. Usually free from insects or disease problems.

D. gracilis (slender deutzia). Hardy to −20F; slender, graceful shrub, to 3 feet. Bright-green leaves, and snow-white flowers. Deciduous.

D. grandiflora (early deutzia). Hardy to −10F; grows to 6 feet, with white flowers. Early blooming. Deciduous.

D. lemoinei. Hybrid; hardy to −20F. Compact grower to about 7 feet. Toothed leaves and clusters of white flowers.

'Compacta'—Dwarf form.

D. scabra. Hardy to −10F; tall species to 10 feet. Dull-green leaves, with clusters of white flowers. Several varieties. Deciduous.

'Candidissima'—Double white flowers.

EUONYMUS (euonymus). While flowers of this group are small and insignificant, the autumn color is spectacular. Plants grow vigorously in any good garden soil, but they are susceptible to scale and must be sprayed regularly. Some in this group are vines, others shrubs. Most are excellent landscape subjects.

E. alata (winged euonymus). Hardy to −35F; horizontal and branching habit. Grows to 10 feet, with dark-green leaves that turn red in fall. Deciduous.

'Compacta'—Excellent dwarf plant, to 4 feet.

E. bungeanus semipersistens (midwinter euonymus). Hardy to −20F; vigorous, to 15 feet. Light-green leaves and yellow to whitish-pink flowers. Good hedge plant. Deciduous.

E. fortunei. Hardy to −10F; vine or shrub to 15 feet. Dark-green leaves. Good one. Evergreen.

'Berryhill'—Upright grower.

'Sarcoxie'—Upright, to 4 feet.

E. japonica (evergreen euonymus). Hardy to 10F; upright, to 10 feet. Lustrous green leaves; pinkish-orange fruit.

'Albo-Marginata'—Green leaves edged white.

'Grandifolia'—Large dark-green leaves.

E. latifolius (broadleaf euonymus). Hardy to −10F; leaves reddish underneath. Red to orange fruit. Deciduous. Grows to 20 feet.

FORSYTHIA (forsythia). These are popular in many regions because their bright flowers are harbingers of spring when all else is bleak. In the North, blooms appear on leafless stems in March or April, and then the plants are outstanding. While the flowers are their chief assets, many forsythias have a graceful habit of growth. Plants grow rapidly and need space;

intelligent pruning is necessary to keep them looking their best.

Forsythias bloom on previous years' wood, so they are pruned after they flower, *never before.* There are several types of forsythias—dwarf and compact, or upright and spreading. These shrubs survive almost any kind of soil, and are practically trouble free.

F. intermedia (border forsythia). Hardy to −10F; long, arching branches. Pale to deep-yellow flowers. Deciduous. Grows to 10 feet.

'Densiflora'—Upright growth; pale-yellow blooms.

'Nana'—Dwarf form.

'Spectabilis'—Large, bright-yellow flowers.

F. ovata (early forsythia). Hardy to −20F; early yellow flowers. Deciduous. Grows to 8 feet.

F. suspensa (weeping forsythia). Hardy to −10F; grows to 10 feet, with vinelike branches. Golden-yellow flowers. Deciduous.

'Fortunei'—More upright than above type.

ILEX (holly). The hollies are evergreen or deciduous and are very popular because they are amenable plants. European and American hollies have hundreds of varieties. The bright-red or black berries are highly desirable for landscape color. Hollies (with few exceptions) have separate sexes, so both must be present in the area to ensure the fertilization of flowers. (Chinese holly can produce fruit without the pollen of other hollies.) Most plants are easily grown in a good garden soil, but they do need good drainage; they are relatively free of pest and diseases.

I. aquifolium (English holly). Hardy to −5F; grows to 15 feet. Variable in leaf, shape, and color. Many varieties. Evergreen.

I. cornuta (Chinese holly). Hardy to 5F; dense or open growth to 10 feet. Glossy, leathery leaves; bright-red berries. Evergreen.

'Burfordii'—Spineless leaves.

'Dazzler'—Compact; many berries.

'Giant Beauty'—Upright and large.

'Jungle Gardens'—Yellow fruit.

I. crenata (Japanese holly). Hardy to −5F; dense and erect; sometimes to 20 feet. Finely toothed leaves and black berries. Evergreen.

'Compacta'—Densely branched.

'Green Island'—Low and spreading.

'Microphylla'—Tiny leaves.

I. glabra (inkberry). Hardy to −35F; grows to 9 feet. Black berries. Evergreen.

I. verticillata (winterberry). Hardy to −35F; grows to 10 feet. Bright-red berries. Deciduous.

LIGUSTRUM (privet). These are popular hedge plants. The leaves may be evergreen (in the South) or deciduous. Vigorous and fast-growing, with small white flowers followed by blue or black berries, they also make good specimen plants against a fence or a wall. Most of the privets are remarkably free of any problem, and they grow in almost any kind of soil under all kinds of conditions. There are many privets, one hardly distinguishable from the other until they are mature, so ask your nurseryman about them before making purchases.

L. amurense (Amur privet). Hardy to −35F; deciduous in the North, evergreen in South. Grow to 15 feet, with small spikes of white flowers. Small black berries. Similar to California privet, but hardier.

L. japonicum (Japanese privet). Hardy to 5F; dense grower to 12 feet. Clusters of small white flowers. Evergreen.

'Lusterleaf' (texanum)—Very large leaves.

L. lucidum (glossy privet). Hardy to 5F; round-headed shrub that can reach 30 feet. Small white flowers; black berries. Evergreen.

L. ovalifolium (California privet). Hardy to −10F; creamy-white flowers. Black berries, but not in the North. Semideciduous. Grows to 15 feet.

'Aureum' (golden privet)—Leaves with yellow edges.

L. vulgare (common privet). Hardy to −20F; grows to 15 feet. Clusters of white flowers, black berries. Deciduous.

'Pyramidale'—Stellar hedge plant.

LONICERA (honeysuckle) These are vigorous shrubs or vines. While they are popular, they have no autumn color. Some of them turn brown in winter. Most are trailing or scandent; only a few are upright growers. The plants grow in full sun, although some of them tolerate light shade. Some honeysuckles are better than others in the group (*L. japonicum* and *L. amoena* 'Arnoldiana' and these are the ones to have. All need little care, and have no special problems.

L. fragrantissima (winter honeysuckle). Hardy to −10F; grows to 6 feet. Stiff, leathery leaves and fragrant, white flowers. Deciduous, but evergreen in mild climates.

L. henyri. Hardy to −20F; vine with dark-green leaves and yellow to purple flowers, followed by black fruit. Good bank cover. Evergreen or semievergreen.

L. maackii (Amur honeysuckle). Hardy to −50F; grows to 15 feet. White, fragrant flowers, and dark-red berries. Good fall color.

L. nitida (box honeysuckle). Hardy to 5F; seldom grows over 6 feet. Creamy-white flowers, and blue-purple berries. Deciduous in the North, and evergreen in the South.

L. tatarica (Tatarian honeysuckle). Hardy to −35F; twiggy branches, big to 10 feet. Oval blue-green leaves, and pink flowers. Deciduous.

'Alba'—Pure white.
'Rosea'—Rose-pink flowers.
'Sibirica'—Deep-pink blooms.

PHILADELPHUS (mock orange). Grown for their white flowers and heady fragrance, mock oranges are vigorous and bloom when young. There are low growers and tall ones, and most of them can take heavy pruning. The plants take hold in almost any kind of soil. There is great variation in shape; many are sculptural and very handsome. They make excellent screens. All in all, a very valuable group of shrubs.

P. coronarius (sweet mock orange). Hardy to −20F; robust, to 10 feet. Oval leaves and very fragrant white flowers. Deciduous.

P. grandiflorus (scentless mock orange). Hardy to −20F; grows to 10 feet. Scentless flowers. Deciduous.

P. lemoinei. Hybrid; hardy to −10F. Grows to about 6 feet with white single or double flowers. Deciduous.

'Avalanche'—Arching branches; very fragrant flowers.
'Girandole'—Double flowers.

P. virginalis. Hybrid; hardy to −10F. Single or double white flowers.

'Glacier'—Double blooms.
'Minnesota Snowflake'—Double fragrant flowers.
'Virginal'—Fast grower.

RHODODENDRONS. A group of many ornamental woody plants—rhododendrons with broad evergreen leaves, and azaleas with small leaves; evergreen or semievergreen or deciduous. The flowers of both types of plants are well known, and in bloom plants are a striking display. Both kinds of plants thrive in an acid soil and need plenty of water. The rhododendrons dislike hot summers and drying winds and need a partially shaded place with only a little sun. The azaleas, on the other hand, can take more sun; the deciduous types need cooler winters than the evergreen azaleas.

Plant rhododendrons in early spring while they are blooming; azaleas (deciduous) are planted when dormant unless they are in cans. The evergreens can be put into the ground any time of the year except in late spring and summer when buds for the following year are developing.

Rhododendrons and azaleas are shallow rooted, so dry conditions injure them. Keep the soil moist, especially in early summer, when new growth is forming. Use an acid-type fertilizer as specified on the container. (There are many of them.) Always remove decayed blooms from rhododendrons so that seed does not develop.

There are low-growing, spreading, and tall rhododendrons; species and hybrids by the hundreds, so make selections carefully. Azaleas too are offered in many varieties—some for mild climates, others for areas with severe winters, and still others for in-between areas. Check with your local nurseryman.

Azaleas are generally listed as follows:

Kurume azalea. Hardy to 10F; somewhat small flowers and leaves; dense growth.
    'Apple Blossom'
    'Christmas Cheer'
    'Salmon Beauty'
Ghent azaleas. Very hardy. Flower color ranges from pure yellow to white to combinations of pink and red. Usually double form.
    'Altaclarense'
    'Coccinea Speciosa'
    'Fanny'
    'Nancy Waterer'
Mollis azaleas. Deciduous; some hardy in New England. Clusters of flowers in shades of yellow or orange; a few red.
    'Adrian Koster'
    'Christopher Wren'
    'Dr. Jacobi'
Knaphill Exbury azaleas. Deciduous; large flowers sometimes ruffled in color ranges from pink to orange to red and rose, and often with contrasting blotches. Fragrant.
    'Berryrose'
    'Cecile'
    'Toucan'
Southern Indica. Evergreen; for sunny places. Outstanding vigor.
Rhododendrons are generally classified as:

Catawba hybrids. Extremely hardy and dependable.
Griffithianum hybrids. Largest flowered species, but not hardy in northeastern United States.
Fortune hybrids. Quite hardy, thriving as far north as Cape Cod.

White Rhododendrons	Hardy to:
'Catalgla'	−25F
'Countess of Haddington'	20F
'Dora Amateis'	−15F
'Great Lakes'	−25F
'Sappho'	−5F
'White Pearl'	5F

Pink Rhododendrons	Hardy to:
'Alice'	−5F
'Cadis'	−15F
'Countess of Derby'	−5F
'Kate Waterer'	−10F
'Pink Pearl'	−5F
'Scintillation'	−10F

Red Rhododendrons	Hardy to:
'America'	−25F
'Brittannia'	−5F
'Caractacus'	−25F
'Holden'	−15F
'Lady Bligh'	0F
'Mars'	−10F

Blue and Purple Rhododendrons	Hardy to:
'Barto Blue'	5F
'Blue Ensign'	−10F
'Blue Jay'	−5F
'Lee's Dark Purple'	−5F
'Sapphire'	0F

Yellow Shades of Rhododendrons	Hardy to:
'Butterfly'	0F
'Crest'	−5F
'Devonshire Cream'	0F
'King of Shrubs'	5F
'Unique'	5F

ROSA (rose). Without doubt, roses are the most popular garden flower, and their value is well known. There are thousands of hybrids—teas, floribundas, grandifloras—and ample information on them; all require a definite program of maintenance to keep them at their best. The native or wild roses are easier to grow, and do not have as many problems as the hybrids. Many wild species can be grown as hardy shrubs for almost all-year color. They have single or double flowers in a range of colors, pure white to pale yellow to pink and the reddest-purple. Plants vary greatly in size, will grow in a poor soil if necessary, and do not need a great deal of attention. While the hybrids certainly have their place in the garden, the wild or shrub roses have immense interest too, and should be grown more.

R. banksiae (Banks rose). Hardy to 5F; climber to 20 feet. Glossy, leathery leaves, and small yellow or white flowers. Evergreen.
    'Alba plena'—Double white fragrant flowers.
    'Lutea'—Double yellow flowers; no scent.
R. centifolia (cabbage rose). Hardy to −10F; grows to 6 feet with prickly stems; Double pink flowers. Deciduous.
    'Muscosa' (moss rose)—Stalks and bases have mossy texture.
R. chinensis (China rose). Hardy to 5F; prickly or smooth stems. Glossy, green leaves and single flowers. Deciduous.
    'Minima' (fairy rose)—Single or double rose-red bloom; grows to 10 inches.
R. damascena (damask rose). Hardy to −20F; grows to 6 feet. Pale-green leaves and fragrant double flowers. Deciduous.
    'Trigintipetala'—Semidouble red flowers.

R. gallica (French rose). Hardy to −10F; grows to 4 feet. Smooth, green leaves; red or purple flowers. Deciduous.

R. hugonis (Father Hugo rose). Hardy to −10F; grows to 8 feet. Deep-green leaves; yellow flowers. Deciduous.

R. multiflora (Japanese rose). Hardy to −10F; grows to 10 feet. Flowers usually white. Floriferous and vigorous. Deciduous.

R. odorata (tea rose). Hardy to 5F; grows to about 12 feet. Pink double flowers. Evergreen or semi-evergreen.

R. rugosa (rugosa rose). Hardy to −35F; vigorous grower to 8 feet. Glossy, green leaves. Single or double flowers in a wide range of colors. Deciduous.

SPIRAEA (spiraea). Spiraeas with red or white flowers are versatile plants that add a high note of outdoor color. There are two groups: spring blooming and summer blooming. Some spiraeas have a lovely branching habit and are small; others reach 15 feet. Most are vigorous, not particular about soil conditions, nor demanding about light. They grow in sun or light shade; in general they need little pruning, nor are they bothered by insects. Summer bloom comes at a time when few other woody plants are in color, making them especially worthwhile.

S. billiardii. Hybrid; hardy to −20F. Arching branches, to 6 feet, and tiny pale-pink flowers. Deciduous.

S. bullata. Hardy to −5F; dense grower to 2 feet. Round leaves and pink flowers; good rock garden plant. Deciduous.

S. bumalda. Hardy to −10F; grows to 3 feet. Narrow, oval leaves and pale-pink blooms. Deciduous.
    'Anthony Waterer' (dwarf red spiraea)—Bright-carmine flowers.

S. prunifolia (bridalwreath spiraea). Hardy to −20F; leaves turn orange in fall. Double white flowers. Deciduous. Grows to 6–9 feet.

S. thunbergii (Thunberg spiraea). Hardy to −20F; grows to 5 feet. Leathery branchlets and single white flowers. Deciduous.

SYRINGA (lilac). Every homeowner has a spot in his heart and in his garden for fragrant lilacs. There are at least 250 named varieties offered today. Basically, these are vigorous upright shrubs valued not only for their flowers but also for use as screen and hedges. They are easily grown in almost any kind of soil, but have a slight preference for a lime-type soil. And while some lilacs do have insect trouble, there are many new ones that are resistant to pest and disease. Lilacs grow vigorously from the base, and pruning is important to keep them healthy. Flowers become less numerous and smaller if suckers take away plant strength. They can stand severe pruning in early spring and still have a good growing season. However, for best results prune lilacs this way: take out one-third of the old stems of mature plants one year; another third, the next year; and the remaining, the third year. Then the plants will always appear handsome.

S. chinensis (Chinese lilac). Hybrid; hardy to −10F; grows to 15 feet. Fine-textured foliage, and fragrant rose-purple flowers. Deciduous.

S. josikaea (Hungarian lilac). Hardy to −50F; dense, upright grower to 12 feet. Glossy, green leaves; lilac flowers. Deciduous.

S. lacinata (cut-leaf lilac). Hardy to −10F; open growth to 6 feet. Rich green foliage, and fragrant pale-lilac flowers. Deciduous.

S. microphylla (littleleaf lilac). Hardy to −10F; grows to 6 feet. Pale-lilac flowers. Deciduous.

S. villosa (late lilac). Hardy to −50F; dense, upright grower to 10 feet. Rosy-lilac to white flowers. Deciduous.

S. vulgaris (common lilac). Hardy to −35F; bulky shrub to 20 feet. Fragrant lilac flowers. Deciduous.
    'Edith Cavell'—French lilac; white.
    'Cavour'—French lilac; single violet.
    'Ellen Willmott'—French lilac; double white.
    'Clarke's Giant'—French lilac; single blue.

VIBURNUM (viburnum). For every season of the year there is a viburnum for the garden. Many are valued for their spring flowers, and others for their beautiful glossy, green foliage in summer. Almost all viburnums grow without much care, and are tolerant of practically any soil; many grow in light shade. Several have vivid autumn color, and a few hold berries all through winter. The leaves are deciduous or evergreen. Viburnums are rarely attacked by insects. They are dependable shrubs that offer much satisfaction for little effort.

V. carlcephalum (fragrant snowball). Hardy to −10F; grows to 7 feet. Dull, grayish-green leaves, and fragrant white flowers. Deciduous.

V. carlesii (spice viburnum). Hardy to −20F; grows to 6 feet. Sweetly fragrant pink blooms. Deciduous.

V. cinnamomifolium. Hardy to 10F; grows to 20 feet. Glossy, dark-green leaves and pink buds; white flowers. Evergreen.

V. davidii. Hardy to 5F; grows to 3 feet. Dark-green, veined leaves, and white flowers. Evergreen.

V. dentatum (arrowwood). Hardy to −50F; grows to 15 feet. Creamy-white flowers, and red autumn color. Deciduous.

V. dilatatum (linden viburnum). Hardy to −10F; tall and broad. Gray-green leaves and creamy-white flowers. Deciduous.

V. japonicum (Japanese viburnum). Hardy to 5F;

Low-growing shrubs and ground cover plants make this entry court a charming scene.
(Molly Adams)

Although planted only a few years, evergreen shrubs seem to have been at this charming entrance for many, many years.
(Molly Adams)

grows to 20 feet. Glossy, dark-green leaves, and fragrant white flowers. Evergreen.

V. lantana (wayfaring tree). Hardy to −35F; grows to 15 feet. Oval leaves turn red in fall; tiny white flowers. Deciduous.

V. opulus (European cranberry bush). Hardy to −35F; grows to 20 feet. Maple-shaped leaves turn red in fall; clusters of white flowers. Deciduous. 'Nana'—Dwarf.

V. plicatum (Japanese snowball). Hardy to −20F; wide and tall, to 15 feet. Dark-green, veined leaves; snowball clusters of white flowers. Deciduous.

V. trilobum (American cranberry bush). Hardy to −50F; grows to 15 feet. Similar to *V. opulus,* but not as susceptible to aphid damage. Deciduous.

V. wrightii. Hardy to −10F; tall and narrow, to 10 feet. Bright-green leaves and small white flowers. Deciduous.

WEIGELA (weigela). These have brilliant flowers and are vigorous growers. However, they do not have autumn color. Some varieties start blooming in May with flowers until June. A few weigelas are valued for their bronze or variegated leaves.

W. middendorffiana. Hardy to −10F; dense and broad shrubs to 4 feet. Dark-green, wrinkled leaves, and yellow flowers. Deciduous.
  W. 'Bristol Ruby'—Ruby-red flowers.
  W. 'Bristol Snowflake'—White with some pink.
  W. 'Candida'—Pure white.

Shrubs by Common Name

Abelia (*Abelia grandiflora*)
American cranberry bush (*Viburnum trilobum*)
Amur honeysuckle (*Lonicera maackii*)
Amur privet (*Ligustrum amurense*)
Andromeda (*Pieris floribunda*)
Arrowwood (*Viburnum dentatum*)
Aucuba (*Aucuba japonica*)

Banks rose (*Rosa banksiae*)
Bearberry (*Arctostaphylos uva-ursi*)
Bearberry cotoneaster (*Cotoneaster dammeri*)
Beauty bush (*Kolkwitzia amabilis*)
Bellflower (*Enkianthus campanulatus*)
Black barberry (*Berberis gagnepainii*)
Black haw (*Viburnum prunifolium*)
Blue blossom (*Ceanothus thyrsiflorus*)
Bog rosemary (*Andromeda polifolia*)
Border forsythia (*Forsythia intermedia*)
Bottlebrush (*Callistemon citrinus*)
Box honeysuckle (*Lonicera nitida*)
Bridal wreath spirea (*Spiraea vulgaris*)
Broadleaf euonymus (*Euonymus latifolius*)
Buttercup shrub (*Potentilla fruticosa*)
Butterfly bush (*Buddleia davidii*)

Cabbage rose (*Rosa centifolia*)
California mock orange (*Carpenteria californica*)
California privet (*Ligustrum ovalifolium*)
Cape jasmine (*Gardenia jasminoides*)
Carolina jasmine (*Gelsemium sempervirens*)
Chaste tree (*Vitex agnus-castus*)
Cherry elaeagnus (*Elaeagnus multiflorus*)
China rose (*Rosa chinensis*)
Chinese hibiscus (*Hibiscus rosa-sinensis*)
Chinese holly (*Ilex cornuta*)
Chinese lilac (*Syringa chinensis*)
Chinese photinia (*Photinia serrulata*)
Chinese witch hazel (*Hamamelis mollis*)
Common boxwood (*Buxus sempervirens*)
Common camellia (*Camellia japonica*)
Common juniper (*Juniperus communis*)
Common lilac (*Syringa vulgaris*)
Common privet (*Ligustrum vulgare*)
Common white jasmine (*Jasminum officinale*)
Cornelian cherry (*Cornus mas*)
Cranberry bush (*Viburnum trilobum*)
Cranberry cotoneaster (*Cotoneaster apiculata*)
Crape myrtle (*Lagerstroemia indica*)
Creeping mahonia (*Mahonia repens*)
Creeping willow (*Salix repens*)
Cut-leaf lilac (*Syringa laciniata*)

Damask rose (*Rosa damascena*)

Early deutzia (*Deutzia grandiflora*)
Early forsythia (*Forsythia ovata*)
English holly (*Ilex aquifolium*)
European cranberry bush (*Viburnum opulus*)
Evergreen euonymus (*Euonymus japonica*)

Father Hugo rose (*Rose hugonis*)
Flowering currant (*Ribes sanguineum*)
Flowering quince (*Chaenomeles japonica*)
Fountain buddleia (*Buddleia alternifolia*)
Fragrant daphne (*Daphne odora*)
Fragrant snowball (*Viburnum carlcephalum*)
French pussy willow (*Salix caprea*)
French rose (*Rosa gallica*)

Glossy privet (*Ligustrum lucidum*)

Hardy orange (*Poncirus trifoliata*)
Heather (*Calluna vulgaris*)
Heavenly bamboo (*Nandina domestica*)
Hills-of-snow (*Hydrangea arborescens* 'Grandiflora')
Holly osmanthus (*Osmanthus heterophyllus*)
Hungarian lilac (*Syringa josikaea*)

Indian hawthorn (*Raphiolepis indica*)
Inkberry (*Ilex glabra*)

Japanese andromeda (*Pieris japonica*)
Japanese aralia (*Fatsia japonica*)
Japanese barberry (*Berberis thunbergii*)
Japanese boxwood (*Buxus microphylla japonica*)

Japanese holly (*Ilex crenata*)
Japanese pittosporum (*Pittosporum tobira*)
Japanese rose (*Rosa multiflora*)
Japanese skimmia (*Skimmia japonica*)
Japanese snowball (*Viburnum plicatum*)
Japanese viburnum (*Viburnum japonicum*)

Korean barberry (*Berberis koreana*)
Korean boxwood (*Buxus microphylla koreana*)
Korean white forsythia (*Abeliophyllum distichum*)

Late lilac (*Syringa villosa*)
Littleleaf lilac (*Syringa microphylla*)

Magellan barberry (*Berberis buxifolia*)
Magellan fuchsia (*Fuchsia magellanica*)
Mentor barberry (*Berberis mentorensis*)
Midwinter euonymus (*Euonymus bungeanus semi-persistes*)
Mountain laurel (*Kalmia latifolia*)

Nannyberry (*Viburnum lentago*)
Natal plum (*Carissa grandiflora*)
New Jersey tea (*Ceanothus americanus*)

Oleander (*Nerium oleander*)
Oregon holly (*Mahonia aquifolium*)

Pfitzer juniper (*Juniperus chinensis pfitzeriana*)

Red box cotoneaster (*Cotoneaster rotundifolia*)
Rock spray (*Cotoneaster horizontalis*)
Rugosa rose (*Rosa rugosa*)
Russian olive (*Elaeagnus angustifolia*)

Salal (*Gaultheria shallon*)
Sasanqua camellia (*Camellia sasanqua*)

Scarlet firethorn (*Pyracantha coccinea*)
Scentless mock orange (*Philadelphus grandiflora*)
Shadblow service berry (*Amelanchier canadensis*)
Sheep laurel (*Kalmia angustifolia*)
Siberian dogwood (*Cornus alba* 'Sibirica')
Silverberry elaeagnus (*Elaeagnus pungens*)
Silverleaf cotoneaster (*Cotoneaster pannosa*)
Slender deutzia (*Duetzia gracilis*)
Small-leaf cotoneaster (*Cotoneaster microphylla*)
Spanish jasmine (*Jasminum grandiflorum*)
Spice viburnum (*Viburnum carlesii*)
Spreading cotoneaster (*Cotoneaster divaricata*)
Spring witch hazel (*Hamamelis vernalis*)
Strawberry tree (*Arbutus unedo*)
Surinam cherry (*Eugenia uniflora*)
Summer sweet (*Clethra alnifolia*)
Sweet bay (*Laurus nobilis*)
Sweet mock orange (*Philadelphus coronarius*)

Tatarian honeysuckle (*Lonicera tatarica*)
Tea rose (*Rosa odorata*)
Tender viburnum (*Viburnum dilatatum*)
Thunberg spiraea (*Spiraea thunbergii*)

Veitch wintergreen (*Gaultheria veitchiana*)

Warty barberry (*Berberis verruculosa*)
Wayfaring tree (*Viburnum lantana*)
Weeping forsythia (*Forsythia suspensa*)
Winged spindle tree (*Euonymus alata*)
Winterberry (*Ilex verticillata*)
Wintergreen cotoneaster (*Cotoneaster conspicua*)
Winter honeysuckle (*Lonicera fragrantissima*)
Winter jasmine (*Jasminum nudiflorum*)

CHAPTER 13

Perennials and Biennials

If you want bright color in the garden year after year, you will want perennials. These are the flowers that everyone loves; but sometimes in our enthusiasm to brighten the garden, we plant all perennials, and then are faced with blank spots when they are not in bloom. Some perennials have only a short period of bloom, and others die down soon after flowering, so selecting the right varieties becomes an important part of the perennial garden.

For simplicity, we say perennials generally bloom the second year after they are planted and live on for many years, while annuals bloom the first year they are planted and then die. Midway between perennials and annuals is a smaller group of plants called biennials. Generally, these produce flowers in their second year, then gradually die. However, under certain conditions some of them live more than two years. Some popular biennials are hollyhocks and pansies.

STARTING THE PERENNIAL GARDEN

For maximum beauty and color, plant perennials in groups according to their blooming times: one for spring, one for summer, and fall flowers in still another place. Fill in with annuals and bulbs so that there will be color all through the warm months.

The size and form of the garden depend on the surroundings and space available. If the bed is accessible from only one side, it is best to limit the width to about 30 inches so that the flowers at the back may be tended with ease. If it is an island bed that you can approach from all sides, the width can be to 60 inches. Place tall flowers, like delphiniums and stock, in the rear of the bed, medium growers in the middle, and the smallest in the front. Avoid straight rows; instead, use circular or oval masses of

flowers, perhaps a dozen or more to a shape. The groups should run into each other and overlap each other to some degree.

To start, decide on the type of garden you want—whether it is going to be only perennials or a mixed bed, whether it will be a seasonal accent or a continuous flow of color throughout spring, fall, and winter. Height, time of blooming, and color must all be considered. The space to allow between plants is always guesswork; some spread quickly and others slowly. Most perennials can be put about 12 inches apart; but this is a generalization and it varies with the plants. Daylilies go 24 inches apart, and alyssum 12 inches, and so forth.

PLANTING AND GENERAL CARE

Prepare the bed with good soil. Dig at least 20 inches deep, and recondition the soil if it is necessary. Mound the soil so that drainage is assured, or slope the bed so that water will not accumulate and stagnate in the soil. Plants can be put in, in fall or spring. Early blooming varieties are best started in the fall, while late bloomers are generally planted in the spring.

Large holes to accommodate all the plant roots should be dug, and the soil firmly tucked around the collar of the plant. After the first frost, it is a good idea to provide a mulch for the garden, using a light organic matter that will not exclude air. (See Chapter 6.)

Water perennials heavily; most of them are thirsty plants and, especially on hot days, see that they have ample moisture. Do not be concerned about the time of day to water plants. Anytime from early morning to midday to late afternoon is fine; I have never really stuck to a rigid schedule of watering. If the soil has been adequately prepared, little feeding is necessary. Generally, I add a mild fertilizer (5–10–5) two weeks after planting and then again, when plants show buds.

Stake plants that have flexible stems; otherwise, they topple from their own weight, or worse yet, are blown to bits by wind. Try to put the supports in place as unobtrusively as possible. Nurseries carry many types of staking devices, or if absolutely necessary, use twigs of other plants. Tie the stems to the stakes with 'Twistems' wrapped loosely around them. Do not strangle them.

Disbudding is a simple but overlooked part of growing flowers; it merely involves nipping off buds with your fingernail in order for plants to produce bigger flowers and bushier growth.

Perennials and biennials are usually sold as started plants, some of them as roots or rhizomes ready to go into the ground. Plants are at nurseries in late fall and in early spring. Occasionally, they are offered in pots and cans, and then it is possible to see the flowers; but this is not the usual case. However, in the South and in western states where many perennials never go fully dormant, this is done.

LISTS OF PERENNIALS

The list in Table 10 is a practical compilation of many perennials and some biennials. It is by no means, a complete list. Perennial plants that are treated as annuals are shown here, but information on them appears in Table 11, Chapter 14.

While species are mainly listed, plants marked with a dagger (†) are available in many varieties. That is, they have been bred to excel in certain qualities—form, color, bushiness—and you will find varieties by the hundreds in garden catalogs under many names.

The plant list is arranged by botanical name rather than common name, which is often the same for two or three plants and can be confusing. However, common name listings are also included at the end of this section.

Table 10. General List of Perennials

Botanical and Common Name	Approx. Height in Inches	Range of Colors	Peak Bloom Season	Sun or Shade
Acanthus mollis (Grecian urn)	To 60	White, lilac	Summer	Sun or shade
Achillea ptarmica (yarrow)	To 18	White	Summer, fall	Sun
Aconitum anthora (monkshood)	36	Pale yellow	Summer	Sun or shade
Althaea rosea* (hollyhock)	60–108	Most colors except true blue and green	Summer	Sun
Alyssum saxatile (alyssum) (basket of gold)	8–12	Golden-yellow, tinged with chartreuse	Early spring	Sun
Anchusa capensis (summer forget-me-not)	12–18	Pure, bright blue	Early summer	Sun or light shade
Anemone coronaria (poppy-flowered anemone)	To 18	Red, blue, white	Spring	Sun
Anemone hupehensis japonica† (Japanese anemone)	25–48	White, pink, rose	Fall	Sun or light shade
Anemone pulsatilla (prairie windflower) (pasque flower)	9–15	Lavender to violet	Spring	Sun or light shade
Anthemis tinctoria (golden marguerite)	24–36	Yellow	Summer, fall	Sun
Antirrhinum (See Table 11—Annuals, Chapter 14.) (snapdragon)				
Aquilegia alpina (dwarf columbine)	To 12	Blue	Early summer	Sun or light shade
Arabis caucasica (wall rock cress)	4–10	White	Early spring	Sun or light shade
Armeria maritima (sea-pink or thrift)	To 12	White, dark red, pink	Spring, summer	Sun

* Biennial.
† Many varieties.

Table 10 (*Continued*)

Botanical and Common Name	Approx. Height in Inches	Range of Colors	Peak Bloom Season	Sun or Shade
Artemisia albula (wormwood)	24–48	Silvery-gray	Summer, fall	Sun
Artemisia frigida† (fringed wormwood)	12–18	Silvery-white (foliage)	Summer, fall	Sun
Asclepias tuberosa (butterfly weed)	24–36	Orange	Summer	Sun
Aster, dwarf type†‡	8–15	Red, blue, purple	Late summer	Sun
Aster, English hardy†‡ (Michaelmas daisy)	30–48	Blue, violet, pink, white	Fall	Sun
Aster frikartii	30–36	Blue, lavender	Summer, fall	Sun
Aubrieta deltoidea† (common aubrieta)	2–4	Blue	Spring	Sun or shade
Begonia semperflorens (See Table 11—Annuals, Chapter 14.) (wax begonia)				
Bellis perennis (English daisy)	3–6	White, pink, rose	Spring, winter in mild climates	Sun
Bergenia cordifolia (heartleaf bergenia)	12–18	Rose	Early summer	Sun or light shade
Campanula carpatica (bellflower)	8–10	Blue, white	Summer	Sun
Campanula persicifolia (peach-leafed bellflower)	24–36	White, blue, pink	Summer	Sun
Centaurea gymnocarpa (dusty miller)	18–24	Velvety-white leaves; purple flowers	Summer	Sun
Chrysanthemum coccineum (Pyrethrum)‡ (painted daisy)	24–36	White, pink, red	Early summer	Sun
Chrysanthemum maximum (Shasta daisy)†	24–48	White	Summer, fall	Sun or shade
Chrysanthemum morifolium† (florists' chrysanthemum)	18–30	Most colors except blue	Late summer, fall	Sun
Convallaria majalis (lily-of-the-valley)	9–12	White, pink	Spring, early summer	Light to medium shade
Coreopsis grandiflora (tickseed)	24–36	Golden yellow	Summer	Sun
Delphinium hybrid† (Connecticut Yankee)	24–36	Blue, violet; white	Early summer	Sun
Delphinium hybrid†‡ (Pacific Giant)	48–96	Blue, white	Early summer	Sun
*Dianthus barbatus** (Sweet William)	10–30	White, pink, red; zoned and edged	Early summer	Sun or light shade
Dianthus deltoides† (maiden pink)	8–12	Rose, purple, white	Early summer	Sun
Dicentra spectabilis (bleeding heart)	24–36	Pink, rose, white	Spring	Light shade
Dictamnus albus (gas plant)	36	White, pink, purple	Summer	Sun or light shade
*Digitalis purpurea** (foxglove)	18–48	Mixed colors, marked and spotted	Early summer	Partial shade or sun
Echinops exaltatus (globe thistle)	36–48	Steel-blue	Late summer	Sun

* Biennial.
† Many varieties.
‡ See "Additional Comments on Perennials."

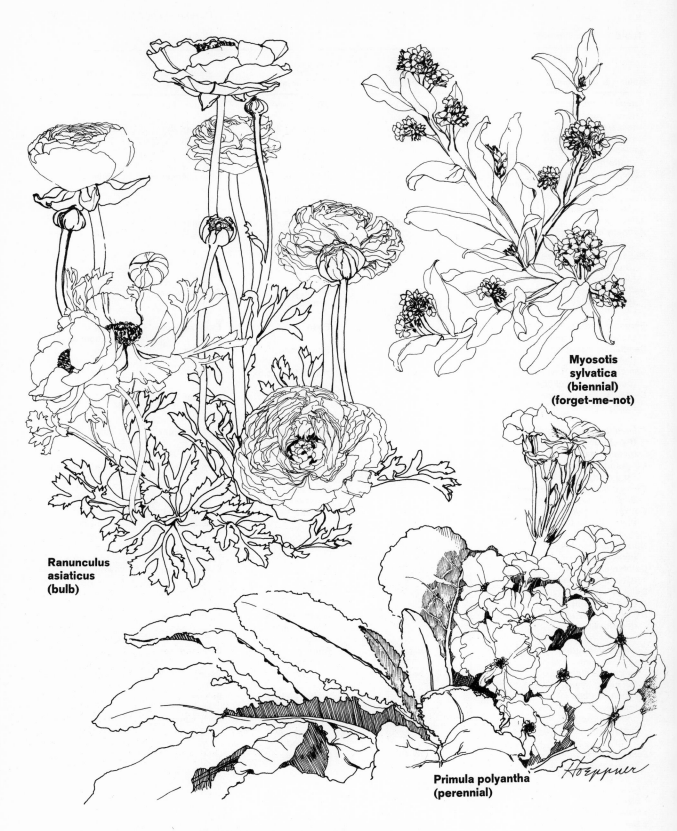

Myosotis
sylvatica
(biennial)
(forget-me-not)

Ranunculus
asiaticus
(bulb)

Primula polyantha
(perennial)

Hoeppner

SPRING-BLOOMING PLANTS

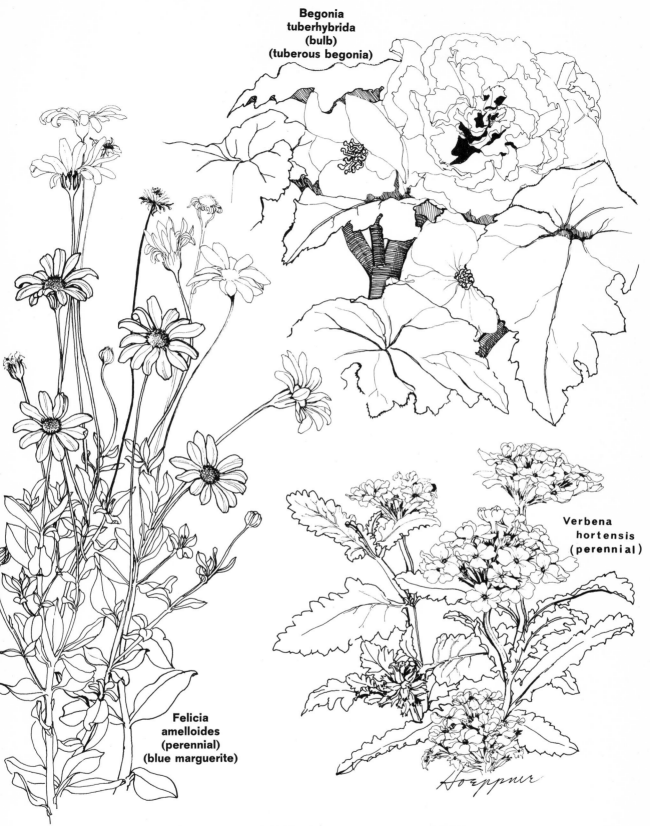

Begonia
tuberhybrida
(bulb)
(tuberous begonia)

Verbena
hortensis
(perennial)

Felicia
amelloides
(perennial)
(blue marguerite)

Hoeppner

SUMMER-FALL-BLOOMING PLANTS

Table 10 (Continued)

Botanical and Common Name	Approx. Height in Inches	Range of Colors	Peak Bloom Season	Sun or Shade
Epimedium grandiflorum (bishop's hat)	12	Red, violet, white	Summer	Light shade
Erysimum asperum (Siberian wallflower)	12–18	Golden-orange	Spring	Sun
Felicia amelloides (blue marguerite)	20–24	Blue	Spring, summer	Sun
Gaillardia grandiflora (blanket flower)	24–48	Yellow or bicolor	Summer, fall	Sun
Gazania hybrids†	10–12	Yellow and brown bicolors	Summer; fall; and spring where mild	Sun
Gentiana asclepiadea (willow gentian)	20–24	Blue to violet	Late summer	Light
Geranium grandiflorum (cranesbill)	10–12	Blue marked red	Summer	Light shade
Geum chiloense (coccineum) (geum)	20–24	Yellow, red-orange	Early summer	Light shade
Gypsophila paniculata† (baby's breath)	24–36	White	Early summer and summer	Sun
Helenium (various) (Helen's flower)	24–48	Orange, yellow, rusty shades	Summer, fall	Sun
Helianthus decapetalus multiflorus (sunflower)	40–60	Yellow	Summer	Sun
Heliopsis (various) (orange sunflower)	36–48	Orange and yellow	Summer, fall	Sun
Hemerocallis (various)†‡ (daylily)	12–72	Most colors except blue, green, violet	Midsummer	Sun or light shade
*Hesperis matronalis** (sweet rocket)	24–36	White, lavender	Early summer	Sun or light shade
Heuchera sanguinea† (coral bells)	12–24	Red, pink, white	Early summer	Sun or light shade
Hosta plantaginea (plantain lily)	24–30	White flowers; yellow-green leaves	Late summer	Light shade
Iberis sempervirens (evergreen candytuft)	8–12	White	Early summer	Sun or light shade
Impatiens (See Table 11—Annuals, Chapter 14.)				
Iris (various) (bearded iris) (See also Chapter 15.)	3–10 (dwarf) 15–28 (intermediate) 24–48 (tall)	Many, many colors	Spring, early summer	Sun or light shade
Iris cristata (crested iris)	6–8	Lavender, light blue	Spring	Light shade
Iris dichotoma (vesper iris)	30–36	Pale lavendar marked purple	Summer	Sun
Iris kaempferi (Japanese iris)	40–48	Purple, violet, pink, rose, red, white	Spring, early summer	Sun or light shade
Liatris pycnostachya (gayfeather)	60–72	Rose-purple	Summer	Sun or light shade
Limonium latifolium (statice, sea lavender)	24–36	Blue, white, pink	Summer, fall	Sun
Linum perenne (blue flax)	20–24	Sky-blue	Summer	Sun
Lithodora diffusa	6–12	Blue	Summer	Sun
Lobelia cardinalis	24–36	Red	Late summer	Sun, light shade

* Biennial.
† Many varieties.
‡ See "Additional Comments on Perennials."

Table 10 (Continued)

Botanical and Common Name	Approx. Height in Inches	Range of Colors	Peak Bloom Season	Sun or Shade
Lupinus polyphyllus	24–48	Red	Summer	Sun or shade
Lythrum (various)	50–60	Rose to purple	Summer, fall	Sun or light shade
Mathiola incana* (See Table 11—Annuals, Chapter 14.) (stock)				
Mertensia virginica (Virginia bluebell)	16–24	Bicolor blue	Early spring	Light shade
Mirabilis jalapa (See Table 11—Annuals, Chapter 14.) (four-o'-clock)				
Monarda didyma (bee balm)	30–36	Scarlet-red, pink	Summer and fall	Sun, light shade
Myosotis sylvatica* (See Table 11—Annuals, Chapter 14.) (forget-me-not)				
Oenothera (various)* (evening primrose)	20–72	Yellow, pink	Summer	Sun
Paeonia (various)†‡ (peony)	18–48	White, pink, crimson, lavender, cream	Early summer	Light shade
Papaver orientale† (Oriental poppy)	24–48	Pink, white, scarlet, salmon, orange	Early summer	Sun
Pelargonium domesticum (Lady Washington geranium)	18–48	Many bicolors; white, pink, red, purple	Summer, fall	Sun
Penstemon (various)† (beard tongue)	18–36	Blue, pink, crimson; mostly bicolors	Summer, fall	Sun
Phlox divaricata† (sweet William phlox)	10–12	Blue, white, pink, rose	Early spring	Sun or light shade
Phlox paniculata†‡ (summer phlox)	36–60	Pink, purple, rose, white, orange, red	Late summer, fall	Sun
Physalis alkekengi (See Table 11—Annuals, Chapter 14.) (Chinese lantern)				
Physostegia virginiana (false dragonhead)	36–48	White and rose bicolors	Midsummer to later summer	Sun
Platycodon grandiflorum (balloonflower)	18–42	Pink, white, purple, blue	Midsummer to late summer	Sun or shade
Polygonatum multiflorum (Solomon's seal)	10–12	White	Spring	Sun or shade
Potentilla atrosanguinea (cinquefoil)	10–12	Red	Summer	Sun
Primula (various)†	10–14	Bicolors, blue, red, yellow, orange, pink	Late spring, summer	Sun or shade
Pyrethrum (various)† (See Chrysanthemum coccineum.) (painted daisy)				
Rudbeckia hirta (coneflower)	36–48	Yellow, pink, orange, white	Summer	Sun
Salvia patens (blue salvia or meadow sage)	24–36	Dark blue	Summer, fall	Sun
Scabiosa caucasica (pincushion flower)	24–30	White, blue, purple	Summer, fall	Sun

* Biennial.

† Many varieties.

‡ See "Additional Comments on Perennials."

Chrysanthemum

Aster

Chrysanthemum

FALL-BLOOMING PERENNIALS

Table 10 (*Continued*)

Botanical and Common Name	Approx. Height in Inches	Range of Colors	Peak Bloom Season	Sun or Shade
Sedum sieboldii	6–8	Pink, coppery foliage in fall	Late summer, fall	Sun or light shade
Solidago (various) (goldenrod)	20–36	Yellow	Summer	Sun or light shade
Tithonia rotundifolia (See Table 11—Annuals, Chapter 14.)				
Kniphofia (various) (torch lily)	24–72	Cream, white, yellow, orange	Early summer	Sun
Verbena hybrida (See Table 11—Annuals, Chapter 14.)				
Veronica (various)†‡ (speedwell)	24–36	Blue, pink, white	Midsummer	Light shade
Viola cornuta† (tufted viola)	6–8	Purple; newer varieties in many colors	Spring, fall	Light shade
Yucca filamentosa (Adam's needle)	36–72	White	Late summer	Sun

* Biennial.
† Many varieties.
‡ See "Additional Comments on Perennials."

Easy-to-Grow Perennials

Achillea (various) (yarrow)
Alyssum saxatile (basket of gold)
Aquilegia chrysantha
Aster (various)
Chrysanthemum (various)
Coreopsis grandiflora (tickseed)
Dianthus (various) (pinks)
Gypsophilia paniculata (baby's breath)
Hemerocallis (various) (daylily)
Lobelia cardinalis (cardinal flower)
Lythrum (various) (loosestrife)
Myosotis sylvatica (forget-me-not)
Phlox subulata (moss pink)
Sedum (various) (stonecrop)
Veronica (various) (speedwell)

Perennials for Wet Soil

Gentiana asclepiadea (willow gentian)
Helenium (various) (Helen's flower)
Iris versicolor (blue flag)
Lobelia cardinalis (cardinal flower)
Lythrum (various) (loosestrife)
Monarda didyma (bee balm)
Oenothera (various) (evening primrose)

Perennials for Dry, Sandy Soil

Achillea (various) (yarrow)
Anthemis tinctoria (golden marguerite)
Coreopsis grandiflora (tickseed)
Dianthus (various) (pinks)

Geranium grandiflorum (cranesbill)
Gypsophila paniculata (baby's breath)
Helianthus (various) (sunflower)
Papaver nudicaule (Iceland poppy)
Phlox subulata (moss phlox)
Potentilla atrosanguinea (cinquefoil)
Rudbeckia hirta (coneflower)
Sedum (various) (stonecrop)
Yucca filamentosa (Adam's needle)

Perennials for Edging

Alyssum saxatile (basket of gold)
Arabis caucasica (wall rock cress)
Bellis perennis (English daisy)
Iberis sempervirens (evergreen candytuft)
Primula (various) (primrose)
Sedum (various) (stonecrop)
Veronica (various) (speedwell)
Viola cornuta (tufted viola)

Perennials for Fragrance

Arabis (various)
Convallaria majalis (lily-of-the-valley)
Dianthus (various) (pinks)
Dictamnus albus (gas plant)
Hesperis matronalis (sweet rocket)
Monarda didyma (bee balm)
Oenothera (various) (evening primrose)
Paeonia (various) (peony)
Phlox (various) (phlox)
Viola cornuta (tufted viola)

Perennials for Background Planting

Althaea rosea (hollyhock)
Aster (various)
Delphinium (various)
Echinops exaltatus (globe thistle)
Helenium (various) (Helen's flower)
Helianthus (various) (sunflower)
Hemerocallis (various) (daylily)
Rudbeckia hirta (coneflower)
Solidago altissima (goldenrod)
Yucca filamentosa (Adam's needle)

Perennials for Naturalizing

Aster (various) (aster)
Convallaria majalis (lily-of-the-valley)
Coreopsis grandiflora (tickseed)
Helianthus (various) (sunflower)
Mertensia virginica (Virginia bluebells)
Monarda didyma (bee balm)
Physostegia virginiana (false dragonhead)

Perennials for Cut Flowers

Achillea (various) (yarrow)
Anemone japonica (Japanese anemone)
Aster (various) (aster)
Chrysanthemum morifolium (garden chrysanthemum)
Delphinium (various) (delphinium)
Dianthus barbatus (sweet William)
Gaillardia grandiflora (blanket flower)
Paeonia (various) (peony)
Pyrethrum (various) (painted daisy)
Rudbeckia hirta (coneflower)

Perennials for Shade

Anemone japonica (Japanese anemone)
Convallaria majalis (lily-of-the-valley)
Dicentra spectabilis (bleeding heart)
Hosta (various) (plantain lily)
Lobelia cardinalis (cardinal flower)
Mertensia virginica (Virginia bluebells)
Polygonatum multiflorum (Solomon's seal)

Additional Comments on Perennials

Because there are so many perennials, many gardeners have a difficult time choosing plants. While most are easy to grow, some are more dependable and offer more color than others. These notes are to guide you in growing some of the more popular perennials.

ASTER. These are now offered in many different colors and heights. They are floriferous and produce daisylike flowers of purple, pink, blue, or white. The Michaelmas daisies (New England hardy asters) thrive in practically any kind of soil and will withstand rough treatment (if necessary). Plant them in fall or spring, 24 inches apart, in full sun in a moist soil. Dwarf asters are another choice, gay and colorful, and like their taller relatives, need minimum care to produce their lovely flowers. Asters start blooming in August and carry through until the end of October.

CHRYSANTHEMUM. "Mums" are outstanding for fall color and they seem to do well everywhere. There are bushy garden kinds and special varieties; cushion types, button-form mums, spoon chrysanthemums and Shasta daisies—a veritable treasure of flowers. Buy young plants in small pots and choose the appropriate variety for your region. If you live in the North where there are early frosts, select varieties that bloom before October 1. (Most catalogs give blooming dates.) Plant "mums" in early spring to about June in a sunny spot; use well-drained fertile soil with a good quantity of humus in it. Space plants about 24 inches apart, and water them copiously at planting time; feed them with a mild solution of 5–10–5 plant food every second week. Pinch back young plants to encourage vigorous shoots.

PHLOX. Summer perennial phlox (there are also annual kinds) bring a rainbow of color to the garden. Plants grow 3 to 4 feet tall, with large clusters of 1-inch flowers—pink, white, purple, red, blue, violet—at the top of leafy stems. Put phlox in a rich soil and give them buckets of water. When they finish blooming, cut off the main cluster to prevent seed falling on the ground and sowing themselves. The seedlings are inferior to the parents and crowd out the good ones. In autumn, cut plants to ground level; divide and reset phlox about every third year.

DAYLILY (hemerocallis). These are becoming bigger and better every year and are desirable summer blooms with varieties for almost every climate. The large flowers come in yellow, orange, red, pink, or combinations, and are borne over an unusually long period. Heat will not cut down daylilies. There are over 300 of them to choose from. Plants can be put in almost any kind of soil, in sun or partial sun; space them 24 to 36 inches apart. Keep the lilies well watered and divide them only when they become so overcrowded that they do not bloom profusely. There are also dwarf daylilies available from suppliers.

PEONY (paeonia). Peonies are long-time favorites, with big fragrant flowers and an extremely long life. In mild winter climates they do not respond because they need a good chill to thrive. One type of peony (herbaceous) dies down to the ground each winter; the other is a shrub with permanent branching growth. The familiar garden kind (herbaceous) needs almost full sun, although some bloom in a partially sunny spot. Space plants about 30 inches apart in a soil that is not overly soggy. Don't expect too much from them the first year; it is the second year that peonies are outstanding. Because there are early- and late-blooming varieties, select them carefully so that you can have a long season of bloom. Do not plant peonies too deep; each root should have 3 to 5 "eyes" at planting time in early fall, and the buds should be set about 2 inches below the surface of the soil. Give plants an early spring feeding and another application after bloom so that they can build strength for the following year. When growth has completely stopped in fall (after the last frost), cut and burn all above-ground parts of the plant. This procedure controls botrytis blight, a disease that nips peonies in bud. The shrub peonies are elegant garden flowers, and now are available from most suppliers. The plants are shrubby and lose their leaves in winter but do not die down to the ground. Tree peonies may be 8 feet high and bear dozens of large translucent flowers—single, double, semidouble —in colors of yellow or lavender, as well as pink, coral, or white. The plants like a rich fertile soil. Put them in the ground in early fall, spaced about 40 to 48 inches apart. Plant them so that the growth buds at the top of the roots are at least 8 inches below the soil surface. If possible, keep plants mulched all year.

DELPHINIUM. These towers of color are a gardener's dream, some growing to 8 feet, with large single or double florets (Pacific hybrids). Stake the plants, or the glorious flower heads, so heavy, will topple over. Other delphiniums such as *D. belladonna* grow to about 4 feet, and are branching and lovely with blue flowers. And still smaller is the Chinese delphinium, *D. grandiflorum,* growing to 24 inches, with blue or white flowers. Buy year-old plants and put them in place in spring in cold winter regions, and in fall in temperate areas. Space them about 24 inches apart in a somewhat sunny place, and be sure the crowns of the plants are not below soil level. When blooming is over, cut stalks below the lowest flower.

VERONICA (speedwell). These plants deserve more attention from gardeners because they have stellar flowers of pink or white carried on lovely tapering spires. Some are trailers, others are branching, and still others reach 3 feet. Put veronicas 8 inches apart in good garden soil. Plant them in the fall or spring in a somewhat sunny spot. Give them plenty of water if rain fails. Magnificent July to September color.

Perennials by Common Name

Adam's needle (*Yucca filamentosa*)
Alyssum (*Alyssum saxatile*)

Baby's breath (*Gypsophila paniculata*)
Balloonflower (*Platycodon grandiflorum*)
Basket of gold (Alyssum saxatile)

Bearded iris (Iris)
Beard-tongue (Penstemon)
Bee balm (*Monarda didyma*)
Bellflower (*Campanula carpatica*)
Bishop's hat (*Epimedium grandiflorum*)
Blanket flower (*Gaillardia grandiflora*)
Bleeding heart (*Dicentra spectabilis*)
Blue flax (*Linum perenne*)
Blue marguerite (*Felicia amelloides*)
Blue salvia (*Salvia patens*)
Butterfly weed (*Asclepias tuberosa*)

Candytuft (*Iberis sempervirens*)
Chinese lantern (*Physalis alkekengi*)
Cinquefoil (*Potentilla atrosanguinea*)
Columbine, dwarf (*Aquilegia alpina*)
Common aubretia (*Aubretia deltoidea*)
Coneflower (*Rudbeckia hirta*)
Coral bells (*Heuchera sanguinea*)
Cranesbill (*Geranium grandiflorum*)
Crested iris (*Iris cristata*)

Daylily (Hemerocallis)
Dusty miller (*Centaurea gymnocarpa*)

English daisy (*Bellis perennis*)
Evening primrose (Oenothera)

False dragonhead (*Physostegia virginiana*)
Florists' chrysanthemum (*Chrysanthemum morifolium*)
Forget-me-not (*Myosotis sylvatica*)
Four-o'-clock (*Mirabilis jalapa*)
Foxglove (*Digitalis purpurea*)

Gas plant (*Dictamnus albus*)
Gayfeather (*Liatris pycnostachys*)
Geum (*Geum chiloense*)
Globe thistle (*Echinops exaltatus*)
Golden marguerite (*Anthemis tinctoria*)
Goldenrod (Solidago)
Grecian urn (*Acanthus mollis*)

Heartleaf bergenia (*Bergenia cordifolia*)
Helen's flower (Helenium)
Hollyhock (*Althaea rosea*)

Indian paintbrush (*Lobelia cardinalis*)

Japanese anemone (*Anemone japonica*)
Japanese iris (*Iris kaempferi*)

Lady Washington geranium (*Pelargonium domesticum*)
Lily-of-the-valley (*Convallaria majalis*)
Loosestrife (Lythrum)
Lupine (*Lupinus polyphyllus*)

Maiden pink (*Dianthus deltoides*)
Meadow sage (*Salvia paterns*)
Michaelmas daisy (aster, English)
Monkshood (*Aconitum anthora*)

Orange sunflower (Heliopsis)
Oriental poppy (*Papaver orientale*)

Painted daisy (*Chrysanthemum coccineum*)
Painted daisy (Pyrethrum)
Pasque flower (*Anemone pulsatilla*)
Peony (Paeonia)
Pincushion flower (*Scabiosa caucasica*)
Plantain lily (*Hosta plantaginea grandiflora*)
Poppy-flowered anemone (*Anemone coronaria*)
Prairie windflower (*Anemone pulsatilla*)

Sea lavender (*Limonium latifolium*)
Sea-pink (*Armeria maritima*)
Shasta daisy (*Chrysanthemum maximum*)
Siberian wallflower (*Erysimum asperum*)
Solomon's seal (*Polygonatum multiflorum*)
Speedwell (speedwell)

Statice (*Limonium latifolium*)
Stock (*Mathiola incana*)
Summer forget-me-not (*Anchusa capensis*)
Summer phlox (*Phlox paniculata*)
Sunflower (*Helianthus decapetalus multiflorus*)
Sweet rocket (*Hesperis matronalis*)
Sweet William (*Dianthus barbatus*)
Sweet William phlox (*Phlox divaricata*)

Thrift (*Armeria maritima*)
Tickseed (*Coreopsis grandiflora*)
Torch lily (Kniphofia)

Vesper iris (*Iris dichotoma*)
Virginia bluebell (*Mertensia virginica*)

Wall rock cress (*Arabis caucasica*)
Wax begonia (*Begonia semperflorens*)
Willow gentian (*Gentiana asclepiadea*)
Wormwood (*Artemesia albula*)
Wormwood, fringed (*Artemesia frigida*)

Yarrow (*Achillea*)
Yarrow (*Achillea ptarmica*)

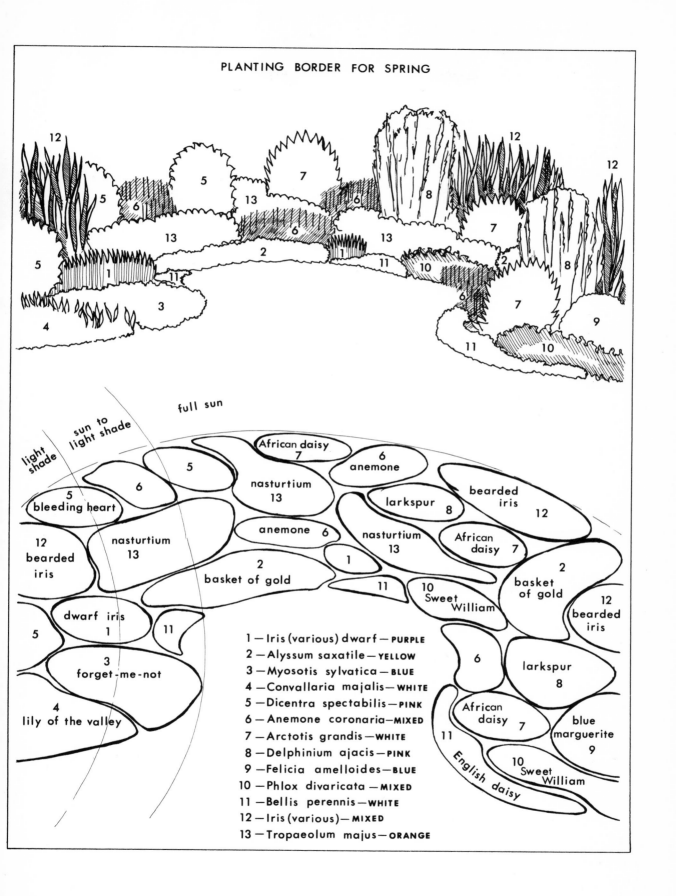

PLANTING BORDER FOR SPRING

full sun

sun to
light shade

light
shade

African daisy
7

5

6

6
anemone

5
bleeding heart

nasturtium
13

larkspur
8

bearded
iris
12

12
bearded
iris

nasturtium
13

anemone   6

2
basket of gold

1

nasturtium
13

African
daisy   7

2
basket
of gold

dwarf iris
1

11

11

10
Sweet
William

12
bearded
iris

5

11

6

larkspur
8

3
forget-me-not

4
lily of the valley

African
daisy   7

11

blue
marguerite
9

10
Sweet
William

English daisy

1 — Iris (various) dwarf — PURPLE
2 — Alyssum saxatile — YELLOW
3 — Myosotis sylvatica — BLUE
4 — Convallaria majalis — WHITE
5 — Dicentra spectabilis — PINK
6 — Anemone coronaria — MIXED
7 — Arctotis grandis — WHITE
8 — Delphinium ajacis — PINK
9 — Felicia amelloides — BLUE
10 — Phlox divaricata — MIXED
11 — Bellis perennis — WHITE
12 — Iris (various) — MIXED
13 — Tropaeolum majus — ORANGE

PLANTING BORDER FOR SUMMER

1—Althaea rosea—PINK
2—Paeonia (various)—ROSE
3—Gypsophila paniculata—WHITE
4—Tagetes erecta—ORANGE
5—Portulaca grandiflora—MIXED
6—Tagetes patula—YELLOW
7—Zinnia elegans—MIXED
8—Lobularia maritima—WHITE
9—Centaurea cyanus—BLUE
10—Salpiglossis sinuata—MIXED

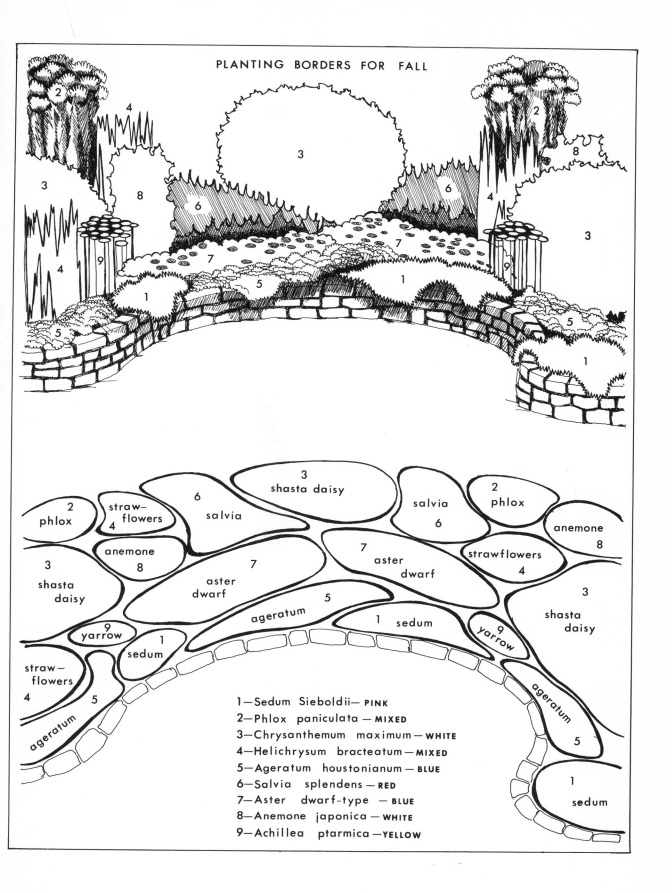

PLANTING BORDERS FOR FALL

1—Sedum Sieboldii— PINK
2—Phlox paniculata — MIXED
3—Chrysanthemum maximum—WHITE
4—Helichrysum bracteatum—MIXED
5—Ageratum houstonianum — BLUE
6—Salvia splendens — RED
7—Aster dwarf-type — BLUE
8—Anemone japonica — WHITE
9—Achillea ptarmica —YELLOW

CHAPTER 14

Annuals

An annual is a plant that produces flowers, matures, and dies in one year. It provides quick color with abundant bloom the same year the plants are put into the ground. Annuals are inexpensive and offer a great deal of satisfaction for gardeners; it is impossible to resist them. Most of them are prolific bloomers that merely have to be set into the ground to give you bountiful color for many months. How can you beat a harvest of petunias that requires little more than water?

Since most annuals are bright and colorful and generally easy to grow, they are indispensable in the garden. During the summer, calendulas, sweet peas, and Chinese asters can glorify the garden (and they also make excellent cut flowers). But with all their desirable traits, if you want color in the garden all year, you will need other plants. Remember that annuals flower only once.

GROWING PLANTS

These plants need as much sun as they can get. In shade, they grow leggy and do not bloom readily. They are not fussy about soil as long as it has some complete fertilizer in it. Some annuals, nasturtiums, for example, are self-sowing. They shed their ripened seed on the ground where they either germinate that year or the following spring. Some plants grown as annuals in severe winter climates are really frost-tender perennials. These include wax begonias, coleus, and others.

Annuals, already growing, are available at nurseries during their season. The most economical purchase is plants that are just showing leafy rosettes. They are ready to go into the ground to mature and bloom. Often it is a good idea to leave the plants in their flats for a few days and gradually accustom them to wind and sun.

To remove annuals from flats, cut them apart like wedges of cake with soil around the roots. Place them in predug holes, firm the soil, and water well. If they are in peat pots with bands of peat, plant them as they are. Do not remove the bands. The idea is to get the plants into the ground without disturbing the roots.

Starting annuals from seed assures you a great harvest of flowers. Packets of seeds are one of the few inexpensive things left in today's society. Once the seeds are sown, you'll have more plants than you know what to do with. Many annuals are seeds sown where they are to grow as soon as the soil is workable, while other annuals which do not tolerate frost are either seeded in cold frames or hotbeds and transplanted later when weather is suitable. With indoor seedlings, harden them off gradually because an abrupt change of temperature and sun is likely to kill them. They need to be acclimated gradually.

PLANTING SEEDS OUTDOORS

The bed for annual seeds should contain good humusy soil. After this is accomplished, rake the surface until all lumps are broken and the soil is almost smooth. Small seeds are scattered on the soil and then sprinkled over with topsoil. Tamp the soil down in place so that seeds will be able to absorb moisture necessary for germination. Large seeds are planted deeper, anywhere from 1/2 to 1 inch, depending on the girth of the seed.

Once seedlings start appearing, they must be thinned so that there is room for them to grow. This is extremely important. Pull the unwanted seedlings;

I usually put them in containers for pot plant decoration rather than discarding them. The distance allowed between the seedlings in the bed depends on the size and habit of the plants (see Table 11).

Sowing seeds outdoors depends upon your climate and the annuals themselves. Some like coolness, others need warmth, and many are just not particular. Generally it is safe to start seeds after the last frost in your region.

LISTS OF ANNUALS

There are so very many annuals it would be impossible to list all of them. Here, I have included the most popular. Additional annuals and varieties can be found in garden catalogs. The plant list is arranged by botanical name rather than common name, which can be confusing. However, common name listings are also included at the end of the section.

Table 11. General List of Annuals

Botanical and Common Name	Approx. Height in Inches	Range of Colors	Peak Bloom Season	Sun or Shade
Ageratum houstonianum (floss flower)	4 to 22 PD* 12″	Blue, pink, white	Summer, fall	Sun or shade
Amaranthus caudatus (love-lies-bleeding)	36 to 84 PD 18″	Red tassel-like flower spikes	Summer	Sun
Amaranthus tricolor (Joseph's coat)	12 to 48 PD 18″	Bronzy-green crown; foliage marked cream and red	Summer	Sun
Anchusa capensis (summer forget-me-not)	12 to 18 PD 6″ to 9″	Blue with white throat	Summer	Light shade, sun
Antirrhinum majus (snapdragon)	10 to 48 PD 10″ to 18″	Large choice of color, flower form	Late spring and fall; summer where cool	Sun
Arctotis stoechadifolia grandis (African daisy)	16 to 24 PD 10″	Yellow, rust, pink, white	Early spring	Sun
Begonia semperflorens (wax begonia)	6 to 18 PD 6″ to 8″	White, pink, deep-rose; single, double	All summer; perennial in temperate climate	Sun or shade
Browallia americana	12 to 24 PD 6″ to 9″	Violet, blue, white	Summer	Sun
Calendula officinalis (calendula or pot marigold)	12 to 24 PD 12″ to 15″	Cream, yellow, orange, apricot	Winter where mild; late spring elsewhere	Sun
Callistephus chinensis (aster or China aster)	12 to 36 PD 10″	Lavender-blue, white, pink, rose, crimson	Late spring where mild; late summer elsewhere	Sun
Catharanthus roseus (Vinca rosea) (Madagascar periwinkle)	6 to 24 PD 12″	White, pink; some with contrasting eye	Summer until early fall	Sun or light shade
Celosia 'Plumosa' (plume cockscomb)	12 to 36 PD 6″ to 12″	Pink, red-gold, yellow	Summer through fall except where very hot	Sun or light shade
Centaurea cyanus (bachelor's button or cornflower)	12 to 30 PD 12″	Blue, pink, wine, white	Spring where mild; summer elsewhere	Sun
Clarkia amoena (godetia) (farewell-to-spring)	18 to 30 PD 9″	Mostly mixed colors; white, pink, salmon, lavender	Late spring; summer where cold	Sun or shade
Clarkia unguiculata (mountain garland)	12 to 48 PD 9″	White, pink, rose, crimson, purple, salmon	Late spring to summer	Sun

* PD = planting distance.

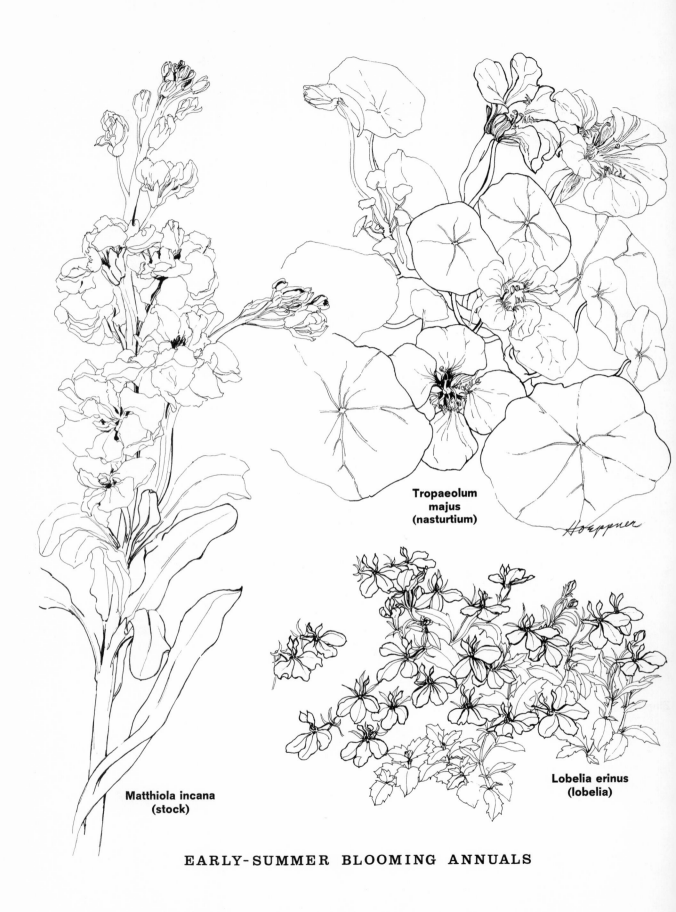

Tropaeolum
majus
(nasturtium)

Hoeppner

Matthiola incana
(stock)

Lobelia erinus
(lobelia)

EARLY-SUMMER BLOOMING ANNUALS

**Tagetes patula
(French marigold)**

Zinnia elegans

**Helichrysum bracteatum
(strawflower)**

Hoeppner

SUMMER-BLOOMING ANNUALS

Table 11 *(Continued)*

Botanical and Common Name	Approx. Height in Inches	Range of Colors	Peak Bloom Season	Sun or Shade
Coleus blumei (coleus)	12 to 30 PD* 9″ to 12″	Grown for its variegated leaves	Midsummer through early fall	Partial shade
Coreopsis tinctoria (calliopsis)	8 to 30 PD 18″ to 24″	Yellow, orange, maroon, and splashed bicolors	Late spring to summer; late summer where cool	Sun
Cosmos bipinnatus (cosmos)	48 to 72 PD 12″ to 15″	White, pink, lavender, rose, purple	All summer	Sun
Delphinium ajacis (larkspur)	18 to 60 PD 9″	Blue, pink, lavender, rose, salmon, carmine, white	Late spring to early summer	Sun
Dianthus species (pinks)	6 to 30 PD 4″ to 6″	Mostly bicolors of white, pink, lavender, purple	Spring, fall; winters where mild	Sun
Dimorphotheca pluvialis *Dimorphotheca sinuata* (African daisy, Cape marigold)	4 to 16 PD 12″ to 18″	White, yellow, orange, salmon	Winter where mild; summer elsewhere	Sun
Eschscholzia californica (California poppy)	12 to 24 PD 9″	Gold, yellow, orange; 'Mission Bell' varieties include pink, rose	Winter and spring in mild climates	Sun
Gaillardia pulchella (rose-ring Gaillardia)	12 to 24 PD 9″	Zoned patterns in warm shades; wine, maroon	All summer	Sun
Godetia amoena (See *Clarkia amoena*)				
Gomphrena globosa (globe-amaranth)	9 to 36 PD 12″	White, crimson, violet, pink	All summer; heat resistant	Sun
Gypsophila elegans (baby's breath)	12 to 30 PD 6″	White, rose, pink	Early summer to fall, but of short duration	Sun
Helianthus annuus (sunflower)	36 to 120 or more PD 3″	Yellow, orange, mahogany, or yellow with black centers	Summer	Sun
Helichrysum bracteatum (strawflower)	24 to 48 PD 9″ to 12″	Mixed warm shades; yellow, bronze, orange, pink, white	Late summer; fall	Sun
Iberis amara (rocket candytuft)	12 to 15 PD 12″	White	Late spring	Sun
Iberis umbellata (globe candytuft)	12 to 18 PD 16″	Pastel pink, lavender, rose, lilac, salmon, white	Late spring	Sun
Impatiens balsamina (balsam)	8 to 30 PD 9″	White, pink, rose, red	Summer to fall	Light shade, sun where cool
Impatiens walleriana Impatiens	6 to 24 PD 9″	Scarlet, mauve, coral, magenta, purple, pink, white	Summer through early fall	Light shade
Lathyrus odoratus (sweet pea, winter flowering)	36 to 72 climber PD* 6″	Mixed or separate colors; all except yellow, orange, and green	Late winter where mild. Not heat resistant	Sun

* PD = planting distance.

Table 11 (Continued)

Botanical and Common Name	Approx. Height in Inches	Range of Colors	Peak Bloom Season	Sun or Shade
Lathyrus odoratus (sweet pea, summer)	Same (new low grow-ing bedding varieties are available) PD 6″	Same	Spring where mild; early summer else-where. Some-what heat resistant	Sun
Limonium bonduellii *Limonium sinuatum* (statice, sea-lavender)	18 to 30 PD 15″	Blue, rose, lavender, yellow, bicolors with white	Summer	Sun
Linum grandiflorum 'Rubrum' (scarlet flax)	12 to 18 PD 9″	Scarlet to deep red, rose	Late spring and fall	Sun
Lobelia erinus (lobelia)	2 to 6 PD 6″ to 8″	Blue, violet, pink, white	Summer	Sun, light shade
Lobularia maritima (alyssum, sweet)	4 to 12 PD 12″	White, purple, lavender, rosy-pink	Year-round where mild; spring to fall elsewhere	Sun, light shade
Lupinus hartwegii (lupine, annual)	18 to 36 PD 12″ to 18″	Blue, white	Early summer	Sun, light shade
Mathiola incana (stock)	12 to 36 PD 9″ to 12″	White, cream, yellow, pink, rose, crimson-red, purple	Winter where mild; late spring elsewhere	Sun
Mirabilis jalapa (four-o'-clock)	36 to 48 PD 12″	Red, yellow, pink, white; some with markings	All summer	Light shade or full sun
Molucella laevis (bells of Ireland)	18 to 30 PD 9″ to 12″	Green, bell-like bracts resembling flowers	Summer	Sun
Myosotis sylvatica (forget-me-not)	6 to 12 PD 6″ to 9″	Blue with white eye	Spring, late fall	Light shade or dappled
Nemesia strumosa (nemesia)	10 to 18 PD 9″	All colors except green	Spring where mild; early summer else-where	Sun
Nicotiana alata *Nicotiana sanderae* (flowering tobacco)	18 to 48 PD 12″	Greenish-white, crimson, magenta	Summer	Light shade, or sun
Nigella damascena (love-in-a-mist)	12 to 30 PD 9″	Blue, white, rose-pink	Spring	Sun
Papaver rhoeas (Shirley poppy)	24 to 60 PD 12″	Red, pink, white, scarlet, salmon, bicolors	Late spring	Sun
Petunia hybrids	12 to 24 PD 6″ to 12″	All colors except true blue, yellow and orange	Summer and fall	Sun
Phlox drummondii (annual phlox)	6 to 18 PD 6″ to 9″	Numerous bicolors. All shades except blue, gold	Late spring to fall	Sun, light shade
Physalis alkekengi (Chinese lantern)	12 to 24 PD 6″ to 12″	White flowers; orange bracts	Late summer	Sun or shade
Portulaca grandiflora (rose moss)	4 to 8 PD 6″	Satiny red-purple, cerise, rose-pink, white, orange, yellow	Summer	Sun
Reseda odorata (mignonette)	8 to 18 PD 12″	Greenish-brown clusters	Late spring to fall	Sun

* PD = planting distance.

Table 11 (Continued)

Botanical and Common Name	Approx. Height in Inches	Range of Colors	Peak Bloom Season	Sun or Shade
Salpiglossis sinuata (painted tongue)	18 to 36 PD* 9″	Bizarre patterns of red, orange, yellow, pink, purple	Early summer	Sun, light shade
Salvia splendens (scarlet sage)	10 to 36 PD 18″	Bright-red, rose, lavender-pink	Summer and fall	Sun
Scabiosa atropurpurea (pincushion flower)	24 to 36 PD 12″	Purple, blue, mahogany, white, rose	Summer	Sun
Schizanthus pinnatus (butterfly flower)	10 to 18 PD 9″ to 12″	White, rose, purple-spotted	Spring	Light shade
Tagetes erecta (hybrids and species) (African or American marigold)	10 to 48 PD 12″ to 18″	Mostly yellow, tangerine, and gold	Generally, all summer	Sun
Tagetes patula (hybrids and species) (French marigold)	6 to 18 PD 9″	Same as African types; and also russet, mahogany, and bicolors	Early summer	Sun
Tagetes tenuifolia signata (signet marigold)	10 to 24 PD 9″ to 12″	Small; yellow, orange	Generally, all summer	Sun
Tithonia rotundifolia (Mexican sunflower)	72 to 100 PD 30″	Orange	Summer	Sun
Trachymene caerulea (blue lace flower)	18 to 24 PD 9″	Blue to violet-blue	Late spring, early summer	Sun
Tropaeolum majus (nasturtium)	12 to 18 Some spread vigorously PD 12″ to 15″	White, pink, crimson, orange, maroon, yellow	Spring and fall; summer where cool	Sun or shade
Verbena hybrida (*hortensis*) (garden verbena)	6 to 12 PD 9″ to 12″	Bright pink, scarlet, blue, purple, some bicolors	Summer	Sun
Viola tricolor hortensis (pansy)	6 to 8 PD 9″	"Faces" in white, yellow, purple, rose, mahogany, violet, apricot	Spring and fall; winter where mild	Sun, light shade
Zinnia angustifolia (Mexican zinnia)	12 to 18 PD 6″ to 9″	Yellow, orange, white, maroon, mahogany	Summer	Sun
Zinnia elegans (small-flowered zinnia)	8 to 36 PD 9″	Red, orange, yellow, purple, lavender, pink, white	Summer	Sun
Zinnia elegans (giant-flowered zinnia)	12 to 36 PD 12″	Same colors as small-flowered zinnia	Summer	Sun

* PD = planting distance.

Annuals for Cut Flowers

Amaranthus caudatus (love-lies-bleeding)
Antirrhinum (snapdragon)
Arctotis stoechadifolia grandis (African daisy)
Calendula officinalis (pot marigold)
Clarkia
Delphinium ajacis (larkspur)
Dimorphotheca (various) (Cape marigold)
Lathyrus odoratus (sweet pea)
Nigella damascena (love-in-a-mist)
Reseda odorata (mignonette)
Salpiglossis sinuata (painted tongue)
Tagetes (marigold)
Zinnia elegans (zinnia)

Annuals for Dry Places

Arctotis stoechadifolia grandis (African daisy)
Coreopsis tinctoria (calliopsis)
Dimorphotheca (various) (Cape marigold)
Helianthus annuus (sunflower)
Mirabilis jalapa (four-o'-clock)
Phlox drummondii (annual phlox)

Annuals for Dry Places (*Continued*)

Portulaca grandiflora (rose moss)
Salvia splendens (scarlet sage)
Zinnia elegans (zinnia)

Annuals for Poor Soil

Amaranthus caudatus (love-lies-bleeding)
Browallia americana (browallia)
Calendula officinalis (marigold)
Celosia 'Plumosa' (plume cockscomb)
Clarkia amoena (farewell-to-spring)
Coreopsis tinctoria (calliopsis)
Eschscholzia californica (California poppy)
Gaillardia pulchella
Impatiens balsamina (balsam)
Mirabilis jalapa (four-o'-clock)
Papaver rhoeas (Shirley poppy)
Portulaca grandiflora (rose moss)
Tropaeolum majus (nasturtium)

Annuals for Edging

Ageratum (various)
Antirrhinum (dwarf kinds) (snapdragon)
Celosia (various) (cockscomb)
Dianthus (various)
Eschscholzia californica (California poppy)
Iberis umbellata (globe candytuft)
Petunia (various) (petunia)
Tagetes (various) (dwarf marigold)
Tropaeolum majus (nasturtium)
Verbena (various) (verbena)

Annuals for Background Planting

Amaranthus caudatus (love-lies-bleeding)
Celosia (various) (cockscomb)
Cosmos bipinnatus (cosmos)
Delphinium ajacis (larkspur)
Helianthus annuus (sunflower)
Nicotiana (various) (flowering tobacco)
Salvia splendens (scarlet sage)
Tagetes (various) (marigold)
Zinnia elegans (zinnia)

Fragrant Annuals

Antirrhinum majus (snapdragon)
Delphinium ajacis (larkspur)
Dianthus chinensis (Chinese pink)
Iberis umbellata (globe candytuft)
Lathyrus odoratus (sweet pea)
Mathiola incana (stock)
Nicotiana (flowering tobacco)
Phlox drummondii (annual phlox)
Scabiosa atropurpurea (pincushion flower)
Tropaeolum majus (nasturtium)

Verbena (various) (verbena)
Viola tricolor hortensis (pansy)

Annuals by Common Name

African daisy (*Arctotis stoechadifolia grandis*)
African daisy (Dimorphotheca)

Balsam (*Impatiens balsamina*)
Baby's breath (*Gypsophila elegans*)
Bachelor's button (*Centaurea cyanus*)
Bells of Ireland (*Molucella laevis*)
Blue lace flower (*Trachymene caerulea*)
Butterfly flower (*Schizanthus pinnatus*)

Calendula (*Calendula officinalis*)
California poppy (*Eschscholzia californica*)
Calliopsis (*Coreopsis tinctoria*)
Candytuft (Iberis)
Cape marigold (Dimorphotheca)
China aster (*Callistephus chinensis*)
Chinese lantern (*Physalis alkekengi*)
Coleus (*Coleus blumei*)
Cornflower (*Centaurea cyanus*)
Cosmos (*Cosmos bipinnatus*)

Farewell to spring (*Clarkia amoena*)
Flowering tobacco (*Nicotiana alata*)
Four-o'-clock (*Mirabilis jalapa*)
Forget-me-not (*Myosotis sylvatica*)

Globe amaranth (*Gomphrena globosa*)
Globe candytuft (*Iberis umbellata*)

Joseph's coat (*Amaranthus tricolor*)

Larkspur (*Delphinium ajacis*)
Lobelia (*Lobelia erinus*)
Love-in-a-mist (*Nigella damascena*)
Love-lies-bleeding (*Amaranthus caudatus*)
Lupine, annual (*Lupinus hartwegii*)

Madagascar periwinkle (*Catharanthus roseus*)
Marigold, African (*Tagetes erecta*)
Marigold, French (*Tagetes patula*)
Marigold, signet (*Tagetes tenuifolia signata*)
Mexican sunflower (*Tithonia rotundifolia*)
Mignonette (*Reseda odorata*)
Mountain garland (*Clarkia unguiculata*)

Nasturtium (*Tropaeolum majus*)
Nemesia (*Nemesia strumosa*)

Painted tongue (*Salpiglossis sinuata*)
Pansy (*Viola tricolor hortensis*)
Petunia (*Petunia*)
Phlox, annual (*Phlox drummondii*)

Annuals by Common Name (*Continued*)

Pincushion flower (*Scabiosa atropurpurea*)
Pinks (Dianthus)
Plume cockscomb (*Celosia plumosa*)
Poppy, shirley (*Papaver rhoeas*)
Pot marigold (*Calendula officinalis*)

Rocket candytuft (*Iberis amara*)

Scarlet flax (*Linum grandiflorum* 'Rubrum')
Scarlet sage (*Salvia splendens*)
Snapdragon (*Antirrhinum*)
Statice (*Limonium*)
Stock (*Mathiola incana*)
Strawflower (*Helichrysum bracteatum*)
Summer forget-me-not (*Anchusa capensis*)

Sunflower (*Helianthus annuus*)
Sweet alyssum (*Lobularia maritima*)
Sweet pea, summer (*Lathyrus odoratus*)
Sweet pea, winter (*Lathyrus odoratus*)

Touch-me-not (*Impatiens balsamina*)

Verbena, garden (Verbena)

Wax begonia (*Begonia semperflorens*)

Zinnia, giant-flowered (*Zinnia elegans*)
Zinnia, Mexican (*Zinnia angustifolia*)
Zinnia, small-flowered (*Zinnia elegans*)

CHAPTER 15

Bulbs, Corms, Tubers

For the gardener who wants early spring color, fall is planting time, for it is then that most of the dependable bulbs—crocus, narcissus, snowdrops—are put in the ground. This is a wealth of beauty for little effort. Bulbs are planted and covered, and that is that—no weeding, no pruning, and generally no battle with the bugs.

Later in the fall, tulips, hyacinths, and scillas are planted, and following them are the summer-flowering bulbs planted in spring, fall bulbs, and some that even bloom in winter in temperate climates. In other words, it is possible to have some kind of bulb blooming in the garden almost all year. No need to stop with the popular spring kinds, beautiful though they may be; but also include callas and cannas, dahlias and gladiolus, for summer color.

Mail-order suppliers and growers' catalogs list all plants with fleshy counterparts under the term bulbs. Actually, this catch-all category includes bulbs, corms, tubers, and rhizomes. But no matter how you define these plants, the makings for the flowers are already in the bulbs, and all you do is plant them.

Many of the most beautiful bulb flowers are winter hardy and are left in the ground year after year. They need cold weather to grow; others must be planted and lifted each year. The life-cycle of a bulb can be stated as (1) blooming, (2) foliage growth, which is stored in the bulb, and (3) the resting period.

PLANTING BULBS

Basically, all bulbs need a moisture-retentive but rapid-draining soil of high organic matter. They do not grow as well in clay soil, and few of them thrive in sandy soil. Dig holes for bulbs with caution; they should be round holes with a concave bottom rather than pointed holes that leave an air pocket below the bulb. There is some confusion among gardeners about which end of the bulb goes into the ground and how deep to plant it. A 3-inch depth means that the bulb has its top, not its bottom, 3 inches below the ground level. Plant the growing side up; in most cases, this is the pointed end or the one that is showing growth. Firm the soil over the bulb; do not leave it loose. Many gardeners make this common mistake that can easily be avoided with a few minutes' more time.

When you buy bulbs, purchase top-quality ones from reputable dealers; avoid bargains. Actually, you are buying an unseen product and you must trust the dealer to give you healthy, robust bulbs that will bloom for years rather than tired bulbs that may come up without flowers (blind).

For the most part bulbous plants can live off their own storehouse of food for some time, but they should not be neglected when they are in active growth. Water them regularly from the time they start growing and after the flowers have faded. Then taper off watering gradually rather than abruptly. Dormant bulbs do not need any more water than natural conditions provide for them. Spring bulbs can be fertilized once a season (I do not do this but some growers recommend it). Summer bulbs can and should be fertilized as soon as growth appears and again in the few weeks before they bloom. Use a balanced feeding mix with a low nitrogen content.

LISTS OF BULBS

Spring-flowering Bulbs

Spring-blooming bulbs are the most popular because they give early color and are easy to manage.

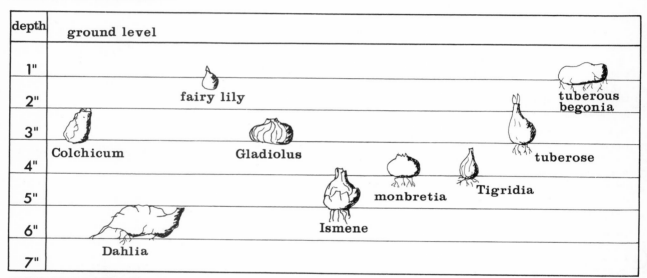

depth	ground level				
1"					
2"					
3"	Chionodoxa	Crocus	grape hyacinth	Scilla	snowdrop
4"					
5"		hyacinth			
6"					tulip
7"	daffodil		lily		

SPRING-FLOWERING

depth	ground level				
1"					tuberous begonia
2"	fairy lily				
3"	Colchicum	Gladiolus			tuberose
4"				Tigridia	
5"			monbretia		
6"	Dahlia	Ismene			
7"					

SUMMER-FLOWERING

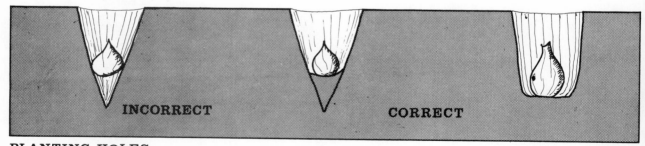

INCORRECT   CORRECT

PLANTING HOLES

ADRIÁN MARTÍNEZ

Bulbs, Corms & Tubers

① DIG UP AFTER LEAVES
   WILT; CUT OFF

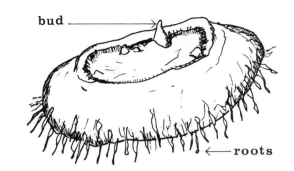

bud ———

←— roots

tuber

② STORE LOOSELY IN
   COOL DRY PLACE

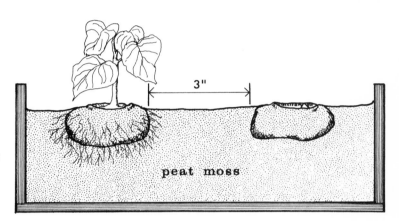

3"

peat moss

③ START INSIDE IN DAMP
   PEAT MOSS; TRANSPLANT
   WHEN 4 LEAVES SPROUT

starting in flats

④ OR, PLANT DIRECTLY
   IN LOAMY SOIL IN
   SEMISHADE

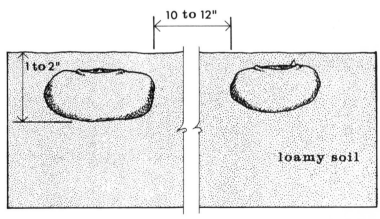

10 to 12"

1 to 2"

loamy soil

planting in ground

ADRIÁN MARTÍNEZ

Storing & Planting Tuberous Begonias

① DIG UP WHEN LEAVES
START TO TURN BROWN,
DO NOT CUT OFF

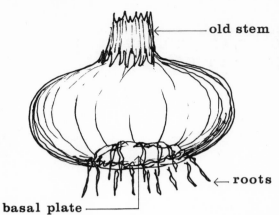

old stem

roots

basal plate

single corm

② STORE IN COOL AIRY
PLACE FOR 8 WEEKS
UNTIL DRY

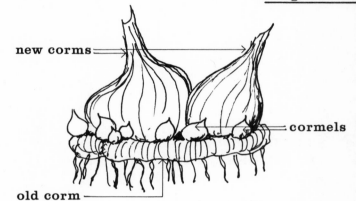

new corms

cormels

③ CUT OLD STEMS, DUST
CORMS & STORE IN
DRY PEAT MOSS, SAND,
ETC.

old corm

④ PLANT AS SHOWN IN
WELL-DRAINED SOIL,
6" APART

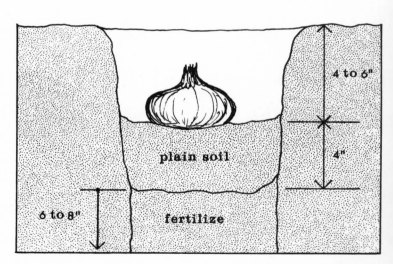

4 to 6"

plain soil

4"

6 to 8"

fertilize

planting depth

ADRIÁN MARTÍNEZ

Storing & Planting Gladiolus

1. AFTER DIGGING UP, LET DRY FOR A FEW HOURS

2. STORE IN DRY PEAT MOSS, SAND, VERMICULITE, ETC.

clump of tubers

3. EACH CUT TUBER SHOULD INCLUDE PART OF THE OLD STEM & AN "EYE"

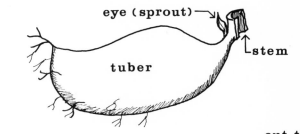

eye (sprout)

stem

tuber

4. PLANT AS SHOWN IN WELL-DRAINED SOIL; WATER

cut tuber

5. KEEP COVERING THE SPROUT AS IT GROWS TO THE SURFACE

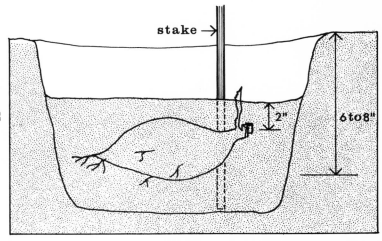

stake

2"

6 to 8"

ADRIÁN MARTÍNEZ

planting depth

Storing & Planting Dahlias

They are classified as spring bulbs because they bear color in late winter or very early spring. They are left in the ground all year, and are called hardy bulbs. However, some bulbs hardy in one climate may not be hardy in another climate. With two exceptions (winter aconite and dogtooth violet that are planted at the end of August or early September), spring bulbs are put in the ground from September until the ground freezes.

With spring bulbs, remember that after they bloom, the foliage must ripen for several weeks. Do not cut off the leaves, or the bulb will not be able to regain strength that went into growing and blooming. If you object to the unsightly foliage fold it over and put a rubber band around it to keep it neat.

See Table 12 for a list of spring-flowering bulbs.

Summer-flowering Bulbs

Generally, in most of the United States, summer-flowering bulbs must be dug up in fall and stored over winter. They can be left in the ground only if the temperature does not go below freezing. Most of these bulbs are planted outdoors after all danger of frost is past. However, some such as tuberous begonias and agapanthus can be started indoors and then transplanted to the garden later.

When foliage dies down in fall, dig up summer bulbs and let them dry off in an airy place. If there is foliage, cut it off to about 5 inches. Remove all dirt from the bulbs and store them in a dry, cool place (50F) in boxes of dry sand or peat or on open trays or in brown paper bags.

See Table 13 for a list of summer-flowering bulbs.

Table 12. Spring-flowering Bulbs

Botanical and Common Name	When to Plant	Depth in Inches	Sun or Shade	Remarks
Allium (flowering onion)	Fall	3	Sun	Prettier than you think
Crocus	Fall	3	Sun	Always dependable
Chionodoxa (glory of snow)	Fall	3	Sun	Do not disturb for several years
Daffodil (jonquil, narcissus)	Fall	6	Sun	The name daffodil is used for all members
Eranthis (winter aconite)	Early fall	3	Shade	Very early bloom
Erythronium (dogtooth violet)	Early fall	6	Shade	Good for naturalizing
Fritillaria	Fall	4	Shade	Overlooked but lovely
Galanthus (snowdrop)	Fall	3	Shade	Blooms while snow is on ground
Hyacinthus (hyacinth)	Fall	6–8	Sun	Protect from wind and mice
Leucojum (snowflake)	Fall	3	Shade	Flowers last a long time
Muscari (grape hyacinth)	Early fall	3	Sun	Easy to grow
Scilla	Fall	2	Sun or light shade	Once established, blooms indefinitely
Tulipa* (tulip)				

* See "Additional Comments on Bulbs."

Table 13. Summer-flowering Bulbs

Botanical and Common Name	Depth in Inches	Sun or Shade	Remarks
Agapanthus (flower-of-the-Nile)	1	Sun	New dwarf varieties available
Alstroemeria	4	Sun	Good cut flowers
Begonia (tuberous)*			
Caladium	4	Shade	Lovely foliage plants; many varieties

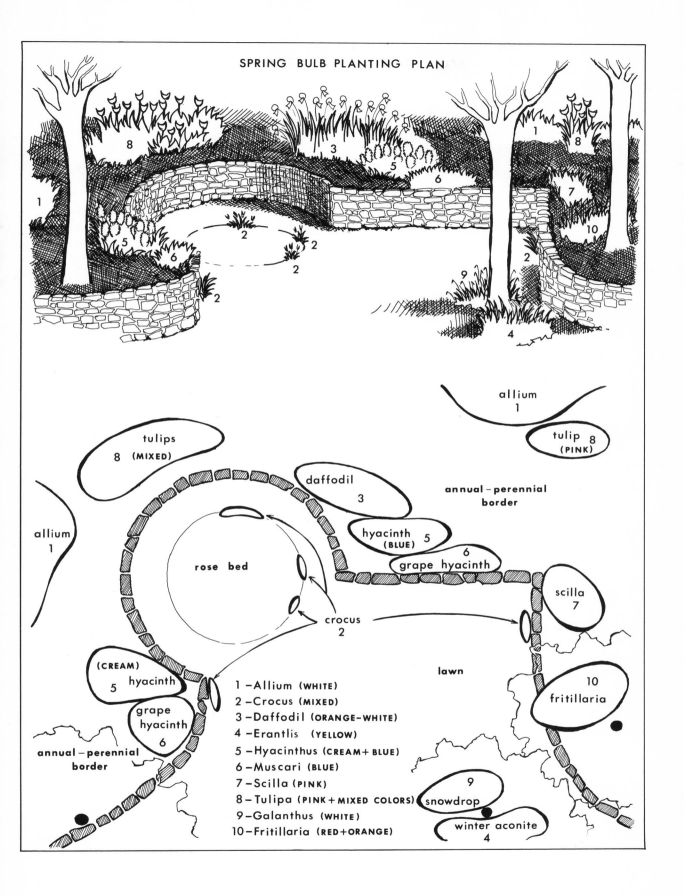

SPRING BULB PLANTING PLAN

allium
1

tulip 8
(PINK)

tulips
8 (MIXED)

daffodil
3

annual – perennial
border

hyacinth
(BLUE) 5

grape hyacinth 6

scilla
7

allium
1

rose bed

crocus
2

10
fritillaria

(CREAM)
5 hyacinth

lawn

grape
hyacinth
6

1 – Allium (WHITE)
2 – Crocus (MIXED)
3 – Daffodil (ORANGE-WHITE)
4 – Erantlis (YELLOW)
5 – Hyacinthus (CREAM + BLUE)
6 – Muscari (BLUE)
7 – Scilla (PINK)
8 – Tulipa (PINK + MIXED COLORS)
9 – Galanthus (WHITE)
10 – Fritillaria (RED + ORANGE)

annual – perennial
border

9
snowdrop

winter aconite
4

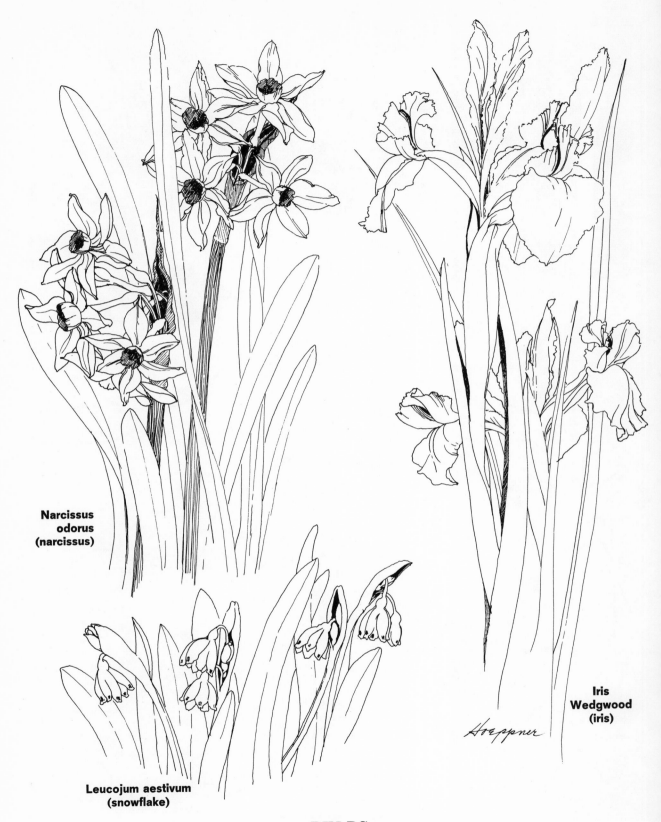

**Narcissus
odorus
(narcissus)**

**Leucojum aestivum
(snowflake)**

**Iris
Wedgwood
(iris)**

Hoeppner

BULBS

Hyacinth   Narcissus   Tulip

BULBS

Table 13 (Continued)

Botanical and Common Name	Depth in Inches	Sun or Shade	Remark
Canna	2	Sun	Showy flowers; lift bulbs after frost kills tops
Dahlia*			
Galtonia (summer hyacinth)	6	Sun	Buy new bulbs yearly
Gladiolus* (gladiola)			
Iris*			
Lilium* (lily)			
Polianthus tuberosa (Tuberose)	1	Sun	Plant after danger of frost
Sprekelia formosissima (Jacobean lily)	3	Sun	Good in pots
Ranunculus	1	Sun	Lovely colorful flowers
Tigridia (tiger flower)	2–3	Sun	Plant in early May
Tritonia (montbretia)	2–3	Sun	Plant in early May
Zephyranthes (zephyr lily)	1	Sun or light shade	Plant after danger of frost

* See "Additional Comments on Bulbs."

Additional Comments on Bulbs

The following information is to supplement data already given on bulbs in this chapter. Here you will find general growing instructions on the more popular bulbous type plants to help you understand their needs.

GLADIOLUS (gladiola). Popular garden plants because they seem to grow in any soil without too much attention, but they do need sun. Plants grow quickly, are dependable, and bear flowers 10 to 12 weeks after planting. There are tall varieties and charming small ones in a wide selection of color. When freezing weather is over, plant the corms 4 to 6 inches deep and about 6 inches apart in a well-cultivated deep bed (at least 15 inches). Keep plants moist; gladioluses can take copious watering. When buds appear between the leaves, use a complete fertilizer. In fall, dig up and store the corms if you are in a cold climate; in mild climates they can remain in the ground. When the foliage turns brown, cut off the tops, then dry the bulbs in an airy, shady place for a few weeks. You will see new corms on top of the old dried withered ones; store the new corms in paper sacks in a dark place at about 45F to 50F until planting time.

G. coviellei. Baby gladiolus; flowers white, pink, red, or lilac. Loose spikes on 18-inch stems.

G. hybrida. Common garden type with wide color range; many varieties.

G. primulinus. Tropical African species with yellow flowers.

G. trista. Small with 2- to 3-inch yellow flowers, purple-veined.

LILIUM (lily). Lilies are synonomous with grace and beauty, and in recent years hybridists have given us some stellar plants. Easy to grow, lilies may be left undisturbed for years while they increase in display. As soon as you get bulbs—and buy the best you can afford—plant them, whether it is spring or fall. Give them a rich neutral soil—neither too acid nor too alkaline—that drains readily. Sun is necessary for a bountiful crop of flowers, and thorough soakings bring lilies to perfection. Plant lilies at a depth of 3 times the height of the bulb; use 3 to 5 bulbs to a group, with tall varieties in the rear, and low-growers in the middle and front of a planting arrangement. Do not be concerned if plants do not bloom profusely the first year; they are at their best the second and third years. Eventually, the plants must be lifted and divided; do this about 4 weeks after they bloom and then replant the bulbs after a reasonable length of time. Exposure naturally weakens them. Before or during the blooming season, a light feeding with a 5–10–5 or similar type commercial fertilizer is beneficial, but do not overdo it. While lilies may have their pests and disease problems, it is nothing drastic, and a regular spraying or dusting program with appropriate insecticide will be necessary. Of more concern are mice. They love the bulbs, so if rodents are prevalent in your area, place the bulbs in hardware cloth or put them in pots.

At its peak bloom, this lovely spring bulb garden has hundreds of
tulips against a natural woodsy scene.
(Molly Adams)

There are several ways to increase lilies; the easiest is just to divide the established bulbs. Or use the scale method; that is, remove 4 or 5 outside thick scales of old bulbs at replanting time. Then put the scales in trenches about 4 inches deep and cover them with sand.

L. auratum (goldband lily). Flowers waxy white and fragrant, with spots and golden bands on each segment. August or September bloom.

L. candidum (Madonna lily). Beautiful white, fragrant blooms; plants die after flowering but make new growth in autumn.

L. longifolium (Easter lily). Fragrant, trumpet-shape flowers on short stems. Several varieties. Not for severe climates.

Aurelian hybrids. June and July flowering; colors range from white to yellow, with many orange shades. Grow 3 to 6 feet tall.

Bellingham hybrids. Yellow or orange or orange-red flowers spotted reddish-brown. June and July bloom.

Fiesta hybrids. A vigorous group of sun-loving lilies that bloom in July with nodding flowers. Colors range from mahogany and amber to red and burgundy to lemon-yellow.

Harlequin hybrids. Wide-open flowers in a color range from ivory-white through lilac to violet and purple. Plants grow to 5 feet and bloom in July.

Martagon hybrids. Many flowers to a stem; color range includes yellow, orange, lilac, tangerine, purple, and mahogany.

Olympic hybrids. Trumpet-shaped flowers in a gamut of colors—white, cream, yellow, pink, shaded on the outside with greenish brown. July and August bloom. Grow 6 feet tall.

Oriental hybrids. Mammoth flowers with segments in white or red, often banded with gold or red and spotted deep-red. Sweetly scented; August and September flowers.

TULIPA (tulip). If you think tulips are anything like they were even a few years ago, you are in for a surprise. There are many new varieties, and the tulip has climbed from an ordinary flower to an extraordinary one. There are parrot kinds, fringed ones, tall ones, small ones, cottage-type, Darwin, Mendel, and so on. Some are so utterly beautiful they stagger the imagination. Such is the varied world of tulips these days.

Because there are so many, choose the ones that appeal to you—the small ones for a woodsy planting, the tall regal type for borders, or perhaps the lily-shaped ones if these are a favorite with you. Do select early and late ones so that you can enjoy the flowers for many months rather than a few weeks. Give plants a sunny place where they are protected from strong winds. Use a light, well-drained soil; tulips will not grow in very sandy or clay soil.

Generally, it is best to plant the bulbs deep, say, 10 to 12 inches below the surface because then there is less danger of botrytis starting, and it is possible to have annuals in the same place after the tulips have bloomed. Set early-flowering types 4 inches apart, Darwins about 6 inches apart. And if you are planting large areas of tulips, it is best to dig out the entire area and then insert bulbs and replace with soil rather than planting them one at a time.

Plant bulbs in a prepared soil bed between October and the middle of November. They can be left in the ground or lifted for other plantings if you desire. In this case, lift them with roots and leaves and then keep them in a shady place to ripen. When the foliage has turned brown, store them in a cool, dry place until planting time in the fall. Tulips need cold weather; in all-year temperate climate, you must buy precooled bulbs or store bulbs in the refrigerator for six weeks before planting them.

For simplicity, tulips can be classed as follows:

Early single. Old favorites; easy to grow.
Early double. Large, wide-open flowers; long-lasting.
Mendel (mid-season). Lovely shapes and beautiful colors.
Triumph (mid-season). Robust; good range of colors.
Darwin tulips (May flowering). Most popular; globular in shape. Average size.
Darwin hybrids (mid-season). Giants with stiff stems.
Lily-shaped tulips. Beautiful reflexed and pointed petals.
Cottage tulips. Flowers large and almost egg-shaped.
Variegated color tulips. Dramatic; lovely.
Parrot tulips. Fringed and scalloped flowers.
Late double. Peony-type tulips.
Fosteriana. Dainty; many unusual hybrids.
Kaufmanniana. Large flowers, early blooming.

DAHLIAS (dahlia). These plants have tuberous roots, and rest between seasons. The next year's flower is produced by the fleshy extension of the old stem. For best results, grow dahlias in a sandy soil; give them plenty of water and sun. Feed them regularly and put some bone meal in the soil.

Make plantings early but not so early that the plants will get chilled. Soak the tubers in water for a day before you plant them in 3- to 4-inch predug holes. Set the tuber in the ground horizontally. Insert a stake in the ground beside the plant because most dahlias need support. Keep the plants weed-free and when watering, soak them.

As soon as the tops are killed by the first frosts in fall, cut the plants back to about 4 inches above the crown and then dig them up in a few days. Dry them in a well-ventilated place for a day before storing them in peat moss or vermiculite in a cool, but not freezing, area. In spring, divide the bulbs, allowing one eye or bud to each root, and replant.

Dahlias have been bred extensively. Before making selections, study all groups: giant formal, cactus type, sweetheart dahlias, dwarf ones, miniatures, the lovely pompoms, single-bedding type. The color range of the flowers is incredible.

BEGONIA TUBERHYBRIDA (tuberous begonia). For sheer drama and intense summer color, these plants are star performers. Tuberous begonias today have been bred to near-perfection in flower form, size, and color. The choice is vast, one prettier than the other: Camelliaeflora, Ruffled, Cristata, Fimbriata, Marginata in two forms (Crispa Marginata with frilled single flowers; and Double Marginata with petals lined and edged with bands of contrasting colors). Other forms include: Narcissiflora, Picotee, and Rose.

In March, select large tubers and put them in a 2-inch layer of peat moss and sand, 1 to 2 ratio, in a wooden flat or other suitable container. Set the tubers in place 2 inches apart and about 1/2 inch deep, with the dented side up. Cover them with about 1/4 inch of the starting medium. Place the container in good light in 60F to 70F and keep the tubers just barely moist. Too much water causes rot, and not enough moisture will curtail growth. When the sprouts are about 2 inches tall (in about 2 weeks) shift them to the garden (after danger of frost is over). If plants develop too fast and become too large before they can go outside, they can be held back by cool temperatures. On the other hand, if they are not growing fast enough, warmth accelerates growth. Place plants where there is scattered sunshine, and while tuberous begonias will survive some heat during the day, they do need cool nights of 55F to 60F. Water the plants heavily in bright weather, but not so much when it is cloudy. When they are actively growing, use a 5–10–5 commercial fertilizer mixed half-strength every second week.

After blooming, when leaves turn dry and yellow, water plants sparingly; let growth continue for as long as possible. When foliage is completely yellow, dig up tubers, wash off soil, remove stems, and place them in an airy, sunny place for a few days. Then store them in a cool, frost-free location until time to start them again.

IRIS. The bulbous irises are superior cut flowers, and their color and form are highly desirable in the garden. (Other irises are discussed in Chapter 13.) The most popular and frequently grown kinds are the Spanish, English, and Dutch types.

Spanish iris (*I. xiphium*) have narrow and grassy leaves about 12 inches tall. The flower color is blue, but there are many shades available; all have the characteristic yellow blotch on the fall; bloom time starts in May and ends in early June. The plants need good drainage, full sun, and shelter from wind.

English iris (*I. xiphioides*) have larger leaves, and the large showy flowers are produced in several colors, with blue predominating. They bloom after the Spanish iris. They need a moist, acid soil and coolness; they do not respond in heat or drought.

Dutch iris plants are hybrids, and although they resemble the Spanish type, they are more robust and floriferous. Flower color ranges from white to yellow to blue. Dutch hybrids need good drainage, sun, and a light-type soil. They put on their colorful display in March and April.

The Spanish, English, and Dutch irises should be planted 4 inches deep and about 4 inches apart. In regions where freezing occurs, mulch over the plants in winter. After foliage ripens, plants can be dug up, dried, and stored in a cool place. Or the plants can be left in the ground.

Iris reticulata is another lovely type which blooms early in spring. The bulbs are planted in September or October, spaced 4 to 6 inches apart in a semishady location. The flowers resemble the Spanish and Dutch iris, but are smaller; plants rarely grow more than 6 inches.

Iris tingitana, known as the Wedgwood iris, is another lovely group of plants.

A sasanqua camellia on a redwood trellis for espalier growing.
(Phil Palmer)

Espaliered camellias in informal pattern decorate a long wall.
(Phil Palmer)

CHAPTER 16

Espaliers, Vines, and Standards

Training plants to specific patterns is not new, but it is certainly an overlooked part of gardening. Yet a well-groomed espalier against a wall can be more attractive than a row of foundation plantings, and a healthy plant grown to tree form (standard) is an asset for any terrace.

Gardening with espaliers and standards takes time and patience, but the results are well worth the effort. Espaliered plants are graceful and charming, take a minimum of space, and to cover bare walls—prevalent in today's architecture—they cannot be beat.

A plant grown to an espalier pattern needs training and trimming to a desired shape. Generally, it is tied to a trellis that is parallel to a flat surface, with 4 to 6 inches of air space behind the plant. (In some cases, espaliers are applied directly to a wall.)

If possible, buy an espalier already started at a nursery. It is much easier to train a tree or shrub that is already started than to initiate the pattern yourself. Do not be in a rush with espaliers; they take time to grow and cover an area, but once established, they are indeed handsome.

Espaliers let you use certain trees and shrubs where space would not permit them to develop naturally. It is gardening with an artist's eye, for the texture of the stems, the variations of leaf pattern and color, and the line of the design must be given careful consideration. It is somewhat like painting a surface with leaves and flowers.

ESPALIER PATTERNS

Years ago, there were rigid espalier patterns, but now the design is almost a personal choice. The formal patterns, although still seen, are not as popular as the informal or free-form espaliers. The formal patterns are quite symmetrical and include the following:

The double horizontal cordon. A center shoot about 20 inches high, with two horizontal branches in each direction.

The vertical U-shape. A vertical stem on each side of a central trunk. Double and triple U-shapes are also seen.

The palmette verrier. A handsome candelabra pattern.

The palmette oblique. Branches trained in a fan shape.

The horizontal T. A multiple horizontal cordon with several horizontals on each side of a vertical trunk.

Belgian-espalier. A diamond pattern.

Arcure. A series of connecting arcs.

Informal espaliers are more natural and, to my eye, more pleasing for most properties. The patterns are casual or free-form. Espaliering is somewhat like bonsai growing except that you are working with mature plants against a flat surface. The informal espalier does not require as much trimming and training as the formal pattern, but creating an open and beautiful design is still the goal. Supports are generally not necessary; you can tie stems of plants to surfaces with special nails or copper wire.

Select suitable plants for espaliering. Some, such as morning glories, grow too rapidly, and others with large leaves do not make good espalier subjects. Dwarf fruit trees are especially suitable, and camellias and pyracantha are often seen. Magnolias, laurel, and *Carissa grandiflora* are other possibilities.

Espaliers can be grown in containers or in the ground. Provide them with a well-drained, rich soil and choose appropriate plants for the conditions you can give them. Use sun lovers against a south wall, and plants that need shade at a north or west exposure. Do not fertilize espaliers; too much feeding will make it impossible to keep them trained to the desired shape.

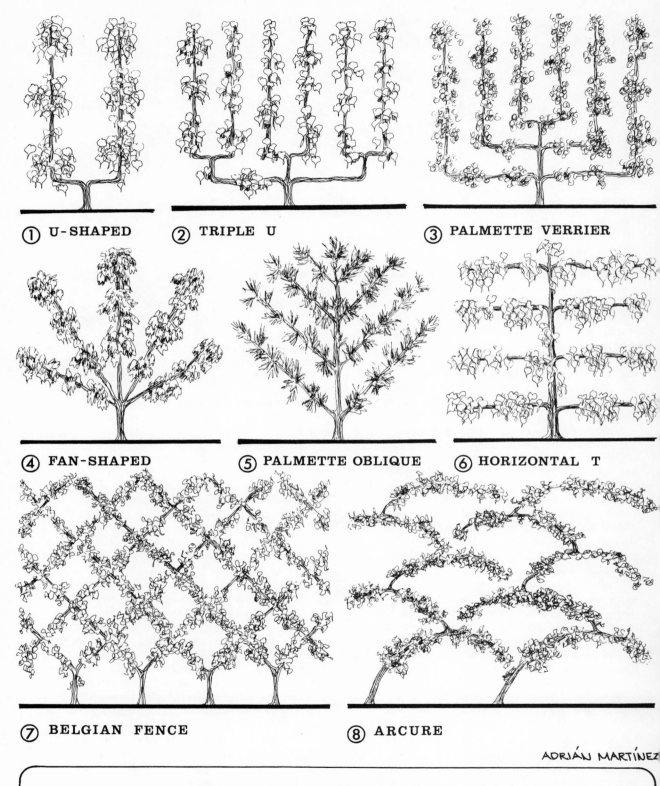

① U-SHAPED   ② TRIPLE U   ③ PALMETTE VERRIER

④ FAN-SHAPED   ⑤ PALMETTE OBLIQUE   ⑥ HORIZONTAL T

⑦ BELGIAN FENCE   ⑧ ARCURE

ADRIÁN MARTÍNEZ

Formal Espaliers

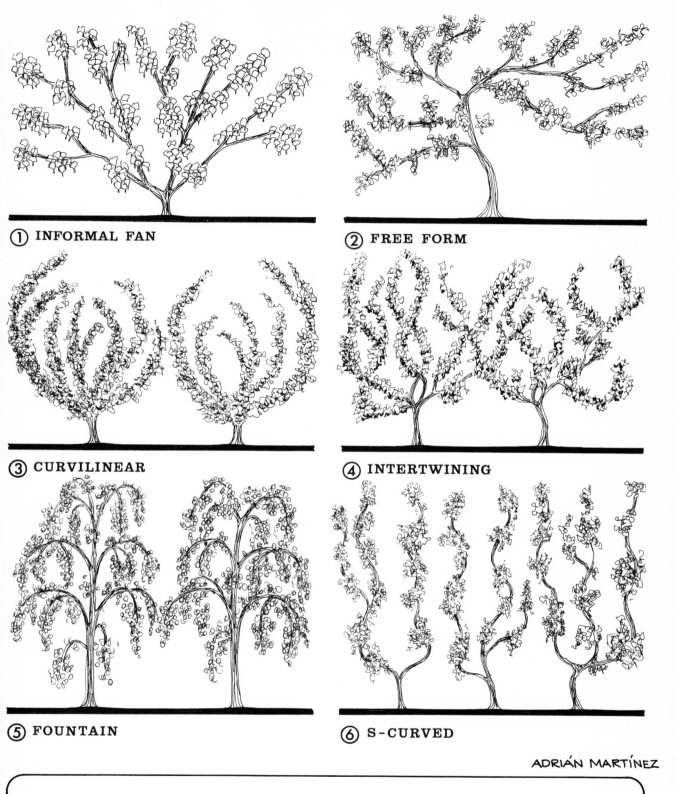

① INFORMAL FAN

② FREE FORM

③ CURVILINEAR

④ INTERTWINING

⑤ FOUNTAIN

⑥ S-CURVED

ADRIÁN MARTÍNEZ

Informal Espaliers

All espaliers trained in formal patterns and most of those in free-form patterns need a framework to support them and to hold the branches. You can obtain commercial trellises at nurseries. Or you can make supporting devices. Redwood strips, wire, or bamboo are excellent materials for the framework. Plunge the base of the trellis several inches into the ground or, if in a pot, into the soil. Be sure the supporting device is at least 6 inches away from the wall so that there will be space for you to tie and prune the plant and so that the building can—when necessary—be painted.

To attach the frame to the wall use wire or some of the many gadgets available at nurseries specifically for this purpose. For a masonry wall, rawl plugs may be placed in the mortared joints, and screw eyes inserted. You will need a carbide drill to make holes in masonry. Branches may be held in place with raffia or soft cotton twine.

The objective with espaliers is to develop a flattened plant that is beautiful in design and generally open enough to allow the background wall to show. To maintain this effect, thinning of twigs and branches, sometimes even denuding of leaves, is necessary. Trimming espaliers differs from regular tree pruning. Training and trimming require a light touch, with careful attention to every twig, branch, and leaf.

When a plant is dormant before new foliage has started in spring, do the heavy pruning. Or, on mature plants, wait until after flowering to start shaping them. With most plants, light pruning can be done every month during the growing season. Do not prune plants in late summer, as this would encourage new growth that would not have time to mature before cold weather.

Root pruning is not usually necessary with espaliers unless you have erred in choice, and the plant grows larger than you want it for a desired place. Do root pruning in early spring by spading out the ground 3 to 4 feet away from the base of the plant. This cuts off feeder roots and curtails rampant growth.

STANDARDS

Standards are plants trained to tree form; generally, the plant is one crown on a central stem. However, the tree-form shape can take on many patterns—a single ball on top, double ball, pyramidal shapes, a poodle trim—and so on. The idea remains the same no matter what kind of shape is selected—to create a neat sculptural effect.

Many plants adapt to the standard form, but azaleas, fuchsias, and geraniums are perhaps best known. Chrysanthemums, oleanders, acacias, and abutilons are other possibilities.

You can grow and train your own standard; this takes time and patience. Or you can buy standards already started in 5-gallon cans at nurseries. There are some basic rules for training the tree if you start your own. Early spring is the best time; choose a young plant with strong top growth. Decide on the shape—ball, cone, umbrella—and remove all side shoots as they form on the new plant to encourage the trunk to grow rapidly. Stake the plant when it is about 8 inches high. When the trunk reaches the height you desire, remove the main growing tips so that branches can form. In a few months, pinch out the branch tips to start shaping the top of the standard.

If you decide on a ball or cone shape rather than an umbrella form, purchase metal wire forms at nurseries. These are put in the container, and the plant is trained to the wires.

Geraniums

Select small plants in 5-inch pots. As growth starts, pinch off side shoots, forcing activity to the top. When the plant is about a foot high give it bamboo support. Tie the geranium stem to it with plastic ties. Fertilize the standard every other watering to encourage foliage growth. Transfer the plant to an 8- or 10-inch container and allow branches to develop at the tip.

In mid-September, except in all-year temperate climates, place the tree in a sunny window. Continue to maintain the proper ball form and remove side shoots. In spring, when the tree is in its second year, bloom starts. Move the standard to the patio for the summer festival of color. This display has taken time and patience, but once you see a geranium tree in bloom, you will feel it was well worth it.

Many of the single or double zonal geraniums make fine standards:

'Scarlet Flame'
'Lavender Ricard'
'Masure's Beauty'
'Orange Ricard'
'Missouri'
'Summer Cloud'
'Will Rogers'

LISTS OF PLANTS FOR ESPALIER GROWING

See Tables 14, 15, and 16 for lists of plants for espaliers that need sun, those that need shade, and espaliers that are suitable for contemporary architecture.

Table 14. Espaliers for Sun

Botanical and Common Name	Approx. Height in Ft.	Min. Night Temp.	Remarks
Acer palmatum atropurpureum (bloodleaf Japanese maple)	10–30	—10 to 0F	Colorful in autumn
Cercis chinensis (Chinese redbud)	3–8	—10 to 0F	Loads of color
Chaenomeles sinensis (Chinese quince)	10–30	—10 to 0F	Colorful in autumn
Cotoneaster divaricata (spreading cotoneaster)	6–15	—20 to —10F	Attractive summer foliage
Cotoneaster horizontalis (rock cotoneaster)	1–4	—10 to 0F	Robust grower
Eriobotyra japonica (loquat)	6–12	Tender	Bold leaves
Ficus carica (common fig)	6–15	—10 to 0F	Good, bold leaf plant
Forsythia intermedia spectabilis (border forsythia)	6–15	—20 to —10F	Bright colors, big flowers
Hibiscus rosa-sinensis (rose of China)	6–12	—10 to 0F	Sweetly scented
Jasminum nudiflorum (winter jasmine)	6–12	—10 to 0F	Sweetly scented
Juniperus chinensis sargenti (Sargent juniper)	1–6	—30 to —20F	Attractive
Magnolia grandiflora (southern magnolia)	10–30	0 to 10F	Large flowers
Magnolia stellata (star magnolia)	6–15	—10 to — 5F	Handsome white flowers
Malus atrosanguinea (carmine crab apple)	10–30	—30 to —20F	Early spring bloom
Pinus aristata (bristlecone pine)	1–4	—40 to —30F	Good in city
Prunus subhirtella pendula (Japanese weeping cherry)	10–30	—10 to 0F	Lovely shape
Taxus cuspidata (Japanese yew)	3–8	—20 to —10F	Handsome summer foliage
Viburnum prunifolium (black haw viburnum)	10–30	—40 to —30F	Spring bloom
Viburnum sieboldi (siebold viburnum)	10–30	—20 to —10F	Ornamental fruit

Table 15. Espaliers for Shade

Botanical and Common Name	Approx. Height in Ft.	Min. Night Temp.	Remarks
Camellia japonica (Japanese camellia)	10–30	0 to 10F	Many varieties
Carissa grandiflora (natal plum)	6–15	Tender	Bold green leaves
Chaenomeles speciosa (flowering quince)	6–12	—20 to —10F	Very colorful
Cornus mas (cornelian cherry)	10–30	—20 to —10F	Amenable plant
Euonymus alatus (winged euonymus)	6–15	—40 to —30F	Good in city
Ilex crenata (Japanese holly)	10–30	—10 to 0F	Handsome
Pyracantha coccinea lalandi (firethorn)	6–15	—20 to —10F	Colorful berries
Stewartia koreana (Korean stewartia)	10–30	—10 to 0F	Versatile, for many areas
Taxus baccata repandens (spreading English yew)	3–8	—20 to —10F	Bold, branching
Viburnum plicatum	6–15	—10 to 0F	Versatile, for many areas

Table 16. Espaliers for Contemporary Architecture

Botanical and Common Name	Approx. Height in Ft.	Min. Night Temp.	Remarks
Camellia japonica (Japanese camellia)	10–30	0 to 10F	Handsome against cement or stucco wall
Cedrus atlantica glauca (blue Atlantic cedar)	10–40	0 to 10F	Good for almost any background
Chaenomeles sinensis (Chinese quince)	10–30	—10 to 0F	Attractive against wood background
Cornus mas (cornelian cherry)	10–30	—20 to —10F	Nice in front of white wall
Ficus carica (common fig)	6–15	—10 to 0F	Easy to train
Ilex crenata (Japanese holly)	10–30	—10 to 0F	Easy to train
Magnolia stellata (star magnolia)	6–15	—10 to 10F	Amenable plant
Poncirus trifoliata (hardy orange)	10–30	—10 to 0F	Handsome against wood background
Pyracantha coccinea lalandi (firethorn)	6–15	—20 to —10F	Bright berries
Stewartia koreana (Korean stewartia)	10–30	—10 to 0F	Nice against wood background
Taxus baccata repandens (spreading English yew)	3–8	—20 to —10F	Robust grower
Viburnum species (viburnum)	To 30	—40 to —30F	Check with nursery for best ones in your region

Fuchsias

Tree fuchsias are for the shady area of the patio where geraniums cannot grow. With their dark-green leaves and balls of flowers, they are eye-stunning at walks leading to the patio; or try a pair of them near a doorway for a cheery welcome. As shade plants, they can be placed in areas where most plants would not succeed.

Grow fuchsias from tip cuttings or one upright main stalk. While the fuchsia is growing, remove all side branches. When the stalk has reached three-quarters of its desired height, allow the top branches to grow to form the head of the tree. Provide a stake to support the stem, and place a wire ball (sold at garden centers) on top of the stem for the plant to conform to desired shape. Tie the plant loosely to the stake.

It will take some time to develop a sizable standard. It is best to purchase young ones started at nurseries. They are sold in 5-gallon cans and can be enjoyed immediately on the patio. In winter, after flowering, move the fuchsia to a basement or a cool, dark location. Cut the plant back and dust wounds with benzene hexachloride.

Almost any strong fuchsia variety with arching growth is good as a standard. Here are some I have used:

'Carnival'
'Flying Cloud'
'Gypsy Queen'
'Leonora'
'Pink Bountiful'
'Swingtime'

Azaleas

Azaleas make any outdoor area a garden. They are floriferous, grow quickly, and make outstanding patio plants. As standards, there are some for shady areas and others for sunny locations. Give them somewhat more humidity than fuchsias and geraniums but less moisture at the roots.

For tree-form azaleas, follow the same starting procedure as for geranium trees or, once again, you might want to buy them already started at nurseries.

Like fuchsias, azaleas have a regal appearance, and a pair on the patio do much to give the area a formal appearance.

The Kurume azaleas, although having smaller flowers, will tolerate sunlight and make excellent standards. 'Falling Waters' and 'Pink Fountain' have been very satisfactory for me. For shady areas, try the wonderful azalea 'George Tabor'.

Roses

Everyone likes roses; they are the backbone of a good garden and, used as pot plants, they can be the focal point of the patio. Whether in bushes for accent or used as standards, they demand attention. The bushes are sold bare root at most nurseries starting in February. They are pruned and ready for potting.

It is difficult to start your own tree roses; it takes patience and a knowledge of grafting. Generally, tree roses are grafted twice; this is a lengthy procedure, so it is best to buy them already started at nurseries. They still have a long way to go before they leaf out and bloom to glorify your patio, so basically they will still be your project.

For planting a rose standard put a screened wire in the bottom of the chosen tub or pot; this keeps sowbugs from entering the soil. Insert drainage material and use a soil mix that has a good amount of leafmold. After potting, water the soil thoroughly.

Protect tree roses from wind and severe rains. Put them in patio corners close to the house where there will be some buffer against severe weather conditions. However, be sure they are placed where there is some sunlight. Only a very few varieties tolerate shade. To feed and protect roses, use the new double-duty systemic granules, which are sold under several trade names. Merely sprinkle the granules on the soil, and water the plant. Within 30 minutes, the systemic pesticide is in the leaves, and the plant is fed at the same time. Use once a month after the rose tree has started growth.

Some varieties I find best for tree growing are:

'Charlotte Armstrong'—Pink
'Eclipse'—Yellow
'Granada'—Yellow with red
'Peace'—Yellow with pink
'Tropicana'—Orange-red

(See Chapter 29 for rose gardens.)

VINES IN THE LANDSCAPE PLAN

With contemporary architecture that often uses bare expanses of walls and sometimes rather sterile lines, vines become an essential part of any good landscape plan. They are stellar decoration for screening walls or fences, or for blocking out an objectionable view. They fit into small spaces, can assume many shapes, and flowering kinds are breathtaking in bloom. For pergolas, trellises, and fences, vines are natural plants and will quickly add color to the scene. The trouble with vines, however, voiced by many gardeners, is that they require constant pruning and attention. This may be true if you select the wrong ones; many are rampant growers that take over an area unless properly trained. But there are many others that stay within bounds with little care.

Some of the climbing vines—like clematis, bougainvillaea, and morning glory—can, with proper care, become screens of living color, and are a delight in the garden. There are also vines, such as stephanotis, wisteria, and sweet pea, that have a dainty loveliness about them, a fragile quality, often necessary to soften harsh garden walls and house lines. And many vines—euonymus, bittersweet, pyracantha—have colorful winter berries that are indispensable in the snow landscape.

Many vines climb by means of twining stems that need support; others have tendrils or discs. Some have leaflike appendages which act as tendrils grasping the object on which they grow. Other plants, like jasmine, have long, slender, arching stems and need support; and some, such as ivy geranium and trailing lantana, are prostrate in growth. Along with growth habit, vines may be open and delicate or heavy with masses of foliage. Several varieties grow rapidly in a few months while others take years to fill a space. Select vines carefully; do not choose them indiscriminately because then constant care will be needed.

Plant woody vines in a deep planting hole to a depth of about 3 to 4 feet so that the roots will have ample space to grow. Replace the dug-out soil with good topsoil, but do not include manure or fertilizers that may burn the plants. When the plant is in place, tamp the earth gently around the collar of the plant so that air pockets will not form. Water thoroughly and deeply, and for the first few weeks give the plant some extra attention. This merely means watching it to see that it is getting started. Once established, it can be given routine care.

Put vines in the ground at the same level at which they were growing in the nursery, and by all means, try not to disturb the roots. Keep the root ball intact, and the chances of the vine becoming established with little trouble are excellent. If roots are disturbed, then the vine will need more time to adjust to its new condition.

Prune, thin, and shape vines at regular intervals to keep them looking handsome.

LISTS OF VINES

Information on when to prune vines is given in Table 17.

Twining Vines

Akebia quinata (five-leaf akebia)
Aristolochia durior (Dutchman's-pipe)
Celastrus species (bittersweet)
Mandevilla suaveolens (Chilean jasmine)
Smilax species (horse brier)

Twining Vines (*Continued*)

Trachelospermum species (star jasmine)
Wisteria floribunda (Japanese wisteria)

Climbing Vines

Ampelopsis species
Bignonia capreolata (cross vine)
Clematis species
Doxantha unguis-cati
Parthenocissus quinquefolia (Virginia creeper)
Passiflora species (passion flower)
Vitis species (glory grape)

Rapid-growing Vines

Akebia quinata (five-leaf akebia)
Ampelopsis acontifolia
Aristolochia durior (Dutchman's-pipe)
Bignonia capreolata (cross vine)
Clematis species
Doxantha unguis-cati
Ficus pumila (creeping fig)
Hedera helix (ivy)
Lonicera species (honeysuckle)

Trachelospermum jasminoides (star jasmine)
Vitis species (glory grape)
Wisteria floribunda (Japanese wisteria)
Wisteria sinensis (Chinese wisteria)

Vines for Flowers

Bignonia capreolata (cross vine)
Bougainvillaea
Clematis species
Hydrangea petiolaris (climbing hydrangea)
Mandevilla suaveolens (Chilean jasmine)
Passiflora caerulea (passion flower)
Plumbago capensis (plumbago)
Rosa (rose)
Stephanotis floribunda (Madagascar jasmine)
Trachelospermum species (star jasmine)
Wisteria floribunda (Japanese wisteria)

Vines for Colorful Fruit

Celastrus scandens (American bittersweet)
Euonymus fortunei (wintercreeper)
Kadsura japonica (scarlet kadsura)
Smilax species (horse brier)

Table 17. General List of Vines

Botanical and Common Name	Min. Night Temp.	General Description	Sun or Shade	Remarks
Akebia quinata (five-leaf akebia)	—20 to —10F	Vigorous twiner; fragrant, small flowers	Sun or partial shade	Needs support; prune in fall/early spring
Allamanda cathartica	Tender	Dense w/heavy stems, lovely tubular flowers	Sun	Prune annually in spring
Ampelopsis breviped-unculata (porcelain ampelopsis) (blueberry climber)	—20 to —10F	Strong grower w/dense leaves	Sun or shade	Prune in early spring
Antigonon leptopus (coral vine)	Tender	Excellent as screen	Sun	Needs light support; prune hard after bloom
Aristolochia durior (Dutchman's-pipe)	—20 to —10F	Big twiner w/ mammoth leaves	Sun or shade	Needs sturdy support; prune in spring or summer
Clytosoma *Bignonia capreolata* (cross vine) (trumpet vine)	—5 to 5F	Orange flowers	Sun or shade	Thin out weak branches in spring; clings by discs
Celastrus scandens (American bittersweet)	—50 to —35F	Light-green leaves, red berries	Sun or shade	Prune in early spring before growth starts
Clematis armandi (evergreen clematis)	5 to 10F	Lovely flowers and foliage; many colors	Sun	Needs support; prune lightly after bloom
Doxantha unguis-cati	10 to 20F	Dark green leaves, yellow blooms	Sun	Needs no support; prune hard after bloom
Euonymus fortunei (wintercreeper)	—35 to —20F	Shiny leathery leaves; orange berries in fall	Sun or shade	Needs support; prune in early spring

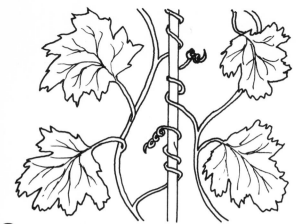

① **COILING TENDRILS** e.g., grape

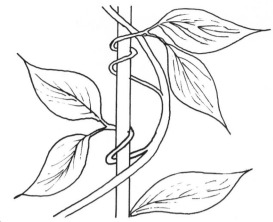

② **COILING LEAFSTALKS** e.g., clematis

③ **TWINING STEMS** e.g., honeysuckle, hall's

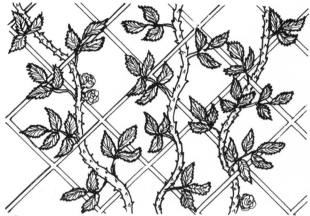

④ **WEAVING STEMS** e.g., climbing rose

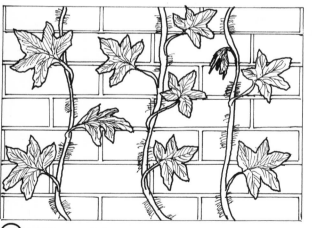

⑤ **AERIAL ROOT HOLDFASTS** e.g., Eng. ivy

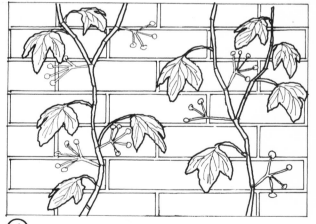

⑥ **ADHESIVE DISCS** e.g., Boston ivy

ADRIÁN MARTÍNEZ

How Vines Cling

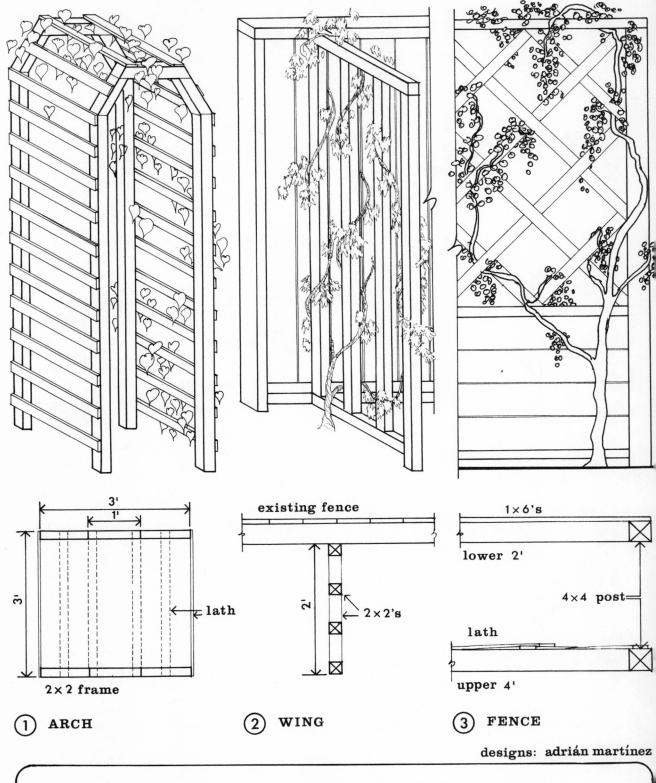

3'

1'

3'

→ lath

2 × 2 frame

existing fence

2'

← 2 × 2's

1 × 6's

lower 2'

4 × 4 post →

lath

upper 4'

① ARCH   ② WING   ③ FENCE

designs: adrián martínez

Trellises & Plant Supports

Table 17 (Continued)

Botanical and Common Name	Min. Night Temp.	General Description	Sun or Shade	Remarks
Fatshedera lizei	20 to 30F	Grown for handsome foliage	Shade	No pruning needed
Ficus pumila (repens) (creeping fig)	20 to 30F	Small heart-shaped leaves	Partial shade	Thin plant in late fall or early spring
Gelsemium sempervirens (Carolina jessamine)	Tender	Fragrant yellow flowers	Sun or partial shade	Needs support, thin plant immediately after bloom
Hedera helix (English ivy)	—10 to —5F	Scalloped neat leaves; many varieties	Shade	Prune and thin in early spring
Hydrangea petiolaris (climbing hydrangea)	—20 to —10F	Heads of snowy flowers	Sun or partial shade	Thin and prune in winter or early spring
Ipomoea purpurea (Convolvulus) (morning glory)	Tender	Flowers are white, blue, purple, pink, or red	Sun	Bloom until frost
Jasminum nudiflorum	—10 to —5F	Yellow flowers	Sun or shade	Needs strong support, thin and shape annually after bloom
Jasminum officinale (white jasmine)	5 to 10F	Showy dark-green leaves and white flowers	Sun or shade	Provide strong support, thin and shape after bloom
Kadsura japonica (scarlet kadsura)	5 to 10F	Bright red berries in fall	Sun	Needs support, prune annually in early spring
Lonicera caprifolium (sweet honeysuckle)	—10 to —5F	White or yellow trumpet flowers	Sun	Prune in fall or spring
Lonicera hildebrandiana (Burmese honeysuckle)	20 to 30F	Shiny dark-green leaves	Sun or partial shade	Needs support, prune in late fall
Lonicera japonica 'Halliana' (Hall's honeysuckle)	—20 to —10F	Deep-green leaves, bronze in fall	Sun or shade	Provide support, prune annually in fall and spring
Mandevilla suaveolens (Chilean jasmine)	20 to 30F	Heart-shaped leaves and flowers	Sun	Trim and cut back lightly in fall; remove seed pods as they form
Parthenocissus quinquefolia (Virginia creeper)	—35 to —20F	Scarlet leaves in fall	Sun or shade	Prune in early spring
Passiflora caerulea (passion flower)	5 to 10F	Spectacular flowers	Sun	Needs support; prune hard annually in fall or early spring
Phaseolus coccineus (scarlet runner bean)	Tender	Bright red flowers	Sun	Renew each spring
Plumbago capensis (plumbago)	20 to 30F	Blue flowers	Sun	Prune somewhat in spring
Pueraria thunbergiana (Kudzo vine)	—5 to 5F	Purple flowers	Sun or partial shade	Provide sturdy support; cut back hard annually in fall

Ivy trained in a formal pattern gives vertical accent to a small deck where there would not be space for standard-size plants.
(California Redwood Assoc.; design by G. Page, John Hartley photo)

Dutchman's pipe, a robust vine, adorns an overhead shelter.
(Molly Adams)

Table 17 (Continued)

Botanical and Common Name	Min. Night Temp.	General Description	Sun or Shade	Remarks
Rosa (rambler rose)	—10 to —5F	Many varieties	Sun	Need support; prune out dead wood, shorten long shoots and cut laterals back to 2 nodes in spring or early summer after bloom
Smilax rotundifolia (horse brier)	—20 to —10F	Good green foliage	Sun or shade	Prune hard annual any time; needs no support
Trachelospermum jasminoides (star jasmine)	20 to 30F	Dark-green leaves and small white flowers	Partial shade	Provide heavy support; prune very lightly in fall
Vitis coignetiae (glory grape)	—10 to 5F	Colorful autumn leaves	Sun or partial shade	Needs sturdy support; prune annually in fall or spring
Wisteria floribunda (Japanese wisteria)	—20 to —10F	Violet-blue flowers	Sun	Provide support and prune annually once mature to shorten long branches after bloom or in winter; pinch back branches first year

Flagstone steps bordered with roses
add charm and interest to a lawn area.
(Star Roses)

This stone step arrangement adds a graceful curve
to a natural garden; although man-made, it is a
total part of the landscape.
(Joyce R. Wilson)

This charming retaining stone wall is a feature of the
garden; with ground cover plants on top and rock-growing
plants between the crevices it is a double-duty wall.
(Woodard Furniture Co.)

CHAPTER 17

Garden Essentials

Although a garden is essentially a thing of beauty, it is also an outdoor living area, and certain conveniences for you and your family should be considered. To enjoy the outdoors, you must be able to get from one place to another easily, so paths and walks are necessary. Plan convenient routes for reaching flower beds and the patio from the house or from different parts of the grounds.

Privacy is a prime factor in the plan, too. Screens and fences are usually necessary, not only to block neighbors' view but also as a decorative feature. Protection from sun and wind are other considerations. While man-made screens are most often used—they can be put in place quickly—many people prefer a natural barrier. Tall hedges are effective in the landscape, but it takes them many years to mature and most of them will need frequent pruning to keep them within bounds.

Today, patios and terraces are much more important than even a few years ago; 70 percent of all new homes are designed with a patio. This outdoor room is now an integral part of the contemporary home and is discussed in Chapter 18.

And just as we furnish the indoors, the outdoors needs furniture too for family activities.

PATHS AND STEPS

Paths and walks must be part of the total design, so think about them before you start to landscape. Be sure they give you full access to all of your grounds; do not waste a secluded spot in back of the house because it is difficult to get to. Here, a secret garden with a path leading to it, is infinitely charming.

Use some imagination in planning paths. Too often a path is selected haphazardly; yet it can be used as a decorative feature rather than merely as a means of getting from one place to another. It can be a subtle turn and graceful curve to accent an area, to frame a flower bed, or to lead the eye to a garden feature. It can be an attractive pattern to break the monotony of a large area, or it can be a finely detailed ornate path with colorful tile.

The construction of the path is important, too—its suitability to the site and use, its cost, and the question of its upkeep.

Paths should have a beginning and lead to a point of interest or connect with other paths. Make the path broad enough—at least 3 to 5 feet wide—for two people to walk abreast. There is nothing more frustrating than a narrow path. The width should have some relation to the length; good proportion is important. (See drawings for patterns and kinds of paths.)

Brick is a popular material for paths because it harmonizes well with nearly every outdoor situation. It is easy to install and can simply be laid on a well-tamped-down sand or cinder base. It can be put down in many patterns to add an interesting note to the garden, and it lasts for years.

Concrete is durable, but it is not always suitable because of its sterile gray color. It must be installed with a good foundation so that it is not cracked by frost. Concrete stepping-stones are decorative and easy to put in place; so are patio pavers and patio blocks. Investigate local building supply yards carefully because there are many new types of stepping-stones available.

Flagstone or gravel or grass paths are handsome, but flagstone is rarely inexpensive, and gravel has to be replaced frequently. And grass has limitations if there is heavy foot traffic. Before you make a final choice, determine the following:

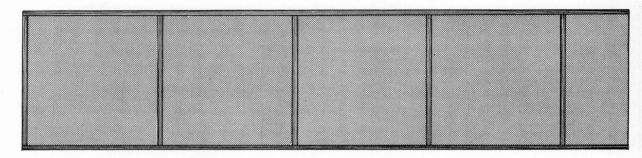

(1) CONCRETE w. redwood

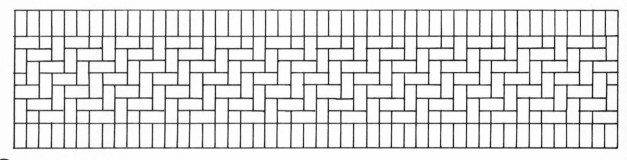

(2) BRICK

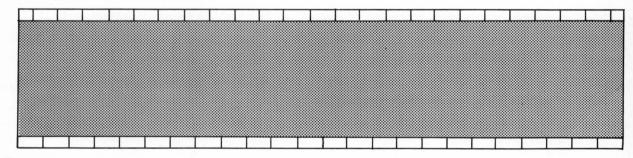

(3) ASPHALT w. brick edging

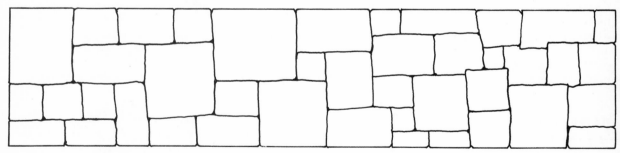

(4) CUT STONE

ADRIÁN MARTÍNEZ

Paths to Guide Traffic

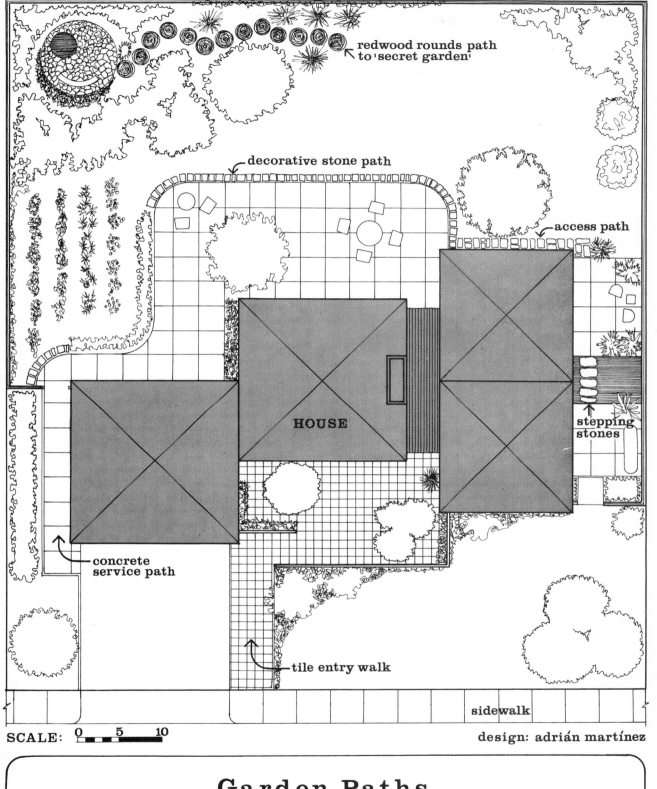

redwood rounds path
to 'secret garden'

decorative stone path

access path

HOUSE

stepping
stones

concrete
service path

tile entry walk

sidewalk

SCALE: 0 5 10

design: adrián martínez

Garden Paths

- Will the paving have a pleasant feel underfoot?
- Will the color, pattern, and texture blend with other surfaces?
- Will it withstand weather?
- Will it last a long time?
- Will it be easy to clean?
- Will you be able to install it yourself?
- Will weeds grow through it?

Steps in the garden are necessary where there is a change of levels. They can be more than steps. They can break the monotony of a landscape with graceful and sweeping lines to add visual interest to the plan. They do not have to be straight nor precise unless you have a very formal garden.

There are many unusual arrangements for steps and several are illustrated in drawings in this chapter. A straight flight of steps is hardly pleasing; turns and angles with wide or low treads are more effective in the landscape. Generally, a 14-inch tread with a rise of about 6 inches is fine but not mandatory in the garden.

If there is a long flight of steps, break it up with landings between with a change of direction perhaps. There is a vast array of materials for steps—concrete or pieces of brick, precast slabs, logs or railroad ties, to mention a few.

As a rule, steps do not require perfect detailing because plants can be used to soften the rough edges.

FENCES AND SCREENS

A fence is the frame of the garden as well as a screen for privacy, or a buffer against the wind. Make it ornamental as well as functional. Manufacturers offer many materials for fences, and you can make countless styles to make them attractive embellishments in the landscape. The choice of the screening depends on the degree of decorativeness desired.

A fence is no longer simply a barrier or a dividing line; it is a vertical line in the garden and, in some cases, can become part of the architectural scheme as well. Indoors, we use walls to partition different areas, and outdoors we use fences and screens.

Put fences where you need them. They can be 5 feet long in the middle of an area, or they can be at the sides of the property. They can be wing walls or extend over a large area. Design, line, and color are all part of a fence. There are as many reasons to have a fence as there are materials to make them from. Is the screen for privacy, or is it to help thwart wind? Do you want wing walls to create areas of seclusion, or is a complete enclosure needed to hide an unsightly view, or should it be freestanding, a short screen, temporary or permanent, curved or straight, covered with vines or natural wood?

Picket and grapestake. These fences are popular standbys that are easy to install and have a rustic charm.

Slat fence. A dramatic and versatile screening; it can be of a formal or informal design. Basically it is constructed of 1- by 1-inch strips nailed over a frame set either closely together or slightly apart. The slat design can be a combination of vertical and horizontal slats, using 4 by 4 upright supports and capped with 1 by 6 stock. Or it can be a horizontal pattern or a curved one.

Board fence. A board fence is easy to build; it is useful, but it needs some skillful design to make it appear more than a barrier. A solid board fence, although affording absolute privacy, gives a person a feeling of being imprisoned behind it. Make the fence interesting by using patterns on it. A decorative grid overlay is one idea. Battens spaced horizontally at given places will add interest too. Basically, the board fence is set with 4 by 4 posts set 6 to 8 feet apart. For rails, use 2 by 4's. Substantial foundations are needed for board fences because they are heavy.

Louver fence. The louver fence is handsome and affords privacy without shutting off light or air. The angle of the louvers is determined by the kind of fence you want. They can be set to furnish maximum light and shade, or, by facing them across the path of prevailing wind, they can act as a buffer. Because of its design the louver fence is dramatic with alternating strips of shadow and light that change as the sun's angle changes. A louver fence is built by attaching the top and bottom rails to posts and nailing the louvers in place at top and bottom. The accepted angle for the louvers is 45 degrees and 2 by 4 or 2 by 6 boards are generally used.

Basketweave. The basketweave fence is attractive from both sides, and offers the homeowner many pattern variations. However, if it is used extensively, the effect can be dizzying, so use this type with discretion. There are many designs, but generally the wooden strips are crisscrossed in a tight weave. The weave effect can be subtle with a flat type design, or it can be more pronounced. The fence is constructed with 1/2-inch or 1-inch rough-finished lumber 4 to 12 inches wide, and any standard length from 14 to 20 feet. Four by 4 posts are the backbone. Nail the strips only at the posts alternating the centers and ends. Halfway between the posts, separate the strips with 1-inch spacers.

Other fence patterns are rail-type, lattice-type, board on board, or shadow box.

A plastic or fiberglass panel fence affords privacy and eliminates glare, but still lets some light through. There are flexible and rigid plastics, translucent or colored, flat and corrugated panels. What you select depends on your own tastes. However, be wary of flexible plastics because they rarely last more than a

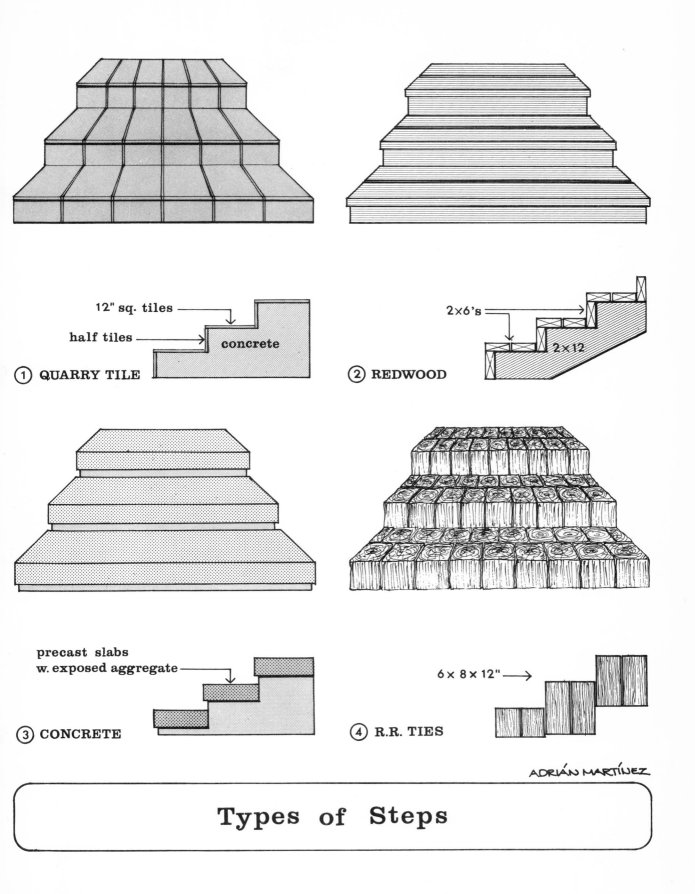

12" sq. tiles
half tiles
concrete

① QUARRY TILE

2×6's
2 × 12

② REDWOOD

precast slabs
w. exposed aggregate

③ CONCRETE

6 × 8 × 12"

④ R.R. TIES

ADRIÁN MARTÍNEZ

Types of Steps

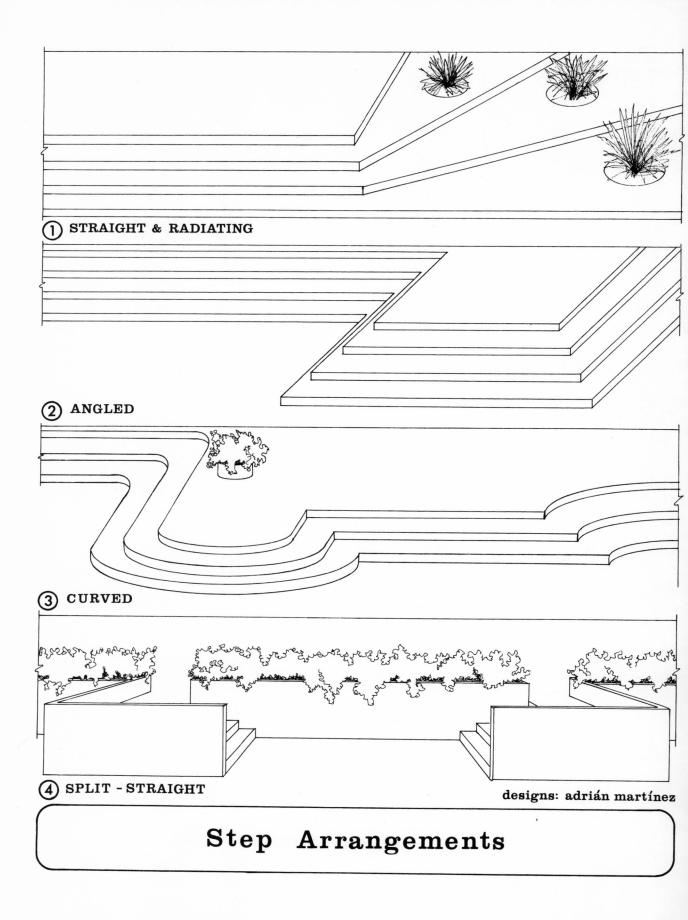

① **STRAIGHT & RADIATING**

② **ANGLED**

③ **CURVED**

④ **SPLIT - STRAIGHT**

designs: adrián martínez

Step Arrangements

few months, and they are a bother to work with. Basically, rigid plastic has a fiberglass core sealed between layers of polyester resin. It can be nailed or sawed or drilled; it is lightweight and generally impervious to weather. Fiberglass colors fade, which some people object to, and unlike wood, the look of plastic is not really in keeping with garden surroundings. Still, these panels are expedient and inexpensive.

Glass screens preserve a view and at the same time afford protection from the wind. The general look of glass adds a note of elegance to the garden, and it blends well with plants. If you are concerned about safety, use tempered glass, which is five times as strong as ordinary glass. Investigate some of the handsome patterned glass if view is not important.

Use substantial foundations and strong posts and frames for glass because in quantity it is heavy. Small panes are less expensive and easier to handle than large ones. Thickness of the glass must be considered; double-strength window glass is 1/8-inch thick and can be used satisfactorily for openings to 16 by 20 inches. For larger areas, 3/16- or 7/32-inch thick crystal sheet glass is best; it does have slight waviness, so if view is a primary factor, select 1/4-inch thick polished plate glass which does not have any distortion. Glare-reducing glass—blue, gray, bronze-tinted—is also available if sun is a problem.

HOW TO BUILD A FENCE

Plot the exact course of the fence and mark the line with string and stakes. Run mason's twine between the stakes, draw it tightly, and tie it to the stakes. Locate the sites for the posts and mark them with stakes. When the fence line is set and the post-hole sites marked, it is time to start digging holes for the posts.

Dig holes large enough to accommodate the size of the post and to allow water to drain away from it. In sandy soils, where drainage is no problem, make the hole only slightly larger than the post; but in clay soil that does not drain readily, prepare a large hole and put 2 inches of gravel at the bottom. The gravel encourages water to drain away from the post rather than trapping it at the bottom.

Dig holes with a spade or a pick, or if the soil is very hard, rent a post-hole digger; select the two-handled clam-shell digger because it is easier to work than the auger type.

Putting the posts in place is a critical part of fence building; they must be plumb and straight and solidly embedded in the soil so that the fence will not lean or buckle.

Posts can be held securely in place by soil or gravel, by cleats nailed to underground portions of the post, or by concrete. A concrete footing assures a strong fence that stands for years. Put 2 to 3 inches of gravel in the bottom of the hole as described and place the post on top of it. Fill in with another 3 inches of gravel around the post to hold it upright. Settle the post in position and check the sides with a carpenter's level. Pour concrete on top of the gravel pad, with the post set in place. Fill in and around the post with concrete and bring it a few inches above the grade. Check the straightness of the post as you fill in and around it with concrete, and make alignments immediately. After 20 minutes or so, the post will be impossible to move.

GARDEN WALLS

Although fences are usually wooden or plastic or glass, garden walls can be made of brick or stone or concrete blocks or clay tile. Masonry walls have an old-world charm and take the edge off the sometimes sterile architecture of some contemporary homes.

The purpose of a garden wall varies considerably, but essentially it is used as a partial screen or as a place for pot plants or for vines, or perhaps a nook for a wall fountain or sculpture. A wall can also carry out the corner of a house across a side yard, or it can hold back a piece of sloping ground. It can also be a screen to hide the carport from the patio or it can substitute for a wooden fence. Walls are more decorative and more substantial than fences; they are pleasing in the landscape if they blend in with the total plan.

New materials—concrete, decorative blocks, tiles—have revolutionized wall designs. These blocks come in lattice or grid patterns of various motifs, such as fleur-de-lis, Mediterranean, Oriental. The conventional solid wall of brick or concrete or stone is still with us too and certainly has its uses, but it is more difficult to construct and usually more costly than a block wall.

The kind of wall—large, small, high, low—dictates how to build it. A wall that holds up a considerable amount of earth needs more solid construction than a freestanding wing wall; but, generally, most walls must have adequate footing and foundation below the frost line. Check local building codes for frost lines.

Unless you are skilled with tools, building a wall is usually a job for a professional mason. Footings must be placed, foundations must be carefully constructed, and any wall over 3 feet tall needs reinforcing rods embedded in the concrete. An exception to the professionally built wall would be a wall of concrete blocks (mentioned above). These are easily put in place by the homeowner once the footings and foundations are in.

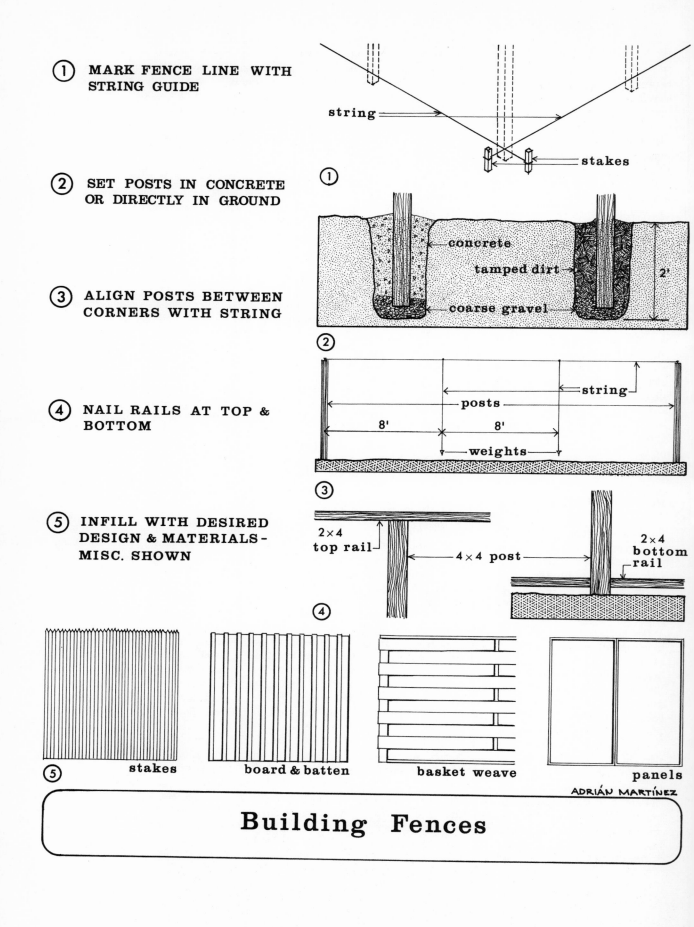

① MARK FENCE LINE WITH STRING GUIDE

② SET POSTS IN CONCRETE OR DIRECTLY IN GROUND

③ ALIGN POSTS BETWEEN CORNERS WITH STRING

④ NAIL RAILS AT TOP & BOTTOM

⑤ INFILL WITH DESIRED DESIGN & MATERIALS - MISC. SHOWN

string

stakes

① concrete   tamped dirt   2'   coarse gravel

② string   posts   8'   8'   weights

③ 2×4 top rail   4×4 post   2×4 bottom rail

⑤ stakes   board & batten   basket weave   panels

ADRIÁN MARTÍNEZ

Building Fences

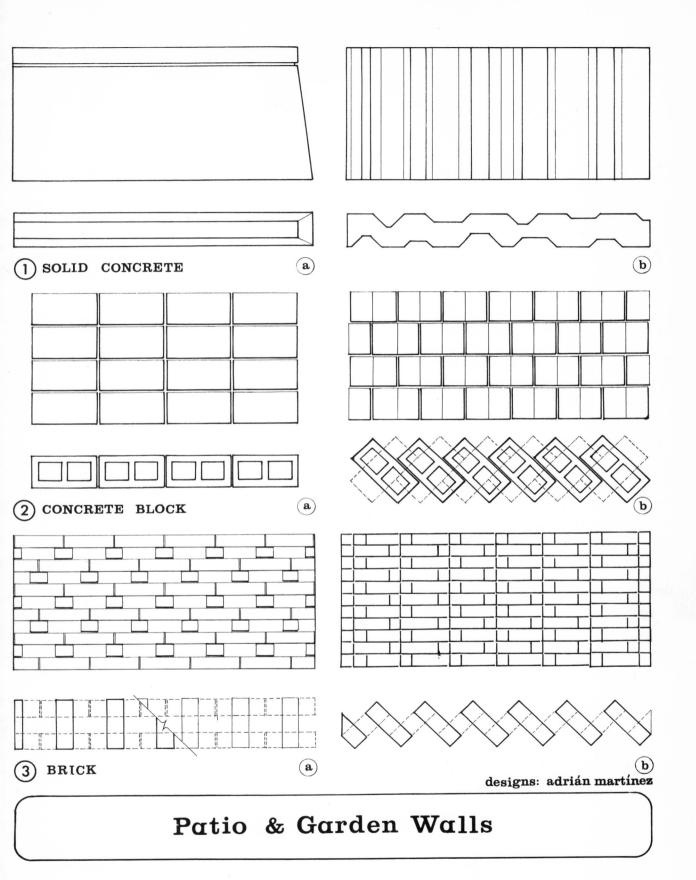

① SOLID CONCRETE ⓐ ⓑ

② CONCRETE BLOCK ⓐ ⓑ

③ BRICK ⓐ ⓑ

designs: adrián martínez

Patio & Garden Walls

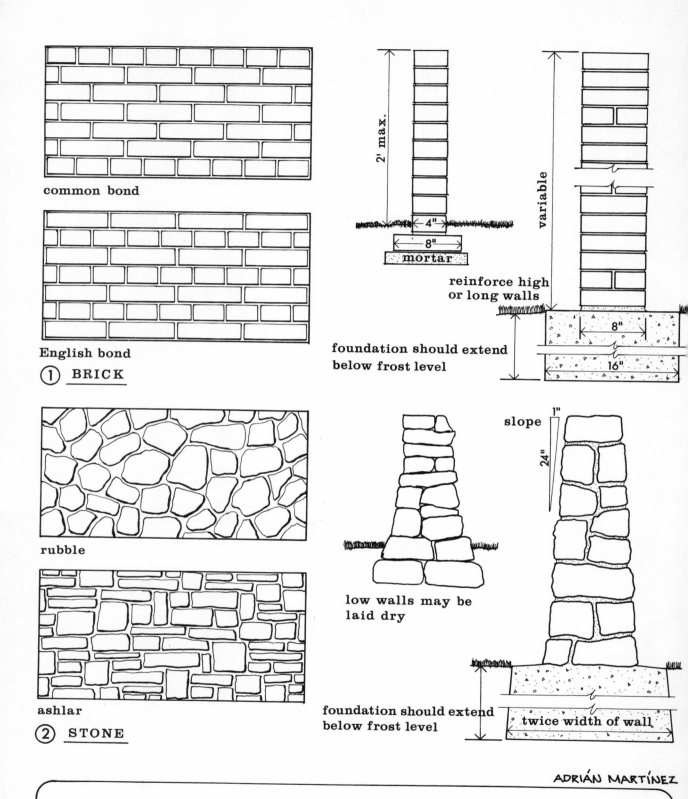

common bond

English bond

① BRICK

rubble

ashlar

② STONE

2' max.

4"

8"

mortar

variable

reinforce high
or long walls

foundation should extend
below frost level

8"

16"

slope

1"

24"

low walls may be
laid dry

foundation should extend
below frost level

twice width of wall

ADRIÁN MARTÍNEZ

Brick & Stone Walls

Complete privacy is attained with a handsome painted plywood
fence; vertical wood batens provide eye interest.
(American Plywood Assoc.; Charles Pearson photo)

Easy to build and a handsome addition to the patio, a 1 by 2
redwood fence gives privacy to a garden corner and blends
well with a concrete-aggregate floor.
(Roger Scharmer)

A decorative concrete block wall provides seclusion; the interesting
pattern is pleasant to see indoors or out.
(National Concrete Masonry Assoc.)

(Left) A wide overhang provides needed shade on this patio; it
makes the outdoor area seem part of the indoors.
(Woodard Furniture Co.)

(Right) This lath-type ceiling is easy to build; it affords
protection from sun but still admits light for
plants to grow.
(Joyce R. Wilson)

FURNITURE

A barren patio is uninviting. New outdoor furniture includes many different kinds of pieces to make living outdoors comfortable. Tables and chairs and accessories come in many styles and in many different materials. Select pieces that are resistant to weather and best suited to your individual needs.

Choose outdoor furniture as carefully as you would choose indoor pieces. Refinement in scale, style, and lightness makes it possible to have attractive furniture outdoors. Often the pieces can be used indoors too.

New materials have made possible sturdier construction. The choices range from polyvinyl cording and metal mesh for seats to sculptured polypropylene for chair arms. Fiberglass or tempered glass tops for safety and soft fabrics treated to resist stain and weather are all part of the outdoor scene. There is pool furniture, patio furniture, tables, chairs and ottomans, and other varied pieces.

Wrought iron, one of the first materials used for outdoor furniture, now has special joints sealed to keep out moisture. There are many styles to choose from including Early American, contemporary, and Oriental. Bamboo, rattan, and wicker—popular old standbys—are still with us, but they are improved to last longer.

Most outdoor furniture can stay in the rain without rusting or showing signs of deterioration, but ask about this anyway. Seat cushions no longer become soggy and mildewed. Polyvinylchloride seat and back wraps are sturdy and guaranteed for longevity. Padded slat construction suspended in steel frames is almost indestructible. Vinyl coverings in many bright colors for seat cushions are also available.

Aluminum tubing and hardwood parts covered with weatherproof vinyl make long-wearing pieces. Furniture of round or square welded tubular aluminum is another innovation. There are several manufacturers, many designs, and a dozen different themes to choose from.

Some furniture will blend into any setting. Other types must be placed in a specific area. Look at garden magazines and visit local showrooms and then make your selections. Outdoor furniture is no longer either bulky redwood pieces or flimsy aluminum. It is highly styled and attractive, and the garden is simply not complete without it.

OVERHEAD SHELTER

A patio overhead affords shade as well as privacy if there are neighbors above. This partial roof is generally supported by posts and beams, or if it is a canvas canopy, by rods and iron pipe. Although wood is most popular, the overhead can be made of plastic or aluminum screening or painted aluminum panels. The "open" roof—eggcrate or basketweave design—is frequently seen because it affords both shade and sun and does not interfere with the free flow of air while still creating a feeling of shelter.

The eggcrate design leaves the overhead open to the sun and can, if necessary, be fully covered at a later time. It is easy to build; all you do is nail blocking between the rafters. The lattice and lath pattern gives more protection from the sun and breaks the force of wind without stopping air circulation. It makes the patio cooler in summer and warmer in winter, and climbing vines can be trained on it.

Corrugated and flat plastic panels are popular for overhead roofs. This material is easily cut and sawed and merely nailed to a skeleton frame. This type of roof gives complete protection from the sun, but in severe wind it rattles. There are many colors available; some of the newer flat sheets are almost transparent.

An aluminum screened overhead can be used by itself or put over a grid or lattice roof. It gives little protection against strong sun but still affords a feeling of shelter. Air passes easily through the screen. This type of overhead is easily installed and inexpensive. There are all types of screening at suppliers, so choose carefully. The plastic-coated aluminum resists corrosion and helps to reduce sun penetration.

Canvas canopies are handsome and now come in many designs and colors. The canvas is pulled taut and laced through grommets to pipe supports. Another variation is strips of heavy canvas woven in a basketweave fashion over a rigid frame.

A many-sided patio and random-cut slate make this area especially inviting.
(Buckingham Virginia Slate Co., Taylor Lewis and Assoc. Architects, Norfolk, Virginia)

CHAPTER 18

The Patio

The size and nature of the lot and your personal needs will dictate the kind of outdoor living area to have and where it should be. It can be a simple exposed area with a few plants, adjacent to the living room to provide a pretty picture. It can be a fully enclosed or partially roofed terrace convenient to the dining room or kitchen if you enjoy outdoor cookery and dining. A patio can also be an intimate fenced or walled area off the bedroom, decorated with flowering plants.

Whether large or small, for lounging or for dining, for growing plants or merely for viewing, the outdoor area is an extension of the home. In all cases, it must have easy access to the house.

SIZE AND LOCATION

Sun, rain, and wind dictate the placement of the patio. The patio that bakes in the sun most of the day offers little pleasure for daytime use. And a patio that is in constant wind is not a comfortable place for either plants or people. Screens, fences, canopies, and trees and shrubs can modify the elements and offer shade, privacy, and protection.

Although an outdoor area should be large enough to fulfill the uses you have for it, it should not become a bleak prairie with a paved floor. These patios are more of a chore than a charm. A general guide to the size of the outdoor area is twice the size of the average living room, but this too can be altered to fit the family's needs.

If the lot is vast, break it up into several patios. Keep them to a sensible size and treat each one individually. One can be small and charming, the other more elaborate with statuary or a fountain, perhaps, but be sure the areas are interrelated in some way. Use the same paving blocks or patterns. If the space

for the patio is small, the area can seem visually larger with clever designing. Tall screening and terraced beds will give it height and volume, make it seem more than it really is.

A south patio basks in sun; in chilly climates it can be a blessing, but in arid regions it becomes an annoyance. A west patio is ideal in the morning, but during the day it may become uncomfortably warm. A patio that faces east is an ideal area; there is morning sun, but in the afternoon it is cool and shady. Northern exposures need not be neglected. Many plants thrive in shade.

Generally, most patios are in the rear of the house, but rear patios are not mandatory. There are many fine front patios screened by fences from the street. Terraces alongside the house—long and narrow—have their uses too. If cleverly designed, they can be very handsome.

The enclosed court or atrium surrounded by the house is well known and has many advantages because from all rooms it offers a pleasant view. It gives protection from wind for plants and people. And with a roof, the court becomes a conservatory, a splendid place for all kinds of tropical plants.

PATIO SHAPES

Square or rectangular patios are popular, but there is no set rule that says a floor must be in these forms. Circular patios and elliptical ones, half-moon shaped and curving surfaces are graceful and certainly effective. The shape of the paved area depends on the overall garden plan. Give some thought to the patio before you accept the conventional square design.

Concrete, brick, tile—almost any paving material —can be set to almost any pattern. If the area to be covered is large, use a pattern within a pattern to

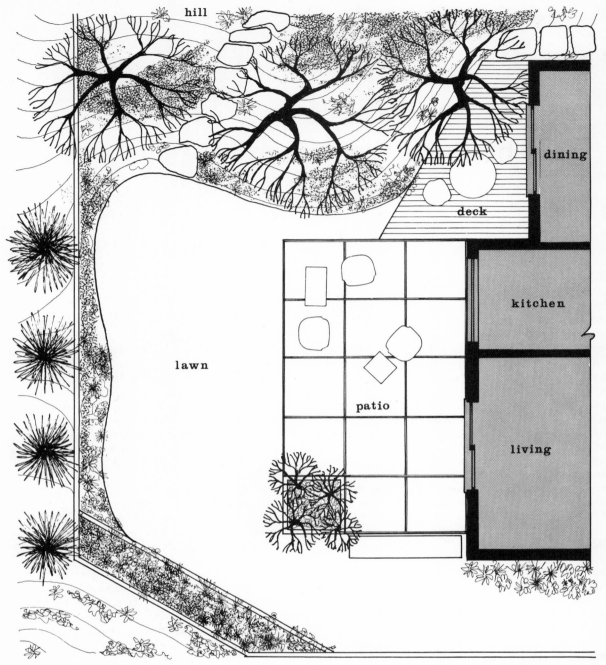

hill

dining

deck

kitchen

lawn

living

patio

PLAN

design: adrián martínez

Backyard Patio

A rather steep downslope called for impressive landscaping in this plan. Here, the sculptural effect of the trees is used as a dominant theme. The trees appear like statues that guard the deck side of the house; stepping-stones lead down the ravine. The somewhat stark effect is softened with a graceful curving lawn and low planters of flowers. The overall picture of very tall trees and low horizontal plantings is not displeasing. Ironically, the combination of these design elements heightens the setting.

The concrete block patio holds one corner tree, a sentinel that adds scale, and there is an uninterrupted view from the patio to the larger trees.

This somewhat flamboyant plan combining height and low mass works well and at the same time is a low maintenance garden. A fence surrounds the property on three sides, a further line of demarcation in this restrained yet well-planned garden.

avoid a monotonous effect. For smaller areas, select a material and a pattern that will make the patio seem larger.

Before you start actual construction, draw rough sketches on paper to be sure the patio is pleasing in all aspects. Put in shrubs and trees and decide whether an unorthodox shape is suitable for your situation or whether a simple layout is best.

PLAN ON PAPER

A rough sketch on paper is all that is necessary to decide just what the patio should be and where it should be. It is far easier to erase pencil lines than to reconstruct an outdoor area once it is installed.

A patio or terrace that is part of the house is desirable. As an occasional dining room it is close to the kitchen. For parties, it can act as an overflow if there are too many guests. It gives children a place to play close to the house where you can watch them.

The patio away from the house assumes a different character. It is more intimate and tends to become a feature in the landscape; it provides a pretty picture to look at from the house or grounds. This patio does not have the advantage of closeness to a structure and depends on a frame of trees or shrubs so that it does not appear merely as a slab of paving in the garden.

A patio that adjoins a bedroom or a bath has its own character too. This area is generally small and charming; it is a snapshot of nature from your window. Generally, it is filled with lush green plants and surrounded with walls or fence for absolute privacy. It is a place for growing plants and a scene to afford a relaxing view.

PATIO PAVINGS

There is a wide selection of materials for outdoor floors. Brick, tile, concrete, paving blocks, fieldstone, and flagstone are all part of the paving picture. So is indoor-outdoor carpeting, which now comes in many colors and designs and in easy-to-install squares. There are also temporary coverings such as loose-fill materials, gravel chips, fir bark, cinders, plastic stones, lavarock, dolomite, and crushed brick.

Because there are so many outdoor floor materials, choose carefully. Select a paving that is in character to the house and overall landscape plan and choose it for durability and service. A floor that is not comfortable to walk on and needs constant cleaning is a bad choice. And, finally, in selecting the patio floor, consider the cost and installation fees. Can you do it yourself, or will it be necessary to hire professional help?

The following information on paving materials includes the most popular floors—concrete, tile, brick, wood, patio blocks, wood blocks and rounds, and loose-fill materials—and how to set them. It also touches on less popular, but equally attractive, floors of flagstone, fieldstone, slate and all-weather carpeting.

Concrete

Concrete is a low-cost and very permanent surface. It is easy to clean and can be completely installed by a paving contractor in a few hours. It can be mixed with color or covered with paint. Or the top layer can be dyed with a liquid that seeps deeply into the pores of the concrete. A rough or textured finish is also possible when using concrete.

The main objection to a poured concrete floor is its monotonous appearance in large areas. A solid pad of gray is hardly attractive or decorative. Do divide very large areas into modular squares with wooden dividers so that the floor will have pattern. Then it is appealing, and the sterile look is eliminated.

An aggregate floor is another idea. In this case, the concrete has small stones on the surface; the resulting textured finish is handsome and blends with plantings and lawns. The uneven texture breaks the monotony of a large area of paving, and the pebbly surface eliminates glare and ensures sure traction in wet weather. This paving collects dirt between the stones, but it is easy to wash it clean with a strong hosing. Or one of the new resin sealers can be used. With a protective coating it is easy to sweep and wash dust away that would otherwise collect between the stones.

Tile

The brown or red color of most tile is especially pleasing with green plants. Tile is smoother than brick and easier to clean. It is virtually impossible to stain it. If the patio floor extends into the house, tile is always the decorator's choice. It has a lovely finished look when properly installed.

Outdoor tile is almost always rough-surfaced and usually 3/4-inch or 7/8-inch thick. Of all the tiles, quarry type makes the best patio floor. It is a heavy-duty ceramic material that comes in squares or rectangles or in special shapes. Standard sizes: 3 by 3 inches to 9 by 9 inches. Some have lightly textured surfaces; others fired-in designs. Colors run from off-white to blue-green, with the red hues the most popular.

Although you can install large patio tiles on a bed of sand and earth, most tiles need a mortar bed to be safe from cracking. It is best to have the work done by a professional.

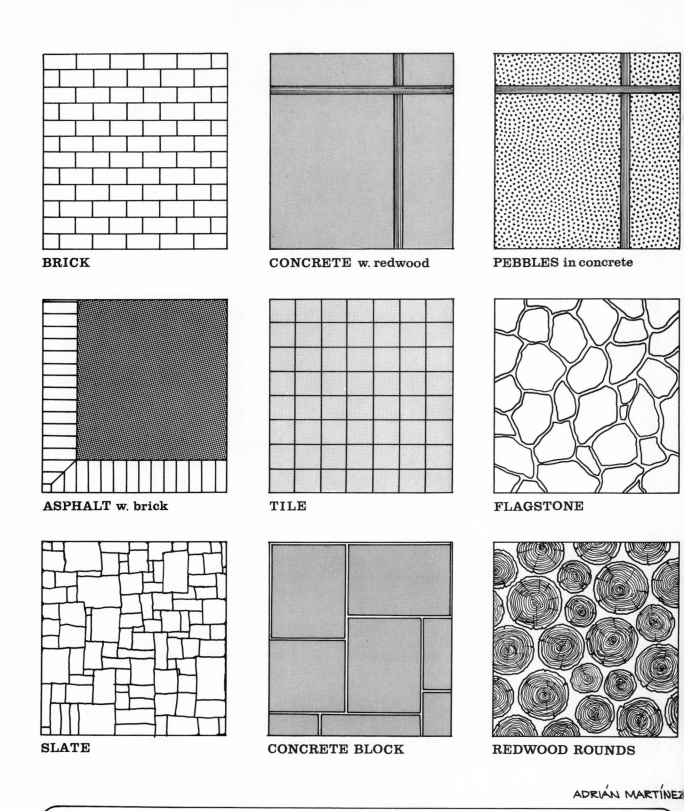

BRICK

CONCRETE w. redwood

PEBBLES in concrete

ASPHALT w. brick

TILE

FLAGSTONE

SLATE

CONCRETE BLOCK

REDWOOD ROUNDS

ADRIÁN MARTÍNEZ

Types of Paving

Ozite outdoor carpeting is
luxuriant to walk on and resists
stain; the plywood platforms are
simple in design and handsome.
*(American Plywood Assoc.;
Charles Pearson photo)*

Brick and concrete complement each
other in a modular patio pattern
accented with planting boxes
of geraniums.
*(California Redwood Assoc.;
design by Douglas Baylis)*

Aggregate patio blocks are available at nurseries and come in many
shapes and sizes.
(Joyce R. Wilson)

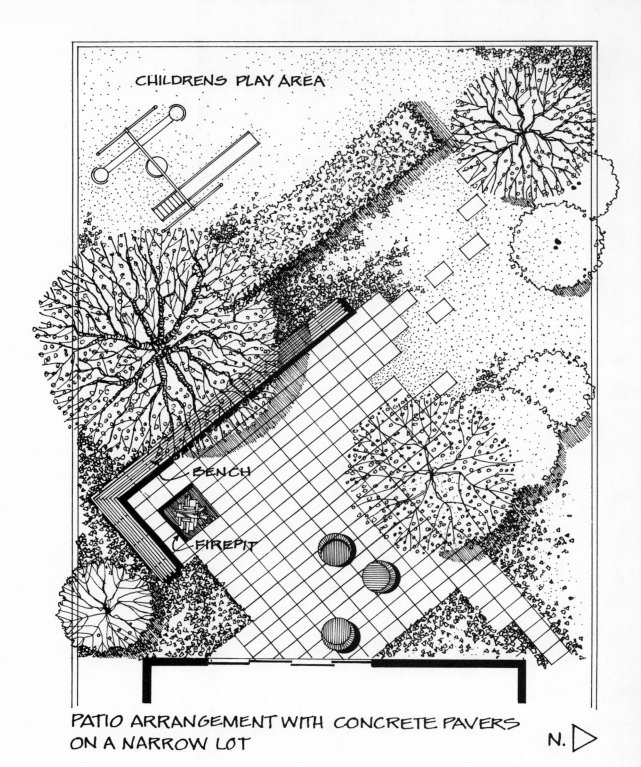

CHILDRENS PLAY AREA

BENCH

FIREPIT

PATIO ARRANGEMENT WITH CONCRETE PAVERS ON A NARROW LOT

N.

Narrow lots can make problem gardens but not in this plan. The landscape architect used textures to great advantage. The terrace is concrete pavers set off by a lawn. Plants include ground cover with tiny leaves, hedges and shrubs and trees in gradual leaf sizes from small to large.

The tree off the terrace stands alone and sets the scale for the plan. It is large for the site but purposely so, and thus imparts drama. Two groups of trees dominate the other side of the plan to assure balance in design. The stark manicured row of hedges separates the play area from the terrace and at the same time provides

a very necessary design line. Wooden benches repeat this line on the terrace to assure a marriage of plant materials with paved area.

The terrace at an angle is visually pleasing where a rectangular area would have been monotonous. There is no defined edge of the terrace but rather, stepping-stones placed in random pattern in the lawn. The stepping-stones further join all elements of the plan.

Within the narrow confines of this site there is a charming woodsy setting and although it is a garden that requires care, it is usable and handsome in all aspects.

Quarry tile in random pattern makes this patio a handsome accent in the garden.
(Westinghouse)

Small but charming, a brick patio becomes an extension of the house.
(Pella Wood)

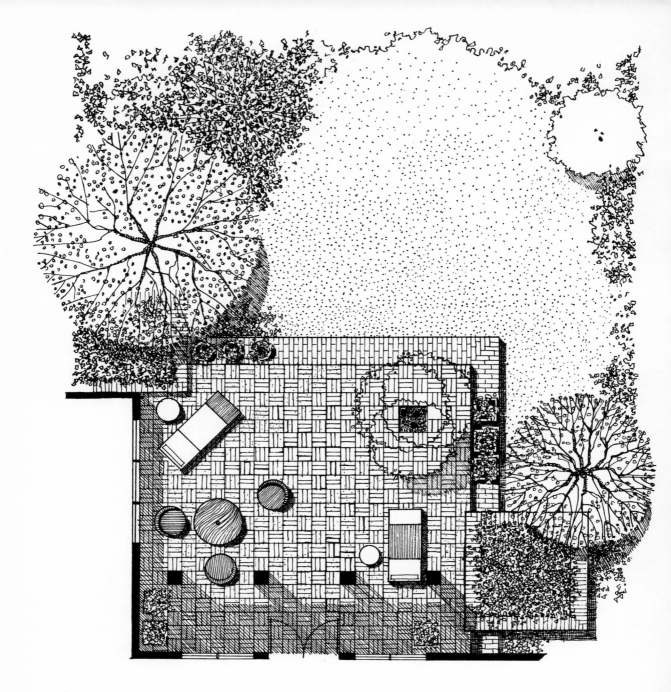

PATIO ARRANGEMENT WITH BRICK PAVING FOR AN "L" SHAPED HOUSE

N.

This garden plan for an L-shaped house depends on texture of materials and plantings for its beauty. The feature of the area is the brick patio with its block-within-a-block design. It is highly architectural and dramatic. To soften and contrast the brick there is ample planting and a spacious lawn.

Small-leaved, medium-leaved and large-leaved trees and shrubs are used and they are placed in concentrated masses so there is movement in the design. Flower masses of color are at the edge of the lawn for accent and background plantings are tall to provide privacy.

Planting boxes brimming with greenery on the patio soften the transition from paving to plantings. The large brick planter at the right of the patio and the tree anchor the plan to the setting. There is continuity, harmony and balance throughout. The setting is lush and provides a handsome vista from the living area of the house.

If the soil is flat and stable and you want to try to lay a tile floor, by all means do so. Here is the tile-on-sand process:

Dig out the soil to about 1 inch below the desired grade. Tamp down or roll the earth smooth. Set the outer border in place—rows of tile or header boards —and allow a drainage slope of 1/8-inch per foot. Pour in sand and level it with a board. Do not use more than a 1/2-inch bed of sand, or the tiles will tilt when you step on them. Start in a corner and set the tiles in place; butt them tightly against each other. Tap each one with a wooden block to bed it into the sand firmly.

Brick

Brick is a most popular paving material because it is difficult to commit a serious error when paving with it. Using the simple method of brick-on-sand, if the first attempt is not pleasing or accurate, it is easy to take up sections and relay them.

Brick comes in a variety of earthy colors. There are rough- and smooth-surfaced bricks, in glazed or unglazed surfaces. New shapes are available too— hexagons, octagons, fleur-de-lis. And colored brick— green, blue, olive—is also offered now.

Smooth-surfaced or rough-textured common brick is the best kind for patio floors. Face brick, including Roman and paving brick, is easy to work with and less expensive than slick kinds. Actually the choice depends upon your own tastes.

Generally, try to choose hard-burned rather than green brick. It should be dark red in color rather than salmon color which indicates an underburned process, and is less durable. When you decide on the kind of brick for the floor, be sure the dealer has a sufficient quantity to complete the area. There is usually some dimensional variation and color difference between bricks, so do not complicate your project.

If you are in a climate where winters are severe specify SW (severe weathering) brick.

It is simple to install a brick on sand paving, but it is not a job to do in haste. Do it in sections—a small piece at a time—rather than try to finish an entire floor in a day. Grading and leveling must be done first and pains taken to have a perfectly level sand base of 2 to 3 inches. Otherwise, the floor will be wavy and visually distracting.

Brick can be laid in an incredible number of patterns. Herringbone, basketweave, and running bond are only a few choices. Brick can also be combined with other materials—squares of grass or cinders—in endless designs. The herringbone pattern looks good in large areas; smaller patios look best with running bond or a basketweave design. Or the area can be broken by fitting bricks into redwood or cedar grid patterns.

To cut or trim bricks use a cold chisel or a brick hammer. Cut a groove along one side of the brick with the chisel and then give it a final severing blow. Smooth uneven bricks by rubbing the edges with another brick.

Brick on sand is installed as follows: grade the soil with a board and tamp it down thoroughly. Slope the floor away from the house—1 inch to 6 feet of paving—to allow for drainage. Put in a 2- to 3-inch cushion of sand; level the sand. Set the bricks as close together as possible and check each row with a level as you go. Then dust sand into the cracks.

For edgings, I use 2- by 4-inch wooden header strips held firmly in place with stakes. Or, should you prefer, use a border of bricks set in concrete.

Brick can also be set in mortar, but this is usually a job for a bricklayer.

WOODEN FLOORS

A wooden floor is a maintenance-free floor. And although a deck is logical for a hillside home, it can also be serviceable on a level site.

Wood has a warm feeling, is easy to clean, dries quickly in rain, and is easier on the feet than concrete or brick. The deck that is raised above grade is especially attractive. It becomes a green island when decorated with pot plants.

Use lumber of good quality. Redwood does not need a preservative and stands up well against weather. But the deck does not have to be redwood. Other woods coated with preservatives will last for many years. Ask the lumber dealer in your area to recommend the best quality wood for the deck.

There are many ways to build a deck, and several styles to choose from. The raised deck is handsome, and the platform is visually pleasing in the landscape. A deck at the same floor level as the house gives an illusion of space. An L-shaped deck affords a view from two sides of the home.

The basic steps in building a deck are given here. (Lumber and construction details will vary depending on how big the area is and how it will be used.)

Outline the area with stakes and strings to locate the posts. Dig holes 18 inches deep. You can use concrete piers (available at lumberyards) and set them into the holes. Or put 6 inches of gravel into the holes and then cut 4- by 4-inch posts to length and set them in place with poured concrete. Set posts in rows 4 feet apart (with posts spaced not more than 6 feet in each row). Bolt 2- by 8-inch beams to the posts.

Planking can be 2 by 3's, 2 by 4's, or even 2 by 6's if you need a very sturdy deck. Lay the planks about 1/2 inch apart so that water will drain off readily, and arrange them at right angles to each other, or vary the size and placement across the area to create

A deck does not have to be uninteresting; this one has an appealing pattern and is easy to build.
(California Redwood Assoc.)

A handsome island deck provides a sunning area for bathers and is well designed so it becomes a total part of the outdoor plan.
(California Redwood Assoc.; Phil Palmer photo)

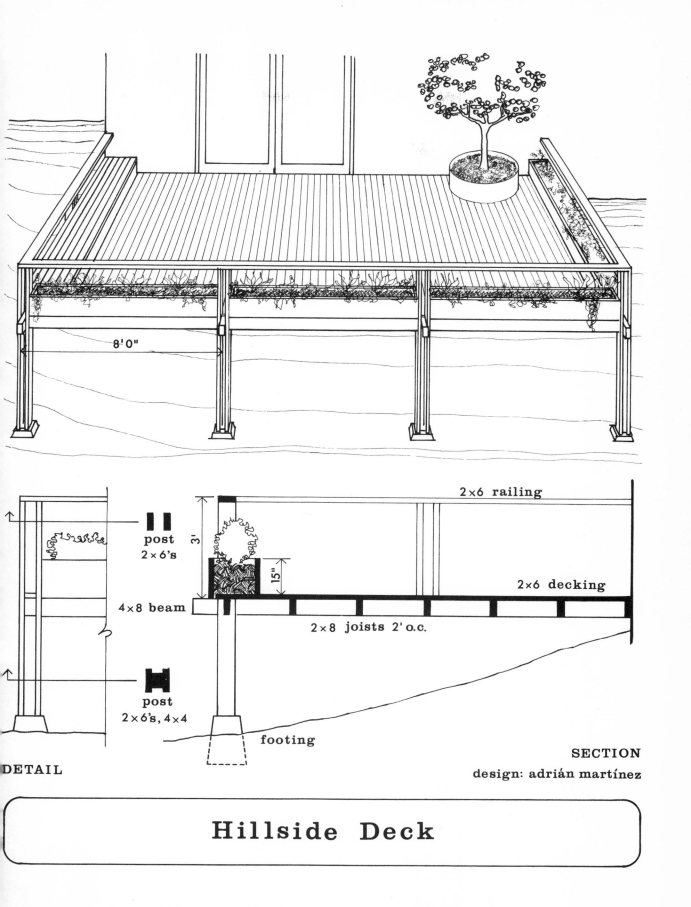

8'0"

2×6 railing

post
2×6's

3'

15"

2×6 decking

4×8 beam

2×8 joists 2'o.c.

post
2×6's, 4×4

footing

SECTION
design: adrián martínez

DETAIL

Hillside Deck

interesting patterns. Nail planking in place with 16-penny nails.

PATIO BLOCKS

Thick patio blocks or pavers are new; they are made of concrete that has been vibrated under pressure. They are uniform in thickness and have straight edges. And they are made in several shapes—hexagon, round, and random—in several colors. The pavers are laid directly on a sand base so that they are free to move and are not rigid in place. This almost eliminates the cracking that can result from a poured concrete floor.

To install patio pavers, mark the boundaries with string and stakes. Take out about 2 inches of soil to accommodate a sand base. Dampen the soil and then add the sand and tamp it down. Level the sand and establish a slope away from the house for drainage. Place a sheet of polyethylene over the sand to prevent weeds or grass from growing up between the blocks. Start in a corner, and be sure that each block is put in place absolutely level.

WOOD BLOCKS AND ROUNDS

Blocks and rounds of wood look natural in a woodland setting. The rounds, about 4 inches thick, are cut from trunks of redwood, cedar, or cypress, and can be placed in a random fashion on a sand base. The square blocks are usually strips of lumber or cut-up railroad ties. Even coated with preservatives, wood paving only lasts about 5 years. It is likely to crack in intense sun, or split in severe frosts. Yet, wood rounds and pieces of railroad ties are different and can easily be removed and replaced with other paving material when the time comes.

Redwood rounds come in sizes from 6 to 36 inches. They are easily set in place. Grade the soil and put in a 2-inch sand base. Place the rounds in a random pattern and fill in between them with soil or crushed gravel.

To install wood blocks, dig out the soil to a depth of 1 inch greater than the thickness of the blocks. Tamp down the ground and fill with a 1-inch sand base. Place the blocks in the desired pattern. Fill spaces between them with sand.

LOOSE-FILL MATERIALS

Loose-fill flooring is generally temporary, but it is easily installed in a few hours. It can be attractive too. There are many materials for soft flooring. New ones appear periodically.

Wood chips are very popular because they are easily put into place. They come in small, medium, or large-grade sizes. The large-grade size is the most satisfactory and lasts for about two years. Installed in a wooden grid pattern, wood chips are handsome. The brownish-red color adds warmth to an area. The chips are sold under different trade names such as firbark, tanbark, and so on.

Lavarock is chunks of porous stone available under different names and in different colors. It is difficult to walk on, and in time wears away. However, it is a simple, inexpensive covering that can be replaced with a more durable surface when necessary.

Dolomite, or pieces of clean limestone, is bright white. In squares combined with other materials, this surfacing is dramatic. But with wear, dolomite discolors and must be replaced.

Crushed brick has a bright-red color that gives striking accent to planting. The brick eventually breaks down and wears away. Yet, it is perhaps the best of the loose-fill materials for durability.

Gravel or marble chips conform to the contour of the ground and are strictly temporary pavings. Loose gravel or pebbles or granite washes out of place, so use a high border to keep it confined—wooden strips or bricks are fine.

To install a loose-fill material, dig out 6 to 8 inches of ground. Cover the area with heavy polyethylene plastic to keep weeds out. Then pour 2 to 3 inches of fine gravel over the plastic. Put the chips in place, level, and rake them so that the surface is easy to walk on.

Plastic stones coated with vinyl are yet another recent innovation for outdoor coverings. In many colors, the stone is made from igneous rock, and can be used for paths, driveways, and patios. The material is said to be fade-proof and will not chip or chalk for 7 to 12 years. It is nonallergic and nontoxic to plants and people, and comes in 50- and 100-pound waterproof bags.

Installation is simple: a shallow bed is prepared, and the stones are laid in place and then raked or brushed level with a board. Edging strips can also be put down to keep the stones confined.

INDOOR-OUTDOOR CARPETING

Indoor-outdoor carpeting is a fresh approach in patio flooring. New innovations appear frequently. Originally, the material was available in only a few colors and in a few standard widths. It now comes in many colors and designs and in easily installed block sections, 12 by 12 inches square.

However, indoor-outdoor carpeting is more costly than most conventional outdoor surfacing; there is no definite data on just how long it will withstand weather conditions before deteriorating. The carpet requires a wood or concrete subfloor. There are even some synthetic carpeting products that simulate grass, but at this writing they are extremely expensive if a large area is required.

OTHER PAVING MATERIALS

There are many kinds of concrete patio blocks. Some have a smooth texture; others are covered with small pebbles or have embedded chips. Some are concrete color; others come in pastel shades. Sizes: to 16 inches square, 1 1/2-inches thick.

Slate is available in rectangles, squares, or irregular pieces and in numerous colors, and it makes a striking floor. Slate has a slight-textured finish, is resistant to strain, and comes in 1-inch or 1/2-inch thicknesses. It is elegant in appearance and lasts a lifetime, but it is rarely inexpensive.

Fieldstone makes a casual floor because of its natural variations in shape, texture, and color. Select flat stones for the upper side, with bottom irregularities sunk into the ground. The success of the pattern depends upon your patience in fitting and aligning the stones properly.

Flagstone is hard, stratified stone (sandstone, shale, slate, or marble) split into flat pieces. It may be laid dry on a sand base or in mortar. For masonry installation use stone 1-inch thick; for dry-laying, 1 1/2-inches thick.

Unique pole planters
with graceful dracaenas
are the feature of this garden.
(Architectural Pottery Co.)

Containers come in many shapes
and sizes, glazed or unglazed.
(Joyce R. Wilson)

CHAPTER 19

Container Gardening

Container gardening is not new. The Hanging Gardens of Babylon, the Adonis Gardens of Greece, Domitian's Palace in Rome were decorated with plants in pots. Through the centuries it has proved to be the easy way to garden. A plant is put within the confines of a container and placed where you want it for display. For basket plants, see Chapter 27.

The beauty, ease and practicability of this kind of gardening cannot be ignored. This is instant color for any garden area. There is no need to wait for plants to grow and no need to be concerned if the soil around the house will not support plants. And almost any kind of plant—tree, shrub, flowering kind—can be grown in a tub or box temporarily or permanently. Some plants, such as camellias and azaleas, do better in a box than in the ground. And there are varieties like the Bonanza peach especially bred for tub growing.

For a long time the standard container for a plant was the terra-cotta pot with a maximum size of 16 inches in diameter. Today, there are many kinds of pots and tubs and boxes to decorate the outdoors.

Even where summers are short, plants in containers are the answer when living color is needed. Along paths and walks, on patios and terraces, rooftop gardens or apartment balconies, portable gardening cannot be beat. On movable dollies (available at hardware stores) plants can easily be moved indoors in winter. The lemon tree that decorated the patio can go in the unheated but not freezing enclosed porch. The Norfolk pine that was on the terrace can become part of the living room, and the tree-form azalea can grace an entry hall.

CONTAINERS

There are so many containers, it is wise to select them carefully and have some idea where they go so that they will blend in with the setting. Wooden tubs are more suitable for outdoors than indoors; glazed pots, jardinieres, and urns are perhaps best used in living or dining rooms. To have some idea of just what is available, here is a list of containers.

The standard clay pot is now offered in many variations:

Italian type. This pot has a modified border to a tight-lipped detail. It is simple and good looking. Some have round edges; others are beveled or rimless. This pot comes in sizes from 12 to 24 inches in diameter.

Venetian pots. Barrel shaped, with a concentric band design pressed into the sides. Somewhat formal in appearance. They come in 8- to 20-inch sizes.

Spanish pots. These pots have outward sloping sides and flared lips. They come in 8- to 12-inch sizes. They have heavier walls than conventional pots and make good general containers for many plants.

Cylindrical shape. These are new and are a departure from the traditional tapered design, being perfectly straight from top to bottom. They come in three sizes at present, with a maximum 14-inch diameter.

Bulb pans or seed bowls. Generally less than half as wide as they are high, these shallow containers appear like deep saucers but have drain holes. They are available in 6- to 12-inch sizes.

Azalea or fern pot. A squatty container formerly sold in only a few sizes. It is three-quarters as high as it is wide and is in better proportion to most plants than conventional pots.

Three-legged pots. Another recent offering that brings the bowl shape to the garden. They range in size from 8 to 20 inches.

Donkey or chicken containers. Novelty pots with pockets for soil. Strawberry jars in various sizes are also offered at nurseries.

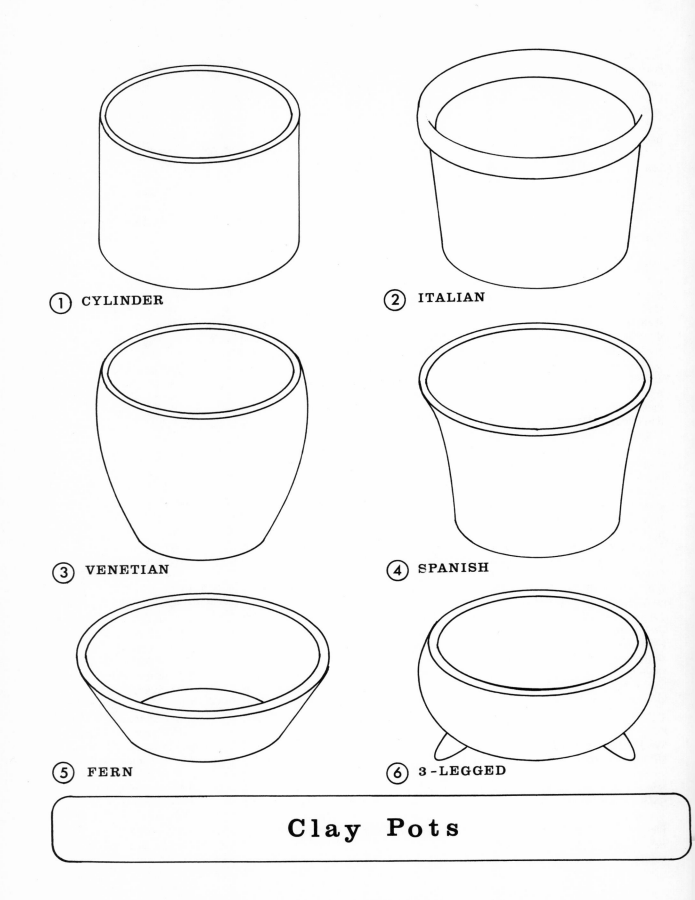

① CYLINDER

② ITALIAN

③ VENETIAN

④ SPANISH

⑤ FERN

⑥ 3-LEGGED

Clay Pots

Plastic pots are lightweight and come in many sizes and colors, in round or square shapes. They are easy to clean and hold water longer than terra-cotta pots, so the plants require less frequent watering—an advantage to some gardeners. They are not suitable for large plants because they have a tendency to tip over.

Most plastic pots are opaque, but there are also some in small sizes (to 10 inches) that are translucent. However, I hardly find these attractive because roots can be seen through them.

TUBS

Tubs may be round, square, or hexagonal. If wooden, be sure they are made of suitable woods, like redwood or cypress, to resist decay; otherwise, they will need a preservative coating. Stone or concrete tubs are ornamental but are very heavy when filled with soil. In several sizes, tapered stone bowls are especially pretty with petunias or marigolds.

Japanese soy tubs are inexpensive and handsome, and plants look good in them. They can be found at nurseries, along with wood and bamboo tubs. Buy the best quality, because cheap versions have a tendency to deteriorate within a few months.

Glazed pots come in a wide variety of colors and in many handsome shapes. These pots, however, usually do not have drainage holes, and soil can become a soggy mess in the bottom, eventually harming a plant. It is better to slip a potted plant into a glazed tub rather than risk overwatering the plant; or take a glazed container to a glass store and have a hole drilled in it.

Sawed-off wine casks and barrels and kegs and washtubs painted dark colors are other possibilities. Oriental urns and jardinieres are always attractive, but they are rarely inexpensive.

Architectural planters of high-fired clay in a wide range of related shapes and sizes keyed to today's architecture are available at garden centers or department stores. They come in an unglazed off-white finish or glazed in colors. Specify drainage holes in them.

BOXES

Wooden boxes are necessary for most trees and shrubs. The largest tub simply does not hold enough soil or carry enough visual weight to balance a tree. Some boxes are perfect cubes, others a low cube. Some of them are detailed; others are plain.

Hanging baskets and self-watering containers complete the assortment of containers. No doubt more new designs and materials will be introduced in the future.

CARE OF CONTAINER PLANTS

Container gardening entails no more work than any other type of plant growing, and perhaps it is easier. Plants are in one area and can be watered easily; tubs and boxes can be moved if there is too much sun or not enough light. Vegetables, herbs, and bulbs are all possibilities for container growing. A whole new world of gardening is at your fingertips.

A good soil is important for all plants, and especially for plants in tubs and pots and boxes that spend their life in a confined space. Here are some basic soils I use:

For most plants:

2 parts garden loam
1 part sand
1 part leafmold
1 teaspoon bone meal for an 8-inch pot

For begonias and ferns:

2 parts garden loam
2 parts sand
2 parts leafmold

For bulbs:

2 parts garden loam
1 part sand
1 part leafmold

For cacti and succulents:

2 parts garden loam
2 parts sand
1 part leafmold
handful of limestone for an 8-inch pot

For bromeliads and orchids:

1 part medium-grade fir bark
1 part chopped osmunda

Potting. Place sufficient drainage material in the bottom of the container so that excess water drains away quickly. Use broken pieces of pots or some crushed stone. Spread a layer of soil over the stones, about 3 inches for a container 16 inches in diameter. Remove the plant to be potted from its original container. Do not pull or tug it loose; try to tease it loose by gently jiggling it back and forth. Center the plant on the bed of soil and fill in and around it with fresh soil, pressing down with your fingers or a blunt-edged piece of wood, to eliminate air pockets. Do not press the soil tightly in place, but be sure it is firm. Add more soil until the pot is filled to 1 inch from the rim. Water thoroughly and place in a partially shaded area for a few days; then move it to its permanent place.

Be sure the size of the plant is in proportion to the container. A small plant will not be attractive in a large pot, and unused portions of the soil are liable to

A long, narrow redwood planter is
striking in this outdoor scene.
It is built to fit the space and
is an integral part of the design.
*(California Redwood Assoc.; Osmundon
& Stanley, Landscape Architects)*

A contemporary architectural
planter brimming with succulents is
an elegant accent on this patio.
(Architectural Pottery Co.)

A pair of wooden boxes hold
graceful ferns in this charming
corner arrangement.
(Hort-Pix)

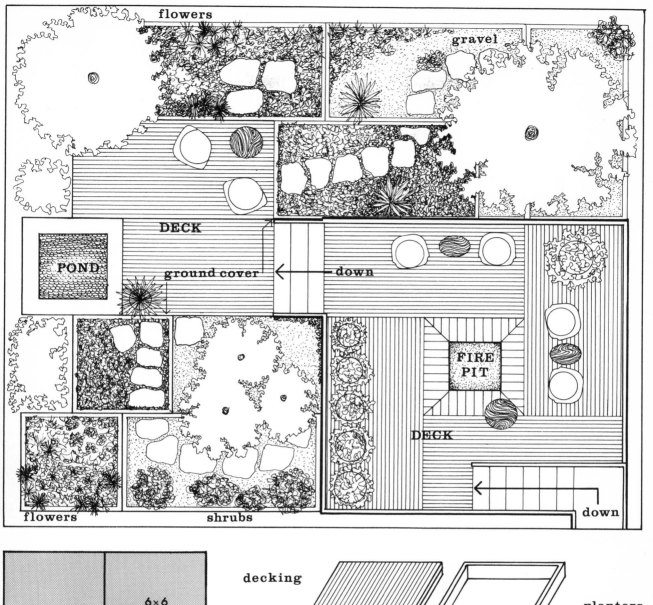

flowers

gravel

DECK

POND

ground cover ← down

FIRE PIT

DECK

down

flowers

shrubs

down

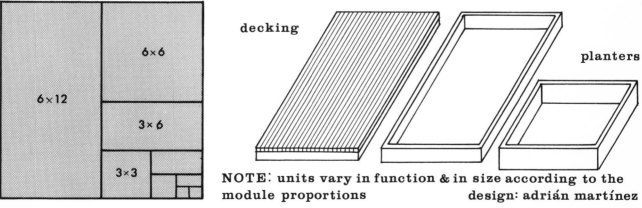

6 × 12

6 × 6

3 × 6

3 × 3

decking

planters

NOTE: units vary in function & in size according to the
module proportions   design: adrián martínez

Modular Container Garden

remove 1" to 2"

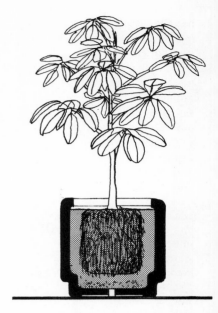

① **REMOVE CAREFULLY**   ② **TRIM ROOT BALL**   ③ **RE·POT W. FRESH SOIL**

Transplanting Container Plants

<u>DO NOT</u> HOSE DIRECTLY INTO SOIL

<u>DO</u> WATER SLOWLY W. A BUBBLER

IF ROOT BALL SHRINKS FROM POT, SOAK IN TUB

Watering Container Plants

become waterlogged, harming the plant. A big plant in a small pot is hardly handsome, and in most cases does not grow well.

Watering. Container plants exposed to the elements dry out more quickly than plants in the ground. Of course, watering them depends on rainfall, the size of the container (large ones dry out more slowly than small ones), and the type of box or tub used. Glazed pots without drainage holes—urns, jugs—need careful watering to avoid a stagnant soil. Wooden tubs and boxes dry out slowly, and metal containers stay wet for many days.

When you water, really soak the plant. Sparse watering results in pockets of the soil becoming wet and eventually waterlogged. Water should run freely out of the drainage hole. A good rule to follow is to water plants thoroughly, and then allow them to become somewhat dry before watering them again. Occasionally hose down the foliage to flush out hiding insects in the leaf axils and veins. Large plants are difficult to move to the water source. With these, use a damp cloth to wipe the leaves.

Feeding. Plants in containers need feeding. Use a commercial soluble fertilizer 10–10–5 (contents marked on bottle) mixed weaker than the directions on the bottle indicate, but use it more often. Avoid a set schedule for feeding plants. In general, large plants in containers 18 to 36 inches in diameter will need feeding about four times in summer and those in smaller pots about once a month during the growing season. Do not feed ailing plants or newly potted ones. Do not feed at all in winter, but light solutions can be given once in early spring and once in the fall.

PLANTS TO GROW

There is no end to the kind of plant that can be grown in a tub or box. Small trees are always desirable for the patio or terrace, and shrubs are essential to make a setting attractive. Plants grown to tree form (standards) and espaliers (shaped plants against a wall) are touches of elegance to make an area unique. (See Chapter 16.)

Large pots filled with soil weigh a great deal. Make provisions for moving them. Commercial dollies are

available at nurseries. Or make your own moving devices for the plants; use 2 by 4 boards with casters under them.

TREES AND SHRUBS

Small trees are basic container subjects. They offer some shade and provide visual background. The relationship of the tree and its tub must be considered. A 4-foot tree would be minimum for a 24-inch container. This gives a satisfying balance. Square or rectangular boxes are best for trees with bold foliage, whereas a lacy-leaved Japanese maple looks best in the graceful outlines of a round container.

Small trees at nurseries come in 5-, 10-, or 15-gallon cans. Decide whether you want a fast-growing or a slow-growing kind. If you are not in an all-year temperate climate, consider where the tree will go in winter. Some of them can be placed in a sunny window, others in an unheated but not freezing garage or porch, and others in a basement with a little light.

In climates with severe winters, and where there is no indoor space for plants, select hardy trees and shrubs. The degree of hardiness of trees and shrubs is difficult to determine; each section of the country has its own definition. However, there are certain plants that are considered hardy where temperatures go well below freezing.

Where shrubs are used, the relationship between the plant and the container should be about equal. Large terra-cotta pots with a lip or without detailing are fine for shrubs. For plants like azaleas and geraniums with little significant height, a low container—a concrete pot, perhaps—is best. Or use three-legged pots.

LISTS OF PLANTS FOR CONTAINER GARDENING

Tables 18 and 19 list container plants that have been selected because they have some outstanding feature or because they grow with little care. The list is by no means complete, but is, rather, a sampling of many fine plants for container growing.

Table 18. Trees for Container Gardening

Botanical and Common Name	Min. Night Temp.	General Description	Remarks
Acer palmatum (Japanese maple)	—10 to 0F	Lovely lacy leaves	Handsome in soy tub or in round container
Araucaria excelsa (Norfolk pine)	Tender	Pyramid shape	Good vertical accent in Spanish flare-lip pot

Table 18 (Continued)

Botanical and Common Name	Min. Night Temp.	General Description	Remarks
Betula populifolia (gray birch)	—20 to —10F	Deciduous; irregular in shape	Fine patio tree or along house wall
Cedrus atlantica glauca (Blue Atlas cedar)	0 to 10F	Needle evergreen, with sprawling habit	Fine accent in large tubs near house corners
Citrus (orange, lemon, lime)	Tender	Dark-green leaves; nice branching effect	Excellent trees, indoors or out
Eriobotrya japonica (loquat)	20 to 30F	Round-headed, w/dark-green leaves	Good for tubs and boxes
Ficus benjamina (weeping fig)	Tender	Tiny dark-green leaves; branching habit	Good special effect in garden or indoors in tubs
Gingko biloba (gingko)	—30 to —20F	Deciduous; lovely foliage	Handsome in containers; nice accent near house walls
Laburnum watereri (golden chain tree)	—10 to —5F	Deciduous; columnar shape	Good patio tub plant
Lagerstroemeria indica (crape myrtle)	—20 to —10F	Deciduous, w/ pink flowers	Showy for patio
Magnolia soulangiana (saucer magnolia)	—20 to —10F	Deciduous, w/ round form, lovely flowers	Good near fence or wall
Malus sargenti (Sargent crab apple)	—30 to —20F	Dwarf; round-topped form	Perimeter decoration for paved area
Phellodendron amurense (cork tree)	—40 to —30F	Deciduous, attractive branching tree	For a special place
Phoenix loureiri (date palm)	Tender	Lovely, arching fronds	An indoor-outdoor favorite
Pinus mugo mughas (mugho pine)	—40 to —30F	Irregular outline; broad and sprawling	To decorate paths, walks, and patios
Pinus parviflora glauca (Japanese white pine)	—10 to —5F	Needle evergreen with horizontal growth	Nice feature in and around garden
Pinus thunbergii (Japanese black pine)	—20 to —10F	Good spreading habit	Excellent container plant
Podocarpus gracilior	Tender	Graceful willowy branches	Good doorway plant
Rhapis excelsa (lady palm)	Tender	Dark-green, fan-shaped leaves	A stellar container plant
Salix matsudana tortuosa (contorted Hankow willow)	—20 to —10F	Lovely sweeping branches	For a special place
Schefflera acontifolia (Australian umbrella tree)	Tender	Graceful stems tipped w/fronds of leaves	Handsome in terra-cotta Spanish pot

Table 19. Shrubs for Container Gardening

Botanical and Common Name	Min. Night Temp.	General Description	Remarks
Abutilon (flowering maple)	Tender	Bell-shaped flowers of paper-thin texture	Give plenty of water and sun
Azalea (See Rhododendron.)	Check with nursery	Brilliant flowers, lush growth; many varieties	Great for portable gardens
Camellia japonica (common camellia)	5 to 10F	Handsome flowers in many colors	Another excellent container plant

Table 19 (Continued)

Botanical and Common Name	Min. Night Temp.	General Description	Remarks
Camellia sasanqua (sasanqua camellia)	5 to 10F	Mostly small white flowers	Many varieties
Cotoneaster (many varieties)	Check with nursery	Glossy leaves; colorful berries	Small and large ones; many varieties
Fatsia japonica (aralia)	Tender	Foliage plant with fanlike leaves on tall stems	Makes bold appearance
Gardenia jasminoides (Cape jasmine)	10 to 30F	Dark-green leaves and fragrant white blooms	New blooming varieties available
Hibiscus rosa-sinensis (Chinese hibiscus)	20 to 30F	Glossy, dark-green foliage; large flowers	Good performer in tubs or boxes
Juniperus chinensis 'pfitzeriana' (Pfitzer juniper)	—20 to —10F	Blue-green foliage	Good screen plant
Juniperus communis depressa (prostrate juniper)	—50 to —35F	Blue-green foliage	Forms dense mass
Ilex crenata (holly)	—5 to 5F	Glossy leaves; bright berries	Many good varieties
Ixora (star flower)	Tender	Small red flowers	Splendid color in white tubs
Nerium oleander (oleander)	10 to 20F	Dark-green leaves and bright flowers	Needs large container and lots of water
Osmanthus ilicifolius (holly olive)	—5 to 5F	Glossy leaves on upright stems	Grows fast in tubs
Pittosporum tobira	10 to 20F	Arching branches	Can be trained to shape
Plumbago capensis (blue phlox)	20 to 30F	Small leaves and blue flowers	Robust grower
Podocarpus macrophyllus	Tender	Bright green leaves	Attractive in tubs
Rhododendron (many varieties)	Check with nursery	Many varieties	Excellent container plants
Rosa (many varieties)	Check with nursery	All kinds and colors	Do very well in containers
Thuja occidentalis (arborvitae)	—50 to —35F	Evergreens	Tough plants for untoward conditions
Viburnum (many varieties)	Check with nursery	Attractive leaves and pretty flowers and berries	Many varieties
Yucca filamentosa (Spanish bayonet) (Adam's needle)	—20 to —10F	Blue-green, sword-shaped leaves	Dramatic in tubs

A sylvan retreat is created in the city with pool, plants, and flowers.
(Eldon Danhausen)

CHAPTER 20

The City Garden

The "Beautify America" program has extended far beyond our streets and sidewalks. City gardens of all types are enjoying renewed popularity. And what is more pleasant than an island of greenery to relieve the monotony of steel and glass! Even new high-rise apartment buildings have balconies or terraces, small though they may be, for plants. With careful planning, even a postage stamp-sized retreat can be charming.

City gardening was the earliest form of ornamental horticulture and the art of landscape design has developed through many centuries. The Persians, Greeks, and Chinese were avid gardeners, and the beauty of the French and English garden is well known. The importance of living plants in past cultures cannot be denied, and the resurgence of interest in gardening today is heartening. More and more, I see fine examples of city gardens.

The advantages of the urban garden—doorway, backyard, or roof area—are evident. Growing plants in the city is somewhat more difficult than in the country; however, the satisfaction of creating a lovely greenery far outweighs any extra work that might be involved.

Because of air pollution and lack of sun in the city, plants must be chosen carefully, and because of space limitations, gardens must be cleverly designed. Yet, these challenges are easily met if you have some knowledge of plants and plan the garden on paper before you start.

SOIL

Buy the best possible soil you can afford and keep it in top condition. In the city, it is difficult to replenish it, so fertilize and use proper chemical additives to keep the soil fertile. Sacks of soil are costly. If you are starting a new garden, it is far more economical to buy soil by the yard. Generally, soil will be delivered by the cubic yard in a truck.

If the topsoil you buy is of good quality, you do not have to do much to it. There may be some stones and debris in it, but these materials are easily picked out. The ideal topsoil is somewhere between a sandy soil, which does not hold moisture, and a clay soil which retains moisture. It should be porous and have a fine texture. (See Chapter 2.)

When you are filling containers with soil, provide materials for drainage. Use gravel, pebbles, clinkers—whatever is handy. The main requirement is that the drainage pieces have curved surfaces so that air and water can circulate between them. Whatever you use for drainage material, spread it evenly over the bottom of the container, about 1 inch for each foot of soil.

In areas where there is existing soil, break it up and add fresh soil; mix it with a rake and hoe. Take your time and do a thorough job.

PLANT MATERIALS

Some plants simply do not grow in city conditions, but there are many others that, with reasonable care, will flourish. Vines are especially good, and so are espaliers to decorate walls and fences. Container plants are the backbone of the city garden. So are seasonal flowering varieties to add color and drama to the area.

Standards—plants grown to tree form—contribute an elegant look to an area. Many of them, such as oleander, rose, fuchsia, and lantana, are available. Placed strategically, they give the garden a profes-

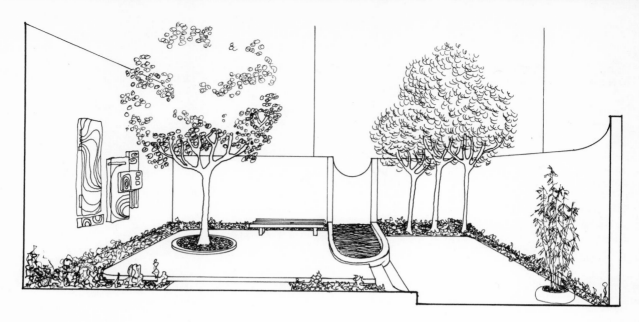

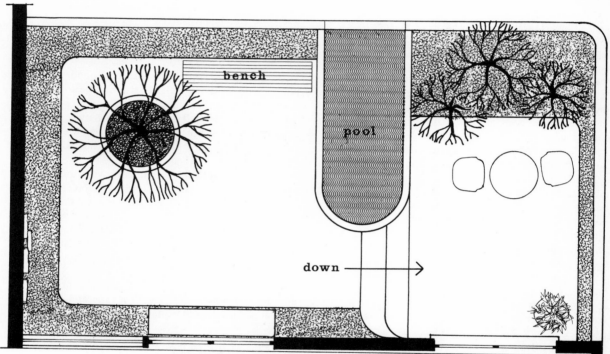

bench

pool

down →

PLAN

design: adrián martínez

City Garden

Simplicity in design and low maintenance keynote this small city garden; yet every feature of a usable outdoor area is in evidence. It is a place to relax or a place to stroll; there is not too much greenery yet just enough to set the scene.

The shaped pool is the feature of the garden and its curved lines are repeated in the step arrangement and again in the wall design. The ample patio area of concrete is purposely on two levels to break the monotony of a concrete pad and to provide eye interest.

Trees are used sparingly, but with purpose, as vertical accents. Three trees in the corner of the garden create a circular mass of green and the tree at the other end of the garden is somewhat large and standing alone heightens the effect of the pool. A container plant adds a needed vertical line in the foreground.

Easy-to-care-for ground cover frames the patios; this is a restrained yet pleasing garden oasis well suited to a city site.

sional touch. Use them; they cannot be beat for decoration. And in the winter, they can be moved to a frost-free garage, or extra room, or even a porch. (See Chapter 16.)

Paths and walks are important in the small city garden, and here is the place for flower beds and borders and well-chosen shrubs. There will not be space for too many plants, so select strong robust species to glorify these areas.

Trees, too, are important. They bring the country into the city. Generally, there will not be room for many of them, but even one Japanese flowering cherry or a pair of magnolias transform an ordinary garden into a special place.

Cascading plants in baskets make the outdoor area especially bright and cheerful. If there is wall space or rafters to hang them from, hanging baskets of petunias or dipladenias are a glorious sight.

Because there are many kinds of plants and so many ways to use them, plan carefully. Decide just what your sylvan retreat will be before you start, but do not despair if you cannot achieve it in the first year. Most gardens take several years before they are truly rewarding.

BACKYARD GARDENS

In the city, space is at a premium, so backyards are generally small. Don't let size or location of the area defeat you. But remember that the full effect of the garden must be complete within the confines of the boundaries. Here, there is no help from nature in the form of backdrops of trees or shrubs.

Select unique pavings to make the small area seem larger. Set up custom planters in step-fashion to accommodate many plants. Use decorative plant stands (many kinds are available at garden centers) with multiple holders. Grow vines and espaliers to transform bare walls into walls of color. Select vertical trees to give illusion of height. And bring in florists' plants like chrysanthemums, cyclamens, and geraniums for seasonal color.

Some gardens will have a section of brick or slate floor; others merely a path with flower beds. Consider what kind of area you want before you start. Observe the sunniest places and reserve them for flowers. Decide on the personality of the area: will it be formal, Japanese, or rustic? Try to follow one dominant theme; it's easier to work with than a combination of ideas. And always, of course, in choosing your theme, be sure it is in keeping with the architecture of your house.

To integrate the garden and the house, planting beds and paved areas are needed. Although the rectangular shape is easiest to work with, it many times lacks the charm and grace that is found in gentle curves or free-form lines. If there are existing trees or shrubs in the yard, try to work around them to create a pleasing setting. Leave an opening, 2 or 3 feet, in the flooring and build a square or circular raised bed around it. However, if the existing shrubbery is really unpleasing, then, and only then, remove it and start fresh.

A city garden usually needs privacy and protection—fences and walls. While most retreats will already have some kind of barrier, fences are bound to need repair. In this case, it is best to start fresh because new materials—plastics, perforated concrete, tempered glass panels—have given us new kinds of barriers. If you have a small shady area, select a fretwork fence so that light can enter. Vines on the fence look good and in time assure privacy.

Be wary of very tall (over 6 feet) fences. They look formidable and your neighbors may object to them. And by all means, consult your neighbors; they may even share part of the cost of the fence.

While an overhead structure like a canopy or trellis is possible for backyard gardens, it usually is not necessary unless there are neighbors above you. Even then, a tree can do the job just as well.

Paths and paved areas are vital in the small garden; consider them first before you do any planting. Because of the limited area, keep paths to a minimum. Paving stones or cross sections of tree trunks, called "rounds," are pleasing. They create design where a straight path tends to be monotonous. Borders for paths or flower beds—brick or concrete stone—are other accents that add attractiveness to the design.

If the soil is bad, put in raised beds for planting. In this way, you add depth to the soil and put plants at a height where they can be seen better by visitors and, at the same time, take much of the backache out of tending the plants. Raised beds can be drywalls of fieldstone or mortar walls of concrete or brick or redwood. All of these are do-it-yourself weekend projects.

In the confines of the city garden, every plant is important. Be sure they are healthy specimens and keep them well groomed. They are always on display. A bench, fountain, or piece of statuary adds a decorative touch to the scene. Do not be afraid to use one; there are many fine examples at garden centers now.

In the city, seasonal container plants are stellar attractions. Group pots of geraniums or chrysanthemums for a real splash of brightness. Put them at corners and in rows along paths and near fences. Use annuals in low redwood boxes, pots of spring bulbs for instant color, and evergreens for winter.

There are many advantages to having a terrace rather than a garden on a small city lot. For example, the outdoor area can be a partial garden with

Secluded and attractive, a brick-wall garden is private and a pretty picture brimming with tulips. An easy garden to maintain and a delight to the eye.
(Hedrich•Blessing)

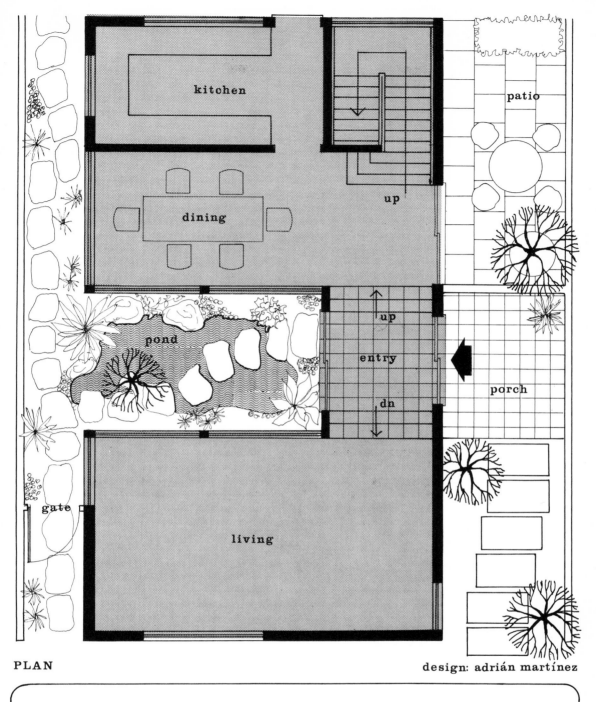

PLAN   design: adrián martínez

Side Yards

This narrow sideyard site was a problem in design; there just wasn't enough space to frame the house in a garden setting. Yet, through clever arrangement, it is done. The narrow site on the entry side was broken into three areas, each with its individual character, and yet totally harmonious.

The entrance walk is wide stepping-stones to give a feeling of space, the porch area utilizes block tile in checkerboard design and the patio too has its own individual paving pattern. Although all areas are rectangular in shape there is no monotony and visual spaciousness has been accomplished. The trees placed strategically at corners soften the wall lines and at the same time are pleasing in scale, neither too small nor too large.

On the left of the site a clever device was used; the garden was brought into the house in an atrium fashion in the form of a highly decorative pool. A visitor at the front door can see through to the pool, once again establishing a feeling of space where there really is little ground. The narrow planting strip that adjoins the pool no longer seems narrow but rather an extension of the atrium garden. Stepping-stones and lush plantings are incorporated throughout this area.

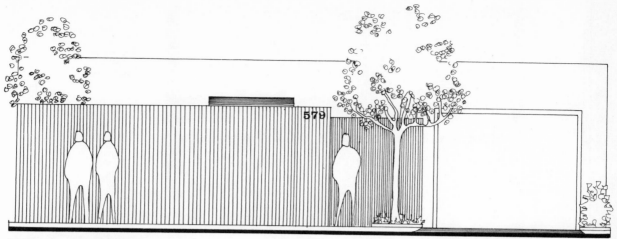

STREET ELEVATION

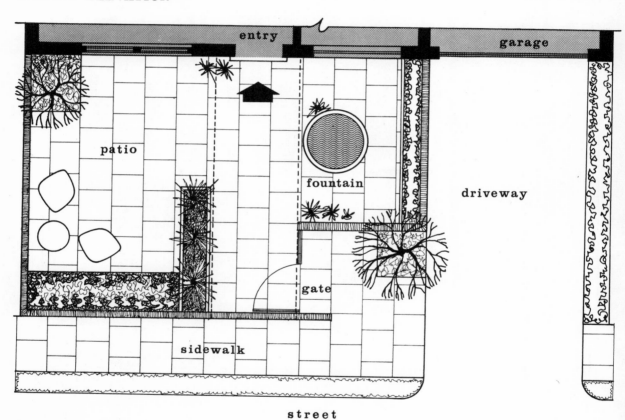

PLAN

design: adrián martínez

Entry Court

For this site, a garden was necessary in the front rather than in the rear. Reminiscent of Spanish courts, the plan provides complete privacy although it faces the street.

The setting is intimate, with L-shaped planters of low hedges; they appear in four places to provide greenery and pattern. The square-shaped site is never monotonous; there is eye interest in every angle.

The fountain, like the court, is small but decorative, its circular shape a pleasing contrast in an otherwise geometrical arrangement. Two small trees in planters further the design and offer visual accent.

Abrupt changes of directions of entries are purposeful here; they provide constant interest and changing scenes at every direction.

A quiet retreat is a stellar attraction in crowded city conditions. Although only a few trees and shrubs are used, the area is picturesque.
(Molly Adams)

Even on a narrow lot, a charming city garden is possible; there is no lawn (gravel is used) and there is little maintenance.
(Eldon Banhausen)

container plants; the paved surface can be a place for outdoor cookery with a table and a few chairs. No matter how small, the terrace adds more interest to a home than a garden. Even a 5- by 10-foot garden can become a handsome greenery instead of a massive tangle of weeds and other plants. A redwood platform bench or a planter box, an overhead trellis with attractive vines, a brick floor, and a few potted plants quickly reclaim the land from the house to the lot line for shaded, private outdoor living. Sliding glass doors from the house to the terrace add to the effectiveness of the area.

Plants in the city suffer from smoke and soot and are further hindered by lack of sun; most city gardens are shaded. Use robust plants like funkia and hosta that tolerate adverse conditions and still remain beautiful.

DOORWAY GARDENS

The doorway area is a small piece of hospitality, so don't leave this area barren. This is where the guest receives the first impression of what is to come. Plan this garden, small though it may be, with utmost care. Entry gardens or courtyards are indeed lovely, but most houses do not have space for them. The immediate area around the door becomes the focal point where green plants and colorful flowers can be a tremendous asset to the house.

Twin ceramic tubs of simple design filled with ivy or fatshedera are perfect for gracing a simple white door of a Colonial house. Be wary of the plant's scale. Height and mass should be in good balance with the size of the door. In winter, the tubbed plants can be moved indoors.

If there are steps leading to the doorway, use twin tubs of foliage that have mass and volume, but do not impede traffic.

A formal entrance porch with a roof needs some low and round box hedges in front of it and then, perhaps, a pair of big white boxes with small gingkos.

Antique urns filled with flowering plants set on brick platforms (two high and two square) do much to make any entrance charming. If your doorway is severely plain, consider the use of a long redwood plant box filled with foliage plants; this arrangement smooths the transition from outdoors to indoors.

ROOFTOP GARDENS

Start with a good structural framework; often the inherited rooftop garden is a conglomeration of decayed boxes and tubs. Or the rooftop is nothing— just a roof and a parapet and sky. There is no tree or shrub or land contour to get you started. Railings,

floors, and other features must be constructed, and they are rarely inexpensive. Yet, while there are problems involved in developing a garden in the sky, what a joy it is to be able to step out of your living room onto a terrace filled with greenery.

To begin with, be sure the roof is strong enough to support a patio with plantings. Ask your building superintendent or an architect about placing additional weight on the structure. The matter of drainage is also important; generally, most roofs will have a slight slope; if not, drainage facilities must be installed to carry away excess water. Water that accumulates on rooftops can cause severe damage to ceilings. The surface of the roof must be completely watertight; a coat of asphalt does the job quickly. Flooring can be any of the materials mentioned in Chapter 18.

Most rooftop gardens will be container gardens. It is just too expensive to bring in enough soil to have a regular countryside scene. Suitable framework to contain the soil is necessary and must be incorporated in the total plan. Masonry—brick, stone, concrete—or wood-retaining walls are the choices, and each kind of planter or trough has its uses.

For a natural effect, use masonry planters; they last for years, and plants look good in them. Featherock or lavarock (weightless rocks) can be used too, and with good effect. Wood containers are fine, especially if the area is long and narrow, or if it is a small space. Here, masonry would be too heavy and too massive. You can make all kinds of containers for plants—shallow boxes for bulbs, deep planters for annuals or perennials, boxes for trees and shrubs. Red cedar or California redwood are the best woods to use for boxes.

Most roof gardens will have their share of wind; provide substantial fencing. Avoid plastic in this case; it rattles and makes a bothersome noise in the wind (even if it is properly installed). Try to use an open-work fence because plants need filtered sun and air; on very hot summer days, ventilation is important. Although trellises are certainly handsome, they are often fragile, so be sure they are firmly set in place. Open-ironwork screens are appealing; so is reed fencing, which makes a handsome background for flowers and plants. If you want to save the view and still have protection from wind, consider using tempered-glass panels set in wood frames.

With roof gardens, if trees are not possible, you may want an arbor or some form of awning as a shelter from sun and rain and, sometimes, from the neighbors' view. An overhead shelter also adds to the appearance of the area; it completes the setting. But before you decide on the structure, remember that a completely covered area will prevent rain from reaching plants and watering every day—in summer—will be necessary.

Concrete planters make this rooftop
garden a pleasant inviting place.
(National Concrete Masonry Assoc.)

This rooftop terrace, small though
it may be, is cleverly landscaped
with container plants for seasonal
color.
(Potted Plant Information Service)

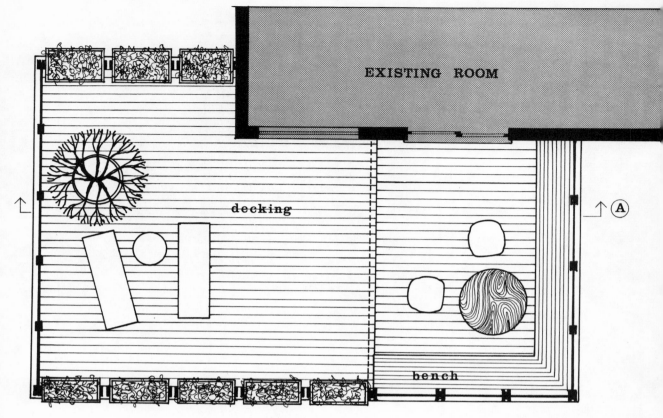

EXISTING ROOM

decking

PLAN

bench

note: the new structure is supported on existing bearing walls

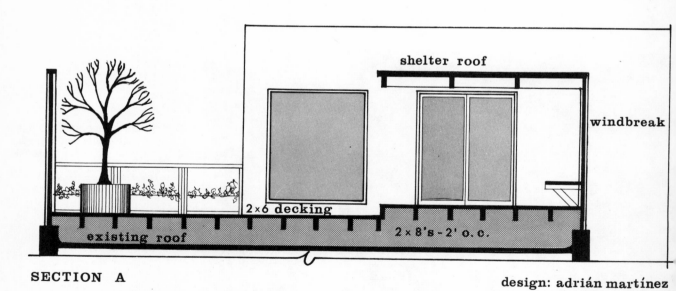

shelter roof

windbreak

2×6 decking

existing roof

2×8's-2' o.c.

SECTION A

design: adrián martínez

Rooftop Deck

Wood overhangs in a grid design are attractive and will allow some moisture to reach plants. With vines, grid construction is especially handsome, and there are so many vines with colorful flowers. Adjustable awnings on iron-pipe framework is another possibility. Today, canvas and awnings come in pleasing colors and designs.

In all cases, when selecting the shelter from sun and rain, be sure that there will be sufficient light to grow plants. Decide how the garden will be used—for dining and sitting, or for growing plants—and then select suitable coverings.

Whether you have planters, boxes, or tubs for the plants, raise them slightly above the patio floor so that air can circulate around the containers and there will be proper drainage. Use bricks or tiles or 2- by 4-inch wood blocks.

Tubs come in an array of different sizes and shapes; there are standard containers for trees and large shrubs. Clay pots can also be used. Today, there is no limit to different kinds of plant containers. Choose the one that suits the design of your garden. Very new are Duraclay pots, which are impervious to freezing and will not crack if left outdoors in winter.

Wind and intense summer sun are roof-gardening hazards. Select plants that can survive these conditions. (See Tables 20 and 21 below.)

When planning the garden, remember that it will be seen from indoors too. Make planting arrangements inviting. Don't forget perennials like hosta, iris, and rose-mallow. And do use annuals, even though they must be discarded in a season; they cost

little and brighten any area. Geraniums, fuchsias, petunias, and marigolds are other good possibilities.

BALCONY GARDENS

New apartment buildings with narrow balconies give the gardener little space for living plants. Yet, these long areas can be cleverly camouflaged to appear like green havens. It isn't easy, but it can be done. Here, vines and trainers are essential to cover bare walls, decorate railings, and in some cases to afford privacy from close-by neighbors. A small canvas or fiberglass awning is sometimes desirable, but one should first check with his building superintendent to see if this structure is allowed.

For balcony gardens, pots of seasonal flowering plants are indispensable; do not use one large pot; group several small ones together for a colorful display. If there is space, you might want window boxes on the sides of the balcony. A hanging basket on the wall, perhaps two, is another note of decoration. Often there is not space for much more on the narrow balcony, but even this small greenery is a welcome sight on a crowded street of brick buildings.

LISTS OF PLANTS FOR THE CITY

I found the plants listed in Tables 20 and 21 are more suitable to city conditions than other kinds. The majority of them can be grown in pots or boxes or, of course, they can be put into the ground if there is space.

Table 20. Trees for the City*

Botanical and Common Name	Approx. Height in Ft.	Min. Night Temp.	Remarks
Abies concolor (white fir)	120	—20 to —10F	Stiffly pyramidal
Acer platanoides (Norway maple)	90	—35 to —20F	Rounded dense tree; many varieties
Ailanthus altissima (tree of heaven)	60	—20 to —10F	Rounded; grows anywhere
Catalpa speciosa (western catalpa)	90	—20 to —10F	Loosely pyramidal
Crataegus oxyacantha (English hawthorn)	15	—20 to —10F	Spreading; round-headed
Crataegus phaenopyrum (Washington hawthorn)	30	—20 to —10F	Broadly columnar
Elaeagnus angustifolia (Russian olive)	20	—50 to —35F	Wide-spreading habit
Euonymus europaea (spindle tree)	20	—35 to —20F	Retains leaves late in fall
Fraxinus americana (white ash)	120	—35 to —20F	Erect with round top

* For espalier and vine plants, see Chapter 16.

Table 20 (*Continued*)

Botanical and Common Name	Approx. Height in Ft.	Min. Night Temp.	Remarks
Gingko biloba (gingko)	120	—20 to —10F	Wide-spreading
Gleditsia triacanthos (honey locust)	100	—20 to —10F	Broad and open; many varieties
Magnolia grandiflora (southern magnolia)	90	5 to 10F	Pyramid
Magnolia soulangiana (saucer magnolia)	25	—10 to —5F	Open with many stems
Phellodendron amurense (Amur corktree)	30	—35 to —20F	Open branching
Picea pungens (Colorado spruce)	100	—50 to —35F	Pyramid
Platanus acerifolia (London plane tree)	100	—10 to —5F	Wide-spreading branches
Quercus borealis (red oak)	75	—35 to —20F	Broad when old; pyramid when young
Rhamnus davurica (davurica buckthorn)	30	—50 to —35F	Vigorous
Taxus cuspidata (Japanese yew)	50	—20 to —10F	Pyramid
Tilia cordata (small-leaved linden)	90	—35 to —20F	Dense pyramid
Tsuga caroliniana (Carolina hemlock)	75	—20 to —10F	Compact pyramid

Table 21. Shrubs for the City

Botanical and Common Name	Approx. Height in Ft.	Min. Night Temp.	Remarks
Aesculus parviflora (bottlebrush buckeye)	8–12	—20 to —10F	White flowers in July
Aralia elata	45	—35 to —20F	Small black berries
Berberis thunbergii (Japanese barberry)	8	—10 to —5F	Bright-red fruits
Buddleia davidii (butterfly bush)	15	—10 to —5F	Lovely summer flowers
Chaenomeles japonica (Japanese quince)	3–5	—20 to —10F	Scarlet flowers in spring; many varieties
Clematis paniculata	30	—10 to —5F	Easy to grow
Cornus paniculata (gray dogwood)	3–15	—30 to —20F	Upright in form, with many branches
Cornus sanguinea (bloodtwig dogwood)	12	—30 to —20F	Blood red foliage
Cornus stolonifera (red-osier dogwood)	7	—35 to —20F	Bright-red winter twigs
Cotoneaster horizontalis (rock spray)	3	—20 to —10F	Graceful plant
Deutzia scabra 'Candidissima' (snowflake deutzia)	8	—10 to —5F	White double flowers in June
Elaeagnus angustifolia (Russian olive)	20	—50 to —35F	Fragrant flowers
Euonymus (many varieties)	3–20	Check with nursery	Good evergreen
Fatsia japonica	15	5 to 10F	Handsome leathery foliage
Hydrangea quercifolia (oakleaf hydrangea)	6	—10 to —5F	Handsome foliage
Ilex glabra (inkberry)	9	—35 to —20F	Evergreen foliage

Table 21 (Continued)

Botanical and Common Name	Approx. Height in Ft.	Min. Night Temp.	Remarks
Juniperus chinensis 'Pfitzeriana' (Pfitzer juniper)	10	—20 to —10F	Evergreen
Kerria japonica (kerria)	4–6	—20 to —10F	Yellow flowers
Lagerstroemia indica (crape myrtle)	20	5 to 10F	Bright flowers in September
Lonicera species (honeysuckle)	to 20	Check with nursery	Ask nursery
Mahonia aquifolium (Oregon grape holly)	3–5	—10 to —5F	Yellow flowers; black berries
Malus sargenti (Sargent crab apple)	6	—10 to —5F	Pure white flowers in May
Philadelphus coronarius (sweet mock orange)	10	—20 to —10F	Scented blooms
Pieris japonica (Japanese andromeda)	9	—10 to —5F	Showy flowers
Potentilla fruticosa (cinquefoil)	4	—50 to —35F	Yellow flowers in May; many varieties
Prunus subhirtella (rosebud cherry)	25–30	—10 to 0F	More a small tree
Rhododendron obtusum amoenum (azalea)	3	—5 to 5F	Superior flowering shrubs
Rosa multiflora (Japanese rose)	10	—10 to —5F	Robust
Rosa rugosa (rugosa rose)	6	—50 to —35F	Many varieties
Spiraea thunbergii (thunberg spiraea)	5	—20 to —10F	Bright-white flowers
Syringa vulgaris (common lilac)	20	—35 to —20F	Many varieties
Viburnum dentatum (arrowwood)	15	—50 to —35F	Nice autumn colors
Viburnum lantana (wayfaring tree)	15	—35 to —20F	Grows in dry soil
Weigela (many varieties)	5–12	—10 to —5F	Does well in shade
Wisteria sinensis (Chinese wisteria)	25	—10 to 5F	Floriferous

This free-standing greenhouse away from the home is perfect as
a working garden area; note shade screens.
(Aluminum Greenhouses, Cleveland, Ohio)

CHAPTER 21

The Greenhouse

The greenhouse is many things: primarily it is a place to grow plants, but it can also be a garden room where you can have morning coffee, or where you can enjoy an evening stroll surrounded by greenery. It can be a place to experiment with plants or a place for a year-round garden. Or it can be a combination of all these things.

Once greenhouses were expensive. Today a complete 5′ by 3′ by 8′ by 7′ prefabricated unit with heater and vents and growing benches costs as little as $650. This is a small investment for the many kinds of gardening that can be done in a greenhouse. Having bright flowers in the dead of winter, hybridizing plants, and getting a head start on spring with garden plants are a few of the exciting avenues open to the greenhouse gardener. And not to be forgotten is that this structure also offers a pleasant retreat from a world of tensions.

WHERE TO PUT THE GREENHOUSE

Many manufacturers recommend a south exposure for a greenhouse, but I have seen lovely glass gardens on the east and west sides of a home. Even in a north light, you can grow lovely foliage plants and many shade-tolerant species; all plants need light, but not all of them require sun.

In a south or southeast exposure the greenhouse benefits from winter sunlight; an eastern exposure is good because there is morning sun; and the unit that faces west will have bright light and some afternoon sun.

Select a location for the greenhouse that suits your needs. As has been mentioned, it can be a combination plant room and growing area—a table and chairs, with only a few plants—or an extra room decorated with greenery or a place to experiment with plants. However, be sure that the type of green-house you choose blends in with the architecture of the home and looks like part of the total picture (if it is a lean-to) rather than a tacked-on structure.

Many families prefer the growing area adjacent to the kitchen, and this is certainly a good idea; it offers a lovely view from the windows. But greenhouses next to the living room are popular too, and even the intimate glassed-over area adjoining a bedroom or a bathroom has its merits.

GREENHOUSE STYLES

Numerous types and styles of greenhouses are offered by manufacturers. In the last ten years, new designs have appeared. Octagonal units, A-frames, greenhouses that look more like teahouses, are all possibilities in the detached style. There is even a greenhouse that revolves with the sun, if you want a fancy one.

For practical purposes the two popular styles are the freestanding (or detached) unit and the lean-to building. The freestanding house resembles a small house with pitched eaves from a central ridge; the attached or lean-to unit is always constructed with a wall of another building as a support.

The glass-to-ground unit is new and rests on a shallow concrete footing; it is not recommended for severe climates. But it is fine for regions where temperatures do not go below 20F. It comes in a lean-to style or as a detached house.

The lean-to greenhouse rests on a brick or masonry wall on three sides and uses the wall of your home to complete the enclosure. If you have a wooden home, the foundation wall can be wood reinforced with steel, and the framing made of redwood instead of aluminum.

The advantages of the lean-to garden are many: you can enter it from your home even if the weather

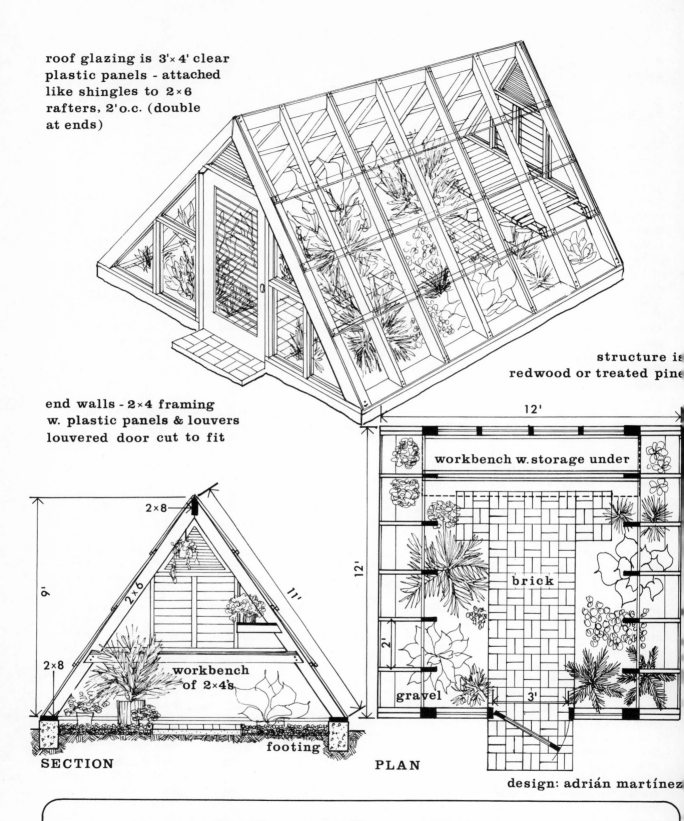

roof glazing is 3'× 4' clear
plastic panels - attached
like shingles to 2×6
rafters, 2'o.c. (double
at ends)

structure is
redwood or treated pine

end walls - 2×4 framing
w. plastic panels & louvers
louvered door cut to fit

2×8

9'

2×6

11'

2×8

workbench
of 2×4's

footing

SECTION

12'

workbench w. storage under

12'

brick

2'

gravel

3'

PLAN

design: adrián martínez

A−frame Greenhouse

is severe, it is easier to heat than the separate unit, and it becomes an integral part of the home.

PACKAGED GREENHOUSES

The packaged, or prefabricated, greenhouse includes glass (or plastic) aluminum headers and channels, and hardware—all the parts needed for the above-the-ground unit. It is shipped "knocked-down," that is, in packages. When you buy this unit, remember that a concrete slab or a foundation wall is necessary. This, of course, must be prepared by you or someone hired to do the job.

The lean-to must be attached to an outside wall, and generally this construction too must be done by you.

Detailed instructions come with all prefabricated greenhouses, but putting the unit together is not as easy as the pictures indicate. But it is not impossible either. Take your time, read the instructions carefully, and think out the project before you start building. If you are not handy with tools, hire someone to do the construction for you. He might also prepare the foundation. The pad or foundation, how it is built and what it is, depends on the style of the greenhouse and the climate.

In large cities you can find professionals to build greenhouses; that is, if you have a design or some idea that cannot be secured from local manufacturers.

FOUNDATIONS

Whether you select a ground-to-glass or wall-and-glass model, attached or freestanding, it must rest on a foundation. This can be poured concrete, steel, or redwood. The footings extend from the ground level to a few inches above the grade down to frost level or a few inches below the frost line. In Illinois, the frost line is 48 inches; call your local building department to find out the frost line in your area. Frost lines must be observed for footings, or alternating freezing and thawing of the ground will cause walls to crack. And building codes require that frost lines be observed. As mentioned, greenhouse prices do not include foundation or footings.

If you do not want to hire a professional to do all the greenhouse construction, have him dig out and pour the footings and then you can install the foundation wall. This is not difficult. Use premixed mortar and prepare a little at a time. Add water to the mix and with a hoe work the moisture throughout the mortar to get a heavy paste consistency. If you are having a brick foundation wall, lay the bricks moist, never dry. Put mortar on the footings for the first course or row of bricks. Using the trowel

upside down, press ripples into the mortar; this gives a good gripping surface for the bricks. Remove excess mortar with a trowel. Lay brick number one for the second row and use the trimmed mortar to smear the edge of the next brick. Be sure to keep the rows of brick even and level. Remove all loose bits of mortar from the wall before they have a chance to set. Cover the wall with wet burlap for a few days to permit a slow cure and to prevent cracks. A few weeks later clean the walls with muriatic acid, then hose them down thoroughly. Install a concrete capping for the top. (Do not use mortar when temperature is below 40F; it will cause cracking in the wall.)

In mild climates, greenhouses can be installed on poured concrete slabs.

Although a dirt floor covered with gravel or crushed stones is adequate, a brick or tile floor is more attractive. Or use stepping-stones (patio blocks) embedded in gravel. These materials retain moisture, and evaporation of water on the floor creates humidity in the greenhouse.

CONTROLS

Be sure there are adequate facilities to assure ventilation easily controlled with a minimum of drafts. Ridge ventilators along the length of the roof are best because when the vents are open, warm air flows out and cools the greenhouse, providing a constant change of air. An automatic system controlled by a thermostat, although more expensive than a manual-type installation, is almost essential, unless you are at home every day.

If possible, supplement the vent system with corner jalousie windows that can be opened or closed, depending on the weather. Remember that a greenhouse must cool slowly, imitating the natural pattern of outdoor climate. A drastic change of temperature is to be avoided.

There are many different types of heating for the greenhouse: hot water heat, warm air heat, electric heat, oil-fired heat, and gas heat. Select a system for your individual conditions. If you use gas heat, make certain that the supply of gas is 100 percent natural gas; artificial gas harms plants. Install thermostat controls to keep temperature from fluctuating radically. Oil burners should be used where natural gas is not available; electric freestanding heaters also have their uses in greenhouses. The variety of heating devices is so wide, it is best to call in a professional and let him recommend the best system for the greenhouse.

Automatic watering sprinklers are a convenience, but they are expensive and generally are not needed for the small greenhouse. There are other ways of almost duplicating these costly systems. A length of plastic hose with perforated holes (available at hard-

This greenhouse is very much a part of the home; masonry foundation adds to its charm.
(Aluminum Greenhouses, Cleveland, Ohio)

A small lean-to greenhouse easily accesible from the home affords plenty of space for growing many different plants.
(Aluminum Greenhouses, Cleveland, Ohio)

ware stores) can be attached to a faucet and placed in and around the pots. Turn on the faucet, and plants are watered. Either method can be made automatic by installing an electric water valve and a time clock. I have never used automatic water systems. The most practical way, and one I have used for years to water plants, is a garden hose connected to the water outlet. However, I do use different nozzles—a spray-type device, a fogger, and so on.

There are also bench watering systems and watermatic kits to apply water to plants. Most greenhouse manufacturers supply these devices.

Fine spraying or misting is beneficial for many tropical plants; several control systems are available at suppliers. The mist cycle is automatically regulated by time interval on the weight of the water; the mist goes on and shuts off by means of a screen that tilts down and actuates a mercury switch which closes the solenoid valve and stops the water from the nozzles.

Humidifiers come in many different shapes. Basically, these units have built-in float valves which automatically regulate the water supply. Water in the container is broken into minute particles discharged into the air, and gives rapid evaporation of the particles into humidity. Although I do have one of these units, I rarely use it; many plants growing together create humidity, and most of the time my greenhouse-garden room has more than adequate moisture in the air, from 40 to 60 percent.

Shading greenhouses in the summer is a bother. Whether it is done with paste and powder, with sprayer, paintbrush or roller, I find it a time-consuming chore. I have found a better way; I made lattice units (trellises) that have been applied to the ceiling; I leave these up all year because they are decorative and offer a support for vines and they afford almost perfect protection from the sun.

Without some protection against the sun—roller blinds, trellises, etc.—plants burn in summer sun, so you must apply shading. Two applications of paste or powder are necessary: one in the spring and another in July. Powder or paste is available in white or green; the paste is sold by the gallon, and the powder comes in cartons. Both are inexpensive.

Wood or bamboo roll-up shades are functional. Although they are expensive, they are more convenient and attractive than the powder or paste application. They are made of redwood slats with nonrusting metal clips. All hardware is included in a kit, and the shades are ready for installation on delivery.

Plastic sheets are still another means of protecting plants from sun scorch. In a variety of materials—Saran cloth, fiberglass, mesh plastic—they do the job. Generally, application of these materials is simple. Apply the plastic to the inside of the glass over a wet surface and set it in place with a wallpaper

brush. The surface tension of the water between the glass and the plastic holds the shading in place. When it is no longer needed, loosen the corners and peel the plastic from the glass. The location of the greenhouse and your individual climate dictate when to apply shading.

Benches or some kind of table to hold plants are another part of the greenhouse. Benches can be of wood, metal and wood, hollow tiles, or concrete. The redwood benches are the most attractive, and generally the type furnished by greenhouse suppliers. Whatever kind of bench you use, be sure it affords free passage of water. You can plant directly into some benches; others are designed to hold a layer of pebbles, and potted plants can be placed on top of these benches.

PLASTIC GREENHOUSES

Many of the prefabricated greenhouses are available with either glass or fiberglass-reinforced plastic. The plastic is corrugated or flat and comes in different colors—white, green, beige. The most translucent plastic you can get is the best for plant growth. While plastic eliminates the broken glass problem, it is not as attractive as glass.

There are two kinds of plastic—reinforced and flexible. Some of the rigid reinforced materials sold under various trade names are adequate; the flexible products rarely last through a year and should really be used only for expediency.

GREENHOUSE ROUTINE

The routine work in a greenhouse depends a great deal on the kind of plants being grown; but basically, environmental conditions such as humidity, temperature, ventilation, watering, resting plants, shading, and insect prevention remain the same.

Humidity. If you are growing tropical plants from very moist climates—some orchids and bromeliads, marantas, ferns—keep the humidity about 40 to 60 percent. If the collection is predominantly cacti and succulents, humidity can be as low as 20 to 30 percent. The more artificial heat used the more moisture in the air will be necessary. On very hot muggy days it is a good idea to keep the humidity somewhat high too. At night, humidity, like temperature, can be lower. In fact, it should be lower if you want good plant growth.

Temperature. Generally, most plants will be fine with a daytime temperature of 60F to 75F with a 10 to 15 degree drop at night. Avoid sudden changes in temperature, which are harmful to many plants; the

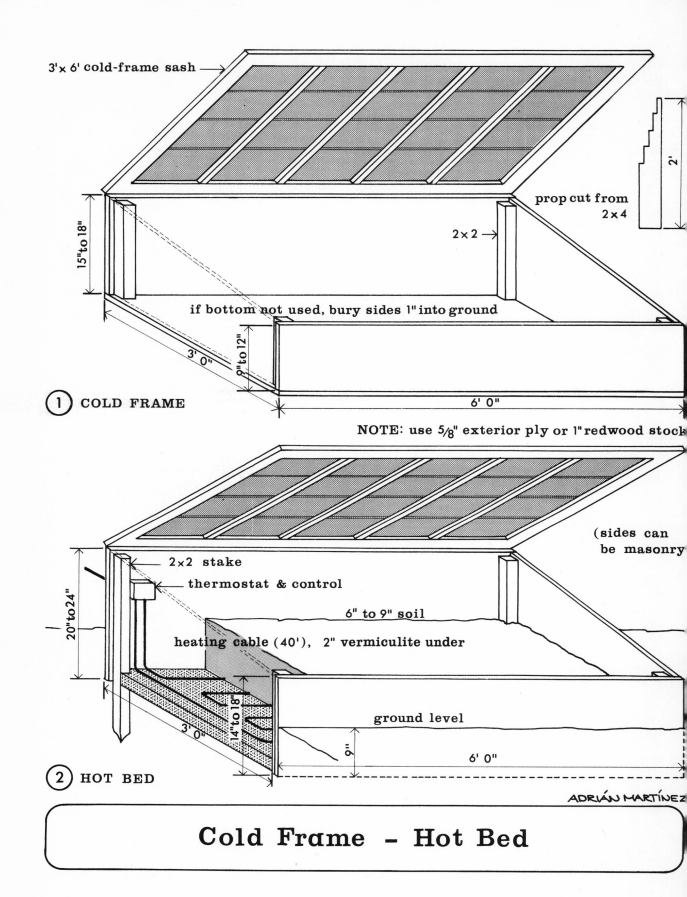

3' x 6' cold-frame sash

2'

prop cut from 2 x 4

2 × 2 →

15" to 18"

if bottom not used, bury sides 1" into ground

9" to 12"

3' 0"

6' 0"

(1) COLD FRAME

NOTE: use 5/8" exterior ply or 1" redwood stock

(sides can be masonry

20" to 24"

2×2 stake

thermostat & control

6" to 9" soil

heating cable (40'), 2" vermiculite under

14" to 18"

ground level

3' 0"

9"

6' 0"

(2) HOT BED

ADRIÁN MARTÍNEZ

Cold Frame – Hot Bed

evening temperature change should be gradual, starting about 6 o'clock and reaching the minimum during the late night hours, rising again gradually in the very early morning hours.

Ventilation. Fresh air is desirable for most plants, so open the ventilators at some time during the day. Even in very cold weather, it is advisable to have some fresh air in the greenhouse. Open the ventilators on the side opposite the side from which the wind is blowing. In early spring, when temperatures fluctuate, unless you have thermostatic controls, vents may have to be closed and opened several times during the day.

Watering. The watering schedule depends upon the plants being grown. It is wise not to keep greenhouse plants too wet because too much shade and too much moisture are an invitation to fungus disease. Try to keep the soil evenly moist for most plants; those that are resting will need a somewhat drier soil. If you mist plants, do it early in the day so that they can dry off quickly in the sun. Some hairy-leaved varieties object to water on the foliage; so do plants in bud. But do mist other plants; it is an effective way of keeping foliage free of insects, and plants looking handsome.

Resting plants. This part of plant growing is often overlooked, and yet it is a vital part of successful culture. Most plants require a period of rest when they will need lower temperatures and less water than at other times of the year. Generally, the resting time comes after blooming, but this is not always the case. Each plant must be treated individually. It is impossible in the confines of this book to list the resting times of all plants. But if your greenhouse is full of leaves rather than flowers, the problem, no doubt, lies in not resting your plants. Make provisions in one part of the greenhouse or solarium where temperatures are lower and where plants can be separated from actively growing ones.

Shading. Years ago, when all greenhouses were essentially of the same design, shading was applied in early spring and removed in fall. Today, the amount of protection from the sun depends not only on your individual climate but also on the design of the greenhouse. Some solariums have partial glass ceilings and will not require extensive shading.

SELECTION OF PLANTS

What you grow depends on your own tastes, but the greenhouse can be used for many things: to display foliage and flowering plants in pots, or to grow cut flowers, or to raise seedlings, or to board plants from outdoors that cannot survive cold. No matter what the plant room is used for, keep it tidy. Pick off dead flowers and wilted leaves; keep plants well groomed.

COLD FRAMES

Cold frames have many uses, but primarily they are used to raise plants from seed and to have them ready for planting in the garden as soon as winter is over. Cold frames are also useful for starting seeds of biennials and perennials during the summer or for starting cuttings of woody and herbaceous plant materials. Cold frames can also be used for hardening-off plants before they go outdoors.

Essentially, a cold frame is a bottomless box with a sloping glass top (sometimes made from old window sash) that conserves heat and sheds water. The frame can be an unglamorous device or it can be a tidy unit, depending upon your skill with a saw and hammer.

Put the cold frame in a place that gets sun but still has some protection from cold winds; since the primary use of the device is to get plants started, warmth is necessary. Place the frames with the high side to the north to receive the greatest benefit from the sun. Be sure it is near the house; in spring you will probably have to adjust the top often for proper ventilation. Temperature buildup is to be avoided, or plants will suffer. Leave space around the frames so that you can remove them when necessary. And remember that the sash will be moved backward and forward, and usually by one person, so leave space around the frames for easy management.

The bed of the cold frame should have ample provisions for water to be absorbed or drained away readily.

Building a Cold Frame

A simple unit can be built by using 12-inch boards on 2 by 4 stakes in the ground to form a backwall, and a 6- or 8-inch board for the front wall. Select redwood for frames; other woods will need preservatives. A good size for the cold frame is 3 by 6 feet; it is large enough to accommodate many plants but not so wide that it is difficult to tend to. Sash is available in two sizes: 3 by 6 and 2 by 4. The front of the frame should be about 9 inches above ground level, and the back about 14 inches above ground level. Keep a stick on hand to prop up the sash on warm days so that it will be well ventilated within. On cold days, cover it; exterior plywood or burlap or canvas is suitable.

Ready-made cold frames are available; these can be set in place with little work.

Managing the Cold Frame

Buy the best soil you can get for the cold frame. If the existing soil is poor, dig it out to a depth of 12 inches and then place a 3-inch layer of crushed gravel on the bottom to facilitate drainage. Cover with topsoil and level it off at the same level as the ground outside so that heat loss through the walls at night will be at a minimum.

Controlling the temperature is a vital part of good frame management. Even on cool days sun can push the temperature to a dangerous point. It is far better to keep the plants cool rather than too hot, because they can recover from a chill but rarely from dehydration.

Be sure there is ample space in the frame for plants; do not crowd them. Plants can dry out in a short time too, so keep a watchful eye on them, especially in bright sunny or in windy weather. Sometimes it is wise to have shading on hand in the form of lattice panels.

HOTBEDS

Hotbeds are very much like cold frames except that they have some artificial means of heat. The most satisfactory heating source is electric cables encased in vinyl or lead jackets. Kits including thermostatic controls are available at suppliers. Incandescent light bulbs (15- or 25-watt) mounted on wooden strips can also be used as a heating source, but they entail somewhat more work than the cables. Use porcelain sockets for the bulbs and wire them to a thermostat that runs to the house. Allow enough clearance between the bulbs and the plants; be sure the lighting strips are movable so that they do not interfere with working in the hotbed.

Be sure the hotbed is of substantial construction and thoroughly insulated. Remember that one of its main functions is to provide heat. Sink the bed deeper into the ground than a cold frame and be sure to provide adequate drainage.

In severe winters, protection in the form of mats or burlap over the sash is necessary to cut down heating costs and to provide a safe place for plants.

The hotbed gives the owner a real head start on gardening. Zinnias and petunias and other tender plants can be planted in midwinter; bulbs for indoors or for the greenhouse, and for raising early vegetable crops are other advantages when you have a hotbed.

CHAPTER 22

Water in the Garden

Water in the garden is one of the basic elements of the Japanese landscape. And in the vast French chateaux and English houses of the past, pools and fountains were part of the outdoor area. These were elaborate showplaces hardly acceptable in today's living scheme.

But water in the garden in one form or another is a decorative feature that is beginning to appear in even small American gardens. What is more soothing to the ear than the quiet trickle of a fountain on a hot day? What is more satisfying to the eye than reflections of sky and trees in a small pond where moving shadows present an ever-changing picture?

Water features can be introduced into the garden in several different ways and for several different reasons. A small reflecting pond is charming and opens new avenues of gardening for the homeowner. There are many lush background plants for pools and many exotic flowers for the surface of the water.

Traditional pools, somewhat large and formal, are indeed handsome. They become the dominant feature in the garden. But use them only if you have the appropriate space for them. They must belong in the landscape and not appear as though they were an afterthought. These pools are rarely inexpensive and often require professional help to build them. Yet, they are impressive, especially if embellished with statuary or with floating water lilies.

Fountains are delightful additions to the plan too. They can be added as pools or be a complete assembly with bowl, recirculating pump, and fountain-heads. Actually, very little plumbing skill is necessary to install them. Pumps for moving water for fountains are somewhat more complex; they are certainly more sophisticated than they were even a few years ago. Most of them can be easily put in place without professional help.

GARDEN PONDS AND POOLS

Small pools to about 24 inches in diameter have their limits. They are generally not deep enough for true water plants nor for goldfish, but they can be attractive. Use them for what they are—a charming picture placed near a path or a patio where they can be seen. Embellish them with ground cover plants at the edges, or seasonal container plants in the background.

Small stone or metal bowls or rigid plastic ones are available at nurseries. Generally, these are shallow receptables about 8 inches deep, with a maximum 24-inch diameter. They can be placed below grade so that the water level is even with the soil or they can fit into a concave mound of soil for a raised pool. These small pools are attractive as a spot of water in the landscape. They are inexpensive and usually do not require plumbing connections; they can be filled and emptied with a garden hose.

Salvaged pool forms for small amounts of water are in the same category as the bowls mentioned above. These include photographers' darkroom trays, surplus plastic bubble domes, laundry tubs, wine barrels, and so on. Or you can make your own pool, provided you keep it small. The general procedure is to pour a concrete mixture into a bowl lined with wire mesh; then another identical form is set on top with the concrete between the metal sandwich. Provide edge clamps to hold the shells together. After the concrete hardens (about two days) remove the bottom form and leave the inner form in place. Cure the concrete by keeping it wrapped in moist burlap for a few days.

Other circular pools can be made, using a sand-and-concrete method. Here, sheet metal or wood acts as a collar to hold the sand in a cardboard base. To

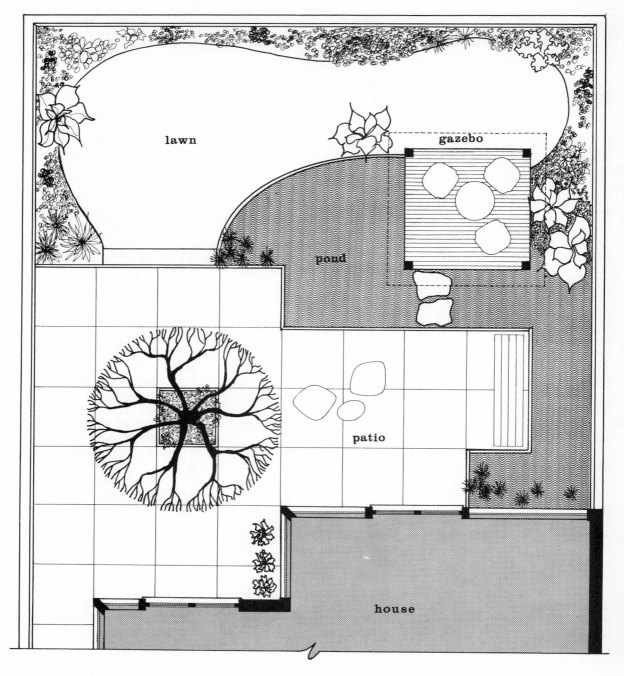

lawn

gazebo

poud

patio

house

PLOT PLAN

design: adrián martínez

Water in the Landscape

The pool is the dominant feature of this elegant garden and is enhanced with a gazebo where visitors can enjoy the water silhouettes and plants. The shape of the pool deserves special attention. It is linear where it joins the terrace and at the same time curving where it flanks the garden area. Natural plantings at the end of the pool are lush and carry the eye around the garden.

The geometrical patio fits well into the water setting; it is bold and massive to balance the large water area.

One large tree in the planter box is the accent and its massive structure enhances the effect of the pool.

The view from the house encompasses a sweep of water and thence to the lawn and background plantings. Every design element is in pleasing proportion here. There are no jarring accents, no barriers, no disruption of nature, but rather a handsome marriage of water, greenery and sky.

shape the sand into a bowl, work it with a template, and then pour concrete on the base to a layer of even depth. Put wire mesh on top to reinforce the pool and then add another layer of concrete. Trowel the material in place and smooth it with a wooden trowel.

Small pools are infinitely charming, but they require attractive backgrounds to show them off. Border the sunken pool with low-growing plants so that it appears natural in the landscape, or put gravel chips around the pool edges. For a tropical effect, put in lacy-leaved plants around the pool.

Most natural pools are free-form shells of reinforced concrete. They are irregular in design and have sloping walls. The edges are always hidden either with stones or by lush plant material. The shell is concrete, 4 to 6 inches thick, reinforced with wire mesh or rods. Smaller pools can be made from one-piece-molded shells, available at nurseries.

Make the rim of the pond a gentle slope so that it looks natural and so that it will not be shattered by a strong frost. The outline of the pool must be graceful, so a circle, or ellipse, or even a kidney shape is best. If possible, try to make only the water surface visible. Cover all concrete edges with stone or plants.

Choose a site for the pool that is a low spot in the garden, for this is the trend most often seen in natural landscapes. Before doing any planting, cover most of the cement edge of the pool with flat rocks or stones and fill in between them with soil. Leave some open approaches to the water's edge for lush plantings.

For the sides of the pool, use a thinner concrete of 1 part cement to 3 parts sand without any stones. But before you start lining the sides with the mix, beat down the sides of the hole with a spade to get rid of loose soil. Put some plastic liner around the edges of the excavation so that loose soil will not fall into the concrete. Use rubble backfill to strengthen the walls and to act as a textured surface so that cement will adhere to the sides. Use 2 layers of cement for the lining. Make the first one 3 inches thick and allow it to dry 48 hours. Then set chicken or stucco wire in place as reinforcement. Put it over the 3-inch layer of wet concrete and spread it out up the sides so that the whole pool is lined with mesh. Then spread the second 3-inch layer of concrete over the wire to cover it. Trowel it and allow it to harden. Seal with plastic cement and water, or paint with special pool paints. Cover the pool with burlap kept moist for about 10 days. Before fish or plants are added, the pool must be cured so that lime in the concrete does not harm wildlife.

ONE-PIECE-MOLDED POOLS

These are generally of irregular design, and fall into the category of informal or natural pools. The largest I have seen holds about 200 gallons of water and is approximately 8 by 6 feet by 18 inches deep; the smallest is about 5 feet in diameter and holds about 50 gallons of water 7 inches deep. They are all one-piece-molded construction of tough resin bonded fiberglass and look like oversized bathtubs.

The small pool in my garden was put in years ago before rigid plastics were available, but from what I am told by gardeners the new molded containers are quite satisfactory, and they are much easier to put in place. Deep digging is not necessary, for the pool can be sunk in a depression in the ground half its depth. The excavated soil is then packed around the sides. When preparing the excavation for the resin pools, remove all sharp-pointed stones, for in time they may penetrate the base and cause damage.

These pools are landscaped the same way as concrete pools so that they appear natural in the landscape. Edges are camouflaged with stones or rocks or a ground cover, and background plants are used as frames for the water.

Although the pools are easy to put in place and certainly suitable for gardens, they have no drainage or overflow apparatus, so you must change the water by a siphoning operation or do it with a bucket.

FLEXIBLE MATERIALS FOR POOLS

Also in the class of informal pools are polyethylene or butalene materials that conform to the shape of the excavation and are loosely held in place with heavy stones. Water is put in gradually, the weight taking the liner down till it is molded to the shape of the depression. The flap around the edges is concealed with stones or rocks. Or some of the liners come with metal edging.

For this pool, dig a hole about 24 inches deep in the shape desired. Slope the sides gradually at an angle of about 30 degrees. Remove any stones and cover the floor with fine sand or tamped-down soil. Then stretch the material into place. This is a quick easy way to have a pool in the garden for a few summers. It is uncertain how the materials will wear over the years.

TRADITIONAL POOLS

These are generally large pools, square or rectangular, occasionally free-form. They differ from informal pools because they have straight walls. While they can be reflecting pools, they will be the feature of the garden and are distinct from small pools. More traditional, they can either be sunken or raised. The shape of the pool is dictated by surrounding shapes and the owner's preference. Square or rectangular pools look best in a plan of similar design; an oval pool suits the

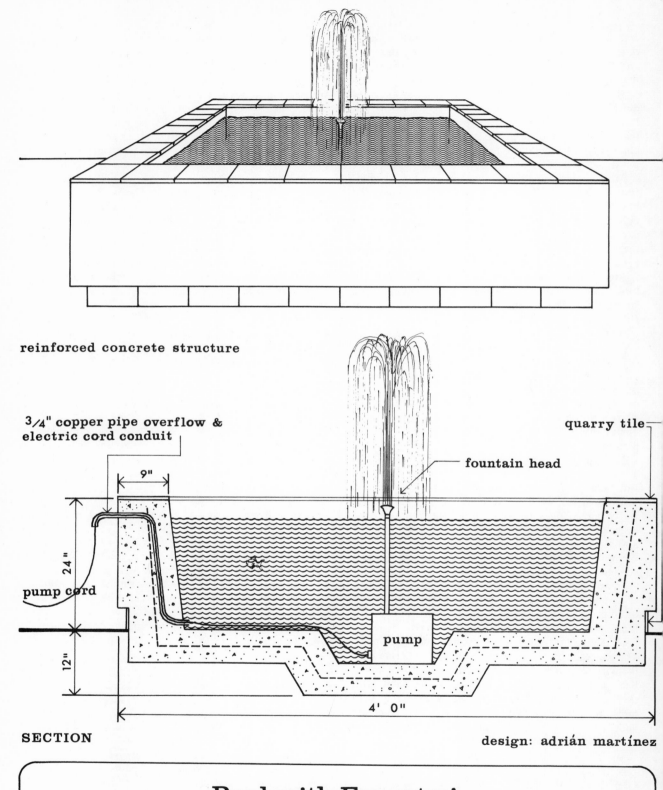

reinforced concrete structure

3/4" copper pipe overflow &
electric cord conduit

quarry tile

fountain head

9"

24"

pump cord

12"

pump

4' 0"

SECTION

design: adrián martínez

Pool with Fountain

A traditional pool in a formal
garden delights the eye. It
is bordered with bricks and
accentuated with clipped hedges.
The sculpture provides needed
vertical accent.
(Hedrich•Blessing)

A small pond with a background of
water plants is a dominant feature
of this garden; stone steps and
gravel mulch add to the effectiveness of the scene.
(Plastic Pool, Inc.)

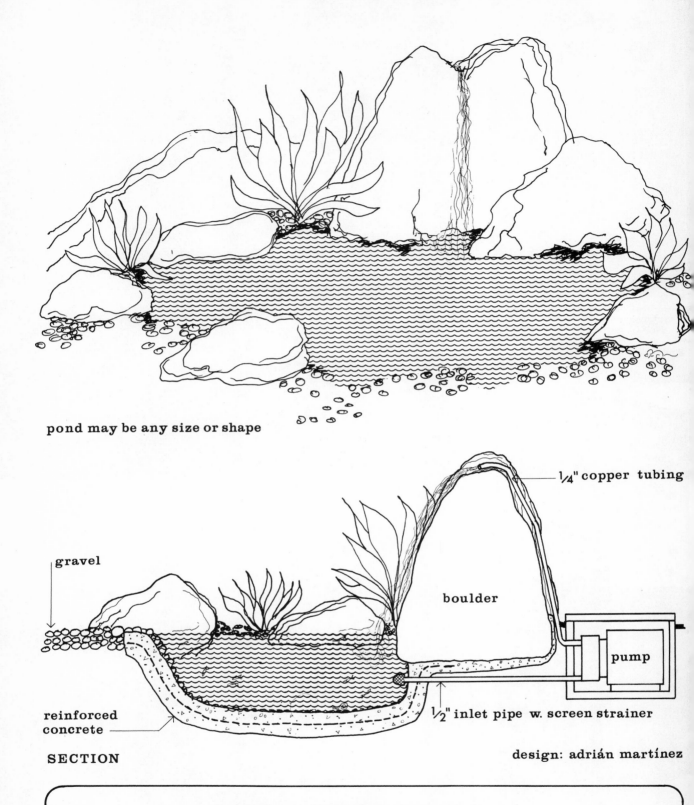

pond may be any size or shape

gravel

1/4" copper tubing

boulder

pump

reinforced
concrete

1/2" inlet pipe w. screen strainer

SECTION

design: adrián martínez

Pond with Waterfall

Resplendent with water lilies and water plants, a pool is a
handsome addition to any garden.
(Featherock, Inc.)

Featherock creates a pleasing waterfall in a pool setting;
note lush greenery used as background.
(Featherock, Inc.)

circular plan. Do not make the pool elaborate; a simple design is best.

What you put into the pool and around it is part of the composition too. It can be merely a reflecting surface for prize pot plants bordering the edges. For a more graceful picture it can contain water plants such as papyrus or horsetail or it can be exotic with water lilies and lotus flowers. If the pool is large, sculpture in the form of concrete stepping-stones projecting above the water, or figures can embellish the setting.

The decorative garden pool is usually a job for a professional mason, but if you are handy with tools there is no reason not to try your skill. First, consider that the walls of the pool must withstand soil pressure and at the same time resist the pressure of frost. If the walls crack, the coping is thrown out of level.

Be sure the ground around the pool is absolutely level; part of the charm of a pool is achieved by maintaining the surface as a silvery sheet.

Concrete is perhaps the best material for patio pools. It is plastic and easy to shape and it is durable. (If desired, it can be covered with brick or tile facing.) For a small area, the bottom should be 5 to 6 inches thick, the sides or walls at least 8 to 9 inches thick. Large pools require reinforcing rods; smaller ones can be made without them.

To build a small pool, excavate the soil to a depth of about 30 inches. Try to make the sides of the hole absolutely vertical. Put in a 3-inch layer of cinders and tap them in place firmly. The cinders keep groundwater away from the undersurface of the concrete and eliminate the danger of heaving in frost. When the excavation is finished, rent wooden forms (or metal ones) and place them around the top to maintain a neat edge and to form the walls. Be sure the joints of the forms are tightly joined so that concrete does not leak through them.

When the wood forms and pipes are in place, gradually pour a 6-inch bed of concrete into the depression for the floor. Start at one end and put in concrete to the full thickness of the floor, then go on to the next section. Place the concrete in the depression; do not throw it in because it will separate in midair. Fill in the floor to the full width and length of the excavation. Trowel the concrete smooth. Wire mesh or steel rods used for reinforcement of the concrete should definitely be used for pools over 24 inches square. (Set the reinforcing material in place before you pour the floor.) If the concrete dislodges the material, reach down and put it back into position and tamp down the concrete around it as you proceed.

When the pool floor is in place, set wire mesh or steel rods into the wall forms. Fill the forms with concrete, tamping it in place with special care where the walls join the floor. This is where most pools leak; a solid bonding of concrete will prevent problems later on. Work around the pool and add 6 or 8 inches of concrete to the walls each time around. Work the concrete into the form with a tamping hoe so that the walls will have a smooth face.

Allow the concrete to set at least 48 hours before removing the forms. Then cover the concrete with burlap and keep it moist for about 10 days with frequent sprinklings of water.

Finish off the pool with a coping or an ornamental rim of stone or brick or tile.

Before fish or plants can live in the water of a new pool, the concrete must be cured so that lime will not injure them. There are several ways to do this. One way is to fill the pool to the brim and let the water stand for 2 days. Repeat this process three times and the last time, allow the water to stand for 5 days. Then rinse the pool thoroughly. Refill it and allow the tap water to remain for another 24 hours before putting in fish or plants.

Another curing method is to fill the pool and allow the water to stand for 5 days. Drain and refill and repeat the process. Then drain the pool again. Now mix 1 part vinegar with 4 parts water and with a stiff brush, scrub all parts of the pool interior. Do not be alarmed if vinegar causes bubbling in the lime; it does not weaken the concrete.

Now rinse the pool thoroughly with a strong jet of water from a garden hose. It is now ready to be filled with water for plants and goldfish. If this sounds like too much work, you can buy chemical solutions at nurseries that will speed up the process.

Most large pools need a drain pipe because they must be cleaned occasionally. Siphoning water from them with a garden hose or pumping the pool clean is a tedious chore. Put pipes into place at the time the forms are built because they will extend through the concrete. Make the joints tight with flanges where the pipe passes through the concrete. The inlet pipe can be below the surface of the water or it may be above the surface of the pool to create a fountain or jet of water. One pipe will serve as both an outlet and an overflow if it is fitted with a branch pipe which rises to the height of the water surface and reruns to the main pipe again. A valve is required on the main pipe between the point of branching and the return pipe. When closed, the valve regulates the overflow; when open, it allows the water to drain from the pool.

FOUNTAINS

The fountain or waterfall adds still another element to the landscape—the sound of water in motion. Today, fountains are enjoying a renaissance. The simplest kind is a single stream rising in a jet from the center. There are also spray-type, splash-type and

Glowing with sunlight, a traditional pool with a fountain jet accents a
well-designed patio. The sculptural tree provides a perfect complement
to the pool.
(Natural Concrete Masonry Assoc.)

A lovely jet stream fountain is a sparkling addition to the garden.
(General Electric)

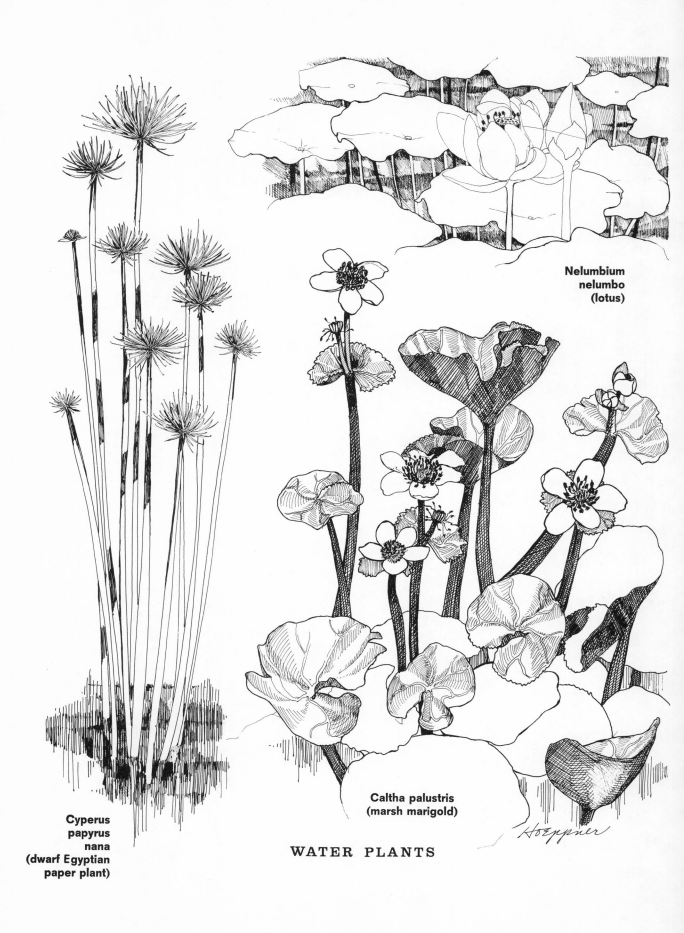

Nelumbium
nelumbo
(lotus)

Caltha palustris
(marsh marigold)

Cyperus
papyrus
nana
(dwarf Egyptian
paper plant)

WATER PLANTS

Hoeppner

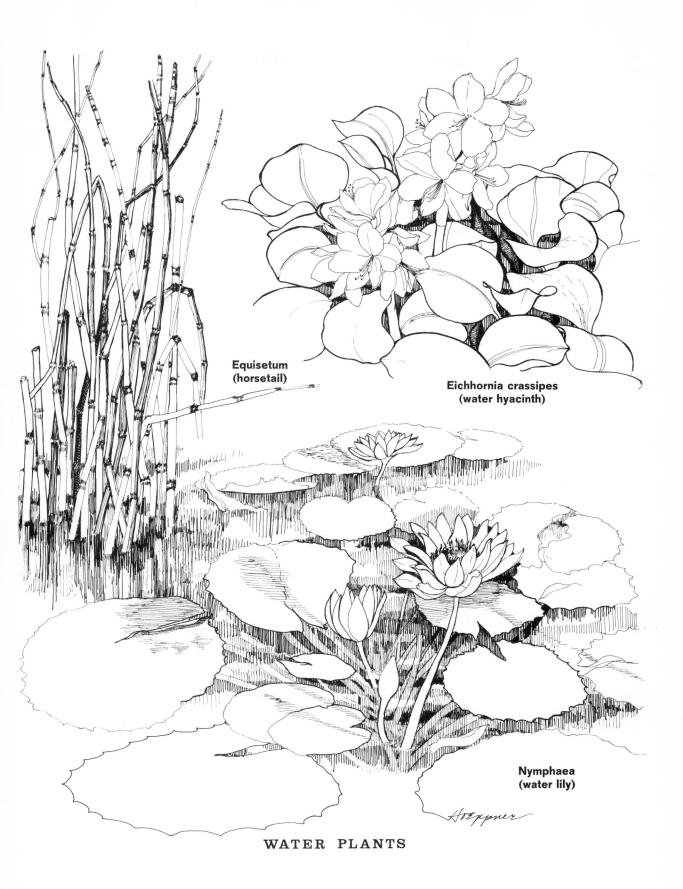

Equisetum
(horsetail)

Eichhornia crassipes
(water hyacinth)

Nymphaea
(water lily)

WATER PLANTS

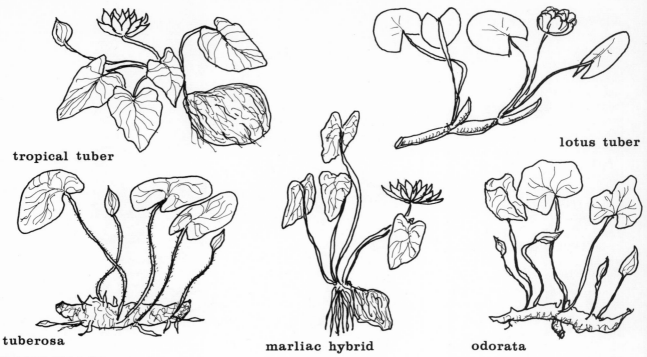

tropical tuber

lotus tuber

tuberosa

marliac hybrid

odorata

ADRIÁN MARTÍNEZ

ROOT STOCK

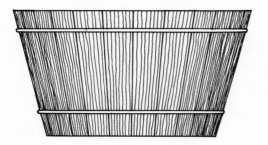

wooden box   12"x18" sq.

barrel section

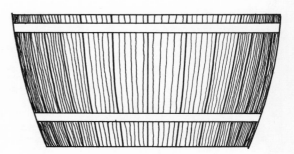

wooden tub

galvanized tub

PLANTING CONTAINERS

Water Lilies

drip fountains, and dozens of manufactured heads that put water in motion in every shape—from a column to a lacelike spray.

Some kind of power is needed to keep the water moving. A recirculating pump is necessary. These pumps are available at nurseries. They vary in power, capacity, and price. Some of them are immersed in water; others are located above the water line. Read the directions carefully. If necessary, consult the manufacturer or have someone put the unit into operation for you. In any case, select a pump that delivers more water than you originally estimated. And be sure to buy fittings that are the same diameter as those on the pump. If you are going to have underwater lights, have an electrician install them. Running wire in water is a hazardous job.

While the fountain has its own charm, waterfalls are indeed impressive. Here is where you can let your imagination run wild. A waterfall can be created by using tiered concrete or plastic dishes (sold at nurseries). Or it can be a stone or a metal disc set in the wall above the pool. Or it can be a stair-step arrangement of concrete blocks or of rocks with water tumbling over them. Featherock, a lightweight-type stone, weighs only one-fifth the weight of granite, or about 40 pounds to the cubic foot. It is easier to work with than natural rock, and is available at dealers throughout the United States.

The way the water falls is important and so is the sound that it makes when striking the pool surface. A gentle cascade or even a trickle of water from one level to another is more pleasing than a constantly gushing waterfall. Water can fall off several surfaces at one time or cascade from one level to another.

PLANTS FOR POOLSIDE

Border plants like horsetail, Egyptian paper-plant, water irises, and cannas thrive at poolside. The moist earth stimulates growth, and once established, the plants grow with little care. The following list provides some available choices:

Acorus calamus (sweet flag). A grassy plant with attractive foliage. Dainty and charming.

Asplenium (fern). Many fine species for growing around the pool; they like partial shade and moist conditions.

Colocasia esculenta (elephant ears). A showy plant with handsome broad leaves. Only a few are needed to accent a pool.

Cyperus papyrus (Egyptian paper plant). Long reed-like stems crowned with tufts of threadlike hairs. An excellent vertical accent, fragile and decorative.

Equisetum hyemale (horsetail). A favorite pool edging plant and a robust one. Grow in groups for a handsome effect.

Helxine soleiroli (baby's tears). A creeping herb that makes a lush green carpet; tiny white flowers.

Hosta plantaginea (plantain lily). A lovely plant with large heart-shaped leaves; a fast grower.

Iris (Japanese varieties). Unbeatable poolside plants with handsome flowers; easily grown.

Phyllostachya aurea (golden bamboo). A valuable plant for pool landscaping. Looks best if combined with other plants; keep it in tubs as it can grow rampant in the ground.

Sagittaria sagittifolia (arrowhead). This plant grows rapidly and forms large clumps. It has dark green arrow-shaped leaves; highly decorative.

PLANTS IN THE WATER

Azolla. This floats on the water surface and forms compounds of tiny plants. Very ornamental.

Eichornia (water hyacinth). Lovely, with large leaf stalks and erect leaves. The violet flowers are stunning. Plants can be grown at the bottom of the pool or put in boxes.

Hottonia palustris (water violet). Fragrant blue flowers and handsome leaves make this a desirable plant.

Hydrocleys nymphiodes (water poppy). A charming small plant that looks like a water lily. It bears yellow flowers almost all year in warm climates. Needs only about 5 inches of water.

Nelumbo (lotus). Thick stems and handsome round leaves. The flowers are incredibly large and stunning. Grow lotus in shallow boxes of soil and manure; it needs about 10 inches of water. There are many varieties, each one prettier than the other.

WATER LILIES

The beauty of these incredible plants often leads the gardener to believe that water lilies are difficult to grow. Actually, if properly planted at the start, they are amenable subjects that need little attention; they take care of themselves.

This is a large group of plants, and new varieties are frequently introduced, each one prettier than the other. The flowers are magnificent—some are 12 inches across—and they come in vibrant colors. There are hardy water lilies and tropical ones; the latter have the largest flowers and are treated as annuals, planted in late spring or early summer and discarded in the fall. Some bloom during the day, others open at night. Many are very fragrant. Several varieties carry their blooms above the surface of the water. Their foliage is luxuriant, and many of them have toothed or fluted leaf edges. But even if you have a greenhouse, it will be almost impossible to carry over the tropicals through the winter. As I have mentioned, they must be discarded and replaced annually with new plants.

The hardy water lilies bloom during the day and last about three days. Generally, they float on the surface of the water. The blooms are smaller than the tropicals. A few varieties bear stalks above the surface of the water. At the first frost, hardy lilies die back and winter safely under ice, provided the pool depth is at least 28 inches. Then in spring, they come back with fresh growth.

For water lilies (both kinds) the pool should be at least 20 inches deep; 30 inches is better. Plants require a great deal of sun, so don't expect them to be floriferous in shade. They need rich soil and plenty of fertilizer (especially for the tropicals, which have a short period of growth). Rather than planting the lilies at the bottom of the pool, I find it easier to work with them in pine planter boxes. They respond better in their own containers. Do not use redwood boxes; the wood will turn the water black and may kill plants. For container growing, put in an 8- to 10-inch bed of fertilizer and then pour in rich soil. Do not mix the ingredients and do not use sand. Anchor the container to the bottom of the pool, moored by wires to a brick, or use a wooden batten to keep the box from floating.

Hardy lilies come from the supplier about mid-April (depending on where you live) either as a piece of rootstock with leaves and perhaps a few buds or just a section of rootstock. Tropicals are set out later in the season (about mid-June) and should be planted when water temperature holds to about 70F.

Both kinds of lilies should be planted as soon as you get them so that they do not dry out, which might hinder or prevent new growth. If you cannot plant them immediately, keep them in a shady place out of the sun because even an hour of bright sun will harm them.

I have not included a list of water lilies because there are so many of them, and choice of color is more a matter of personal taste. Suppliers' catalogs list many varieties of water lilies. (See the Appendix for names of suppliers.)

CHAPTER 23

Garden Ornaments

Gardens and sculpture have been synonymous in past cultures; stone and metal and wood are natural in the garden. But original sculpture is usually beyond the budget of most homeowners, and until recently even authentic reproductions were costly. Now manufacturers through more sophisticated processes offer many garden oraments including figures, animals, sundials, birdbaths, wall plaques, and containers (urns and jugs, stone baskets).

The charm of garden ornaments brings old-world elegance to the outdoors, but using too many of them defeats the purpose. A few choice pieces strategically placed are highly desirable. As features in the garden, they add character and atmosphere, and they are perfect foils for plants and flowers. Gardening and sculpture combine two arts—one complementing the other.

SCULPTURE

The word *sculpture* includes a multitude of figures and forms; it can mean anything from a stone bird to a painted wooden figure. Eliminating the junk sculpture such as dwarf figures and painted animals, sculpture for the garden can be classified as animals, figures, free-form design, stone lanterns, bowls, and urns in many different materials. Perhaps the best-looking pieces are made of bronze or lead or marble, but there are also handsome wooden sculptures too. Most of these materials are right at home outdoors, and are long-lasting—even wood lasts for many years. Just what kind of piece you choose and what material it is made of depends on your own taste and pocketbook. Do not let anyone tell you what to buy. Select your own art, but keep the goals high.

With sculpture, the question of scale is vital. The piece cannot be too large for the space, nor should it be so small as to appear insignificant—it must seem to belong. Contemporary pieces seem to be best suited to woodsy settings; traditional sculpture looks best in a simple scene.

Original sculpture is, of course, the first choice, and artists are using exciting materials and new styles. Welding and riveting are all part of the scene. Limited editions of old masterpieces are also available, and some of these are indeed handsome. Lead reproductions and cast stone pieces are certainly acceptable. So are bronze or stone frogs or turtles piped for water, and terra-cotta or lead urns to lift a garden out of dullness into grandeur. There are numerous choices, pieces, and materials to choose from. (See Source List in the Appendix for catalogs.)

When you have one piece of sculpture in the garden, it must be placed for maximum display. In general, figures should be placed near some man-made object such as a walk or path, a wall, or a pool, and not set alone. In other words, do not isolate the statuary, but, rather, make it part of the total picture.

Provide a suitable base for the piece. The pedestal should be related to the garden and the sculpture. The base must be heavy enough to resist wind, with the sculpture firmly attached to it.

A metal figure looks good against a lattice or a wall of color; it softens the area and adds charm to it. At the side of a reflecting pool, it is handsome too.

Free-form sculpture, if large enough, can be isolated to occupy a special place and become part of the landscape. Place the sculpture in front of, or near, large trees where it has a suitable background. In this case, just as a tree is a part of the landscape, the sculpture becomes an organic part of the total scene.

Cast stone animals and urns and jugs are ideal for

A sculpture of marble and bronze becomes part of this forest-garden scene.
(Eldon Danhausen)

This elegant patio-garden is handsomely decorated with sculpture and urns; a delightful well-designed indoor-outdoor picture.
(National Concrete Masonry Assoc.; Dan Harnat, Jr., Landscape Architect)

Even a birdbath can be sculpture in a garden; this one is set in a shallow pool of water.
(Roche)

Rocks and stones used in Japanese style make this area an attractive and easy-to-care-for garden arrangement.
(B&G International)

terrace walls; or put them on a low base among low-growing plants rather than elevated above them.

BIRDBATHS AND SUNDIALS

These decorative accents are in many guises, some more sophisticated than others. The pedestal, whether it holds a sundial or a birdbath, adds a vertical note to the garden. Many fine ones are offered in fluted or plain columnar designs. The dish for the birdbath is generally—and should be—shallow, with gently sloping edges so that birds will not fall from it. Stone, concrete, terra-cotta, and concrete-aggregate birdbaths with or without pedestals, in several sizes, are available at nurseries.

The birdbath in summer adds activity to an otherwise quiet setting. It should be in a somewhat open spot away from tall shrubbery. Then birds will feel secure because they have ample time to see an approaching cat. At the same time be sure the bath is located near the house so that you can enjoy seeing the birds. A small birdbath does not need a water outlet. Water is easily put into it, and if it overflows, there is no problem in the garden. In winter, there is no need to keep water in the bath for the birds, for with snow, they suffer no shortage of water.

The sundial is a sophisticated accent in the garden and is reminiscent of old-world charm. Select one that is well designed and of a suitable material rather than one of the cheap concrete pieces. By its very nature, the sundial is a piece of sculpture and is best placed in a prominent position, perhaps at the junction of paths or at the end of walks. However, to be effective, it must be in the open, away from shade of the house or tree branches (even though we may not use it for telling time). The base of the pedestal can be in a carpet of greenery to set it off, with some tall plantings in the background.

PEBBLES AND STONES

If sculpture does not suit the garden, consider the use of stones and pebbles to create visual interest. While stone gardening is basically Oriental, many facets of it can make an ordinary American garden extraordinary.

Natural, lightweight lavarock is available as featherock or lavarock at building supply yards. Generally, two men can lift a sizable rock and put it in place; this would be impossible with natural rock. With lavarock you are creating your own sculpture;

the shapes, surfaces, and planes of the stones are used to paint a pleasing picture. You can use one large lavarock or a group with plantings around them or by themselves. When placing rocks be sure at least one-third is buried in the ground so that they appear as part of the landscape.

Featherock is gray with a somewhat striated texture and comes in various shapes and sizes. It lends a contemporary look in the garden, but it is somewhat sterile and needs plantings to bring out its best qualities. Arrange the rocks so that they form interesting compositions; try them at different angles with different planes facing the viewer before putting them in place permanently.

Lavarock is rust color, sometimes black, with darker markings, and has a porous texture. Used strategically, it can be dramatic. It has an advantage over featherock because carved pockets can be dug into it for the plants. Its form is more round and gnarled than flat. It is best used alone rather than grouped with other stones. It is sometimes available in gray, too.

Every region has its own variety of native stone, and a trip to the local building supply yard will get your imagination going. You will indeed find beautiful stones with handsome patinas, but some of them might weigh close to a ton. How to put them where you want them becomes a problem. The supply yard will deliver them to your home, but they will rarely put them in place for you. Getting the rocks or stones to the site is your problem and it is wise to make it someone else's problem. Call a garden contractor who has proper equipment to do the job. And be prepared—it will be costly.

The size, shape, and grain of the stones are all factors to be considered when deciding how they are to be arranged in the garden. They can be used in arrangements with plants for low maintenance gardens; they can accent a curving gravel path; or they can be used by themselves with sand in true Oriental style. Even one very large stone in the proper setting can be extremely effective.

Whatever arrangement you choose for the stones, one thing remains constant: when placing them, try to make them appear part of the landscape. A certain portion of the stone, depending upon its size, must be buried in the ground. Properly set, the viewer should not be able to determine just how much or how little of the stone remains underground. Other considerations are spacing and proportion and rhythm in arrangements. These factors depend on each individual setting and the kinds of stones used.

CHAPTER 24

Garden Shelters

Garden shelters—gazebos, pergolas, lath-and-garden-houses—become more popular as we spend more time outdoors. A shelter can be many things: a place to meditate, a secluded nook for cocktails, or simply a place to putter around with potted plants. Unlike the patio, which is usually adjacent to the house, the shelter is a detached separate building with distinct characteristics. And its prime function, of course, is to shelter; it is a protection against sun, wind, and rain.

The structure should be made from materials that do not require hours of upkeep. Redwood, with its built-in resistance to weather and decay, is a good choice; so is cedar. The design of the building can be elaborate or simple, depending upon your individual needs.

The gazebo that overlooks a swimming pool is a handsome garden feature furnishing seating space and a place to change clothes protected from wind and people's view. The pergola, along a path or framing a view, is an attractive addition, somewhat like a wooden sculpture. Canvas pavilions are popular now; the material comes in many colors, and units supported by poles on posts are easily assembled. An A-frame structure is neat and functional and can serve many purposes—playhouse or a place for plants or a seating area. And the lathhouse garden room is a great convenience for people who like to putter with plants.

LATHHOUSE GARDEN

Too often, this structure is of haphazard design and adds little attractiveness to the plan. Yet, with some careful design, it can be a desirable feature in the landscape. The type of construction—made of open slats—can be used to create pleasing designs; trellis ceilings or walls are indeed decorative. With alternating sun and shade, the lathhouse provides almost ideal conditions for plants. It reduces the intensity of the sun while it provides coolness within it.

The size and shape of the enclosure are determined by the site; a good size is 10 by 12 feet. The width of a single lath is generally the best space for maximum sun control, but a trellis ceiling (laths crossing) is acceptable too and more handsome. Construct the house with a sloping roof so that rain runs down the laths and plants are protected from dripping water. Be sure to include waist-high potting benches, cabinets for supplies, and shelves for plants.

A-FRAME GREENHOUSE

An A-frame greenhouse can be used for plants or as a retreat for the gardener where he can spend a few quiet moments. This structure is made of 2 by 4 redwood rafters and fiberglass panels, and can be assembled in a day. Dig two parallel trenches 12 inches deep and 12 inches wide. Nail four 2 by 4 rafters to a 1 by 10 ridge and raise the skeleton supported by temporary bracing in the ground. Then nail the other rafters to the ridge and fashion bridging between the rafters. Put the 2 by 4 and 2 by 2 cross braces in place between opposite rafters. Now pour a mixture of 1 part cement, 3 parts gravel, and 2 parts sand into the trench around the rafters. Do not remove the braces until the concrete is thoroughly set. At one end put up a frame for a door.

Next, with a saw, cut fiberglass panels to fit the wooden skeleton, and nail them to the frame, allowing one corrugation overlap between them. (If you are using flat material, allow a 2-inch overlap.) To weatherproof the ceiling apply mastic between the panels before nailing them in place, using aluminum

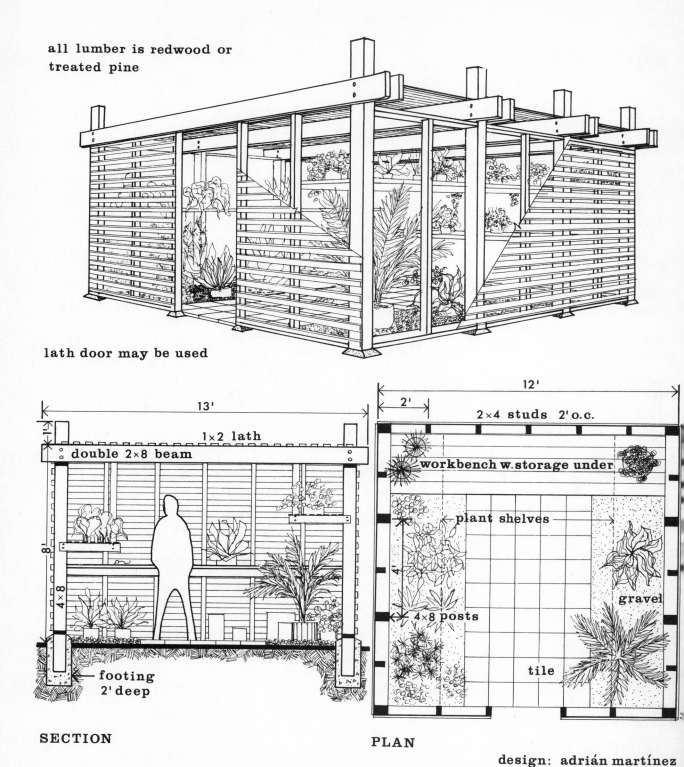

all lumber is redwood or
treated pine

lath door may be used

13'

1×2 lath

double 2×8 beam

8'

4×8

footing
2' deep

SECTION

12'

2'

2×4 studs 2'o.c.

workbench w. storage under

plant shelves

4'

4×8 posts

gravel

tile

PLAN

design: adrián martínez

L a t h   H o u s e

Of lath house design, this simple
structure is attractive and
functional; a pleasant place
to sit in the shade and enjoy
the garden.
(California Redwood Assoc.;
Phil Palmer photo)

This shelter provides protection
from rain and wind, makes the
deck appear more than it is, and
adds additional living space for
the owners.
(California Redwood Assoc.; Pacific
Interiors Design, Phil Palmer photo)

nails so that rust will not occur. The floor of the greenhouse can be gravel or bricks laid on sand. (See drawing.)

THE PERGOLA

The pergola is a covered passageway that can be a desirable garden feature as well as a means of furnishing shade. Or it can be a frame for a particularly good view. Originally, a pergola was made of poles; a simple structure that provided shade with living plants over a path or a terrace. Now it has a variety of architectural designs. I saw one recently, used as an entrance shelter, integrating the house with the site.

Generally the pergola is best placed at one end of a terrace path, though it can even span the length of the terrace. On a southern exposure, it offers considerable shade, and is useful as well as ornamental. The framework should be strong enough to support vines; the green mantle is part of the charm of the structure. The pergola can be made from stone or brick, but the wooden type is more popular because it is easy to put together. However, whatever material you choose, be sure there is plenty of head room for a person walking underneath the beams.

Whether the columns or piers of the pergola are made of wood or stone, a concrete footing at least 12 inches deep is essential. Run strong timbers along the length of the structure and use somewhat lighter-weight wood, crossing them at even intervals. Then you might want several thin laths across the cross-beams so that climbing and trailing plants can be tied to them. Floors can be concrete or gravel.

A simplified type of pergola is shown on the next page.

THE GAZEBO

Gazebos can be of many designs, but basically they are 6- or 8-sided, with a peaked roof, and are 8 to 10 feet in diameter. According to Webster, the gazebo was originally a gazing room. Although the word is somewhat outdated, it is still essentially a small latticed structure. Its beauty, like a trellis, depends on crisscrossed laths which form small squares or triangles. It is, when well done, a very effective if somewhat ornate garden shelter.

The gazebo is perhaps the most difficult of all shelters to build. It must be cleverly designed, and is generally difficult to construct unless you are skilled with tools. Yet, because of its charm and old-world flavor, it deserves consideration if you want a unique feature in the landscape.

Our drawing of a gazebo is a basic shell; lattice or vine supports can be added later. It is a starting place if you want to try to build a shelter yourself. See drawing on page 268.

CANVAS SHELTERS

If you remember canvas as awnings only for grocery or barber shops, you are in for a surprise. Today, canvas comes in a wide variety of weights, finishes, and weaves and in a veritable rainbow of colors. Because the product is so versatile and so many things can be done to it, the hazard lies in too many avenues of use rather than in too few.

The new canvas material is mildew resistant and is also available vinyl-coated for greater soil resistance, easier cleaning, and longer life. Top-grade Army duck is used for most outdoor shelters.

The flexible nature of canvas allows many designs. You can have a cone of canvas, an arc, a tent, a cantilevered roof line—easily assembled on pipe framing. Or you can merely stretch triangles of canvas from a tree with ends staked into the ground, an effective and handsome protection against the sun. A small canvas pavilion for dining is another idea; these are very attractive and can easily be moved if necessary.

BUILDING SIMPLE GARDEN SHELTERS

As has been mentioned, there are many kinds of garden shelters, but basically, framing for these structures is the same: a post-and-beam construction. Posts properly spaced support the roof and are set in the ground in concrete collars. The posts support the horizontal beams which hold the roof rafters at right angles to the beams. Where the structure is a lean-to design against another building, a ledger strip is used, and the building takes the place of posts on one side.

The posts are the backbone of the simple shelter, and 4 by 4 lumber is generally used. For larger structures, heavier posts support the additional weight. A simple way to anchor a post in the ground is to set it into a predug hole and pour a concrete collar around it. The depth of the post depends on the soil conditions and on the frost line in the region. Thirty inches is adequate for a 10-foot structure, but check with your local building authorities first.

Another way to secure posts in the ground is to employ nailing blocks. With these, it is not generally necessary to pour concrete around them. The nailing block is a precast concrete pier with a wood insert; the posts are nailed in place after the pier is set in the hole.

Roof beams, 2 by 6 or 2 by 8, support the rafters

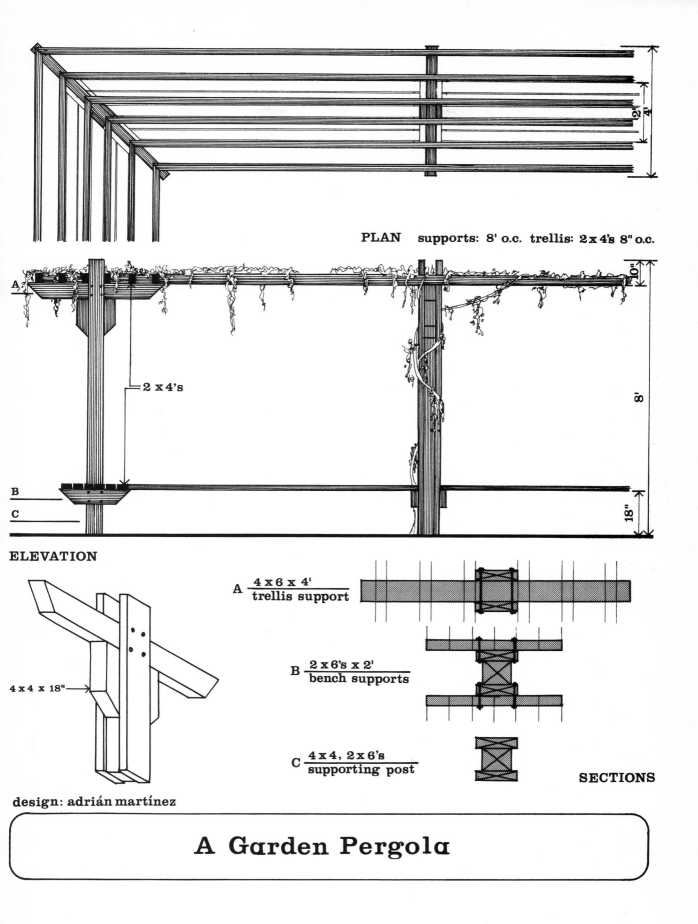

PLAN   supports: 8' o.c. trellis: 2 x 4's 8" o.c.

2'
4'

A

2 x 4's

8'

B

C

18"

10"

ELEVATION

4 x 4 x 18"

A $\dfrac{\text{4 x 6 x 4'}}{\text{trellis support}}$

B $\dfrac{\text{2 x 6's x 2'}}{\text{bench supports}}$

C $\dfrac{\text{4 x 4, 2 x 6's}}{\text{supporting post}}$

SECTIONS

design: adrián martínez

A Garden Pergola

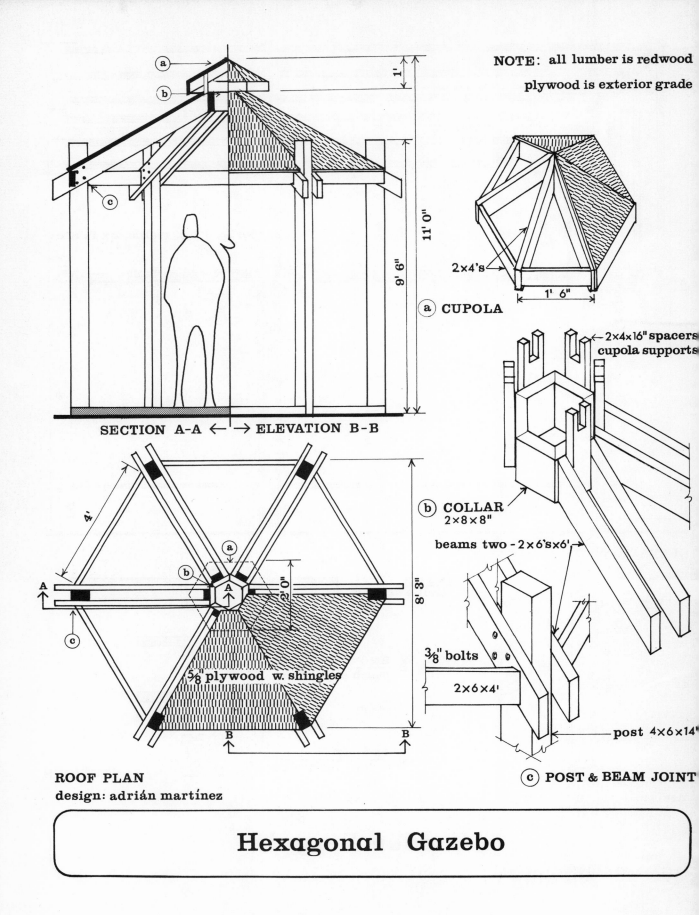

NOTE: all lumber is redwood

plywood is exterior grade

1'

11' 0"

9' 6"

SECTION A-A ← → ELEVATION B-B

ⓐ CUPOLA

2×4's

1' 6"

2×4×16" spacers
cupola supports

ⓑ COLLAR
2×8×8"

beams two - 2×6's×6'

4'

8' 3"

2' 0"

ⓐ

ⓑ

A
↑

⅝" plywood w. shingles

B

B

ROOF PLAN
design: adrián martínez

⅜" bolts

2×6×4'

post 4×6×14"

ⓒ POST & BEAM JOINT

Hexagonal Gazebo

A garden shelter, neither gazebo nor pergola, but intensely dramatic with circular sweeping lines. *(California Redwood Assoc.; George Murata design, Ken Molino photo)*

For the contemporary garden, a unique shelter shades benches. *(California Redwood Assoc.; Frederick Coolidge Landscape Architect, Ken Molino photo)*

and tie the posts together. For best results, place the beam directly on top of the posts. There are several methods of construction, using either wood cleats or by notching the posts. Rafters are normally used to support a roof, but with garden shelters, they are generally used to create roof patterns. Usually the rafters are set on top of the supporting members and toenailed in place. Or, for a finished look, the rafters can be notched out before they are nailed into place. Metal rafter hangers can also be used to hold rafters in place.

Basic roof designs are either flat or shed design. Gable and pyramid roofs are more complicated, so more skill is required to build them.

CHAPTER 25

Making Garden Furniture and Accessories

If you are reasonably skilled with tools, you can make your own furniture and decorations for the garden. Containers for plants, benches and tables, arches and trellises, plant stands and light fixtures are all part of the garden scene. Small bowls for ponds, wall plaques, and birdbaths are some other projects for the ambitious gardener.

Many outdoor decorations are built with wood, but bricks, concrete blocks, and flat glass (available at building supply yards) are also used. Salvage items can be put to work too. Hatch covers are ideal for table tops, railroad ties covered with a pane of glass make an excellent table, and redwood boards on concrete blocks become a fine bench. Birdbaths and small sculptures, and concrete panels cast in sand to decorate fences, are some other ideas.

TABLES AND BENCHES

For a simple table, concrete blocks are an excellent base; adhere them with mortar to any masonry patio floor. Angle irons bolted to a redwood top and cemented to the block complete a sturdy table. Use 2- by 8-inch lumber for the top, or for a more decorative effect build the table with a slant design of 2- by 2-inch boards spaced 1/2 inch apart, covered with a pane of glass. Nail the 2 by 2's to a 3/4-inch piece of exterior plywood supported by angle irons.

Small coffee tables made of tile flues or drainpipes are very easy to make. The tiles are available at builders' yards in different sizes; an 18-inch diameter is quite satisfactory for a small table. Merely set a pane of glass 20 inches in diameter on the tile flue for a table. Small drainpipes 6 inches in diameter can be grouped together in a honeycomb pattern and covered with glass for a unique table.

For a colorful small table, set mosaic pieces in mortar on a plywood base and trim with a wooden molding for an attractive piece. Art stores have special kits containing mosaics and epoxies.

A bench in the garden or patio is a decorative feature as well as a place to rest. A simple bench can be built in a few hours, whether it is freestanding or used as part of the patio design. Bordering the area as it usually does, it becomes a frame; at another level it breaks the monotony of a setting. One end of the bench can serve as a display platform for container plants.

The design of the bench is your choice, but in all likelihood it will not have a back to obstruct a view. Although an ideal place for a bench is along a wall or a fence, it can also be an island design to frame a tree or a piece of sculpture. Even a cantilevered bench is not difficult to make. For color, benches can be covered with bright, weather-resistant fabrics.

Make benches 15 to 18 inches high if they are to be for sitting; for sunbathing, an 8-inch height is ideal. The width can be from 24 to 28 inches depending on its use. A simple bench is made from 2-inch redwood stock for the top, spaced about 1/2 inch apart and set on concrete blocks 3 feet apart.

Another sturdy bench can be made from an 8-foot board. Cut two 12-inch lengths, and you have both legs and the top with a 2 by 4 board for the leg brace. The legs are secured to the brace, and then the three-pieced bottom section is toenailed to the top.

A slat bench is another idea. Use 1- by 2-inch lumber set on edge spaced 1 inch apart in a wooden frame. Bolt the top section to U-shaped straps sunk in 4- by 8- by 16-inch blocks.

There are several designs for benches, and these are some general rules to follow:

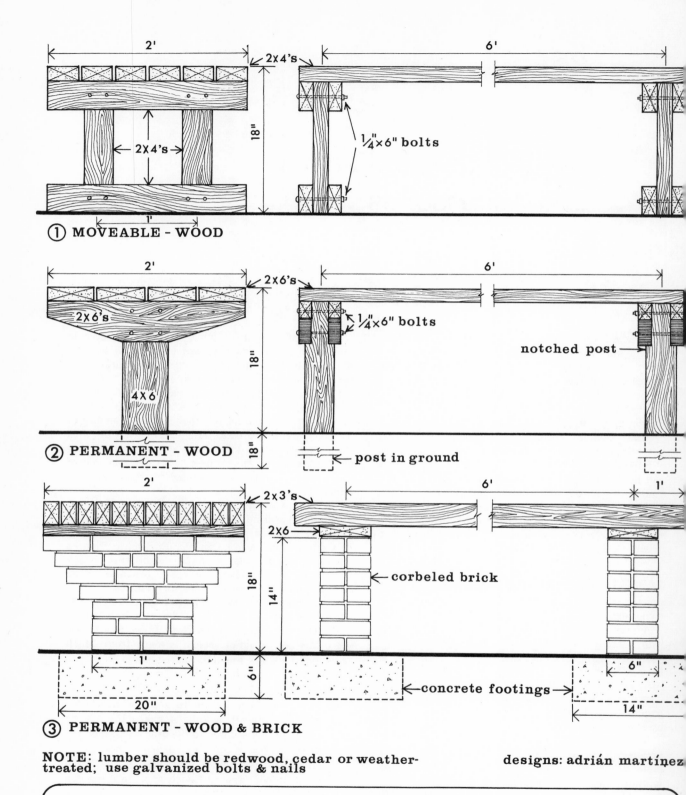

① MOVEABLE - WOOD

2'
2X4's
18"
2X4's
1'

6'
2x4's
¼"×6" bolts

② PERMANENT - WOOD

2'
2x6's
2x6's
18"
4×6
18"

6'
2x6's
¼"×6" bolts
notched post
post in ground

③ PERMANENT - WOOD & BRICK

2'
2x3's
2x6
18"
14"
1'
6"
20"

6'
corbeled brick
concrete footings
6"
14"

NOTE: lumber should be redwood, cedar or weather-treated; use galvanized bolts & nails

designs: adrián martínez

Bench Designs

- Redwood and cedar are the best woods to use. They weather well and usually need no preservatives. Select finished grade for the top; lower grade, such as rough finish, is fine for the lower parts of the bench.
- Where strong support is needed, use 2-inch-thick lumber for bench tops; leave ½-inch spaces between the boards for water drainage.
- To prevent the wood from being stained by nails and screws, use galvanized nonrusting nails and screws.
- Make bench legs sturdy enough to support weight, but keep the legs in scale with the design.
- Space legs about 3 to 5 feet apart for large benches, closer together for smaller ones.
- To finish redwood or cedar, use a water-repellent product and then a sealer—or paint the benches. For a unique bench design, see page 272.

CONTAINERS

Wood is the best material—the most popular—for tubs and boxes and outdoor planters. It lasts a long time, is easy to work with, and the natural finish looks good outdoors. Redwood or cedar need no preservatives. Douglas fir does need a protective coating, and it is much stronger and more costly than redwood. Use it for very large boxes. Pine can also be used, but it too requires a preservative.

Most boxes are nailed together; if you use glue and screws, however, the boxes will last longer. Use brass screws and good quality wood glue. One-inch lumber is fine for most boxes, but for very large ones (over 24 inches), select 2-inch stock.

The container with tapered sides is attractive and suitable for dish gardens and small plantings. An 18-inch top tapering to a 10-inch base is a good size for many arrangements. Use 1-inch redwood for the box and miter the corners. Add a platform made from 1-inch lumber.

A simple rectangular container 3 inches deep built with 1-inch redwood is ideal for flowering bulbs and other low-growing plants. Use 3/4-inch stock for the bottom and 1- by 1-inch platform legs at each corner.

The cube box is functional, neat, and simple. For a 12-inch box, use 1- by 12-inch redwood.

WINDOW BOXES

We think of window boxes in their conventional role as a decorative fixture for a window. But the same type of planter can be used on the roof garden or as a border accent on the patio, or even to act as a boundary line.

There is considerable pressure against the sides of a window box, so build it with care. Use 1-inch lumber and brass screws; nails have a tendency to pull out if the boards warp. Angle irons at the corners give extra strength. The necessary drainage holes must be drilled in the bottom of the box.

For installation against a house wall, place the box 1 to 2 inches from the walls to avoid water-stained surfaces. Be sure the boxes are firmly anchored in place; filled with soil, boxes are heavy, and are a formidable hazard if they ever pull loose from a wall.

You can plant directly into any kind of window box, or you can use a metal pan inside the box if you think it is necessary. When you use boxes on pavings, elevate them with small wooden blocks at each corner. This eliminates hiding places for insects and allows air to reach the bottom of the soil so that a waterlogged situation does not occur.

PERMANENT PLANTERS

Many homes include planter dividers; these are basically the same construction as a window box. In gardens, permanent planters of brick, wood, or concrete are often seen. They are attached to the house walls or built to fit a special place. They can be rectangular, square, triangular, or circular. Like tubs and pots, their value is largely decorative.

Outdoor planters attached to entrances or the front of a house should be in proper scale and proportion to the building. Because they cannot be removed, they should have galvanized metal liners for durability, and adequate facilities for drainage. Although redwood planters are attractive in the garden, brick and stone boxes are superior in appearance.

Raised planter beds of brick look good in the landscape and have several advantages. They make it easier to tend to plants and they provide excellent drainage for them. Furthermore, the retaining walls of raised planters keep out greedy roots of nearby trees and shrubs. Also, raising the beds makes the flowers and foliage appear more attractive, bringing them closer to eye level.

To build a planter, lay out a line you want to follow on the ground and dig a trench about 15 inches deep. Make it 5 inches wider than the wall you are planning. Fill the trench with concrete—1 part cement, 3 parts sand, and 5 parts gravel. When the footing is dry, install the brick on it, using mortar and checking each brick with a mason's level to make sure the brick is evenly placed. When the wall has reached the desired height, trim it with a cap of concrete. Raised planters of this type can be used against a fence as entranceway highlights, or as retaining walls around the edges of patios, terraces, or walks. Circular and free-form designs can be built

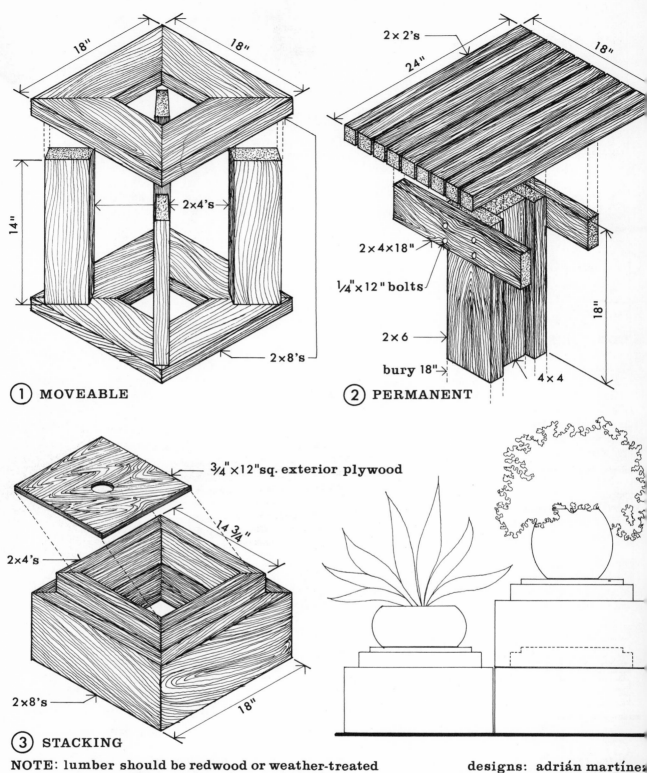

18"   18"

14"

2×4's

2×8's

① MOVEABLE

2×2's   24"   18"

2×4×18"

¼"×12" bolts

2×6

bury 18"   18"   4×4

② PERMANENT

¾"×12"sq. exterior plywood

14 ¾"

2×4's

2×8's   18"

③ STACKING

NOTE: lumber should be redwood or weather-treated

designs: adrián martínez

Plant   Stands

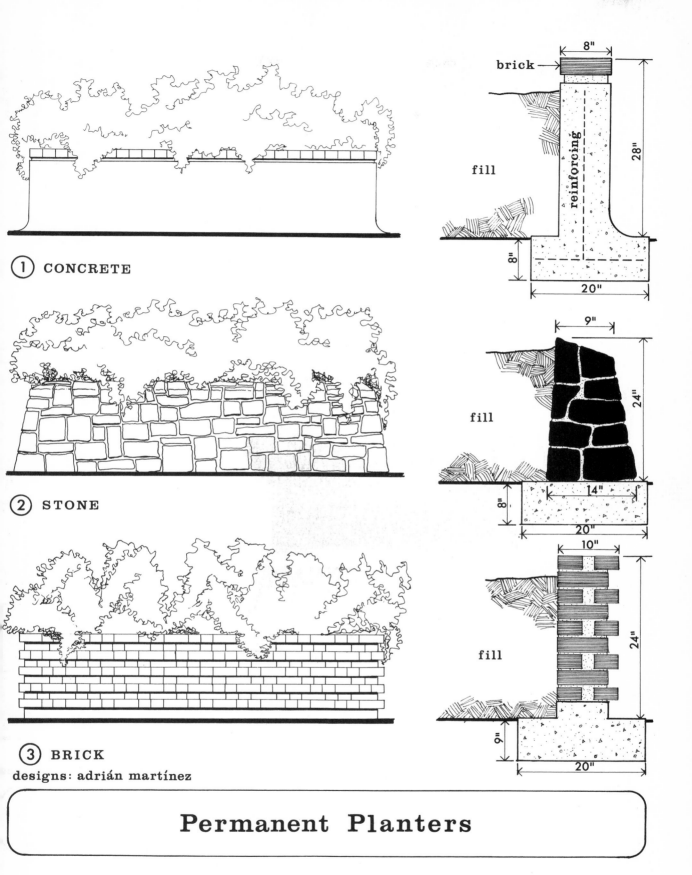

① CONCRETE

brick

reinforcing

fill

8"

28"

8"

20"

② STONE

fill

9"

24"

8"

14"

20"

③ BRICK

designs: adrián martínez

fill

10"

24"

9"

20"

Permanent Planters

around trees or posts. For typical planter construction see page 274.

OTHER DECORATIONS

Select a material for plaques and panel decorations that will withstand sun, wind, and rain. Wood, copper, or brick are suitable choices. So is stone or concrete.

Panels cast in sand make a lovely wall decoration, and they are simple to move. Plaster of paris carved with a design is another idea. Mosaics created from pebbles or pieces of glass or tile embedded in a mortar base on a plywood backing are other possibilities.

Birdbaths and bird feeders are easy do-it-yourself projects, and redwood plant stands and light boxes can be made in a day. See page 275.

CHAPTER 26

Lighting the Landscape

There was a time when lighting property was a complex and expensive undertaking. Today, with low-voltage systems, it is easy and within most home-owners' means. Now you can use the outdoors at night as well as during the day.

A lovely garden demands lighting. By day, it is beautiful, and at night, it can be another scene with dramatic lighting. Trees and shrubs, pools and fountains, patios and paths take on new dimension when properly illuminated. Water gardens sparkle and garden ornaments—statues or figures—become alive. But lighting is necessary not only for beauty but for safety too.

Many principles are involved in the art of landscape lighting, so if your grounds are large, it might be wise to seek professional help. For the homeowner with average property, here are some helpful hints.

Silhouette lighting. Silhouette lighting is light coming from above to create halos below, and light coming from below to silhouette the plants. Light source is directed at a wall, fence, or shrubbery behind the object, with very little brightness at the front.

Etched lighting. Etched lighting is used to emphasize effectively the texture of tree bark, masonry walls, and architectural objects. The light source, at a distance of 4 to 10 inches, is aimed parallel to the surface of the object.

Contour lighting. Contour lighting is used for creating depth and three-dimensional character in a subject. Light is aimed at an object from several directions, with more light coming from one side than from the other.

Colored lighting. The purpose of colored lighting is to emphasize the color of plants; this is achieved with the same color light as the object illuminated.

Occasionally, light itself becomes the object to be seen, adding little illumination; it is used as a substitute for plants to fill spaces with shadow and light rather than with leaf and branch.

The placement of fixtures is vital in outdoor lighting. They should, whenever possible, be concealed from view. Do not use too many lights, but have them in the right places. Paths and walks should be illuminated for safety, and patios and terraces for nighttime use. Certain trees and shrubs—not all of them—deserve a bright spot focused on them.

Select a focal point—a branching tree or a piece of statuary—and start here. Make the light brighter in this area than in other places. The best way to arrange lights is at night by a trial-and-error method. A few inches one way or another makes a big difference.

Create an interplay of light and shadow. Keep the illumination at different intensity levels throughout the garden. Do not light a subject head-on; such lighting washes away the details. Strive for a soft, diffused effect to bring out textures, shadows, and contours. Place fixtures on two sides of an object rather than on one side. Use walls and fences as reflecting surfaces. Follow the basic rule in all lighting; do not aim fixtures at neighbors' property.

TYPES OF LIGHTING

Low-voltage lighting systems are now part of the evening scene, and conventional 120-volt lighting is now more sophisticated. It is no longer necessary to protect wires in rigid conduits. New chemically coated wire can be buried directly in the ground. However, conventional lighting entails more work and time than installing low-voltage systems. Trenches at least 18 inches deep still must be dug to bury wires. Outlet boxes are necessary, and, generally, trench cable must be grounded. These are jobs for a qualified electrician.

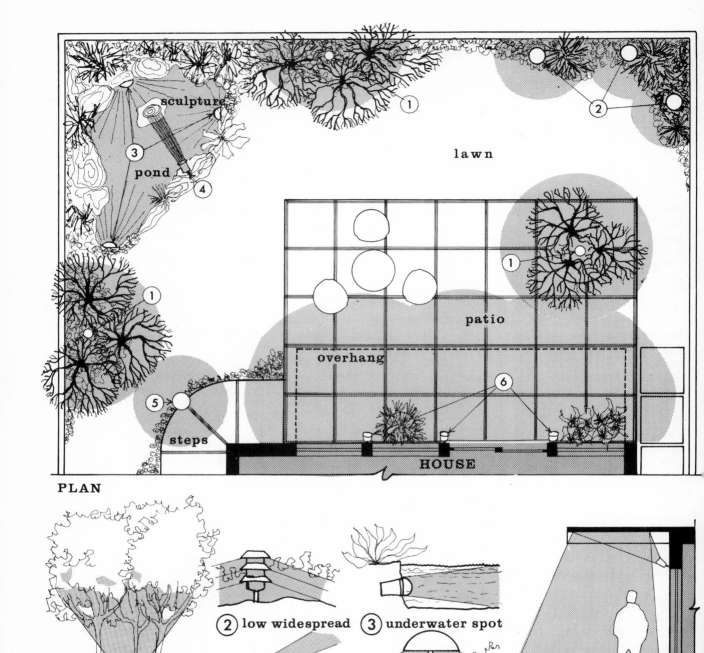

sculpture

③

pond

④

lawn

①

①

patio

overhang

⑥

①

⑤

steps

HOUSE

PLAN

① **wide-beam uplighting**

② **low widespread**   ③ **underwater spot**

④ **spotlight**   ⑤ **high widespread**   ⑥ **reflected floodlight**

120 VOLT LIGHTING FIXTURES

design: adrián martínez

Landscape Lighting

Low-voltage systems are an easier answer to lighting the landscape and a far safer one. Even if you accidentally cut a cable with a spade, there will be a spark but no shock. Or, if you poke your finger inside a fixture, there is little danger of shock. However, for an effective lighting plan, both kinds of systems are usually needed.

The secret of the low-voltage system is a simple transformer that attaches to the side of the house and plugs into any outdoor outlet. This unit reduces the normal 120-volt house system to 12 volts. Unlike the cables for the 120-volt system that must be deeply buried in the ground, low-voltage cables can be set 1 inch below the soil. Just wedge the earth apart with a spade, put the cables in place, and tamp down the soil with your shoe.

The systems come in kits with a transformer and either 4 or 6 or 8 lights, and about 100 feet of cable. The kits have resealing cable; you can clip on fixtures to the cable at any point.

Low-voltage lighting is soft and subdued to dramatize and emphasize the property. It is excellent for decorative effects along flower beds, walks and paths, and steps. But for additional light for large areas, such as lawns and patios, you may need to have the standard 120-volt system.

Sometimes, several kits are necessary to light all outdoor areas adequately. Therefore, set apart each area—garden, patio, pool, walks, and steps—and install a separate system for each place. This makes it easy to shut off areas you do not want lighted.

Decide exactly where you want light before you start buying fixtures. It is a good idea to make a rough plan on paper; decide which area is most important in your scheme of living. Perhaps a mass of light for the patio, with subdued illumination for other areas, is the best answer to your outdoor-living scheme.

BULBS AND FIXTURES

The mainstay for outdoor lighting is the PAR lamp. It is not affected by water, snow, ice, or fluctuating temperatures. It is a sealed unit generally in the shape of a mushroom. Some PAR lamps are for floodlighting an area while others are for spotlighting an object. They come in different wattages: 75, 100, and 150. Higher intensities are also available for landscapes; these include 200-, 300-, and 500-watt. Install all lamps in fixtures with waterproof sockets.

The common household bulb can be used outdoors too. Bulbs of 15 watts or 25 watts used for wall brackets and path fixtures do not need protection from weather, but bulbs of higher wattages do. Where lines of light are needed, say, along a flower bed or a path, fluorescent lamps from 15 to 40 watts can be used in weatherproof sockets. For outdoors, cool white or daylight types are the best. Underwater fixtures come in the same bullet shape as PAR fixtures or as separate housings. Colored bulbs are available too. Avoid strong colors such as red, blue, and green, which will create a carnival effect. Pink, blue-white, yellow, and amber are better choices.

Fixtures come in a variety of designs: some are very ornamental and simulate flowers or leaves, rocks, or frogs. The standard fixture and the one you will work with most is a bullet reflector type. Canopy fixtures, cone fixtures, and mushroom design, as well as louvered kinds, are also available at suppliers'. Some are portable, mounted on metal spikes that stick into the ground, while others are for permanent installation on a tree or post or a house eave. Also available are recessed units and flush-mounted fixtures for areas where there is little natural shielding.

ILLUMINATING TREES AND SHRUBS

Many trees and shrubs are natural light subjects. Those with feathery foliage or gnarled branches are better than others. Plants with dense foliage generally do not look good illuminated. Deciduous trees and shrubs properly illuminated are always interesting in winter.

If the tree has an umbrella shape, like an elm, aim the light upward into the foliage. The fixture can be at ground level or in the lower part of the tree. If it is a heavy tree with a thick trunk and branching system, put lights at ground level so that the rays graze the limbs, just barely etching them with light. If it is a tall and columnar tree, put the lights in a circle on the ground and aim them upward.

With weeping trees, such as willows, and with smaller trees, such as Japanese maple, direct the light at the delicate foliage. Trees with small leaves are best illuminated in this manner too. For big, heavy trees, etch the branches with light to accent unusual textures and reliefs. If the tree is against a fence or wall, use backlighting to silhouette it rather than lighting the tree itself. Dense-leaved trees appear lovely with halos of brightness, with the illumination aimed at the outer edges of the total form.

Plants, too, can be dramatic at night; they can be backlighted from the ground, making the leaves and branches a tracery of silver light. A single plant can be floodlighted, and others in the same area illuminated with subdued light. With a lighted background such as a fence or a wall, it is possible to silhouette the shape and outline of a plant. And finally for an entirely different effect, try positioning the light source to create shadows.

The many advantages of lighting for safety and show.
(Westinghouse)

Here, mushroom-type lighting on a low-voltage system illuminates planter boxes and small lawn area; a simple, inexpensive method of lighting.
(Westinghouse)

Low-voltage concealed spots are used in this lighting plan with a standard voltage system for complete night illumination of the patio.
(Westinghouse)

A lighted tree, graceful and effective, becomes the feature of an outdoor area.
(General Electric)

To make the small Japanese garden effective at night, four down spots
are used along a house wall.
(General Electric)

House and entrance are well lighted in a contemporary plan; mushroom
spots along the walk, bracket lights at entrance, and can-type down
spots along the window wall make a study in shadows and light.
(General Electric)

A LIGHTING PLAN

To light your garden, separate the plan as follows: entryway and driveway, walks and steps, patio and garden area. In this way, one section can be done at a time, with a definite overall lighting program as the goal as time and money are available. Each of these areas needs a different kind of light treatment. Although there is no formulated approach to lighting a landscape, there are some general rules that apply to all plans.

Lighting the entryway and driveway should be attractive and functional. A pleasing picture is important here, but safety is vital too. Lead the guest to the door with subdued lighting; bright light is not needed. Place fixtures low along paths and walks with a good level (but not bright) illumination on the rest of the area. Avoid spotlights and floodlights. If there is a wall adjacent to the door, bathe the wall in soft light to accent the architectural features. If there are steps leading to the entrance, provide adequate illumination. Place fixtures out of sight; as guests walk to the house, they do not want to be blinded by glare. Use concealed lighting; there are several styles of fixtures—mushroom and dome, to name two.

In the garden there are usually flower beds, trees, and shrubs, and this is the place to paint a picture with light. You want to see a lovely picture from the patio or from within the house. The plantings determine what kind of lighting to use (these techniques have been already covered).

The patio needs bright illumination; this is where you will spend most of your time and where guests will most likely gather. The lighting level should be sufficient to allow people to see one another. Overhead floods balanced with accent lighting give contrast and interest. Generally, the patio has walls that can be dramatically etched with light. Above all, be sure that seated guests are not confronted with light bulbs staring at them; try to conceal all fixtures.

ILLUMINATING STATUES AND POOLS

For a sculpture, spot or floodlight it at a distance with two 75-watt PAR bulbs, one on each side. If you want the lights closer to the subject, use 25- or 40-watt bulbs in reflectors. An overhead brightness might be necessary, too, so that all shadows fall in a normal pattern, but this will depend on the size of the statue. Never place the illumination on one side of the object; it is needed from two angles so that the edges and the contours of the sculpture are emphasized.

There are several ways to light garden pools. The plantings around the pool can be the feature and the water remain in the shadows, or the water can be illuminated from below; or a combination of the two methods for an overall effect can be tried. For garden pools, ponds, or swimming pools, local code regulations must be followed when you are installing lighting equipment. Contact electrical inspectors in your building code office. In general, lighting for pools or any area with water is best done by a professional electrician.

House plants and seasonal plants decorate a breakfast room
in a suburban home.
(Woodard Furniture)

CHAPTER 27

House Plants

The barren look of many indoor areas demands living green plants. They are decorative and add color whether they are at windows or used as floor plants for room accent or as ornamental features for a coffee table.

The world of house plants is huge, and more new plants are offered today than even a few years ago. Many species that were once confined to conservatories have taken their place indoors because most new homes have controlled heating and humidity systems. (And inexpensive room humidifiers for apartments are also available.) We are no longer restricted only to philodendrons and rubber trees or ferns and palms indoors.

There are plants for all kinds of situations. Some tolerate poor light and dry air, others need only a bright place, several need partial sun, and still other species prefer a sunny location. Average home temperatures of 78F by day and 10 or 15 degrees less at night are fine for most plants. There are some species that need constant heat or coolness, but these are the exceptions rather than the rule.

Because there are so many indoor plants, I have classified them as foliage plants, multicolored-leaved kinds, and flowering plants. Also included are gift plants.

FOLIAGE PLANTS

PHILODENDRONS. These have dark-green leaves and can absorb whatever amount of light is available. They live for many months in shady corners where other plants simply will not survive. With 250 species from tropical parts of America, philodendrons offer many different shapes of leaves, and different sizes: small, medium, and large plants. Some species are self-heading, the leaves borne in a central crown.

Most philodendrons will grow into lovely vining plants if trained to a stake. Grow plants in a porous soil of one-third sand, one-third peat moss, and one-third rich loam. Let the plants dry out between waterings. Feed them about once a month during warm months, not at all the rest of the year.

P. andreanum. Handsome, arrow-shaped foliage; needs moisture, warmth. Grows large.

P. cordatum (P. oxycardium). The heart-leaf plant with glossy, green leaves. Grows in water or soil.

P. hastatum variegatum. New, with yellow and green leaves.

P. panduraeforme. Scalloped olive-green leaves; grows low.

P. pertusum. A robust grower with deep-lobed, heart-shaped leaves. Variegated form of yellow and green also available.

P. soderoi. Large or small forms with mottled leaves, red stems.

P. squamiferum. Unusual leaf design; good accent.

P. verrucosum. Exotic satin sheen foliage—outstanding; needs warmth, humidity.

P. wendlandii. Self-heading cabbage type, with dense rosettes of waxy-green, tongue-shaped leaves; grows large.

DRACAENA. From the west coast of Africa, dracaena have plain green leaves or variegated foliage. The plants are extremely decorative, and as they come from an area where there is plenty of rain, they need a moisture-retentive soil of equal parts of loam, peat moss, and sand. Keep the medium moist but not soggy. Repot the plants yearly, as they do not thrive in the same pot too long.

D. deremensis longii. Bright-striped, green and white leaves on a central trunk.

D. deremensis warneckii. Gray and green leaves; good accent plant.

House plants including African
violets and azaleas make a window
garden a study in color.
(Roche)

Corner of an apartment is an ideal
place for foliage house plants.
(Window Shade Assoc.)

D. fragrans massangeana. The "corn plant" with cream-colored stripes of broad leaves. Grows somewhat like a palm from a central core, and becomes a handsome tree in a few years.

D. goddseffiana. Green leaves spattered with yellow; bush growth, small size.

D. marginata. Handsome decorator plant with clusters of blade-shaped green leaves edged with red. Branches when young.

D. sanderiana. Gray-green, white margined foliage. Especially good for dish gardens.

FICUS. Rubber trees are well-known members of the ficus family, but their relatives, such as weeping fig, common fig, and fiddle-leaf fig are seldom seen. Yet these are amenable house plants. Coming from temperate and tropical countries, ficus plants enjoy warmth (80F day), but will survive a wide range of temperatures, from 55F to 70F. Pot plants in equal parts of loam, sand, and peat moss. Keep the soil barely moist all year; they never like to be too wet. A drastic change of light or temperature causes many ficus plants to drop leaves; repotting sets them back considerably, so leave them undisturbed for 2 to 3 years. Feed moderately only during active growth.

F. benjamina. The weeping fig with long, slender, shiny leaves. Can grow into a tree.

F. carica. A good tub plant with thick-lobed leaves and palmate veining; goes dormant in winter.

F. elastica decora. The common rubber tree, with oval, glossy green leaves and ivory veins.

F. lyrata. Fiddle-leaf fig, with huge dark-green leaves; leathery foliage.

F. radicans variegata. Small creeping type, with white and green foliage.

FERNS. As a group, these plants offer a dazzling array of foliage accent. There are some with lacy fronds, others with bold foliage. In nature, most ferns grow in moist, cool locations in partial shade. Provide plants with a very porous soil of equal parts loam, leafmold, and sand. Keep them moist but never soggy. Fertilizers seem to burn leaf tips of plants, so it is generally wise not to feed ferns. Most ferns rest in winter, so keep the soil then just barely moist. Provide some additional humidity for these plants; place pots on pebble-filled trays.

Adiantum hispidulum. Dwarf maidenhair fern; charming.

A. cuneatum. Old favorite; dark-green fronds; many varieties including *A. cuneatum* 'Excelsum,' 'Goldelse,' 'Matador'—all good; tolerant of adverse conditions.

A. tenurum wrightii. Typical maidenhair; one of the best.

Asplenium nidus. (Bird's Nest fern). Evergreen fronds. Outstanding.

A. viviparum. Very lacy fronds; produces plantlets on leaves.

Blechnum braziliense. Coarse fronds; low-growing. Different.

Davallia fejeensis (Rabbit's Foot fern). Fine feathery foliage and hairy creeping rootstalks. A curiosity.

Nephrolepis exalata 'Fluffy Ruffles'. Heavily ruffled one; choice.

Polypodium polycarpon. Strap leaf fern; best grown on slab of osmunda.

Polystichum setosum. Stiff, glossy fronds of green; compact growth.

Pteris ensiformis. 'Victoriae.' Many forms; this one silver and green.

Woodwardia orientalis. The chain fern; excellent for basket growing.

PALMS. These graceful plants really need little care, and are stellar indoor decoration. Grow them in a soil of equal parts of loam, peat moss, and sand, and repot them every second year. Keep soil quite moist in summer but just barely watered in winter. Feed only moderately, if at all.

Caryota (fishtail palm). Leaves wedge-shaped like a fishtail. Superlative house plant.

Chamaedorea elegans bella. Most popular; dwarf-type, with graceful arching fronds.

Chamaerops humilis. Never grows to more than 3 feet; has fan-shaped, blue-green foliage. Likes a cool, airy spot.

Cocos weddelliana (*Syagrus weddelliana*). Dwarf, with feathery, yellow-green foliage. Graceful plant, but won't be with you for more than a few years.

Howea fosteriana. Pendent flat leaves from central stems; dark-green foliage; grows quickly.

Phoenix roebelenii (date palm). Dwarf variety with dark-green leaves. Outstanding as a pot plant.

Rhapis excelsa. Indestructible, with green, fan-shaped leaves.

MULTICOLORED-LEAVED PLANTS

CROTONS. These plants have foliage in a veritable rainbow of color, with combinations of yellow and green perhaps the most common. Some have broad leaves, others lance-shaped or scalloped patterns. From the tropics, crotons like warmth and humidity, and are extremely sensitive to drafts and fluctuating temperatures. Grow plants in equal parts of loam, sand, and peat moss. Give them plenty of water all year and keep them in small containers undisturbed for several years.

'Cameo'—Semioak foliage; shell-pink.
'Gloriosa'—Red-purple and maroon leaves.

Artificial-light plant stand.
(Tube Craft)

A corner arrangement of
house plants.

'Harvest Moon'—Green foliage with yellow midrib and white veins.

'Jungle Queen'—Red, pink, and maroon; striking plant.

'Monarch'—Broad, irregular leaves, brilliant red.

'Spotlight'—Narrow, irregular leaves, green, yellow, and red.

'Sunday'—Large semioak leaf; orange, yellow, and red.

DIEFFENBACHIA. First appearing as house plants in 1830 in Germany, it is only recently we have had a selection of dieffenbachias in this country. The large heart-shaped leaves resemble caladiums, and the plants are usually bushy. They grow from a central trunk, much like a palm. Pot dieffenbachias in equal parts of peat moss, loam, and sand, with a teaspoon of rotted cow manure to an 8-inch pot. Keep them watered in summer but somewhat dry in winter.

D. amoena. Deep-green leaves blotched white.
D. arvida. White leaf pattern.
D. bowmannii. Chartreuse foliage.
D. exotica. Mottled green and white foliage; compact growth.
D. hoffmanni. Showy white leaf pattern.
D. splendens. Velvety green foliage with white dots.

MARANTA and CALATHEA. These are fine decorative plants, but the nomenclature for this large family is confusing. The group also includes calathea and ctenanthes. No matter how they are listed in catalogs, do try these fine house plants. Grow them in equal parts of rich loam and sand; keep moist all year; repot them annually.

C. argyrala. Silver-gray and green foliage.
C. concinna. Dark-green leaves with feather design.
C. insignis. Light green, with olive-green markings.
C. lietzei. Light-green feather design, purple underneath.
C. makoyana. Olive-green, pink, silver, and green foliage. Outstanding.
C. oppenheimiana. Silver and green.
C. ornata. Pink or white stripes; striking.
Maranta leuconeura massangeana. Pearl-gray-green foliage.
Ctenanthe 'Burle Marx'. Gray-green, dark-green leaves.

Other fine foliage plants include podocarpus, nepthytis, schefflera, syngonium, aglaeonema, succulents, bromeliads, peperomia, pandanus, fatsia, pilea, and too many more to list.

FLOWERING PLANTS

SAINTPAULIA (African violets). Small though they may be, these are tremendously popular, rewarding plants. They come in thousands of varieties. Foliage may be velvety or smooth, lance-shaped or heart-shaped, green or variegated. Flowers are single, double, or semidouble in shades of pink, blue, lavender, and purple. Use sterilized soil or mixes especially prepared for these plants. Give bright light in spring and summer, some sun in fall and winter, and keep plants where there is good air circulation. Water soil moderately and be sure pots have perfect drainage. Keep humidity at 40 to 60 percent.

'Alakazam'—Double lavender flowers.
'Big Boy Blue'—Splendid double blue blooms.
'Bloom Burst'—Semidouble pink.
'Cochise'—Semidouble red star-shaped.
'Flash'—Double rose-pink.
'Happy Time'—Double pink.
'Purple Knight'—Single, dark purple.
'Red Honey'—Double red flowers.
'Spitfire'—Single deep pink, fringed white.
'White Perfection'—Immense double.
'Zorro'—Double lavender blossoms.

BEGONIA. Favorites for house decoration, with several hundred species and thousands of varieties. Plants have glossy dark-green or mahogany-colored leaves and single or semidouble or double blooms in shades of white to fiery red. Give them small pots and some sun; avoid overwatering. They like to be quite dry; too much water rots them quickly. Prune back tops as plants get leggy. Propagate by cuttings or seeds.

Semperflorens or Wax Begonias

'Andy'—To 6 inches; grass-green leaves, single rose flowers.
'Apple Blossom'—To 12 inches; pale-pink, double flowers.
'Ballet'—To 12 inches, bronze leaves, double white flowers.
'Cinderella'—To 12 inches; pink single blossoms tipped red.
'Green Thimbleberry'—Pale-green leaves and crested double pink blooms.
'Jack Horner'—To 12 inches; dark-green leaves, pink double flowers.
'Little Gem'—To 6 inches; bronze leaves, double pink flowers.
'Lucy Locket'—To 14 inches; double pink flowers.
'South Pacific'—To 10 inches; bright orange-red double flowers.

Hirsute, or hairy-leaved begonias. These have furry foliage and whiskered flowers, the leaves are lobed or tapered; the blooms, red or pink or white; always impressive. Plants perform superbly even in apartments; they can live with dry air if they must and they can tolerate coolness if they have to. Just be sure they get some winter sun so that they will bloom. And a word of caution: keep them only moderately moist; overwatering causes rot. Propagate by stem cuttings.

B. 'Alleryi'. To 30 inches; dark-green leaves with white hairs and pale pink flowers.

B. drostii. To 30 inches; very hairy leaves and pink flowers.

B. prunifolia. To 30 inches; cupped leaves and white blooms.

B. scharffiana. To 30 inches; green-red plush leaves; ivory blooms.

B. viaude. To 36 inches; leaves green on top, red below with fine white hairs; white flowers.

Rex begonias. These are mostly rhizomatous, grown for their exquisite patterned leaves. Provide warmth (75F daytime, 65F nighttime), and high humidity (60 percent); bright light but not much sun; a north window is fine. Keep soil evenly moist. Most kinds drop their leaves and go dormant in winter; don't try to force them to grow then. Water sparingly and wait for new growth. It will appear about mid-March. Propagate from leaf cuttings or seeds.

'Autumn Glow'—To 14 inches; rose-colored leaves with silver.

'Baby Rainbow'—To 12 inches; cupped silver-green and purple leaves.

'Berry's Autumn'—To 8 inches; olive-green leaves with silver spots.

'Calico'—To 8 inches; crimson, green, and silver foliage.

'Cardoza Gardens'—To 16 inches; large purple, silver, and green foliage; a striking plant.

PELARGONIUMS (Geraniums). These provide almost constant color if given full sun and grown rather cool, with frequent airing and no crowding at the window. Plant in a rather firm soil mixture of 3 parts loam to 1 part sand plus a little peat moss slightly on the acid side, say, pH 6.0 to 6.5, with some leeway in either direction acceptable. Water freely, then let dry out a little before watering again. Geraniums bloom best when pot-bound, so grow in as small pots as possible. Martha Washingtons and the ivy-leaved rest somewhat in winter; water them moderately then and do not feed. Feed the others every other week when they are in active growth, which is most of the time in sunny weather. Geraniums are sometimes troubled by edema; water-soaked spots appear on the leaves, and cells burst when moisture collects in the plants faster than it is transpired from the leaves. Avoid overwatering and high humidity; don't mist the foliage. Do investigate the new Carefree geraniums that come true to type and color from seed. Vining geraniums in mixed colors can also be grown from seed. Propagate most other geraniums from cuttings

taken in spring for winter bloom, August or early September for spring and summer flowering. Geraniums are usually classified in the following groups:

Zonals. Fancy-leaved geraniums, with green leaves variegated with white or foliage in shades of brown, bronze, and gold, or very fancy tricolor combinations. Miniatures of the zonal type to 3 inches are also available; ideal for a windowsill.

'Alpha'—Dwarf; yellow and brown foliage.
'Alphonse Ricard'—Semidouble scarlet blooms.
'Happy Thought'—Green and yellow bicolor.
'Salmon Irene'—Lovely pink.
'Skies of Italy'—Gold and silver leaves.
'Snowball'—White blooms.
'Tu Tone'—Dwarf, pale-pink flowers.

Martha Washington geraniums. Varieties of *Pelargonium domesticum,* with all-green leaves and large flowers in late spring.

'Easter Greeting'—Cerise blooms.
'Gardener's Joy'—Pink blooms.
'Madame Layal'—Purple and white blooms.
'Salmon Splendor'—Lovely salmon shade.
'Senorita'—Orange-pink flowers.

Ivy-leaved geraniums. Varieties of *Pelargonium peltatum,* with trailing stems of glossy ivy leaves and luxuriant bloom in summer. Excellent for hanging baskets.

'Charles Turner'—Rose-pink.
'Mexican Beauty'—Semidouble red.
'Santa Paula'—Lavender-blue.
'Sunset'—Lavender flowers.

Scented-leaved geraniums. Decorative shrubs, with heady fragrance. Many leaf forms and growth habits.

P. graveolens (rose-scented varieties)
'Grey Lady Plymouth'
'Little Gem'
'Rober's Lemon Rose'

EPIPHYLLUM (Orchid-cactus). Large hanging plants, mostly epiphytic, to 4 feet, or upright growers (if staked) to 20 inches; famous for evening blooms, red or pink, purple or white, with peak in May and June. Hybrids have also been developed for day bloom. Keep plants pot-bound and in a bright windowsill or grow as natural trailers in baskets. Don't miss these mammoth flowers; they do bloom indoors with little care; and always cause comment in my garden room. Take cuttings in spring for new plants.

'Conway Giant'—7-inch magnificent purplish-red day bloom.
'Eden'—6-inch white and yellow day flowers.
'Luminosa'—5-inch day blooms.

Window garden featuring cacti.
(Roche)

Trailing plants in brackets.
(Roche)

'Nocturne'—6-inch purple and white night blooms.
'Parade'—6-inch pink day blooms.
'Royal Rose'—6-inch rose-buff day flowers.

GIFT PLANTS

Today, gift plants are year-round plants. From Easter to Christmas there is a colorful array of blooming plants for almost every month. Cineraria, azalea, cyclamen, daffodil, Easter lily, poinsettia are a few of the many available for festive giving. The problem is to make gift plants permanent house plants. Several of them can be grown to decorate your home for many years. Others, like calceolaria and cineraria, are only temporary visitors.

Gift plants are in bloom when you receive them, and they have been grown under ideal greenhouse conditions. The adjustment from greenhouse to your home is quite a shock to them. Almost all of them require a cool, airy place at an east or west window away from heat.

Christmas begonias. These plants are smothered with flowers and make a pretty picture indoors. The new cultivars have been bred for heat tolerance, and these stay handsome for many months. Keep them cool (about 60F) and provide an evenly moist soil for them.

Azalea. A successful year-round indoor plant. Grow cool and spray foliage frequently. Flood plants, then allow them to dry out between waterings. When flowers fade, cut them off, but continue to water plants. In late April or early May, put them in the garden or on a porch in a shaded place. In summer, give them plenty of water and repot them in an acid soil mix in September. Return them to the house and fertilize moderately.

Christmas poinsettia. A beautiful plant valued for its red bracts rather than the tiny yellow flowers. When you receive it, do not put it in a warm place. It must have coolness (about 60F). After blooms fade, dry out the plant and store it at about 50F in north light until April. Then cut it back to 3 or 4 inches and put it in sun. Water lightly, increasing moisture with growth. When it is warm outdoors, put the poinsettia in a sunny spot and fertilize it. Prune it again, allowing only a few strong branches to grow on through summer. When the weather turns cool, about 55F, move the plant to a semishady window and increase moisture until buds form.

Cyclamen. These are glamorous but temperamental plants that will need buckets of water and a very cool (50F) place. When flowers fade, plants must be discarded.

Gloxinia. Beautiful flowering plants, and the new varieties are better than ever before. Keep them cool

and shaded, and they will be attractive for many months. Water them moderately; soil should be evenly moist. When blooms fade, store the tubers in their pots at 60F, and water them about once a week. Too much moisture rots the tubers. When new growth appears, repot them and return to a window.

Hydrangea. Lush and colorful, these plants need copious watering. Stand the pot in a saucer of water once a day. When flowering stops, cut back the plants to about a 4-inch height. Repot in fresh soil in a larger container. In summer, sink the pot in a semishaded place in the garden; water and feed well. Let it stay out until the first frost. Return the pot indoors to a cool place, about 40F, and keep the soil barely moist. It must have low temperatures for at least 8 weeks to initiate flower buds. In January, put it in a sunny cool (60F) window and increase moisture. Feed twice a month.

Easter lily. This lily must be kept cool, about 50F. Keep the soil evenly moist, and when flowering stops, cut off the withered blooms. Keep the leaves growing at a sunny window. In spring, when weather permits, take the plant from its pot and place it in a sunny garden spot. Water and feed it like other garden flowers. Blooms may appear in late summer. To keep it indoors, in late fall dig up the bulb and store it at 40F. Pot it again right after Christmas with top of bulb 2 inches below the soil.

Kalanchoe blossfeldiana. Available at Christmas, this flame-colored flowering plant is a favorite. Grow it cool and keep the soil evenly moist. After flowering, let it rest with a somewhat dry soil until March. Then start watering and feed it. A second set of flowers will appear in April.

Calceolaria. This annual has showy flowers in standard sizes or in a dwarf variety. Needs somewhat more warmth than most gift plants and plenty of water. Strictly a temporary plant that must be discarded after it blooms.

GROWING PLANTS UNDER ARTIFICIAL LIGHT

If window space is limited at home or buildings shut out light, you can still have house plants. Artificial light makes it possible to have greeneries in closets, basements, attics or pantries. You can make your own arrangements with light fixtures and homemade trays, or you can buy commercial units from suppliers: table models or movable carts.

With artificial light, remember that plants still need humidity, ventilation, and warmth by day, coolness at night. Put the plants where there is easy access to water and where you can tend them without bumping into furniture.

If the garden is in the living room or dining room,

it must be used decoratively. More suitable areas perhaps where you can experiment and where there is more space are in a basement or an attic.

Almost any plant can be grown under artificial light; however, some fare better than others. African violets, gloxinias, some begonias, and seedling orchids do remarkably well. Choose plants that appeal to you and try them; experimenting is half the fun of this kind of gardening.

While the choice of plants is up to you, cultural factors such as humidity, temperature, ventilation, and moisture must be provided with care—perhaps with more care than if you are growing plants at windows. With constant light there must be constant care. Plants grow all the time in artificial gardens. At windows, if there is a series of cloudy days and you forget to water plants, little harm is done.

Ventilation is vital for plants in light gardens. Plants are comfortable at windows if we are. In an area of their own where there are many plants together, use a small fan to keep air moving or open a window (weather permitting) for ventilation.

Light and Plants

When sunlight passes through a prism, we see the colors of the solar spectrum. We know that visible colors are violet, blue, green, yellow, orange, and red. There are additional rays we do not see. Plants make various uses of the parts of the solar spectrum at various times in their life cycle. Generally, plants absorb more red and blue light than green and yellow. Plant scientists have discovered that red and blue light stimulate plant growth. Blue light promotes the production of sugar and starches (photosynthesis), and red light causes germination and growth; it also controls a plant's photoperiodism (the response of organisms to the relative length of day and night). Plants exposed to their proper photoperiod grow faster, bloom better. Some plants need photoperiods of long duration, 14 to 18 hours; some, of intermediate duration, 12 to 18 hours; and others require short photoperiods of 10 to 13 hours. Therefore, the time that plants will be exposed to lamps varies accordingly with each species.

Photoperiods

Long (14–18 hours)	Intermediate (12–18 hours)	Short (10–13 hours)
dahlia	geraniums	poinsettia
nasturtium	African violet	morning glory
some begonias	roses	chrysanthemum
calceolaria	gloxinia	gardenias
	coleus	Christmas begonia

There is a bewildering array of fluorescent lamps. Some are cool white; others are daylight kinds or warm white or natural light lamps. Tubes designed specifically for plant growth with more red and blue light are most popular with growers. These are Plant-Gro by Westinghouse Electric, Gro-Lux by Sylvania Electric, and Duro-Lite Naturescent tubes. More recent introductions have brought wide-spectrum Gro-Lux lamps.

BASKET PLANTS

The beauty of plants at eye level cannot be denied; they are easily seen and add color and interest to otherwise barren areas. In handsome containers, they complete the garden picture. There are many trailers and climbers that can be used for baskets; some for flowers, others for foliage. And there are dozens of different containers for them.

Here are a few of the many plants for baskets.

(Plants marked with an asterisk are especially recommended for outdoor decoration.)

Asparagus sprengeri (emerald fern). One of the choice trailers with feathery leaves and tiny white flowers followed by red berries.

Begonia tuberhybrida 'Pendula.' Cascades of colorful flowers; unbeatable summer color but difficult in parts of the country with hot summers. Needs coolness and shade.

Campanula fragilis (bellflower). Blue flowers and lush foliage make this a perfect basket plant. Needs only a little sun.

Chlorophytum elatum (spider-plant). This one grows as easily as a weed and within a year will fill a basket with bright-green sword-shaped foliage.

Cissus rhombifolia (grape-ivy). One of the toughest indoor basket growers; it has glossy toothed and pointed leaves and will trail or climb. Needs a bright spot.

*Fuchsia (lady's-eardrops). Many fine trailers; easy plants in partial shade but need buckets of water in growth.

*Geraniums (ivy-leaved types). Many kinds with abundant bloom and handsome leaves.

Hedera (ivy). Pretty foliage plants that do well in partial shade. Many varieties. Check catalogs.

Hoya carnosa (wax-plant). A popular trailer with gray-green oval leaves. Only mature specimens will bear the handsome, scented, waxy-white flowers. After bloom fades do not remove flower spurs; subsequent flowers can come from the same spurs.

Lantana montevidensis. A robust grower that blooms for months with attractive lavender flowers.

*Petunia (cascading varieties). Absolutely the finest annual for baskets. Many kinds and flowers get bigger and better every year. Needs sun.

Rosmarinus officinalis 'Prostratus' (rosemary). Not often seen but a fine creeping plant that cascades

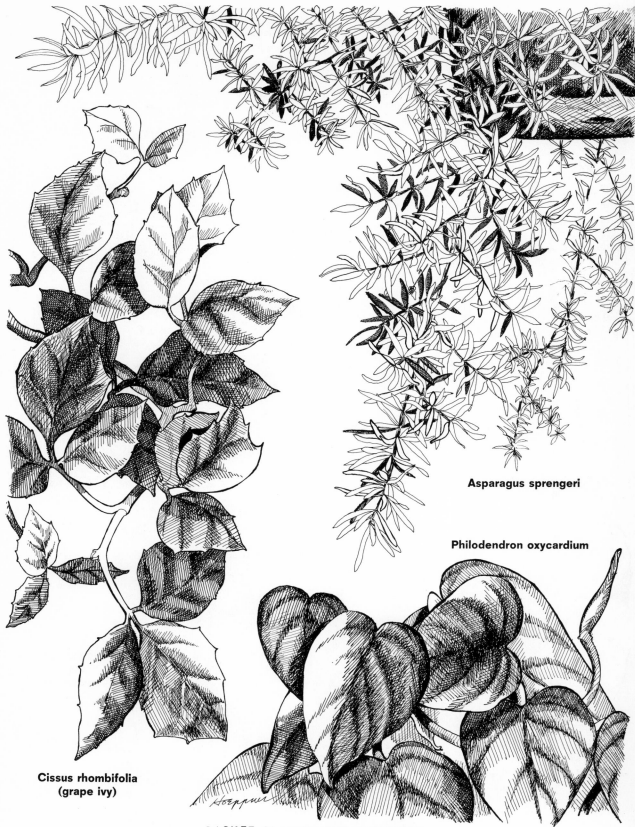

Asparagus sprengeri

Philodendron oxycardium

Cissus rhombifolia
(grape ivy)

BASKET PLANTS FOR INDOORS

**Begonia tuberhybrida
(tuberous begonia)**

**Lobelia
erinus**

**Tropaeolum
majus
(nasturtium)**

BASKET PLANTS FOR OUTDOORS

over the pot rim with dark-green leaves and bright lavender flowers.

Saxifraga sarmentos (strawberry geranium). This is neither a strawberry, nor a geranium, nor a begonia but a member of the Saxifragaceae. The plant sends out runners from a clump of basal leaves, and it is these runners that make the plant effective for hanging. Keep in the shade.

Scindapus aureus (ivy-arum). A fine plant with heart-shaped dark-green leaves marked with yellow. Many varieties; all easy plants to grow and highly effective in baskets.

*Tropaeolum majus (nasturtium). Bright and lovely; makes a big splash of color. Needs sun.

SUCCULENTS AND CACTI

This is a big family of plants with many overlooked gems that come to life in pots and tubs. Where something is wanted that is unusual, cacti and succulents are the answer. Some of the big agaves and aloes are particularly desirable because of the leaf color—blue, green, purple-green—and their sculptural qualities.

Select mature plants; these are slow growers and, unlike other plants that require frequent watering, cacti and succulents can, if necessary, go without water for weeks. Grow them in a sandy soil; or if they are epiphytes such as Epiphyllum, grow them in equal parts of fir bark and soil. Most species rest in winter and need lower temperatures, about 55F, and little, if any, water.

Here is a list of some amenable cacti and succulents:

Aeonium arboreum. Decorative rosettes on tall stems that appear like full-blown roses. Need almost no care.

Agave americana marginata (century plant). Big spiny giant, with sword-shaped leaves, yellow and green. Dramatic in the right container.

Agave victoriae reginae. Small but lovely globe of handsome olive-green leaves delicately penciled along the edges. Beautiful symmetry.

Crassula argentea (jade plant). Old favorite, with bright-green, leathery leaves. Nice tree form when mature.

Dudleya brittoni. Big white rosette of leaves. Striking display in white tubs; mature plants only.

Epiphyllum (orchid cactus). Epiphyte; superb flowers in May and June. Color range incredible, size mammoth. Don't let the sprawling growth of the plants scare you away from them. They can be staked to grow vertically. Many new varieties. Pot in fir bark and soil.

Euphorbia grandicornis. An oddity, with branching stems armed with heavy spines.

Kalanchoe tomentosa (panda plant). Long, tapering leaves covered with hair; edges dark brown. Unusual; pot in fir bark and soil.

Zygocactus (Christmas cactus). Another superb flowering group of many varieties, some of them making a solid sphere of color. Grow in·equal parts of fir bark and soil.

BROMELIADS

Bromeliads are plants with bright leaf color and gaudy flowers. Many of them are rosettes, others tubular or vase-shaped. Some are medium-size; others, giants. But all of them need almost no care, and add a lot of color to an area for little cost.

Bromeliad care is simple. Most of them have a bowl or vase formation of leaves. Keep the vase filled with water; that is all there is to it. Pot the plants in equal parts of shredded fir bark and soil.

Here are some dependable species that I grow, all of which require a minimum night temperature of 45F.

Aechmea chantini (silver king). To 40 inches; variegated vase-shaped plant; red and yellow flowers. Needs some sun.

Billbergia venezuelana. A giant with broad leaves and mosaic patterns of chocolate brown with silver bands. Needs large tub. A spectacle in bloom.

Guzmania monostachia. To 30 inches; satiny green leaves in a rosette. Tall flower spike, with white flowers and green bracts, tipped red. Will take shade. Handsome in white pot.

Hohenbergia ridleyi. To 5 feet; with golden-yellow leaves and a tall branched yellow-and-red flower head. Fine accent plant for patio or terrace.

Pitcairnia carolinae. To 36 inches; tubular growth. Incredible red flowers; nice leafy growth.

Portea petropolitana extensa. To 48 inches; fan-shaped growth. Lush green foliage and multicolored flower spike. Needs sun and a large tub.

Streptocalyx poepeggi. To 48 inches; a dense rosette of spiny leaves. Whitish-rose flowers. Needs bright light.

Vriesia fenestralis. To 40 inches; green leaves delicately figured with darker green and lined purple. Big and bushy. Ideal for wooden box.

ORCHIDS

Orchids are splendid plants—no more difficult to grow than ferns or palms and perhaps easier to tend to. The orchid flower is well-known and outstanding in the plant world. More and more, these are becoming popular indoor plants.

The majority of orchids are epiphytic (growing on

trees); some are terrestrial (growing in the ground). The epiphytes must be potted in fir bark or osmunda (available in packages at nurseries). It is imperative that water does not linger at the roots of plants, so be sure drainage is perfect when planting orchids.

Containers—open-slatted baskets, slotted pots —that permit air to circulate around the roots are best for these plants. If they are in standard pots, be sure to provide for bottom ventilation. Orchids will not thrive in pots set directly on the floor. Use florist wire stands or make wooden platforms for them so that air can circulate around the base of the pot.

Some species need a great deal of sun; others will bloom in bright light. Most of them do not tolerate temperatures below 50F.

These orchids are dependable robust plants, easy to grow indoors.

Ansellia africana gigantea (spider orchid). To 40 inches; delightful patio plants with cane growth and evergreen leathery leaves. Bright yellow-and-brown flowers in spring. Grow in fir bark; give sun and warmth. Spring or fall bloom.

Bletilla hyacinthina. Low-growing to 16 inches; good in small boxes. Grassy leaves and bright lavender-purple flowers. Grow in equal parts of soil and fir bark. Need some sun for flowers in summer.

Cattleya. Many, many hybrids in dozens of colors including white, lavender, orange, red, apple-green. Plants grow to 36 inches. Need bright sun and copious water except for about a month after flowering. Grow in fir bark. Varieties for bloom in all seasons.

Coelogyne massangeana. To 36 inches. Decorative, broad evergreen leaves and pendent spikes of small beige-and-brown flowers. An easy one to grow in shade and coolness (58F). Pot in fir bark. Fall bloom.

Cymbidium. Many varieties in several different color combinations, with yellow and orange shades predominating. Standard plants grow to 40 inches, miniatures to about 28 inches. Give cool nights (45F) while buds are setting in fall. Winter and early spring flowering. Grow in equal parts of soil and shredded fir bark.

Dendrobium phalenopsis. An exquisite flowering plant. To 40 inches, with magenta-purple, open-faced blooms. Needs some sun and ample water all year. Grow in fir bark.

Epidendrum O'Brienianum. To 60 inches; reedlike stems crowned with bunches of tiny flowers. Needs sun. Grow in fir bark. Spring and summer flowers.

Lycaste aromatica. One of the finest indoor orchids, with yellow scented flowers. Grow in a somewhat shady place, and give plant a dry rest (about four weeks) after it blooms. Plant in fir bark.

Odontoglossum grande (tiger-orchid). Big brown-and-yellow flowers on a 30-inch plant. Needs some sun and even moisture all year. Grow in fir bark.

Phaius grandiflora (nun's orchid). To 40 inches, with big decorative leaves and large multicolored flowers. Grow in equal parts of soil and fir bark. Fall blooming.

Rhyncostylis gigantea. Straplike leaves to 30 inches. Plant bears pendent scapes of small white flowers dotted red. Grow in fir bark. Makes a colorful spring display. Needs sun or a bright spot.

Sobralia leucoxantha. To 48 inches; dark-green, papery leaves, with 4-inch rose-purple flowers. Grows in fir bark in a bright location. Summer blooming.

Handsome ceramic tile in striking designs accentuate this swimming
pool, bordered with turf on one side. Next to a sun porch, the
entire picture is appealing.
(Tile Council of America)

CHAPTER 28

Swimming Pools

Even in short summers the swimming pool is a desirable outdoor feature. No longer are pools only for the few. Today manufacturers have new construction techniques, and new materials have reduced costs considerably from even a few years ago. It is now possible to have a swimming pool for as little as $3,000. A pool can change your living patterns considerably: it affords a tremendous amount of recreational and entertainment pleasures.

Because the swimming pool industry has grown so rapidly, most homeowners are sadly misinformed about suitable standards and necessary qualifications for a pool. Not everyone can have a pool. A suitable site is tremendously important—and a hole in the ground filled with water does not constitute a swimming pool. Excavations and piping, pumps and filters, trim and accessories, pavings and decks, plantings around the pool, and in some cases, pool fences, are all part of the total swimming picture.

PLANNING THE POOL

A pool must fit into your landscape plan without destroying the patio and garden area. It must not compete with it but rather be part of it. The solution is, of course, to include the pool in your original plan; if you cannot afford it at the time, do it later. But often the property is already landscaped, and placing the pool properly becomes a challenge.

The pool is not a minor addition to the site. It will, in most cases, be the feature of the plan. Remember that the size and shape of the pool cannot be changed, and once it is installed, it cannot be moved. Trees and shrubs can be dug up if necessary, and even a patio can be reconstructed, but a pool is as permanent as the house.

Before you decide on the pool, select the size and shape you want and decide what minimum and maximum depth it will be. Do not leave this to the contractor; it is your pool and you know best whether there will be many children in it, whether it will be seldom used, and so on.

Trim and decking for the pool are other considerations that are often forgotten in the first enthusiasm of planning a swimming area. These are necessary and sometimes expensive items. So is equipment for the pool such as filters, pumps and motors, heaters, electric hookup, fittings, and other technical facets generally taken care of by the contractor. And once the pool is in place, you might want poolside structures.

SELECTING THE SITE

As I have mentioned, not all homeowners can have a pool. A house on a lot 50 by 70 feet can hardly accommodate an attractive pool.

Assuming the site is adequate for the pool, the first step is to decide just where it will be. There are several factors to think about before positioning the pool. Is the location the most effective so that life can go on normally during winter when the pool is not in use? Is your property suitable for a below-grade excavation? Construction will require a building permit and must abide by local zoning ordinances and building codes. These vary from state to state.

A pool involves digging deep into the ground, and it must not interfere with drainage lines, telephone lines, gas lines or water mains. These can be moved, but it is an expensive project. Usually, most pools are in the rear of the house where there is sufficient space and privacy. But actually, if necessary, a pool can be in the corner or to the side of the house, and even between the front of the house and a wing wall.

As with landscaping, plot the layout of all existing buildings, trees, and shrubs on graph paper to plan the pool site. Indicate the direction of prevailing winds and location of sun. The pool should receive as much sun as possible in summer and be free of shade from trees and other buildings during the time of its greatest use.

However, around the pool, some shade is welcome as a relief from constant heat. Plant small trees or shrubs, or build cabanas or overhead structures. Even mild summer breezes can be annoying and feel quite chilly to bathers in and around a pool. A wind screen or some sort of portable or permanent windbreak may be necessary.

When the pool is being placed, consider the view from the inside of the house. Do you prefer to have the pool out of sight when it is not in use, or do you want to have full view of the swimming area? Also consider that if the pool is between the house and the setting sun, there will be a sufficient amount of glare to make inside viewers uncomfortable. If your site has a very fine view, try to use it as a frame for the pool.

Be sure the pool is near the dressing area. Having wet swimmers track up the house is to be avoided. See that there is easy access to dressing rooms and showers.

A pool needs a filter and a pump; these mechanics should be located near the deep end so that there are short pipe runs for the recirculating system. In some cases, the filter system is massive and has to be hidden; try to put it behind a fence or in a corner.

The drainage area around the pool is often overlooked, and yet it is vital to good maintenance. If water collects under the base of the excavation, cracking and weakening can occur quite rapidly. Be certain there is a system of drain tiles around the pool to carry off underground water and to take care of surface water on the deck or paving. Prepare for drainage facilities for the deck while the pool is being excavated and before the decking is poured.

SIZE AND SHAPE

The size and shape of the pool are determined by several factors: space, site, and use by the family. The basic shapes usually developed by the pool manufacturer, and sometimes referred to as "packaged pools," specify a rectangular or kidney shape. However, these are not the only forms. The L-shaped, tear-drop, circle, free-form, and triangle are all suitable shapes for a pool. If the landscape plan is unorthodox, a unique pool is better than a stereotyped one. It adds drama to the setting.

Rectangle. While this shape is most popular and excellent for swimming, it is difficult to landscape and work around.

L-shaped. Adds a great deal of interest to an area, and affords interesting corners and planes for decking and plantings.

Tear-drop. Similar to an oval, this is an attractive shape that works well in the landscape plan.

Kidney. Not as popular as it used to be, but the curves make it a graceful and attractive pool.

Free-form. This shape is usually dictated by the available site and is perhaps the best plan for a crowded or irregular area.

Circle. Not as attractive as one would think; difficult to landscape.

There is only one way to find the maximum size of a pool that will fit your site and that is to take a tape measure, walk outside, and measure the site accurately. Then when you have the measurement and decide on a 20- by 30-foot pool, add 6 feet to each side to be sure. The coping is 12 to 16 inches wide. If a diving board is wanted at a later date, it requires 9 feet beyond the pool edge, with at least 2 feet of walkway around the board. If you are using a shaped pool in lieu of a rectangular one, remember that a 20- by 30-foot size is not all-inclusive. The length remains the same, but the width varies according to the shape of the pool.

The style of your house and your type of landscaping also influence the shape of the pool. If the garden is formal, with geometrical lines, the pool shape should perhaps be a rectangle or a square. A free-form pool is best for the natural landscape plan so that it matches the rounded corners of the land.

PAVINGS AND DECKINGS

The area around the pool is generally overlooked by most homeowners, but it is an important part of the swimming area. It provides a safe walkway for swimmers, and it also acts as a drainage surface. In many cases, the right design of the decking makes the difference between an ordinary pool and one that is outstanding.

The usual rim of coping stone and strip of concrete are no longer in keeping with new swimming pool design. This is the area that is the stepping-stone between the pool and the garden, and it needs careful planning.

Contemporary decks or pavings can extend right to the water's edge to eliminate that tight border line. The paving does not have to be a set width around the pool; the design can vary from narrow rims on one side and broad walks on other sides, to a contour edging. While concrete is suitable around a pool, textured concretes and pebbled surfaces in different colors are attractive too and, more important, safer. They are not as slippery as concrete. Redwood deck-

The shape of this pool delineates the lines of the house and becomes part
of the total composition.
(General Electric)

An oval pool, neither too large nor too small, is pleasing in the landscape.
(General Electric)

An angular-shaped concrete pool is ideal for the small house. *(Woodard Furniture)*

Here, a rectangular pool has redwood decking that frames the water area and is easy to clean. *(Woodard Furniture)*

ing can be used as a decorative border; bricks with a pebbly texture also make a suitable edging. Don't just throw a ribbon of concrete around a pool when so many decorative materials and interesting patterns are available to integrate the pool with the landscape.

PLANTINGS AROUND THE POOL

A pool by itself, no matter how well designed, needs a living frame of green plants to make it more than a hole in the ground with water. If you have a natural background of trees and shrubs, you are indeed fortunate. If you do not, even a few container plants strategically placed take the raw edges off a new pool.

The landscaping must not interfere with the pool itself. Many people immediately put lawns or ground covers at the edge of the pool. It is here, unless you have adequate drainage, that the ground will become saturated and soggy. Wooden headers are a solution; so are raised beds.

Often the raised bed looks better than a planting bed, and it is easier to maintain plants in beds. The choice of material for the beds gives you a chance to use the same paving that is around the pool and, thus, the whole area will appear larger.

When placing plants around a pool, avoid ever-green or deciduous trees that drop leaves; no one wants the continual job of cleaning leaves from the water surface. Set trees far back from the pool when-ever possible, and pay attention to root spread so that it will not interfere with water pipes. And do not use fruiting shrubs or trees. Dropping fruits stain paving and make it slippery; they also attract bees.

The Plants

Concentrate on foliage plants such as philoden-dron, podocarpus, schefflera and pittosporum—in the ground or in tubs, as weather permits. Use ferns and palms; their graceful fronds and tropical appearance are in keeping with the water picture. For flowering plants, select those that bloom in the hot months such as hibiscus, bougainvillaea, agapanthus, chrysanthe-mums, and Shasta daisies. For shady locations, grow fuchsias and tuberous begonias.

MAINTENANCE OF THE POOL

Once you have invested money in a pool, it is wise to keep it in good condition. Maintenance is not diffi-cult if done on a regular schedule. And in winter, care may be nonexistent if you cover the pool in the coldest months. By all means, use pool safety covers (from suppliers) if there are children in the family.

While there are many accessories for the pool, a few basic ones are all that are needed. The vacuum cleaner is essential. One type works from a vacuum inlet that is part of the filter system. The other has its own power source, using a garden hose connected to a house faucet. Each unit has its advantages and costs about the same.

Other pool items to consider:

A leaf skimmer. An aluminum or plastic frame with a skimming net that saves you lots of time and work. It is somewhat like a gigantic spoon with which you can scoop off debris and leaves from the water in a short time.

Brushes. These are needed to clean vinyl or fiber-glass pools. They have nylon bristles and come with or without a handle. For plaster-finished pools, a stainless steel brush is needed. They come in many sizes and designs.

Test kit. This tests the pool water for alkalinity, pH, and disinfectant residual. There are several kits available so buy the one that fits the sterilizing agent you are using.

Automatic pool cleaners. These are becoming more popular and are installed at the time the pool is built. There is also a portable type pool cleaner. This unit eliminates the need for a vacuum cleaner and brushes.

A cleaning once a week with occasional clean-ups before and after days of heavy use generally keeps a pool clean and attractive all summer. For equipment maintenance and water treatment, consult your pool contractor. These are specialized procedures that depend upon the type of equipment installed and the kind of pool built.

POOL CONSTRUCTION

The kind of pool you select is your own choice. There is no set answer. Prices, materials, and your own taste dictate what to buy. But in evaluating pools, the following information will be helpful to you:

Concrete

This is the most popular material for pools. It is strong, permanent, and ideal for below-grade installa-tion. Concrete pools have reinforced steel rods to withstand the pressure of the soil and water. There are five types of concrete construction: gunite, poured, handpacked, block, and precast pools.

Gunite. Gunite is a mixture of hydrated sand and cement applied over steel reinforcing rods directly on the soil. It is put in place with an air gun under great pressure to form a one-piece shell that is considered stronger than other types of concrete. Gunite allows complete freedom of size and shape because the concrete flow follows any earth contour.

Poured concrete. This is a laborious but a popular method of pool construction. Framing forms are necessary and the shape and size of the pool are governed by these.

Hand-packed. This is a process whereby pools are formed by hand-packing concrete against an excavation wall. It is a difficult process, using dry-packed concrete to regulate the concrete flow.

Block pools. These require a formed wall and a slab floor. The blocks are used as forms that become part of the pool structure. This type of construction limits the shape of the pool because you can work only with straight lines.

Precast concrete. These are panel walls cast beforehand and brought to the site, joined there to a slab floor. Then the precast panels are sealed together between the floor and the walls and between the sections themselves. Seals and gaskets wear out in time, and rework is usually necessary.

Vinyl or glass fiber. These are formed shells set in place in an excavation. At one time they were popular, but lately I have not seen them used often.

CHAPTER 29

Special Gardens

What is the reason for a special garden and why include one on your property? Because it gives you a chance to indulge in special flowers or plants. If your extravagance is roses, by all means have an area for them. If you are intrigued with rock gardens, make a tucked-away retreat where you can grow alpine plants. The special garden can become the feature of your landscape. It will give you hours of pleasure. If flower beds and borders are not for you, indulge in a specific interest.

ROCK GARDENS

A rock garden is not the easiest landscape to simulate on your property, but it is certainly a worthwhile undertaking. This garden requires labor, patience and careful construction, but when finished it is a picturesque, highly desirable feature. The secret is to build it slowly and with care so it will become a permanent landscape asset.

The rock garden takes you into the world of alpine plants, which are among the most attractive of hardy subjects. These are intriguing cold weather plants that blaze with color in their season. The garden can take many forms; it can be a many-pocketed structure in a small area—a few rocks and plants—or it can be a large landscape scene where the plants are placed at intervals throughout the area.

Whatever form it is, the garden must be a true representation of natural rock scenery. Find just the right place for it; in the wrong location it becomes an eyesore rather than an attractive picture. A woodland setting is, of course, the most convincing background for the garden, but many times the perfect setting is simply not available. In general, keep rock gardens away from walls and buildings and avoid construct-ing them on a level site; a natural slope is an ideal place.

An important part of assembling the garden and how it will eventually look depends on the individual shapes of the stones used. Plan different levels so that there is constant interest. It is easier to work with a slope or a bank that naturally lends itself to rock treatment than with a flat piece of ground.

The placement of rocks is hard work even if the new lightweight stone, such as featherock and lava-rock, is used. The rocks should be used like a retaining wall—each one set in place with a slight tilt backwards. This gives stability to the structure and allows rain to run into the rock bed behind. Set the stones firmly in place. Most of them should be buried one-third of their height in the ground and placed in a natural design of ledges and abutments.

Designing the Rock Garden

The site for a rock garden should preferably face south or southeast on an irregular slope with natural outcroppings of rocks. This is the ideal location. But ideal conditions are rarely found, and often we must settle for second-best places—perhaps a corner where there are some big trees, or even a bare slope that will in time require plantings to show the rock scene to its advantage.

Now, while the garden is an arrangement of rocks, it is essentially a place to grow alpine plants, those species that grow at high altitudes in cool conditions with lots of sun and with an active but short period of growth. These plants are highly colorful and infinitely charming and to grow well need some approximation of their natural conditions—shade, coolness, moisture. The emphasis on rock gardening is not so much soil as location, and a place where

Bold rocks with severe planes are used to create a handsome rock-garden setting. The planning is perfect; neither rocks nor flowers predominate, but there is a marriage of materials. It is a permanent garden that will be on the property for many years producing beauty for the homeowner, and yet care is at a minimum.
(Molly Adams)

A different kind of rock garden is shown here; plants and stone border the house in a mound effect rather than a true outcropping of rock with plants. The idea is unique and pleasing, and, further, adds color and texture to a predominately green garden.
(Molly Adams)

water continually runs off rather than settles. There must be plenty of moisture in the soil, but it must be moisture in motion that constantly drains through. The soil can be dry on the surface but must be damp below.

A rock garden is three dimensional, and elevations and depressions are vital to the total design. The design itself is a study in heights with appropriate paths and steps to give adequate access to the plants. The paths can be stepping-stones or gravel. The ultimate appearance of the garden depends on the kinds of stones available and the way they are placed to create masses and slopes. Many rock plants are small and require little space; others grow rampant and should be placed within rock barriers. Rocks must be firmly in place without air pockets behind them, which will cause the soil to dry out and the plants to die.

New England areas and the cooler regions of the Great Lakes have favorable conditions for rock gardens. In warmer climates, this special landscape is difficult to create.

In the first year, only grow a few plants rather than dozens of them. Rock gardening requires patience and skill that comes from experience. You are growing alpine plants from high altitudes quite unlike other flowers. However, the flower bed and the rock garden do have one thing in common—good composition. The rock garden should have harmony, unity and balance.

Soil for the Rock Garden

Provide soil for the garden that is porous so that excess water will drain away quickly and yet, at the same time, hold moisture to keep plants growing. I use a mixture of 3 parts loam, 2 parts crushed stone, 1 part sand, and 2 parts humus. You can deviate from this soil mix somewhat, but you cannot deviate from the principle of perfect drainage for these small plants. Without adequate drainage, they simply will not survive. Provisions must be made to carry excess water away from plant roots. A 4-inch layer of cinders under the soil works well in keeping water running below the plants. Or you can use small stones or broken pieces of clay pots as a drainage bed.

After the drainage material is in place, three-quarters of the soil is spread over the excavated site, the remainder left for filling in and between rocks as they are put in place. In the planting area, use soil to a depth of 18 inches. Start at the lowest point and place each rock on its broadest side. Sometimes it will be necessary for you to dig out soil to make space for a stone, or you can leave a free-standing stone and fill in around it with soil. Soil ranging from pH6 to pH8 is suitable for most rock plants.

Rocks

Frequently, when climate is conducive to rock gardening and when there is a suitable location for it, securing and putting rocks in place become the main concern of the gardener. All kinds of rocks and stones are at local building suppliers who will deliver to your home; but moving and putting rocks in place is your project. And indeed it can be a project because rocks are heavy, and even for a small garden some very large ones will be needed. A conglomeration of small stones set into the landscape looks just the way it appears, a mess of stones. Large and formidable boulders are needed to pattern the garden successfully.

There are several ways of lifting and placing rocks. Old-fashioned muscle power is the most inexpensive means, although a laborious way. You will need at least four people to lift a heavy rock. Another way to position the rock is to place a pipe under it, push the rock the length of the pipe, then move the pipe ahead on the ground, and so on. Planks of wood set under the stones is another method where the rocks are pushed along the length of the planks to their location. And, of course, there are derricks and other equipment usually supplied by garden contractors.

Select flat stones of irregular shapes with rough surfaces rather than rounded stones with smooth planes. Absorbent rock is preferred: limestone and tufarock are very suitable; granite is not a good choice. Porous sandstone and split and cracked rocks are good too. Check in your area and see what kind of native stone is available.

Care and Maintenance of Rock Gardens

Most alpine plants need bright light or partial sun, and during the hot summer months will need frequent waterings, for moisture is the key to success. In long hot summers, keep alpine plants as cool as possible. Exposed to wind and sun, they dry out quickly. While they can stand drought if necessary, there will be a better harvest of flowers if ample moisture is supplied.

Because most plants are small, they can get lost in weeds, so keep the rock garden free of weeds; cover bare places with stones to discourage weeds from growing. Nothing destroys the appearance of this garden more than a crop of weeds.

Plants are set in place in fall or in very early spring. In winter, many alpines can go without protection, but others require protection against dampness (not cold) and the ill effects of freezing and thawing. Mulching the plants will conserve moisture and keep the soil cool. Plants that form heavy mats of foliage need no protection, and species that are deciduous can withstand winter, but plants that have

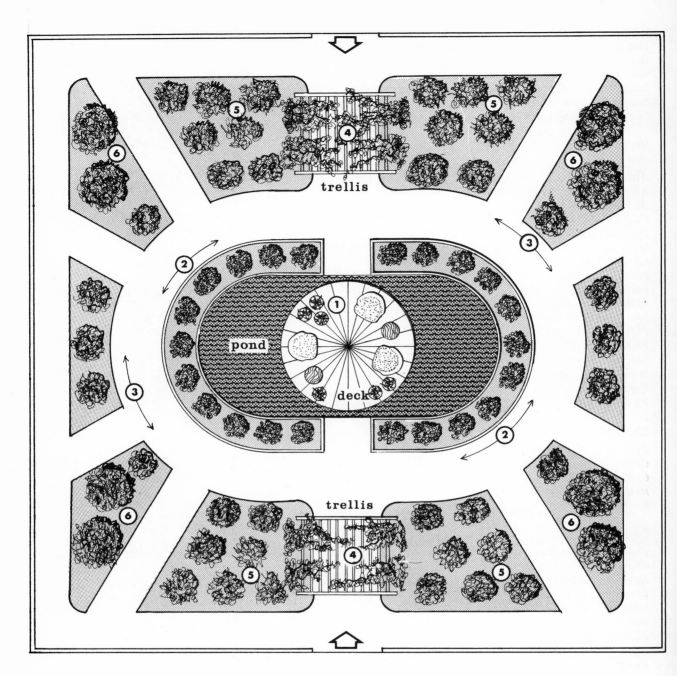

MINIMUM
SPACING :

①	MINIATURES	6"	④	CLIMBERS	6'
②	FLORIBUNDAS	20"	⑤	POLYANTHAS	18"
③	HYBRID TEAS	22"	⑥	GRANDIFLORAS	24"

ADRIÁN MARTÍNEZ

Formal Rose Garden

rosettes of leaves need some mulching. Use a mulch that affords some air circulation. You do not want a wet decaying mat around the plant. Evergreen boughs, salt hay, and oak leaves are satisfactory mulches. Remove them gradually rather than all at once in the spring when danger of frost is over.

Plants for Rock Gardens

Achillea tomentosa (yarrow)
Ajuga repens (bugleseed)
Alyssum saxatile (goldentuft)
Aquilegia vulgaris (columbine)
Campanula carpatica (bellflower)
Dianthus deltoides (maiden pink)
Geranium grandiflorum (cranesbill geranium)
Gypsophila repens (creeping gypsophila)
Iberis sempervirens (candytuft)
Iris pumila (dwarf bearded iris)
Linum perenne (flax)
Myosotis scorpiodes (forget-me-not)
Phlox sublata (moss pink)
Primula polyantha (primrose)
Sedum album (stonecrop)
Sempervivum (many)
Veronica incana (speedwell)
Viola cornuta (viola)

Shrubs for Rock Gardens

Berberis thunbergii minor (barberry)
Cotoneaster microphylla (rock spray)
Cytisus kewensis (broom)
Potentilla fruticosa (cinquefoil)
Spiraea bullata (spirea)

Dwarf Evergreens for Rock Gardens

Calluna vulgaris (heather)
Chamaecyparis obtusa nana (Hinoki cypress)
Erica carnea (heather)
Euonymus fortunei minimus (dwarf wintercreeper)
Juniperus horizontalis (creeping juniper)
Juniperus procumbens nana (creeping juniper)
Pinus mugo compacta (Swiss mountain pine)
Rhododendron facenosum (rhododendron)
Rhododendron impeditum (rhododendron)

Rock Garden Plants for Shade

Ajuga repens (carpet bugle)
Allium moly (lilyleek)
Anemone canadensis (anemone)
Aquilegia coerulea (columbine)
Asarum canadense (wild ginger)
Asplenium trichomanes (maidenhair spleenwort)
Camassia esculenta (camass)
Dicentra eximia (fringed bleeding heart)
Epimedium macranthum (epimedium)
Hepatica triloba (hepatica)

Iris cristata (crested iris)
Mentha requieni (Corsican mint)
Mertensia virginica (Virginia bluebell)
Mitchella repens (partridgeberry)
Phlox divaricata (blue phlox)
Polypodium vulgare (common polypody)
Sanguinaria canadensis (bloodroot)
Sedum pulchellum (stonecrop)
Sedum ternatum (stonecrop)
Trillium grandiflora (trillium)
Viola (violet)

Bulbs for Rock Gardens

Camassia esculente (camass)
Chionodoxa luciliae (glory-of-the-snow)
Colchicum autumnale (autumn crocus)
Crocus, various (crocus)
Fritillaria meleagris (guinea-hen flower)
Galanthus nivalis (snowdrop)
Muscari botryoides (grape hyacinth)
Narcissus species (narcissus, daffodil)
Puschkinia scilloides (puschkinia)
Scilla hispanica (Spanish bluebell)
Scilla nonscripta (English bluebell)
Tulipa kaufmanniana (tulip)

ROSE GARDENS

Roses are popular flowers that have been with us for a long time and continue to be grown and admired. A well-designed and properly cared-for rose garden is a stunning sight in bloom. And it seems that roses, because of their special requirements, do need a place of their own.

In planning the garden, select a place that has good air circulation but is still protected from wind. Choose a natural background so the roses will be seen to their best advantage. Light shade during part of the day is not objectionable but in general give roses all the sun possible. Install paths of brick or flagstone to enhance the beauty of the garden, and decide upon a definite pattern for the beds.

Design of the Rose Garden

Traditionally, a rose garden is a formal design; a geometrical repeat pattern of a definite form. In other words, the garden itself has a beauty independent of the flowers. But today, the strictly formal rose garden is not popular, and with good reason: most lots are small, and the space needed for a formal plan is prohibitive. Somewhat more casual and more varied rose gardens are what we see today. Whatever design you choose—and draw several arrangements on paper before making up your mind— do not make the beds too wide because then it be-

Borders of bright roses set off this charming house; this garden
is hardly formal and certainly not planned, and yet it is completely
inviting and attractive.
(Clint Bryant)

Roses here serve a double purpose—for beauty and for a barrier
separating one building from another. Plants are confined with a
simple brick border.
(Clint Bryant)

comes difficult to reach the plants from the paths, and spraying and pruning them become a chore.

For a successful rose garden, choose an open area that is sheltered on the north and west sides, provide a good soil, and install adequate drainage provisions to carry off water. When you buy plants select vigorous ones. Put them in the ground properly, then follow with good cultural practices—pruning, mulching, fertilizing, and protecting them from insects. A rose garden does not grow by itself; it needs attention and daily observation.

Soil for the Rose Garden

While roses need a fertile, slightly acid soil with a pH range between 5.5 and 6.5, the actual structure and content of the soil are not as important as its drainage capacity and its fertility. Roses require large quantities of water for maximum growth, and simply will not thrive in soil which does not drain readily. To assure good drainage in the beds, put in a 6-inch layer of crushed gravel in the bottom of the trench.

Prepare the soil with utmost care because the more attention you give to preparation, the less trouble there will be later on. If the soil is sandy, improve its water-holding capacity with compost, peat moss, and other organic materials. If it is a heavy soil, add sand and compost. The soil must be porous and somewhat rich (see Chapter 2). Dig the beds at least 20 inches deep; rose roots are long and need depth to grow well.

Planting and Care of the Rose Garden

Planting distances depend upon the type of rose being grown. For hybrid and tea roses a distance of 18 to 24 inches apart is fine. Floribundas and grandifloras need more space, about 18 to 36 inches between each plant. Trim the roses before you plant them; remove broken or injured roots. As I have mentioned, plant roses deep and place them in position so that the crown (point of union between the stock and scion) is between 1 and 2 inches below the surface of the soil. In mild climates the bud union should be just above the surface of the soil. After planting, pack the soil firmly around the roots. Keep the roses well watered the first few weeks until they are established.

Roses need pruning to produce strong roots and shoots; without proper cutting they get leggy and dense. In spring, before growth starts, prune plants just above a node (bud); cut in a slanting direction and leave 3 to 5 buds on each stem. Only light pruning is needed for rambler roses that bloom on old wood. The ramblers that bloom on new wood from the base of the plant need pruning after flowering.

The time to plant roses depends upon your climate. In cold winter areas early spring is best for setting out dormant bushes. In the midpart of the country, early spring or late fall is suggested, and in all-year mild climates, roses can be planted from November to January.

Bare-root plants are most often selected by gardeners. These are dormant and ready to start a new cycle of growth when you get them. If you cannot plant them immediately, keep them cool and be sure the roots are kept moist. Never allow rose roots to become dry before they are planted. Put them in water until you can get the plants in the ground. Packaged roses are often seen, and if they have been stored in a cool place, they are satisfactory. If the branches look dry and shriveled, chances are they have been kept in a hot location. Don't buy them. Container-grown roses are already started for you and cost more than dormant ones. For beginners, these are the best buy.

In cold regions, plants should be protected for the winter. Place mounds of soil about 10 inches high around them. Do not scoop the soil from around the plant, but bring in fresh soil. Remove the covering gradually in spring when growth starts.

Numerous kinds of roses are available today. The following list may help you decide the kind you want.

For display and cutting, garden roses include hybrid teas, floribundas, and grandifloras. The hybrid teas have a sturdy growing habit, and are hardy in the North if given suitable winter protection. They give generous bloom from June to September. Some varieties grow over 3 feet while others are low-growers. A wide range of color and form is available.

Floribunda varieties vary greatly in size, some almost dwarf while others grow to 6 feet. Flower form is single to semidouble in a wide range of colors. These plants are very floriferous and less demanding than most roses.

Grandifloras are very vigorous and free blooming and easy to grow. The flowers are borne in clusters and last very well.

Edging roses are dwarf, generally of the polyantha group. They are very hardy and give generous bloom throughout the season.

Hedge roses are quick growing, tall and bushy, and they require very little care.

Old-fashioned roses are generally with single flowers, and include old favorites such as the provence rose and the damask rose.

Climbing roses can be trained to supports; some are rampant while others are more restrained in growth. Some have a peak season of bloom while others flower intermittently through the season. Some

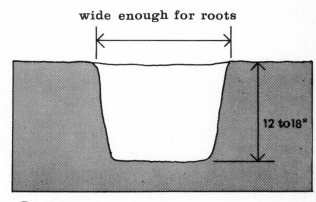

wide enough for roots

12 to 18"

① PRUNE & TRIM BROKEN ROOTS & BRANCHES

② SOAK ROOTS FOR A FEW HOURS; DIG HOLE

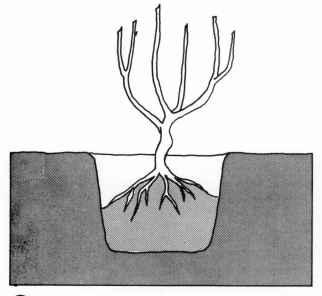

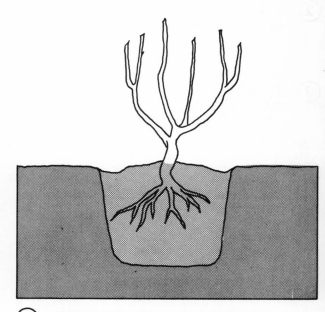

③ MOUND SOIL; SPREAD ROOTS OVER

④ COMPLETE FILLING; WATER

ADRIÁN MARTÍNEZ

Planting Bare-Root Roses

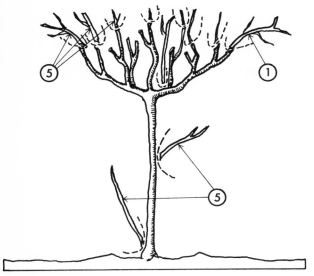

rose tree

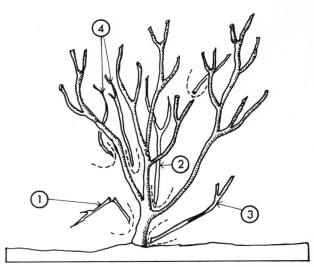

climbing rose

IN THE SPRING, PRUNE:

(1) DEAD, DAMAGED OR DISEASED CANES

(2) OLD CANES THAT HAVE BEEN REPLACED BY NEW

(3) SUCKERS THAT START BELOW BUD UNION

(4) CANES OR TWIGS THAT CROSS & CROWD EACH OTHER

(5) CANES & TWIGS TO MAINTAIN THE PROPER SHAPE

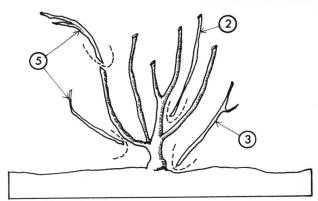

rose bush

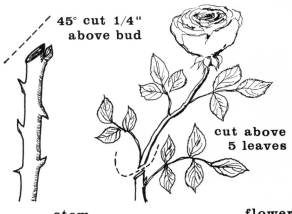

45° cut 1/4" above bud

cut above 5 leaves

stem   flower

ADRIÁN MARTÍNEZ

Pruning Roses

varieties are very hardy; others are suitable only to mild climate regions.

NATURAL GARDENS

Plants in their proper place—in respect to light and moisture—thrive. In the woodland or natural garden the homeowner can create a landscape that is easy to care for and one that will always be an attractive scene. This kind of gardening is not trying to imitate Nature but rather working with her.

The natural garden has a subtle charm and a casual quality. There is no studied grouping of plants; there are no straight lines or studied designs. Curves and drifts of flowers and plants give the scene its informal look. And while the composition of the garden is vital, the choice of plants is indeed important, too. The greenery must belong to the plan; it must appear as though it had been there for years.

Design

Exact plotting of this garden is not necessary, nor should plants be spaced at regular intervals. Allow one mass of foliage to blend into another. Although exactness does not count, composition and balance are still the prime requisites of the natural scene. Place groups of plants that grow well together in the same soil conditions. Try to create a small section with shade, humus, and other ecological factors where woodland plants can thrive.

Search out the shaded area of the property and look for a natural helper—a rock, a stream, a secret niche—to form the background of the garden. Look for trees that will provide filtered sunlight and offer protection for the plants from hot, dry, summer winds. Clear the area of undesirable plants or those that need constant attention. Select anemones and dogtooth violets, Solomon's seal and trilliums; these are nature's spring bounty. Use them to create the natural picture you want.

Do not make the area too large; concentrate on one small portion at a time. Naturalizing woodland plants takes time and patience, but once established, the plants grow year after year without attention. Rely on easy growers such as phlox; put in English primroses and wood hyacinths for a stunning display, and don't forget the stately spires of foxglove for vertical accents.

Soil

Natural woodland soil is rich in humus, and holds many times its weight in water. The crumbly black humus has been developing for years as trees drop leaves, needles, twigs, and branches. If the area you have chosen for your garden does not have these natural conditions, you must provide them. Even for a small area you will need large quantities of leafmold, composted leaves, and old manure. Remember that you are trying to build in a few weeks what nature has taken years to do—a rich humusy soil. You can mix the new humusy soil with the existing soil; dig out the old, turn it and mix it with at least 8 inches of new soil. Or you can remove all the soil to a depth of 12 to 18 inches and replace it with humus and leafmold. (I get my leafmold from the woods, but it can also be purchased in sacks at nurseries.)

While you are preparing the soil be sure that there is adequate drainage in the area chosen. A boggy situation should be avoided. It may be necessary to install a layer of fine gravel or sand to assure proper drainage of excess water. Or you might raise the surface of the garden somewhat so water drains freely.

This all may seem like a great deal of work, but remember, that once established, plants will require little care. You do not have to weed or fertilize or mulch them. You are creating a natural, maintenance-free garden.

For the most part, woodland plants enjoy a slightly acid soil but some such as lady-slipper orchids need a very acid soil. I maintain a slightly acid soil in my woodland area and can cultivate most of the common wildflower plants.

The Plants

In most states, woodland plants are protected by law, so just don't go out and start picking them; check with local authorities first. Even if there is no conservation law with regard to the plants, I think it is preferable to buy them from suppliers rather than to collect them. However, if the bulldozer is coming into an area where plants thrive, gathering them would be considered a rescue mission.

When you dig woodland plants, take as much of the surrounding soil as possible and try not to disturb the roots too much. Expediency is the key to success in getting these gems to grow. They should be put into the ground immediately. The best time to gather the plants is in the fall or immediately after they bloom.

I buy most of my woodland plants. I have found that those from local nurseries or mail-order suppliers succeed better than collected specimens that I have occasionally tried to naturalize. Nursery plants seem less fussy about being transplanted; they are pot-grown and much more robust than wildlings. Try to put new plants into the ground the day you get them. Then keep the soil around them moist and mulched with leaves until the plants become established.

This small natural scene at the side of a home uses evergreens predominately; natural rocks are in place and the entire picture has a natural been-here-for-years look. No care is required; plants are left to grow by themselves. *(Clint Bryant)*

This natural garden scene was created at the edge of the property; most of it was already there. However, the grass path and stepping-stones were added so one could wander and enjoy the plants. Wildflowers and narcissus dot the path with bright colors and shrubs and evergreens give boldness and lushness to the scene. This natural setting, never easy to recreate, is certainly pleasing to the eye. *(Molly Adams)*

Plants for the Woodland Garden

Aquilegia canadensis (American columbine). With cloverlike leaves, columbine has yellow and red flowers on thin stalks. Plants need a neutral soil and partial shade.

Arisaema triphyllum (Jack-in-the-pulpit). A favorite wildling, yellow-green in color with brown-purple stripes. Thrives in a shady place in moist soil.

Claytonia virginica (spring beauty). One of the earliest of the woodland flowers with white to pale pink blooms. Give plants a neutral soil; some sun.

Cypripedium acaule (moccasin flower; lady-slipper orchid). Lovely pink flowers—a real jewel in the garden. Prefers a somewhat dry soil, but I have also seen it respond in very moist places.

Digitalis (foxglove). These plants come in a wide variety of colors—white, primrose, apricot—and can grow to 6 feet. Give them a deep, woodsy soil and light shade.

Epigaea repens (trailing arbutus). In early spring, arbutus bears white or pink phloxlike flowers with a lovely fragrance. Plants need a very acid soil; shade.

Erythronium (dog-tooth violet). With narrow leaves and nodding fragrant blooms these are easy to grow. Give them a neutral soil and a shady place. Many species from suppliers.

Hepatica triloba (liverleaf or liverwort). Tiny plants with cup-shaped flowers; leaves appear before flowers. Needs a rich woodsy soil; shade.

Mertensia virginica (Virginia cowslip). This one gives a fine display of lovely large nodding flowers. It needs neutral soil and can take some sun.

Phlox divaricata (wild blue phlox). These are favorites in the cultivated garden but are equally at home in the woodland scene; the blue flowers are desirable in any situation. Give sun or shade; neutral soil preferred but not essential.

Ferns for the Woodland Garden

Adiantum pendatum (maidenhair fern)
Asplenium platyneuron (ebony spleenwort)
Asplenium trichomanes (maidenhair spleenwort)
Botrychium virginianum (rattlesnake fern)
Camptosorus rhizophyllus (walking fern)
Dryopteris clintoniana (wood fern)
D. cristata (crested wood fern)
Lygodium palmatum (Hartford fern)
Osmunda cinnamonea (cinnamon fern)
Pellaea atropurpurea (purple cliffbreak fern)
Polypodium virginianum (vulgare) (common polypody)
Polystichum acrostichoides (Christmas fern)

Shrubs for the Woodland Garden

Azalea (rhododendron). Many kinds.
Clethra alnifolia (sweet pepperbush)
Cornus alba (coral dogwood)
Cornus stolonifera (red osier dogwood)
Fothergilla gardeni (dwarf fothergilla)
Hamamelis virginiana (American witch hazel)
Hydrangea arborescens (wild hydrangea)
Ilex glabra
Ilex verticillata (winterberry)
Kalmia latifolia (mountain laurel)
Rhododendron catawbiense
R. maximum

CHAPTER **30**

Fruits, Vegetables, and Herbs

A pear tree in bloom in spring is a breathtaking sight, and apple and other deciduous fruit trees are equally lovely at flowering time. For beauty alone, these trees are desirable in the garden, but they also produce delicious fruit. And the fabulous flavor of home-grown produce far surpasses store-bought kinds.

Of course, all of this bounty does not come without some work. Fruit trees do require some attention if they are to prosper. They need pruning and thinning and generally must be sprayed a few times a year. Still, having the fruit in your own backyard where you can pick an apple or peach or plum when you want it is a satisfying experience.

FRUIT TREES FOR YOUR GARDEN

Years ago, fruit trees were generally for large properties because they needed space. But today, the perfection of the dwarf fruit trees makes it possible for everyone to grow a few of them.

Your climate and soil dictate what kind of fruit trees to have. Some must have a chilling weather; others are injured by freezing. Certain varieties will do better in your specific area than in other regions, so check with your local nurseryman for suggestions.

Some trees do not fruit by themselves, and it is necessary to plant two compatible varieties. Therefore, with fruit trees, ask the nurseryman whether or not they are self-fruitful trees.

How to Plant Fruit Trees

Put fruit trees in a sunny place where they will not be injured by spring frosts after blossoms have opened. Use a soil that drains readily and that is fertile; a porous somewhat clayey soil is best. When you dig holes for the trees, make them large so that roots have space to spread out.

Standard trees can be planted at the depth at which they were previously grown. Except in very cold climates, where spring planting is mandatory, put them in the ground in spring or fall. Keep the soil around the trees deeply watered; it is wise to conserve moisture by applying an organic mulch around the tree at all times of the year.

Spraying and Feeding Fruit Trees

Trees planted in fall should be fertilized for the first time the following spring. Those put in the ground in spring can be fed about a month later. Then fertilize them each spring. Use a mild feeding solution (5–10–5) at the rate of about one pound for each year of tree age.

Because pest problems vary greatly from one state to another, ask your Agricultural Extension Service (see the list at the back of this book) for a schedule to follow for spraying and which preventatives to use. Generally a dormant oil spray is applied when leaves are 1/4 inch long. Then an all-purpose fruit spray is used when blossoms show color, and again when the last petals are falling, and every 10 days thereafter until two weeks before harvesting.

Pruning

After plants have been in the garden for a year, prune them annually each spring. Try to maintain a strong, healthy open tree; the idea is to keep out tangled branches so light gets to all parts of the tree, and to keep several strong trunks going in different directions so the tree will not be subject to splitting. Main branches should grow at an angle of 45 to 90 degrees. Otherwise, the crotch will become weak.

Peaches bear fruit on the previous years' wood, and require heavier pruning than most fruit trees to encourage vigorous new wood. Pear trees, on the other hand, do not need too much pruning.

Dwarf Fruit Trees

Dwarf trees are rarely over 10 feet tall, bear fruit sooner and as big or bigger than those of the same variety of standard trees. And they are easier to spray, maintain, and prune. There are two types of dwarf trees: natural ones such as the Bonanza peach and kumquat, and standard varieties that have been dwarfed by artificial means. They are grafted onto a growth-inhibiting root system, or else a short piece of stem of a dwarfing variety is grafted to a seedling tree which will be the new tree's base and roots. Put dwarf trees into the ground so that the graft joint is 1 to 2 inches above the surface. If the upper part of the tree—the scion—is at ground level, it sometimes takes root and the tree grows larger than it should.

Dwarf trees need a sunny, protected place, as they are susceptible to wind injury. Space them about 10 feet apart. Wrap the trunk with special tree paper or with burlap to protect it from sun scald and rodents. Prune trees at planting time if this has not been done at the nursery. Remove any broken or weak branches and shorten side shoots about one-third.

Apple (Malus). Standard trees grow to about 30 feet spaced about 40 feet apart. (Dwarf varieties can be planted 10 feet apart.) Put trees in a well-drained soil and give them a good deal of attention in the first few years. When the trees bear fruit, a complete fertilizer (5–10–5) can be applied in early spring.

Apricot (*Prunus armeniaca*). Grows to 20 feet; space 20 feet apart. Plant in a deep, rich soil that drains readily. Start with a year-old tree and allow about five main branches to develop. Follow pruning data as mentioned in earlier section.

Peach (*Prunus persica*). Grows to 15 feet; space 20 feet apart. Fruit is borne on previous year's growth. Annual pruning in spring is necessary once the tree has attained its basic shape and has started to produce fruit. Peach trees need a well-drained location in light, fertile soil. In sod, borer attack is possible. Do not overfeed. (Treat nectarine fruit trees the same way.)

Pear (Pyrus). Grows to 25 feet; space 25 feet apart. These are robust trees that need a well-drained, loamy soil free of manure or rich fertilizers. Lush growth is more susceptible to attack by fire blight disease. Prune only when the trees have started to bear fruit.

Plum (Prunus). Many kinds to 25 feet; space 25 feet apart. Trees vary in adaptability to soil and weather conditions, so check your local nursery.

Generally, all need a well-drained, somewhat sandy soil.

Quince (*Cydona oblonga*). Grows to 15 feet; space 20 feet apart. Highly susceptible to fire blight and borers. Best to use other fruit trees, or be satisfied with lovely spring blossoms.

Small Fruits

Small fruits, most of which are called berries and used for making pies, jellies, and preserves, are popular, and once established, grow readily. There are some for cool climates and others that need warmth.

The plants need full sun and a well-drained soil. Early spring is planting time except in the Deep South, where fall planting is permissible. Set the plants in place as you would plant shrubs: modest holes for small plants and larger holes for the big ones like blueberry. Fertilize in early spring a few weeks after plants are in the ground, and then 2 or 3 more times until August. Do not feed afterwards unless you live in a warm climate. Keep plants copiously watered, and use a mulch for them to conserve moisture and keep out weeds. It is virtually impossible to eliminate weeds because the roots of small fruits lie close to the ground.

Strawberries (Fragaria). These are perennials. Some bear in late winter or early spring while others ripen over many months, primarily in the spring. Where you live dictates what variety to grow. In cold winter climates, plant in early spring, using dormant plants. Keep the roots moist until they can get in the ground. In mild winter areas, fall planting is recommended, with fruit coming the following spring.

Plant strawberries in a sunny area in a deep, loamy, sandy soil that will drain readily. You can space the plants 16 to 18 inches apart in long rows and let baby plants which develop at the tips of the runners fill in the space between. Or you can plant them 6 inches apart and cut off runner plants as they develop. You can also arrange plants in the hill method by spacing them 1 foot apart in rows 2 feet apart and cut runners as soon as they form.

Feed all new strawberries about a month after planting with a fertilizer recommended by your Agricultural Extension Service. Feed again in early August. On spring-bearing varieties, remove the blossoms during the first year; on ever-bearing varieties, remove the blossoms until mid-July so that the plant can use all its energy for growing and making runners. In fall, after the ground is frozen but before it is too cold (below 20F), cover the plants to a depth of 2 to 3 inches with hay or salt hay and leave until spring.

Ever-bearing varieties generally produce fruit in

the fall of the first year and in the spring and fall of the second year. They should then be discarded. The spring bearers usually have one good crop in the spring of the second year, and then can be replaced with new plants.

Grape (Vitis). There are grapes for both mild and cold climates. Buy vigorous one- or two-year-old plants with good root systems.

In cold climates, plant in very early spring; in mild climates, in late winter—mid-February on. Give grapes a sunny site with very well-drained soil, and space them about 10 feet apart in 12-inch-deep holes, 12 inches across. Prune before planting and leave only the strongest cane with 2 buds or nodes. This will assure vigorous new shoots. Set the plants in the ground 2 inches lower than they were previously grown; spread the roots out, tamp the earth firmly in place, and water thoroughly.

In the first year, give plants plenty of water to encourage as much growth as possible. In the second spring, they must be trained. After they are mature and have produced their first crop, grapevines must be ruthlessly pruned, as otherwise there will be a great deal of future growth and very little fruit.

Grapes are usually trained on wires (or grown on trellises and arbors.) Select the best long cane, fasten it into a vertical position to become the trunk, and prune out all other branches. When the trunk develops side shoots, choose the most robust ones, fasten them horizontally along the supports, and remove all others. In the fourth year, cut out the previous year's pencil-sized branches which developed from the horizontal branches and tie the new pencil-sized branches which developed to the wires. Trim these branches back to about 8 buds. Save one newly formed spur near each branch and remove all other growth. In succeeding years, repeat this procedure.

Blackberry (Rubus). Blackberry brambles require a great deal of attention, but the fruit at its prime is gourmet eating you will never forget. Blackberries will ramble all over if you let them; they send up suckers from their roots, and these must be removed periodically. Pull them up; cutting will only tend to make more suckers grow from the stumps. Put plants in good garden soil that has plenty of humus. In spring, reduce the canes to one every 2 feet; pull up others. Then pinch the tips of the plants to make them branch low, or better yet, fasten them to wires. After the canes have borne fruit, cut them close to the ground. In spring shorten bushes not on wires to about 16 inches. Blackberries start to bear in the second season.

Blueberry (Vaccinium corymbosum). Blueberry shrubs offer breathtaking red color in autumn. They need acid soil (pH4 to 4.8) with a high amount of organic material. They revel in moisture. Set blueberries 4 to 6 feet apart in hedge fashion. You will need a few varieties for cross-pollination. When the shrubs are established, annual spring pruning is necessary. Cover the bushes, or birds will get most of the fruit. Plastic or hemp netting is available at nurseries.

Currants (Ribes sativum) Gooseberries. These 3- to 5-foot plants are easy to grow. They like moist cool conditions, so give them a mulch at the base to conserve moisture. Grow them in rows 5 feet apart or in groups. Put them in the ground in early spring (select 1- or 2-year-old plants). Set them slightly lower in the ground than they grew in the nursery and prune the tops by one-third. Feed in spring with a complete fertilizer (5–10–5). When bushes mature prune in very early spring. Cut away oldest branches (4 or more years old) and leave 6 or 8 strong younger ones. (Some states have restrictions on currants and gooseberries to protect white pine trees from blister rust. This disease can only live by growing one stage of its life on gooseberries or currants to complete its growth cycle.)

Raspberry (Rubus). Plant raspberries in spring or fall in well-drained, somewhat loamy soil. Apply fertilizer each spring. Red raspberries are best planted 2 feet apart; fruit is borne on second-year canes. After bearing, remove canes and burn them. Ever-bearing varieties produce fruit in fall on new growth made that summer. Then they bear again on the same canes the following year. Purple and black raspberries are planted 4 feet apart. After the first year, when canes reach 2 feet, cut them back to about 18 inches so side branches will grow. In early spring, shorten these side branches to 6 inches of the main stem. After the crop is harvested, cut away canes and burn them. When new shoots start to grow, select the best 4 or 5 of them and then prune them back to 20 inches. With all raspberries, keep them protected with netting.

VEGETABLES

One of the rewards of your own garden is a place for vegetables. Home-grown varieties are the tastiest you will ever eat, inexpensive, and nutritious. You can grow superior varieties that you simply cannot obtain in markets. The rewards of vegetable growing are large, and the effort to maintain the garden is small.

Many people shy away from vegetables, thinking they require a great deal of space and need constant care. Actually, an area of 10 by 10 feet gives your family enough salad greens for the summer, with some left over. A rectangular bed of 10 by 15 feet supplies me with more vegetables than I need. If necessary, even a few vegetables can be grown in tubs or in with your flowers.

Time Guide for Growing Vegetables

If possible, designate a separate patch for the vegetable garden. Prepare the ground thoroughly; spade, break up, and turn the soil to a depth of about 12 inches, mix the soil with a commercial fertilizer recommended for vegetables, and make sure the plot has good drainage. The pH of the soil should be about 6 to 7.

To give you a head start, many vegetables are sold as seedlings in pots or little boxes. However, it is extremely easy to have vegetables from seed—beans, radishes, peas, lettuce, cucumbers, beets, carrots, cabbage, etc. Some vegetables, like lettuce and peas, grow best in cool weather, while tomatoes and lima beans prefer hot weather. Some varieties are planted before the last frost, others after the last frost. Eggplant and peppers, which take longer to mature than some other vegetables, generally must be started indoors or in a cold frame. Depending upon what you plant, you can harvest vegetables in spring, summer, and fall; it is wise to work out a schedule so that the garden works for you most of the time. Plan a rotating crop system by planting late plants between early maturing kinds and using cool weather vegetables and warm varieties. There is variation in the time it takes different varieties of the same vegetable to mature, so it is possible to keep the vegetable garden working almost all year. (See Table 22 for a time guide for growing vegetables.)

How to Plant and Care for Vegetables

Rake the prepared soil into a fine seed bed. Most of the vegetables will be sown in shallow trenches or "drills" (furrows) of suitable depth. Try to maintain a straight row so that plants will be easy to cultivate. Place the seed evenly in the drills and scatter fine soil over them; firm the soil. Some vegetables—pole beans, cucumber, squash—are planted in hills rather than in drills. A hill is a circle of seeds about 12 inches across.

Thinning out young plants is necessary as soon as they are large enough to handle so that remaining ones have room to develop. Do not neglect the thinning process; it is the only way to get a good yield from crops. When the garden is on its way, weeding and cultivation to conserve moisture are necessary.

Here are some suggestions for the vegetable garden:

- Place tall-, medium- and small-growing vegetables so that all can have sun.
- Put quick crops between slow-growing crops to conserve space.
- Rotate crops rather than leaving them in the same place each year. This is done to conserve nutrients in the soil.
- Mulch the garden with organic materials to keep down weeds and to conserve moisture.
- Side-dress vegetables with a balanced fertilizer after the seedlings are thinned out.
- *Choose chemicals for insect prevention that do not leave a poisonous residue.*

Table 22. Time Guide for Vegetable Growing

Vegetable	Buy Plant or Seed Depth	WS*	CS†	Space after Thinning	Days from Seed to Harvest
Asparagus	BP		X	3′–4′	2 years
Beans, lima	1–2″	X		5″	120
Beets	1–2″		X	2″–3″	50–60
Broccoli	BP		X	1 1/2″–2″	60
Brussels sprouts	1/4″		X	18″–24″	
Cabbage	BP		X	1 1/2″–2″	60–100
Cantaloupe	1″	X		3″	75–80
Carrots	1/2″		X	2″–3″	70–75
Cauliflower	1/2″		X	18″	95
Chard	1″		X	6″	75
Corn, sweet	1–2″	X		10″–12″	75–90
Cucumber	1″	X		3″	70
Lettuce	1/2″		X	6″–15″	20–40
Peas	1–2″		X	2″	65–75
Pepper	BP	X		18″	115
Radish	1/2″		X	1″–2″	20–30
Spinach	1″		X	3″	60–70
Squash	1″	X		3″–4″	60–65
Tomato	BP	X		3″–4″	100–120
Turnip	1″		X	3″	60–80

* WS = Warm-season vegetable.
† CS = Cool-season vegetable.

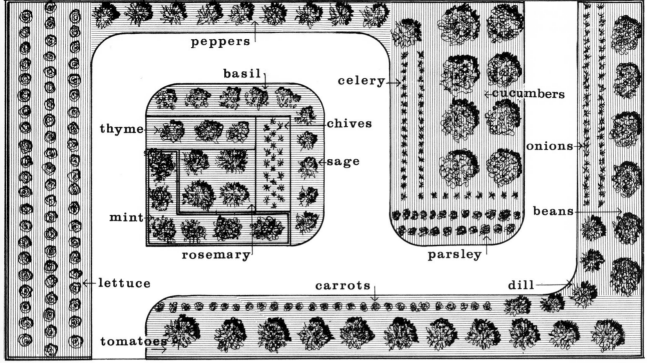

peppers
basil
celery→
←cucumbers
thyme→
chives
←sage
onions→
mint
beans
←rosemary
parsley
←lettuce
carrots
dill←
tomatoes→

PLAN ⬆N

VEGETABLES					
plant	when to plant	depth	spacing		days to mature
			plant	row	
POLE BEAN	after last frost	2"	3'	4'	60
CARROT	ʺ	1/2"	2-4"	18"	100
CELERY	ʺ *	1/4"	8"	30"	190
CUCUMBER	ʺ	1"	3-4'	3-4'	140
LETTUCE	ʺ	1/4"	1'	18"	70/90
ONION	ʺ	1/2"	1-3"	1'	50/60
PEPPER	ʺ *	1/2"	30"	3'	60/80
TOMATO	ʺ *	1/2"	30"	3'	60/90

HERBS, ETC.					
plant	when to plant	depth	spacing		har-vest
			plant	row	
BASIL	after last frost	1/4"	9"	9"	#
CHIVES	ʺ +	–	4"	4"	#
DILL	ʺ	1/4"	9"	18"	#
MINT	ʺ +	–	keep contained		#
PARSLEY	ʺ	1/4"	6"	1'	#
ROSEMARY	ʺ +	–	3'	3'	#
SAGE	ʺ +	1/4"	9"	9"	#
THYME	ʺ +	1/4"	9"	9"	#

✳ start indoors
ADRIÁN MARTÍNEZ

+ buy plants to set out   # use as needed

Vegetable & Herb Garden

- Harvest vegetables just before they reach maturity so that they are at their prime when you eat them.

HERBS

You can buy herbs in bottles from your grocer. But harvesting them from your own garden is a satisfying experience. Home-grown herbs have more flavor and taste than those bought in stores. Not only are there herbs for flavoring, but there are many—lavender, geranium—for fragrance.

Herbs are attractive plants that are easy to grow in average conditions, they take little space, and can be grown directly in the ground or in pots. Put them near the kitchen so you can snip fresh herbs you want quickly for a stew or salad, or stroll outside for a refreshing scent whenever you want.

You can buy small plants of herbs or start seeds which germinate easily. Grow them in a somewhat sandy soil that drains readily, and where they will get at least 3 hours of sun. Keep the soil moist and divide and prune the plants occasionally to keep them within bounds and to prevent them from crowding out other plants.

Cut herbs just as the flowers are about to open, as this is when the essential oils are the most plentiful. To save the herbs for future use, properly cure and store them. Wash the leaves or stems in cold water, and then dry them thoroughly by spreading out leaves over a wire mesh in a warm place. Or, put them on a baking sheet in a 200-degree oven with the door open. When they are dry, strip the leaves from the stems and put them in airtight containers. Do not overdry the leaves; they should barely reach the crumbling stage. Or, tie stems in bunches and hang them from the ceiling in an attic or other dark place until it is time to use them. (See Table 23.)

Table 23. Guide for Herbs

Herb	Biennial, Perennial, Annual	Height	Flavoring Fragrance
Ambrosia	A	24″	Fragrance
Basil	A	8″–12″	Flavoring
Chives	P	10″	Flavoring
Dill	A	24″–30″	Flavoring
Geranium	P	12″–36″	Fragrance
Lavender	P	24″–36″	Fragrance
Lovage	P	6″	Flavoring
Mint	P	30″	Flavoring
Parsley	B	6″–10″	Flavoring
Rosemary	P	36″–72″	Fragrance
Sage	P	24″–30″	Flavoring
Summer savory	A	12″–18″	Flavoring
Sweet marjoram	A	8″–12″	Flavoring
Tarragon	P	12″–24″	Flavoring
Thyme	P	6″–8″	Flavoring
Verbena	P	48″–60″	Fragrance

Plant Selection Supplement

The Plant Selection Supplement is a compilation of the plants in the main book as well as additional varieties and species. Its purpose is to offer you a quick handy reference guide for choosing plants. For easy use it includes plants for special purposes: that is, for dry soils, for shade, for wet soils . . . for specific situations. Flower color and common names are also given where necessary.

In the Supplement we have listed plants by botanical name and by common name. Some plants have several common names and they vary from region to region. However, botanical names remain the same the world over (the common name listings will give you the botanical name) and purchasing plants by these names assures you get the plant you want.

After you have read the main book and decided on your landscaping plans and plantings, the Plant Selection Supplement should be all you need to properly choose plants for almost any landscape situation.

The Supplement is arranged in the following order:

For Wet Soil Conditions

Trees

Deciduous

Acer rubrum (red maple)
Alnus glutinosa (black alder)
Betula populifolia (gray birch)
Gleditsia aquatica (water locust)
Liquidambar styraciflua (sweet gum)
Platanus occidentalis (buttonwood)
Quercus palustris (pin oak)
Salix alba (white willow)
Tilia americana (American linden)

Evergreen

Abies balsamea (balsam fir)
Thuja occidentalis (arborvitae)
Tsuga canadensis (hemlock)

Shrubs

Alnus (various) (alders)
Amelanchier canadensis (shadblow service berry)
Andromeda species (andromeda)
Aronia arbutifolia (red chokeberry)

Calluna vulgaris (heather)
Clethra alnifolia (summer sweet)
Cornus alba (tatarian dogwood)
Cornus stolonifera (red osier)
Cornus sanguinea (bloodtwig dogwood)
Hypericum densiflorum (dense hypericum)
Ilex glabra (inkberry)
Ilex verticillata (winterberry)
Kalmia angustifolia (sheep laurel)
Ligustrum amurense (amur privet)
Pieris floribunda (mountain andromeda)
Rhododendron (rhododendron)
Sabal minor (dwarf palmetto)
Salix (various) (willow)
Spiraea menziesii (spiraea)
Spiraea tomentosa (hardhack)
Vaccinum corymbosum (highbush blueberry)
Viburnum alnifolium (hobblebush)
Viburnum cassinoides (withe rod)
Viburnum dentatum (arrowwood)
Viburnum lentago (nannyberry)
Viburnum sieboldii (Siebold viburnum)

Perennials

Arundo 'Donax' (giant reed)
Asclepias incarnata (swamp milkweed)
Caltha palustris (marsh marigold)
Equisetum hyemale (horsetail)
Gentiana asclepiadea (willow gentian)
Helenium (various) (Helen's flower)
Hibiscus moscheutos (swamp rose mallow)
Iris pseudacorus (yellowflag)
Iris versicolor (blue flag)
Lobelia cardinalis (cardinal flower)
Lythrum (various) (loosestrife)
Monarda didyma (bee balm)
Myosotis scorpioides (true forget-me-not)
Oenothera (various) (evening primrose)
Sarracenia purpurea (pitcher plant)
Saxifraga (saxifrage)
Vinca (periwinkle)

For Dry Soil Conditions

Trees

Deciduous

Acer ginnala (Amur maple)
Acer tataricum (tatarian maple)
Ailanthus altissima (tree of heaven)
Betula pendula (European birch)
Betula populifolia (gray birch)
Carya glabra (pignut)
Cotinus coggygria (smoke tree)
Populus alba (white poplar)
Populus tremuloides (quaking aspen)
Prunus cerasus (sour cherry)
Prunus serotina (black cherry)

Quercus suber (cork oak)
Robinia pseudoacacia (black locust)

Evergreen

Juniperus chinensis (Chinese juniper)
Juniperus virginiana (eastern red cedar)
Picea alba (Canadian spruce)
Picea abies (excelsa) (Norway spruce)
Pinus mugo (Swiss mountain pine)
Pinus rigida (pitch pine)
Pinus strobus (white pine)
Pinus sylvestris (Scots pine)

Shrubs

Acacia
Arbutus unedo (strawberry tree)
Arctostaphylos uva-ursi (bearberry)
Berberis, several (barberry)
Betula glandulosa
Betula nana
Buddleia alternifolia (fountain buddleia)
Ceanothus americanus (New Jersey tea)
Cotoneaster (cotoneaster)
Cytisus (broom)
Elaeagnus angustifolia (Russian olive)
Elaeagnus longipes (goumi)
Euonymus japonica (evergreen euonymus)
Genista tinctoria (dyer's greenweed)
Hamamelis virginiana (common witch hazel)
Hypericum spathulatum (shrubby Saint-Johns-wort)
Juniperus communis (juniper)
Juniperus horizontalis (creeping juniper)
Kolkwitzia amabilis (beauty bush)
Ligustrum vulgare (common privet)
Nerium oleander (oleander)
Pittosporum tobira (Japanese pittosporum)
Potentilla fruticosa (cinquefoil)
Prunus besseyi (western sand cherry)
Prunus maritima (beach plum)
Pyracantha coccinea (scarlet firethorn)
Raphiolepis umbellata (yeddo hawthorn)
Rhamnus alaternus
Rhamnus frangula (alder buckthorn)
Rhus (various) (sumac)
Robinia hispida (rose acacia)
Robinia pseudoacacia (locust)
Robinia viscosa (clammy locust)
Rosa (various) (rose)
Salix tristis (dwarf gray willow)
Tamarix species (tamarix)
Viburnum lantana (wayfaring tree)
Viburnum lentago (nannyberry)

Perennials

Achillea (various) (yarrow)
Ajuga reptans (carpet bugle)
Anthemis tinctoria (golden marguerite)
Artemisia pycnocephala

Asclepias tuberosa (butterfly weed)
Aster novae-angliae (New England aster)
Callirhoë involucrata (poppy mallow)
Cerastium tomentosum (snow-in-summer)
Coreopsis grandiflora (tickseed)
Dianthus (various) (pinks)
Echinops exaltatus (globe thistle)
Echium
Gazania hybrids
Geranium grandiflorum (cranesbill)
Gypsophila paniculata (baby's breath)
Helianthus (various) (sunflower)
Limonium latifolium (statice, sea lavender)
Papaver nudicaule (Iceland poppy)
Phlox subulata (moss pink)
Potentilla atrosanguinea (cinquefoil)
Rudbeckia hirta (coneflower)
Veronica (various) (speedwell)
Yucca filamentosa (Adam's needle)

Annuals

Arctotis stoechadifolia grandis (African daisy)
Browallia americana (browallia)
Centaurea cyanus (bachelor's button or cornflower)
Convolvulus tricolor (dwarf morning glory)
Coreopsis tinctoria (calliopsis)
Cryophytum crystallinum (ice plant)
Delphinium ajacis (larkspur)
Dimorphoteca (various) (Cape marigold)
Eschscholzia californica (California poppy)
Euphorbia marginata (snow-on-the-mountain)
Gaillardia pulchella (rose-ring Gaillardia)
Gypsophila elegans (baby's breath)
Helianthus annuus (sunflower)
Ipomoea purpurea (morning glory)
Mirabilis jalapa (four-o'-clock)
Phlox drummondii (annual phlox)
Portulaca grandiflora (rose moss)
Salvia splendens (scarlet sage)
Zinnia elegans (giant-flowered zinnia)

To Provide Shade

Trees

Acer (various) (maple)
Aesculus carnea (red horse chestnut)
Callistemon citrinus (bottlebrush)
Catalpa speciosa (western catalpa)
Celtis occidentalis (hackberry)
Cinnamomum camphora (camphor tree)
Crataegus oxyacantha (English hawthorn)
Crataegus phaenopyrum (Washington hawthorn)
Fagus sylvatica (European beech)
Fraxinus americana (white ash)
Ginkgo biloba (ginkgo tree or maidenhair tree)
Gleditsia triacanthos (sweet honey locust)

Koelreuteria paniculata (goldenrain tree)
Liquidambar styraciflua (sweet gum)
Magnolia grandiflora (southern magnolia)
Malus (crab apple)
Populus alba (white poplar)
Populus nigra 'Italica' (Lombardy poplar)
Platanus acerifolia (London plane tree)
Prunus sargentii (Sargent cherry)
Quercus (various) (oak)
Sophora japonica (Japanese pagoda tree)
Sorbus aucuparia (mountain ash)
Syringa japonica (Japanese tree lilac)
Tilia americana (American linden)
Tilia cordata (small-leaved linden)
Ulmus americana (American elm)
Zelkova serrata (Japanese zelkova)

For Shady Places

Trees

Deciduous

Acer circinatum (vine maple)
Acer ginnala (Amur maple)
Acer palmatum (Japanese maple)
Acer spicatum (mountain maple)
Albizzia julibrissin (silk tree)
Alnus species (alder)
Betula papyrifera (canoe birch)
Cercis canadensis (redbud)
Cornus alba
Cornus kousa (Chinese dogwood)
Cornus mas (cornelian cherry)
Crataegus oxyacantha 'Paul's scarlet' (hawthorn)
Elaeagnus angustifolia (Russian olive)
Franklinia alatamaha (franklinia)
Fraxinus holotricha
Magnolia stellata (star magnolia)
Malus species and hybrids (flowering crab apple)
Prunus (various) (flowering cherry and others)
Sorbus (various) (mountain ash)

Evergreen

Magnolia soulangiana (saucer magnolia)
Pinus bungeana (lacebark pine)
Taxus species (yew)
Thuja species (arborvitae)
Tsuga species (hemlock)

Shrubs

Acanthopanax pentaphyllus
Amelanchier (various) (service berry)
Aronia (various) (chokeberry)
Azalea nudiflorum (Pinxter flower)
Ceanothus americanus (New Jersey tea)
Cephalanthus occidentalis (buttonbush)
Chionanthus virginica (fringe tree)
Clethra alnifolia (summer sweet)

Cornus alba 'Sibirica' (tatarian dogwood)
Cornus mas (cornelian cherry)
Euonymus fortunei (winter creeper)
Hamamelis virginiana (common witch hazel)
Hypericum (various) (Saint-Johns-wort)
Ilex glabra (inkberry)
Ilex verticillata (winterberry)
Kalmia latifolia (mountain laurel)
Leucothoë catesbaei (drooping leucothoë)
Mahonia aquifolium (Oregon grape)
Mahonia bealei (leather-leaf grape)
Pieris floribunda (Mountain andromeda)
Rhododendron (various)
Rhus canadensis (fragrant sumac)
Ribes alpinum (alpine currant)
Ribes sanguineum (flowering currant)
Vaccinium corymbosum (highbush blueberry)
Viburnum (various) (viburnum)

Perennials (Semishade)

Aconitum anthora (monkshood)
Ajuga (bugle)
Althaea rosea (hollyhock)
Anemone hupehensis japonica (Japanese anemone)
Anemonella thalictroides (rue anemone)
Aquilegia hybrids (columbine)
Asperula (woodruff)
Campanula rotundifolia (harebell)
Convallaria majalis (lily-of-the-valley)
Cornus canadensis (bunchberry)
Dicentra spectabilis (bleeding heart)
Dictamus albus (gas plant)
Epimedium grandiflorum (bishop's hat)
Geranium grandiflorum (cranesbill)
Helleborus niger (Christmas rose)
Hemerocallis (various) (daylily)
Hepatica
Heuchera sanguinea (coral bells)
Hibiscus moscheutos (swamp rose mallow)
Hosta (various) (plantain lily)
Hypericum (Saint-Johns-wort)
Iberis sempervirens (evergreen candytuft)
Lobelia cardinalis (cardinal flower)
Mertensia virginica (Virginia bluebell)
Monarda didyma (bee balm)
Phlox divaricata (sweet William phlox)
Platycodon grandiflorum (balloonflower)
Primula (various) (primrose)
Trollius europeaus (globeflower)

Annuals (Light Shade)

Ageratum houstonianum (floss flower)
Bellis perennis (English daisy)
Catharanthus roseus (*Vinca rosea*) (Madagascar periwinkle)
Celosia 'Plumosa' (Plume cockscomb)
Centaurea americana (basket flower)

Centaurea moschata (sweet sultan)
Clarkia elegans (Clarkia)
Cryophytum crystallinum (ice plant)
Delphinium ajacis (larkspur)
Euphorbia marginata (snow-on-the-mountain)
Gerbera jamesoni (Transvaal daisy)
Godetia amoena (farewell-to-spring)
Impatiens balsamina (balsam)
Lobelia erinus (lobelia)
Lobularia maritima (sweet alyssum)
Lupinus hartwegii (lupine, annual)
Myosotis sylvatica (forget-me-not)
Nicotiana sanderae (flowering tobacco)
Phlox drummondii (annual phlox)
Primula malacoides (fairy primrose)
Salpiglossis sinuata (painted tongue)
Viola tricolor hortensis (pansy)

Vines

Akebia quinata (five-leaf akebia)
Ampelopsis breviped-unculata (porcelain ampelopsis or blueberry climber)
Aristolochia durior (Dutchman's-pipe)
Clytosoma (*Bignonia capreolata*) (cross vine or trumpet vine)
Celastrus scandens (American bittersweet)
Euonymus fortunei (wintercreeper)
Fatshedera lizei
Ficus pumila (*repens*) (creeping fig)
Gelsemium sempervirens (Carolina jessamine)
Hedera helix (English ivy)
Hydrangea petiolaris (climbing hydrangea)
Jasminum nudiflorum (winter jasmine)
Jasminum officinale (white jasmine)
Lonicera hildebrandiana (Burmese honeysuckle)
Lonicera japonica 'Halliana' (Hall's honeysuckle)
Parthenocissus quinqefolia (Virginia creeper)
Pueraria thunbergiana (Kudzo vine)
Smilax rotundifolia (horse brier)
Trachelospermum jasminoides (star jasmine)
Vitis coignetiae (glory grape)

Bulbs (Semishade)

Achimenes (rainbow flower)
Anemone
Begonia (tuberous)
Caladium
Camassia (camas)
Chionodoxa (glory of snow)
Colchicum (meadow saffron)
Colocasia esculenta (taro)
Convallaria (lily of the valley)
Crocus
Cyclamen (various) (Cyclamen)
Eranthis (winter aconite)
Erythronium (dogtooth violet)
Frittilaria

Galanthus (snowdrop)
Muscari (grape hyacinth)
Ornithogalum umbellatum (star-of-Bethlehem)
Scilla (squill)
Trillium
Zephyranthes (zephyr lily)

For Background Planting

Shrubs

Arbutus unedo (strawberry tree)
Callistemon citrinus (bottlebrush)
Ceanothus thyrsiflorus (blue blossom)
Cornus mas (cornelian cherry)
Cornus officinalis (dogwood)
Cotoneaster frigida
Elaeagnus angustifolia (Russian olive)
Enkianthus campanulatus (bellflower)
Euonymus latifolius
Euonymus sanguinea
Euonymus yedoensis
Hamamelis mollis (Chinese witch hazel)
Hamamelis virginiana (common witch hazel)
Ilex cornuta (Chinese holly)
Ilex crenata (Japanese holly)
Ilex glabra (inkberry)
Jasminum officinale (common white jasmine)
Kalmia latifolia (mountain laurel)
Lagerstroemia indica (crape myrtle)
Ligustrum lucidum (privet)
Nerium oleander (oleander)
Osmanthus heterophyllus (holly osmanthus)
Photinia serrulata (Chinese photinia)
Poncirus trifoliata (hardy orange)
Pyracantha atlantioides
Rosa odorata (tea rose)
Syringa chinensis (Chinese lilac)
Syringa vulgaris (common lilac)

Perennials

Althaea rosea (hollyhock)
Aster (various)
Delphinium (various)
Echinops exaltatus (globe thistle)
Helenium (various) (Helen's flower)
Helianthus (various) (sunflower)
Hemerocallis (various) (daylily)
Rudbeckia hirta (coneflower)
Solidago altissima (goldenrod)
Yucca filamentosa (Adam's needle)

Annuals

Amaranthus caudatus (love-lies-bleeding)
Celosia (various) (cockscomb)
Cosmos bipinnatus (cosmos)
Delphinium ajacis (larkspur)
Helianthus annuus (sunflower)

Nicotiana (various) (flowering tobacco)
Salvia splendens (scarlet sage)
Tagetes (various) (marigold)
Zinnia elegans (zinnia)

For Screens and Windbreaks

Trees
Deciduous

Acer ginnala (Amur maple)
Crataegus mollis (downy hawthorn)
Fagus species (beech)
Fraxinus americana (white ash)
Populus alba (white poplar)
Quercus imbricaria (shingle oak)
Quercus palustris (pin oak)

Evergreen

Eucalyptus species (eucalyptus)
Pinus nigra (Austrian black pine)
Pinus thunbergana (Japanese black pine)
Thuja occidentalis (American arborvitae)
Tilia species (linden)
Tsuga canadensis (hemlock)

Shrubs

Acanthopanax pentaphyllum
Elaeagnus angustifolia (Russian olive)
Elaeagnus pungens (silverberry)
Euonymus europaens
Forsythia intermedia (border forsythia)
Forsythia suspensa (weeping forsythia)
Forsythia viridissima (greenstem goldenbells)
Hamamelis vernalis (vernal witch hazel)
Lagerstroemia indica (crape mrytle)
Laurus nobilis (sweet bay)
Ligustrum (various) (privet)
Lonicera fragrantissima (winter honeysuckle)
Lonicera tatarica (Tatarian honeysuckle)
Philadelphus coronarius (mock orange)
Spiraea veitchii (Veitch spiraea)
Syringa henryi 'Lutece' (lilac)
Syringa villosa (late lilac)
Syringa vulgaris (common lilac)
Viburnum (various)

For Hedges

Trees
Evergreen (to 5 feet)

Picea glauca (white spruce)
Pinus mugo (Swiss mountain pine)
Taxus canadensis (Canada yew)
Taxus cuspidata (Japanese yew)

Evergreen (to 30 feet)

Tsuga canadensis (Canada hemlock)
Tsuga caroliniana (Carolina hemlock)

Shrubs

Deciduous (to 5 feet)

Berberis koreana (Korean barberry)
Berberis mentorensis (mentor barberry)
Berberis thunbergii 'Erecta' (Japanese barberry)
Cotoneaster lucida (hedge cotoneaster)
Euonymus alata 'Compacta' (winged euonymus)
Ligustrum vulgare 'Lodense' (privet)
Rosa species (rose)
Salix purpurea Gracilis (dwarf purple osier)

Evergreen (to 5 feet)

Berberis juliane (wintergreen barberry)
Berberis sempervirens suffruticosa (dwarf box)
Berberis verruculosa (warty barberry)
Euonymus kiautschovica
Euonymus fortunei
Ilex crenata (Japanese holly)
Ilex crenata 'Microphylla'
Thuja occidentalis varieties (American arborvitae)

Deciduous (to 30 feet)

Acer ginnala (Amur maple)
Crataegus species (hawthorn)
Hibiscus syriacus (shrub althea)
Lonicera maackii (Amur honeysuckle)
Lonicera tatarica (Tatarian honeysuckle)
Philadelphus coronarius (mock orange)
Spiraea prunifolia (bridal wreath spirea)
Spiraea thunbergii
Syringa persica (Persian lilac)
Syringa vulgaris (common lilac)
Viburnum lantana (wayfaring tree)
Viburnum sieboldii (Siebold viburnum)

Evergreen (to 30 feet)

Abelia grandiflora (glossy abelia)
Buxus sempervirens (common box)
Photinia serrulata (Chinese photinia)
Pittosporum tobira (Japanese pittosporum)
Podocarpus macrophyllus
Pyracantha coccinea (firethorn)

For Best Ground Cover

Shrubs

Akebia quinata (five-leaf akebia)
Arctostaphylos uva-ursi (bearberry)
Calluna vulgaris (heather)
Cotoneaster damaneri
Cotoneaster horizontalis (rock spray)
Euonymus radicans (various) (wintercreeper)
Hedera helix (English ivy)
Hypericum calycinum (Saint-Johns-wort)
Jasminum nudiflorum (winter jasmine)
Juniperus chinensis 'Pfitzeriana' (Pfitzer juniper)
Juniperus communis depressa (spreading juniper)

Juniperus conferta (shore juniper)
Juniperus horizontalis (creeping juniper)
Lantana montevidensis (trailing lantana)
Lonicera japonica 'Halliana' (Hall's honeysuckle)
Rhus aromatica (fragrant sumac)
Rosa carolina (pasture rose)
Rosa multiflora (Japanese rose)
Rosa virginiana (Virginia rose)
Spiraea tomentosa (hardhack)
Thymus (thyme)
Thymus serpyllum vulgaris (lemon thyme)
Thymus serpyllum lanuginosis (mother-of-thyme)

Perennials

Ajuga reptans (carpet bugle)
Anthemis nobilis (chamomile)
Arabis alpina (mountain rock cress)
Campanula (bellflower)
Cerastium tomentosum (snow-in-summer)
Convallaria majalis (lily-of-the-valley)
Drosanthemum floribundum
Gazania splendens (gazania)
Iberis sempervirens (evergreen candytuft)
Lampranthos spectabilis (trailing ice plant)
Malephora croceum (ice plant)
Mentha requienii (mint)
Myosotis (forget-me-not)
Nepeta mussinii
Pachysandra terminalis (Japanese pachysandra)
Phlox divaricata (sweet William phlox)
Phlox subulata (moss pink)
Sedum acre (stonecrop)
Vinca minor (common periwinkle)

For City Conditions

Trees

Deciduous

Acer platanoides (Norway maple)
Aesculus carnea (red horse chestnut)
Ailanthus altissima (tree of Heaven)
Betula alba (white birch)
Carpinus betulus (European hornbeam)
Catalpa speciosa (western catalpa)
Cornus florida (flowering dogwood)
Crataegus oxyacantha (English hawthorn)
Crataegus phaenopyrum (Washington hawthorn)
Elaeagnus angustifolia (Russian olive)
Euonymus europaea (spindle tree)
Fraximous americana (white ash)
Ginkgo biloba (maidenhair tree or gingko tree)
Gleditsia triacanthos (honey locust)
Ilex opaca (American holly)
Magnolia (various)
Malus species (flowering crab apples)
Phellodendron amurense (Amur corktree)

Platanus acerifolia (plane tree)
Populus nigra italica (Lombardy poplar)
Prunus subhirtella (rosebud cherry)
Quercus borealis (red oak)
Rhamnus davurica (davurica buckthorn)
Sophora japonica (Japanese pagoda tree)
Styrax japonica (snowbell tree)
Syringa pekinensis (Pekin lilac)
Tilia cordata (small-leaved linden)
Ulmus pumila (dwarf elm)

Evergreen

Abies concolor (white fir)
Picea pungens (Swiss mountain pine)
Pinus mugo (Swiss mountain pine)
Taxus cuspidata (Japanese yew)
Thuja occidentalis (American arborvitae)
Tsuga caroliniana (Carolina hemlock)

Shrubs

Abelia grandiflora (abelia)
Acanthopanax pentaphyllum
Aesculus parviflora (bottlebrush buckeye)
Aralia elata
Azalea (many)
Berberis thunbergii (Japanese barberry)
Buddleia davidii (butterfly bush)
Buxus microphylla Koreana (Korean boxwood)
Chaenomeles japonica (Japanese quince)
Clematis paniculata
Cornus paniculata (gray dogwood)
Cornus sanguinea (bloodtwig dogwood)
Cornus stolonifera (red-osier dogwood)
Cotoneaster horizontalis (rock spray)
Deutzia gracilis
Deutzia scabra 'Candidissima' (snowflake deutzia)
Elaeagnus angustifolia (Russian olive)
Euonymus (many)
Fatsia japonica
Forsythia (all species)
Hibiscus syriacus (rose of Sharon)
Hydrangea quercifolia (oakleaf hydrangea)
Ilex crenata (Japanese holly)
Ilex glabra (inkberry)
Juniperus chinensis 'Pfitzeriana' (Pfitzer juniper)
Kalmia latifolia (mountain laurel)
Kerria japonica (kerria)
Lagerstroemia indica (crape myrtle)
Ligustrum (various) (privet)
Lonicera species (honeysuckle)
Mahonia aquifolium (Oregon grape)
Malus sargenti (Sargent crab apple)
Myrica caroliniensis (bayberry)
Nandina domestica (heavenly bamboo)
Osmanthus aquifolium (holly olive)
Philadelphus (mock orange)
Pieris japonica (Japanese andromeda)

Potentilla fruticosa (cinquefoil)
Prunus subhirtella (rosebud cherry)
Pyracantha coccinea (scarlet firethorn)
Rhododendron carolinianum
Rhododendron hybrids
Rhus cotinus (smoke tree)
Rosa multiflora (Japanese rose)
Rosa rugosa (rugosa rose)
Spiraea thunbergii (Thunberg spiraea)
Spiraea vanhouttei (Vanhoutte's spiraea)
Symphoricarpos albus (snowberry)
Syringa vulgaris (common lilac)
Tamarix (various)
Vitex agnus-castus (chaste tree)
Viburnum dentatum (arrowwood)
Viburnum lantana (wayfaring tree)
Weigela hybrids
Wisteria sinensis (Chinese wisteria)

Perennials

Astilbe japonica
Bergenia
Chrysanthemum
Coreopsis
Dianthus barbatus (sweet William)
Gaillardia
Hemerocallis (daylily)
Heuchera sanguinea (coral bells)
Hosta plantaginea (plantain lily)
Iris (bearded iris)
Paeonia (peony)
Phlox
Sedum (stonecrop)

Annuals

Ageratum
Antirrhinum (snapdragon)
Cleome
Lobelia erinus (lobelia)
Lobularia
Mirabilis
Nicotiana
Petunia
Phlox
Salvia
Tagetes (marigold)
Verbena
Zinnia

Vines

Akebia quinta (five-leaf akebia)
Clematis paniculata
Cobaea scandens (cup-and-saucer vine)
Hedera helix (English ivy)
Lonicera Japonica 'Halliana' (Hall's honeysuckle)
Parthenocissus quinquefolia (Virginia creeper)
Parthenocissus tricuspidata (Boston ivy)

Phaseolus coccineus (scarlet runner bean)
Polygonum auberti (China fleece vine)

For Soil Between Paved Areas

Shrubs

Cotoneaster dammeri
Juniperus (many) (juniper)
Santolina
Thymus
Thymus serpyllum vulgaris (lemon thyme)
Thymus serpyllum lanuginosus (mother-of-thyme)

Perennials

Ajuga reptans (carpet bugle)
Anthemis nobilis (chamomile)
Arabis alpina (mountain rock cress)
Arenaria montana
Arenaria verna
Armeria maritima (sea-pink or thrift)
Bellis perennis
Campanula glomerata acaulis
Dianthus (pink)
Gypsophila repens
Iberis sempervirens (edging candytuft)
Phlox subulata (moss pink)
Sedum acre (stonecrop)
Sempervivum arachnoideum (cobweb houseleek)
Veronica repens (creeping speedwell)
Veronica rupestris
Veronica serpyllifolia
Vinca minor (common periwinkle)

For Edging

Perennials

Achillea tomentosa (woolly yarrow)
Ajuga reptans (carpet bugle)
Alyssum saxatile (alyssum or basket of gold)
Arabis alpina (mountain rock cress)
Arabis caucasica (wall rock cress)
Armeria maritima (sea-pink or thrift)
Aubrietia deltoide (common aubrieta)
Bellis perennis (English daisy)
Campanula carpatica (bellflower)
Cerastium tomentosum (snow-in-summer)
Dianthus plumarius (grass pink)
Festuca ovina 'Glauca' (blue fescue)
Heuchera sanguinea (coral bells)
Iberis sempervirens (evergreen candytuft)
Papaver nudicaule (Iceland poppy)
Phlox procumbens (hairy phlox)
Phlox subulata (moss pink)
Primula (various) (primrose)
Sedum (various) (stonecrop)

Veronica (various) (speedwell)
Viola (various)

Annuals

Ageratum (various)
Antirrhinum (dwarf kinds) (snapdragon)
Begonia semperflorens (wax begonia)
Brachycome iberidifolia (Swan River daisy)
Browallia americana (browallia)
Calendula officinalis (calendula or marigold)
Celosia (various) (cockscomb)
Centaurea cineraria (dusty miller)
Coreopsis tinctoria (calliopsis)
Cryophytum crystallinum (ice plant)
Dianthus chinensis (China pink)
Eschscholzia californica (California poppy)
Iberis umbellata (globe candytuft)
Linum grandiflorum 'Rubrum' (scarlet flax)
Lobelia erinus (lobelia)
Petunia (various) (petunia)
Phlox drummondii (annual phlox)
Portulaca grandiflora (rose moss)
Tagetes (marigold)
Tropaeolum majus (nasturtium)
Verbena (various)

For Flowers

Trees

Acacia baileyana (Bailey acacia)
Aesculus glabra (Ohio buckeye)
Albizzia julibrissin (silk tree)
Catalpa speciosa (catalpa)
Cercis canadensis (redbud)
Cornus florida (dogwood)
Cornus kousa chinensis
Franklinia alatamaha
Jacaranda acutifolia
Koelreuteria paniculata (goldenrain tree)
Magnolia grandiflora (southern magnolia)
Magnolia stellata (star magnolia)
Malus species (crab apple)
Prunus species (fruit trees)
Sophora japonica (Japanese pagoda tree)

Shrubs

Azalea
Buddleia Davidii (butterfly bush)
Callistemon citrinus (bottlebrush)
Calluna vulgaris (heather)
Camellia
Carpenteria Californica (mock-orange)
Chaenomeles speciosa (flowering quince)
Daphne odora (fragrant Daphne)
Forsythia intermedia (border forsythia)
Fothergilla major
Hamamelis virginiana (common witch hazel)

Hibiscus syriacus (shrub althaea)
Kalmia latifolia (mountain laurel)
Lagerstroemica indica (crape myrtle)
Rhododendron
Rosa (rose)
Spiraea
Syringa chinensis
Syringa vulgaris (common lilac)
Viburnum
Weigela

Vines

Bignonia capreolata (cross vine)
Bougainvillaea
Clematis species
Clytosoma
Hydrangea petiolaris (climbing hydrangea)
Mandevilla suaveolens (Chilean jasmine)
Passiflora caerulea (passion flower)
Plumbago capensis (plumbago)
Rosa (rose)
Stephanotis floribunda (Madagascar jasmine)
Trachelospermum species (star jasmine)
Wisteria floribunda (Japanese wisteria)

For Cut Flowers

Shrubs

Buddleia
Chaenomeles (quince)
Cornus mas (cornelian cherry)
Corylus maxima (filbert)
Deutzia
Forsythia
Philadelphus (mock orange)
Prunus
Salix caprea (French pussy willow)
Salix discolor (pussy willow)
Spiraea
Syringa (lilac)
Tamarix

Perennials

Achillea (various) (yarrow)
Anemone japonica (Japanese anemone)
Aster (various)
Chrysanthemum morifolium (florists' chrysanthemum)
Delphinium (various)
Dianthus barbatus (sweet William)
Gaillardia grandiflora (blanket flower)
Paeonia (various) (peony)
Rudbeckia hirta (coneflower)

Annuals

Amaranthus caudatus (love-lies-bleeding)
Antirrhinum majus (snapdragon)
Arctotis stoechadifolia grandis (African daisy)

Browallia speciosa (*major*) (browallia)
Calendula officinalis (calendula or pot marigold)
Callistephus chinensis (aster or China aster)
Centaurea moschata (sweet sultan)
Chrysanthemum
Clarkia elegans (Clarkia)
Coreopsis tinctoria (calliopsis)
Cosmos
Delphinium ajacis (larkspur)
Dianthus chinensis (China pink)
Dimorphoteca (various) (African daisy, Cape marigold)
Eschscholzia californica (California poppy)
Gaillardia
Gomphrena globosa (globe-amaranth)
Gypsophila
Helianthus annuus (sunflower)
Helichrysum bractaetum (strawflower)
Lathyrus odoratus (sweet pea)
Lupinus (lupine)
Mathiola bicornis (night-scented stock)
Mathiola incana (stock)
Nicotiana sanderae (flowering tobacco)
Nigella damescena (love-in-a-mist)
Papaver glaucum (tulip poppy)
Papaver rhoeas (Shirley poppy)
Phlox drummondii (annual phlox)
Polygonum orientale (princess feather)
Reseda odorata (mignonette)
Salpiglossis sinuata (painted tongue)
Scabiosa atropurpurea (pincushion flower)
Senecio elegans (purple ragwort)
Tagetes (marigold)
Verbena hybrida (*hortensis*) (garden verbena)
Zinnia elegans (small-flowered zinnia)
Zinnia haageana (orange zinnia)

For Fragrance

Shrubs

Abelia grandiflora (glossy abelia)
Ceanothus americanus (New Jersey tea)
Clethra alnifolia (summer sweet)
Daphne odora (winter daphne)
Deutzia gracilis (slender deutzia)
Fothergilla (several) (fothergilla)
Gardenia jasminoides (gardenia)
Jasminum officinale (common white jasmine)
Lonicera (several) (honeysuckle)
Osmanthus heterophyllus (holly olive)
Philadelphus coronarius (sweet mock orange)
Raphiolepis umbellata (yeddo hawthorn)
Rosa (rose)
Skimmia japonica

Perennials

Anthemis nobilis (chamomile)

Arabis (various) (rock cress)
Artemisia abrotanum (southernwood)
Asperula odorata (sweet woodruff)
Convallaria majalis (lily-of-the-valley)
Dianthus (various) (pinks)
Dictamnus albus (gas plant)
Heliotropium arborescens (heliotrope)
Hemerocallis (various) (daylily)
Hesperis matronalis (sweet rocket)
Hosta plantaginea (plaintain lily)
Lathyrus grandiflorus (everlasting pea)
Monarda didyma (bee balm)
Oenothera (various) (evening primrose)
Paeonia (various) (peony)
Phlox (various)
Rosa species (roses)
Viola cornuta (tufted viola)
Viola odorata (sweet violet)

Annuals

Ageratum houstonianum (floss flower)
Antirrhinum majus (snapdragon)
Calendula officinalis (calendula or pot marigold)
Centaurea moschata (sweet sultan)
Delphinium ajacis (larkspur)
Iberis umbellata (globe candytuft)
Lathyrus odoratus (sweet pea)
Lobularia maritima (sweet alyssum)
Lupinus luteus (yellow lupine)
Mathiola bicornis (night-scented stock)
Matholia incana (stock)
Nicotiana sanderal (flowering tobacco)
Oenothera biennis (evening primrose)
Petunia
Phlox drummondii (annual phlox)
Reseda odorata (mignonette)
Scabiosa atropurpurea (pincushion flower)
Tagetes (marigold)
Tropaeolum majus (nasturtium)
Verbena (various)
Viola tricolor hortensis (pansy)

Bulbs

Acidanthera
Convallaria
Freesia
Hedychium (ginger lily)
Hemerocallis (daylily)
Lillium (lily)
Lycoris
Muscari (grape hyacinth)
Narcissis
Puschkinia (white)

Vines

Akebia quinata (five-leaf akebia)
Gelsemium sempervirens (Carolina yellow jessamine)

For Colorful Autumn Foliage

Trees

Purples

Fraxinus americana (white ash)
Liquidamber styraciflua (sweetgum)

Reds

Acer ginnala (Amur maple)
Acer japonicum (Japanese maple)
Acer rubrum (red maple)
Acer saccharum (sugar maple)
Crataegus phaenopyrum (Washington thorn)
Liquidambar styraciflua (sweetgum)
Oxydendrum arboreum (sourwood)
Quercus coccinea (scarlet oak)

Yellows

Acer rubrum (red maple)
Acer saccharum (sugar maple)
Carya glabra (pignut)
Cercidiphyllum japonicum (katsura tree)

Shrubs

Purple

Cornus racemosa (gray dogwood)
Viburnum (various)

Reds (Red, Crimson, Rose, Scarlet)

Acer circinatum (vine maple)
Amelanchier canadensis (shadblow service berry)
Aronia arbutifolia (red chokeberry)
Azalea obtusa kaempferi
Azalea mucronulata (Korean azalea)
Berberis (various) (barberry)
Cotoneaster horizontalis (rock spray)
Enkianthus campanulatus (bellflower)
Euonymus alatus (winged euonymus)
Hydrangea quercifolia (oakleaf hydrangea)
Nandina domestica (heavenly bamboo)
Photinia serrulata (Chinese photinia)
Rhus (various) (sumac)
Ribes alpinum (alpine currant)
Vaccinum corymbosum (highbush blueberry)
Viburnum (various)

Yellows (Yellow, Orange, Bronze)

Acanthopanax pentaphyllum
Chionanthus virginica (fringetree)
Enkianthus campanulatus (bellflower)
Fothergilla
Hamamelis (witch hazel)
Leucothoë catesbaei (drooping leucothoe)
Mahonia aquifolium (Oregon grape)
Spiraea prunifolia (bridal wreath spiraea)
Spiraea thunbergii (thunberg spiraea)
Viburnum dentatum (arrowwood)

For Colorful Fruit

Shrubs

Red Fruit

Arctostaphylos uva-ursi (bearberry)
Ardisia crenata (ardisia)
Aronia arbutifolia (red chokeberry)
Berberis koreana (Korean barberry)
Berberis thunbergii (Japanese barberry)
Berberis vulgaris (common barbery)
Ceanothus ovatus (inland ceanothus)
Cornus mas (cornelian cherry)
Cotoneaster divaricata (spreading cotoneaster)
Cotoneaster horizontalis (rock spray)
Cotoneaster microphylla (small-leaf cotoneaster)
Elaeagnus multiflorus (cherry elaeagnus)
Euonymus (various)
Ilex cornuta (Chinese holly)
Ilex opaca (American holly)
Ilex verticillata (winterberry)
Lonicera fragrantissima (winter honeysuckle)
Lonicera maackii (Amur honeysuckle)
Lonicera tatarica (Tatarian honeysuckle)
Magnolia stellata (star magnolia)
Malus sargentii (Sargent crab apple)
Nandina domestica (heavenly bamboo)
Photinia serrulata (Chinese photinia)
Pyracantha coccinea (scarlet firethorn)
Rosa (many) (rose)
Sarcococca ruscifolia (fragrant sarcococca)
Skimmia japonica (Japanese skimmia)
Virburnum (various)

Blue Fruit

Fatsia japonica
Gaultheria veitchiana (Veitch wintergreen)
Ligustrum obtusifolium (border privet)
Mahonia aquifolium (holly grape)
Vaccinum corymbosum (highbush blueberry)
Viburnum davidii (David viburnum)
Viburnum dentatum (arrowwood)

Black Fruit

Ligustrum vulgare (common privet)
Mahonia repens (creeping mahonia)
Sambucus canadensis (American elder)
Viburnum lantana (wayfaring tree)
Viburnum prunifolium (black haw)
Viburnum sieboldii (Siebold viburnum)

Vines

Celastrus scandens (American bittersweet)
Euonymus fortunei (wintercreeper)
Kadsura japonica (scarlet kadsura)
Smilax species (horse brier)

For Rapid Growth

Trees

Deciduous

Acer negundo (box elder)
Acer platanoides (Norway maple)
Acer rubrum (red maple)
Ailanthus altissima (tree of heaven)
Alnus rhombifolia (white alder)
Betula populifolia (gray birch)
Catalpa speciosa (western catalpa)
Fraxinus americana (white ash)
Ginkgo biloba (maidenhair tree or ginkgo tree)
Gleditsia triancanthos (honey locust)
Grevillea robusta (silk oak)
Larix decidua (European larch)
Liriodendron tulipifera (tulip tree)
Magnolia tripetala (umbrella tree)
Morus alba (fruitless forms) (white mulberry)
Platanus acerifolia (London plane tree)
Populus alba (white poplar)
Populus nigra italica (Lombardy poplar)
Prunus serotina (black cherry)
Quercus palustris (pin oak)
Robinia pseudoacacia (black locust)
Salix alba (white willow)
Salix vitellina (golden willow)
Syringa amurensis japonica (Japanese tree lilac)
Tilia americana (American linden)
Ulmus americana (American elm)
Ulmus parvifoeia (Chinese elm)

Evergreen

Picea abies (*excelsa*) (Norway spruce)
Pinus resinosa (red pine)
Pinus rigida (pitch pine)
Pinus strobus (Eastern white pine)
Pinus sylvestris (Scotch pine)

Shrubs

Acanthopanax pentaphyllum
Elaeagnus angustifolia (Russian olive)
Elaeagnus pungens (silverberry)
Euonymus europaeus
Forsythia intermedia (border forsythia)
Forsythia suspensa (weeping forsythia)
Hamamelis vernalis (spring witch hazel)
Lagerstroemia indica (crape myrtle)
Laurus nobilis (sweet bay)
Ligustrum (various) (privet)
Lonicera fragrantissima (winter honeysuckle)
Philadelphus coronarius (mock orange)
Salix pentandra (bay willow)
Spiraea veitchii (Veitch spiraea)
Syringa henryi 'Lutece' (lilac)
Syringa villosa (late lilac)

Syringa vulgaris (common lilac)
Viburnum (various)

Vines

Akebia quinata (five-leaf akebia)
Ampelopsis acontifolia
Aristolochia durior (Dutchman's-pipe)
Clytosoma (*Bignonia capreolata*) (cross vine, trumpet vine)
Clematis species
Doxantha unguis-cati (cat's-claw)
Ficus pumila (*repens*) (creeping fig)
Hedera helix (English ivy)
Lonicera species (honeysuckle)
Trachelospermum jasminoides (star jasmine)
Vitis species (glory grape)
Wisteria floribunda (Japanese wisteria)
Wisteria sinensis (Chinese wisteria)

To Attract Birds

Trees

Deciduous

Acer platahoides (Norway maple)
Albizzia julibrissin (silk tree)
Alnus (alder)
Betula (birch)
Celtis occidentalis (hackberry)
Cornus florida (flowering dogwood)
Crataegus (hawthorn)
Fraxinus ornus (flowering ash)
Malus (flowering crab apple)
Morus alba (white mulberry)
Platanus (plane tree or sycamore tree)
Quercus rubra (red oak)
Sorbus avcuparia (mountain ash)
Ulmus Americana (American elm)

Evergreen

Abies balsamea (balsam fir)
Juniperus virginiana (eastern red cedar)
Picea abies (Norway spruce)
Picea glanca (white spruce)

Shrubs

Amelanchier (service berry)
Arbutus
Berberis (barberry)
Berberis thunbergii (Japanese barberry)
Cotoneaster (many)
Elaeagnus
Fuchsia
Ilex glabra (inkberry)
Ilex verticillata (winterberry)
Lantana
Ligustrum (privet)
Lonicera (honeysuckle)

Mahonia (grape holly)
Photinia
Pyracantha
Ribes (currant)
Viburnum dentatum (arrowwood)
Viburnum lentago (nannyberry)

Twining and Climbing Vines

Twining

Akebia quinata (five-leaf akebia)
Aristolochia durior (Dutchman's-pipe)
Celastrus species (bittersweet)
Mandevilla suaveolens (Chilean jasmine)
Smilax species (horse brier)
Trachelospermum species (star jasmine)
Wisteria floribunda (Japanese wisteria)

Climbing

Ampelopsis species
Clytosoma (*Bignonia capreolata*) (cross vine)
Clematis species
Doxantha unguis-cati (cat's-claw)
Parthenocissus quinquefolia (Virginia creeper)
Passiflora species (passion flower)
Vitis species (glory grape)

For Flower Boxes

Full Sun

Ageratum
Antirrhinum majus (snapdragon)
Azalea
Bellis perennis (English daisy)
Cheiranthus cheiri (wallflower)
Geranium
Iberis umbellata (candytuft)
Lantana
Lobelia erinus (lobelia)
Lobularia maritima (sweet alyssum)
Myosotis sylvatica (forget-me-not)
Petunia hybrids
Phlox drummondii (annual phlox)
Portulaca grandiflora (rose moss)
Thunbergia alata (clockvine)
Tropaelum majus (nasturtium)
Verbena
Viola tricolor hortensis (pansy)

Partial Shade (but Some Light)

Achimenes
Begonia (tuberous begonia, wax begonia)
Browallia speciosa major (browallia)
Coleus
Ferns
Fuchsia

Hedera helix (English ivy)
Heliotrope
Impatiens
Syngonium
Tradescantia (spiderwort)

For Containers (Tubs, Pots, and Boxes) on Patio and Terrace

Trees

Deciduous

Acer circinatum (vine maple)
Acer davidii (David maple)
Acer ginnala (Amur maple)
Acer japonicum (full-moon maple)
Acer palmatum (Japanese maple)
Albizzia julibrissin (silk tree)
Betula nigra (river birch)
Betula populifolia (gray birch)
Betula verrucosa (pendula) (European white birch)
Betula verrucosa dalecarlica (cutleaf weeping bush)
Cercidiphyllum japonicum (Katsura tree)
Cercis canadensis (eastern redbud)
Chionanthus virginica (fringe tree)
Cornus florida (flowering dogwood)
Cornus nuttallii (Pacific dogwood)
Cotinus americana (smoke tree)
Crataegus lavallei (lavalle hawthorn)
Crataegus oxyacantha (English hawthorn)
Crataegus phaenopyrum (Washington hawthorn)
Erythrina americana
Gingko biloba (maiden hair tree or gingko tree)
Jacaranda acutifolia (sharp-leaf jacaranda)
Koelreuteria henryi (Chinese flame tree)
Koelreuteria paniculata (goldenrain tree)
Laburnum watereri (goldenchain tree)
Lagerstroemia indica (crape myrtle)
Liquidambar formosana (Formosa sweet gum)
Liquidambar styraciflua (sweet gum)
Magnolia soulangeana (saucer magnolia)
Magnolia stellata (star magnolia)
Malus (crab apple)
Pistacia chinensis (Chinese pistache)
Prunus (various) (stone fruits)
Punica granatum (pomegranate)
Robinia pseudoacacia (false acacia)
Sophora secundiflora (mescal bean)
Stewartia koreana (Korean stewartia)
Styrax japonica (Japanese snowball)
Styrax obassia (fragrant snowball)

Evergreen

Acacia baileyana (Bailey acacia)
Acacia pendula (weeping acacia)
Acacia retinodes (water wattle)
Agonis flexuosa (peppermint tree)
Arucaria excelsa (Norfolk Island pine)
Bauhinia variegata (mountain ebony)

Cedrus atlantica glauca (Blue Atlas cedar)
Citrus (dwarf forms)
Clethra arborea (lily-of-the-valley clethra)
Eriobotrya deflexa (bronze loquat)
Eriobotrya japonica (loquat)
Eucalyptus caesia
Eucalyptus cornuta (yate tree)
Eucalyptus erythrocorys (red cap gum)
Eucalyptus leucoxylon 'Rosea' (white ironbark)
Feijoa sellowiana (pineapple guava)
Ficus benjamina (weeping fig)
Ficus retusa (Indian laurel fig)
Juniperus chinensis (Chinese juniper)
Laurus nobilis (laurel)
Leptospermum laevigatum (Australian tea tree)
Magnolia grandiflora (southern magnolia)
Magnolia grandiflora lanceolata
Olea europeae (common olive)
Phellodendron amurense (cork tree)
Pinus (various) (pine)
Pittosporum crassifolium (karo)
Pittosporum phillyraeoides (willow pittosporum)
Pittosporum rhombifolium (Queensland pittosporum)
Podocarpus gracilior
Rhapis excelsa (lady palm)
Sophora secundiflora (mescal bean)

Shrubs

Abutilon (flowering maple)
Arbutus unedo (strawberry tree)
Azalea (many)
Callistemon citrinus (bottlebrush)
Callistemon viminalis (weeping bottlebrush)
Camellia japonica (common camellia)
Camellia sasanqua (sasanqua camellia)
Cotoneaster (many)
Fatsia japonica (Japanese aralia)
Gardenia jasminoides (Cape jasmine)
Hibiscus rosa-sinensis (Chinese hibiscus)
Ilex crenata (Japanese holly)
Ixora (star flower)
Juniperus chinensis 'Pfitzeriana' (Pfitzer juniper)
Juniperus communis depressa (prostrate juniper)
Ligustrum lucidum (glossy privet)
Nerium oleander (oleander)
Osmanthus ilicifolius (holly olive)
Pittosporum tobira (Japanese pittosporum)
Plumbago capensis (blue phlox)
Podocarpus macrophyllus
Rhododendron (many)
Thuja occidentalis (arborvitae)
Viburnum (many)
Yucca filamentosa (Adam's needle)

House Plants (for Hanging Baskets)

Abutilon megapotamicum (flowering maple)
Achimenes

Aeschynanthus lobbianum (lipstick vine)
Begonia (angel-wing begonia)
Begonia foliosa
Campanula isophylla
Cissus discolor
Cissus rhombifolia (grape ivy)
Coleus (many)
Columnea banksii
Dipladenia amoena (Mexican love vine)
Episcia (many)
Ferns (many)
Fuchsia (many)
Hedera helix (English ivy)
Hoya carnosa (wax plant)
Lantana montevidensis (trailing lantana)
Maranta massangeana
Pelargonium peltatum (ivy geranium)
Saxifraga sarmentosa (strawberry geranium)
Schizocentron elegans (Spanish shawl)
Scindapsus aureus (pothos)
Sedum morganianum (burro's tail)
Syngonium (many)
Tolmiea menziesii (pickaback plant)

House Plants That Require Sun

Abutilon hybridum (flowering maple)
Achimenes (many)
Aerides odoratum
Agave filifera
Agave picta
Agave victoriae-reginae
Astrophytum ornatum (star cactus)
Begonia (many)
Beloperone guttata (shrimp plant)
Cattleya (many)
Cephalocereus palmeri (woolly torch)
Chamaecereus silvestri (peanut cactus)
Coleus (many)
Crassula argentea (jade plant)
Croton (many)
Dieffenbachia (various)
Dracaena fragrans massangeana (dracena)
Dracaena goddseffiana
Echeveria (many)
Echinocereus ehrenbergii
Echinocereus rigidissimus (rainbow cactus)
Epiphyllum (orchid cactus)
Ficus benjamina (fig)
Ficus carica (common fig)
Haworthia tessellata
Mammillaria bocasana (powder puff cactus)
Nutocactus haselbergii (scarlet ball)
Parodia sanguiniflora
Pelargonium (geranium)
Rebutia miniscula (crown cactus)
Vanda (many)

House Plants That Require Coolness
(60–65° F. by day, 50–55° F. by night)

Abutilon hybridum (flowering maple)
Acorus gramineus pusillus
Araucaria excelsa (Norfolk Island pine)
Asparagus sprengeri (emerald fern)
Aspidistra elatior (cast-iron plant)
Camellia
Campanula (bellflower)
Coelogyne lawrenceana
Coelogyne massangeana
Eucharis grandiflora (amazon lily)
Fatshedera litzei
Hedera helix (English ivy)
Lantana montevidensis (trailing lantana)
Schlumbergera gaertneri (Easter cactus)
Streptocarpus rexii (Cape primrose)
Tolmiea menziesii (pickaback plant)
Zygocactus truncatus (Christmas cactus)

For Bottle Gardens

Calathea species
Episcia varieties
Ficus radicans variegata
Ficus pumila
Fittonia species
Koeleria varieties
Maranta species
Miniature orchids
Polystichum tsus-simense
Pteris ensiformis victoriae (sword brake)
Rex begonias (miniatures)
Selaginella species

Flowering and Blooming Calendar

Shrubs
Early Spring
Daphne odora (fragrant daphne)
Hamamelis mollis (Chinese witch hazel)
Hamamelis vernalis (vernal witch hazel)

Spring
Amelanchier canadensis (shadblow service berry)
Amelanchier gandiflora (apple service berry)
Andromeda polifolia (bog rosemary)
Chaenomeles japonica (Japanese quince)
Chaenomeles speciosa (flowering quince)
Cornus mas (cornelian cherry)
Cytisus decumbens
Enkianthus perulatus
Epigaea repens (trailing arbutus)
Forsythia intermedia (many) (forsythia)
Forsythia ovata (early forsythia)
Jasminum nudiflorum (winter jasmine)
Lonicera fragrantissima (winter honeysuckle)

Mahonia species (holly grape)
Pieris floribunda (mountain andromeda)
Pieris japonica (Japanese andromeda)
Rhododendron

Summer

Abelia grandiflora (glossy abelia)
Kalmia latifolia (mountain laurel)
Kolkwitzia amabilis (beauty bush)
Philadelphus (various) (mock orange)
Potentilla fruticosa (bush cinquefoil)
Rosa (shrub type) (rose)
Spiraea (various)

Fall

Clethra alnifolia (summer sweet)
Hamamelis virginiana (common witch hazel)
Hibiscus syriacus (althea or hibiscus)
Hydrangea (various)
Prunus subhirtella
Spiraea billiardi (billiard spirea)
Tamarix (various)

By Color

Perennials

White

Achillea ptarmica (yarrow)
Althaea rosea (hollyhock)
Anemone hupehensis japonica (Japanese anemone)
Anemonella thalictroides (rue anemone)
Aquilegia (columbine)
Arabis alpina (mountain rock cress)
Arabis caucasica (wall rock cress)
Arctotis
Artemisia frigida (fringed wormwood)
Asperula odorata (sweet woodruff)
Aster
Astilbe
Bellis perennis (English daisy)
Bergenia cordiflora (heartleaf bergenia)
Campanula persicifolia (peach-leafed bellflower)
Cerastium tomentosum (snow-in-summer)
Chrysanthemum coccineum (painted daisy)
Chrysanthemum maximum (Shasta daisy)
Chrysanthemum morifolium (florists' chrysanthemum)
Convallaria majalis (lily-of-the-valley)
Cornus canadensis (bunch berry)
Delphinium hybrid (Connecticut Yankee and Pacific Giant)
Dianthus barbatus (sweet William)
Dianthus deltoides (maiden pink)
Deltoides plumarius (grass pink)
Dicentra spectabilis (bleeding heart)
Dictamnus albus (gas plant)
Gypsophila paniculata (baby's breath)

Helleborus niger (Christmas rose)
Heliotropium arborescens (heliotrope)
Hemerocallis (daylily)
Hesperis matronalis (sweet rocket)
Heuchera sanguinea (coral bells)
Hosta plantaginea (plantain lily)
Iberis sempervirens (evergreen candytuft)
Iris (bearded iris)
Iris kaempferi (Japanese iris)
Kniphofia uvaria (torch lily)
Lathyrus latifolius (perennial pea)
Limonium latifolium (statice, sea lavender)
Monarda didyma (bee balm)
Paeonia (various) (peony)
Papaver orientale (Oriental poppy)
Pelargonium domesticum (Lady Washington geranium)
Penstemon (various) (beard tongue)
Phlox divaricata (sweet William phlox)
Phlox paniculata (summer phlox)
Phlox subulata (moss pink)
Platycodon grandiflorum (balloonflower)
Primula malacoides (fairy primrose)
Polygonatum multiflorum (Solomon's seal)
Rudbeckia hirta (coneflower)
Scabiosa caucasica (pincushion flower)
Saxifraga (saxifrage)
Viola cornuta (tufted viola)
Viola odorata (sweet violet)
Yucca filamentosa (Adam's needle)

Blue

Anchusa capensis (summer forget-me-not)
Aquilegia (columbine)
Aquilegia alpina (dwarf columbine)
Aster frikartii (aster)
Aster novae-angliae (New England aster)
Aubrieta deltoidea (common aubrieta)
Campanula carpatica (bellflower)
Campanula rotundifolia (harebell)
Delphinium hybrid (Connecticut Yankee and Pacific Giant)
Echinops exaltatus (globe thistle)
Felicia amelloides (blue marguerite)
Gentiana asclepiadea (willow gentian)
Heliotropium arborescens (heliotrope)
Limonium latifolium (statice, sea lavender)
Linum perenne (blue flax)
Lithodora diffusa (gromwell)
Lupinus polyphyllus (lupine)
Mertensia virginica (Virginia bluebell)
Myosotis scorpioides (true forget-me-not)
Penstemon (various) (beard tongue)
Phlox divaricata (sweet William phlox)
Phlox subulata (moss pink)
Platycodon grandiflorum (balloonflower)
Primula malacoides (fairy primrose)

Primula polyantha (polyanthus)
Salvia patens (blue salvia or meadow sage)
Veronica (speedwell)
Viola cornuta (tufted viola)

Lavender

Althaea rosea (hollyhock)
Anemone pulsatilla (prairie windflower, pasque flower)
Aquilegia (columbine)
Aster frikartii (aster)
Aster novae-angliae (New England aster)
Aubrieta deltoidea (common aubrieta)
Bergenia crassifolia
Chrysanthemum morifolium (florists' chrysanthemum
Dianthus (pink)
Digitalis purpurea (foxglove)
Hesperis matronalis (sweet rocket)
Hosta plantaginea (plantain lily)
Iris dochotoma (vesper iris)
Paeonia (peony)
Pelargonium domesticum (Lady Washington geranium)
Phlox subulata (moss pink)
Primula malacoides (fairy primrose)
Primula polyantha (polyanthus)
Tulbaghia fragrans
Valeriana officinalis (common valerian)
Vinca minor (common periwinkle)
Viola cornuta (tufted viola)

Violet

Anemone pulsatilla (prairie windflower, pasque flower)
Delphinium hybrid (Connecticut Yankee and Pacific Giant)
Epinedium grandiflorum (bishop's hat)
Gentiana asclepiadea (willow gentian)
Iris kaempferi (Japanese iris)

Lilac

Acanthus mollis (Grecian urn)
Althaea rosea (hollyhock)

Purple-Lavender

Bergenia crassifolia

Purple-Violet

Aquilegia (columbine)
Aster novae-angliae (New England aster)
Aubrieta deltoidea (common aubrieta)
Chrysanthemum morifolium (florists' chrysanthemum
Dianthus (pink)
Digitalis purpurea (foxglove)
Heliotropium arborescens (heliotrope)
Helleborus niger (Christmas rose)

Pelargonium domesticum (Lady Washington geranium)
Platycodon grandiflorum (balloonflower)
Primula polyantha (polyanthus)
Viola cornuta (tufted viola)
Viola odorata (sweet violet)

Purple

Althaea rosea (hollyhock)
Armeria maritima (sea-pink or thrift)
Iris kaempferi (Japanese iris)
Liatris pycnostacha (gayfeather)
Lupinus polyphyllus (lupine)
Lythrum (loosetrife)
Phlox paniculata (summer phlox)
Scabiosa caucasica (pincushion flower)

Red-Purple

Callirhoë involucrata (poppy mallow)
Lathyrus grandiflorus (everlasting pea)
Lathyrus latifolius (perennial pea)

Red

Althaea rosea (hollyhock)
Anemone hupehensis japonica (Japanese anemone)
Aquilegia (columbine)
Aster
Astilbe (various) (meadowsweet)
Aubrieta deltoidea (common aubrieta)
Digitalis purpurea (foxglove)
Epimedium grandiflorum (bishop's hat)
Gaillardia grandiflora (blanket flower)
Geranium grandiflorum (cranesbill)
Hemerocallis (daylily)
Heuchera sanguinea (coral bells)
Iris kaempferi (Japanese iris)
Kniphofia (various) (torch lily)
Lobelia cardinalis (cardinal flower)
Lupinus polyphyllus (lupine)
Monarda didyma (bee balm)
Paeonia (peony)
Papaver nudicaule (Iceland poppy)
Papaver orientale (Oriental poppy)
Pelargonium domesticum (Lady Washington geranium)
Penstemon (various) (beard tongue)
Phlox paniculata (summer phlox)
Phlox subulata (moss pink)
Primula malacoides (fairy primrose)
Primula polyantha (polyanthus)
Saxifraga (saxifrage)
Sedum spectabile (stonecrop)
Senecio (cineraria)
Viola cornuta (tufted viola)

Rose

Acanthus mollis (Grecian urn)
Althaea rosea (hollyhock)

Bellis perennis (English daisy)
Bergenia cordifolia (heartleaf bergenia)
Bergenia crassifolia
Dianthus deltoides (maiden pink)
Dianthus plumarius (grass pink)
Dicentra spectabilis (bleeding heart)
Hibiscus moscheutos (swamp rose mallow)
Iris kaempferi (Japanese iris)
Lythrum (various) (loosestrife)
Phlox paniculata (summer phlox)
Physostegia virginiana (false dragonhead)

Pink

Althaea rosea (hollyhock)
Anemone hupehensis japonica (Japanese anemone)
Anemonella thalictroides (rue anemone)
Aquilegia (columbine)
Armeria maritima (sea-pink or thrift)
Aster
Astilbe (various) (meadowsweet)
Aubrieta deltoidea (common aubrieta)
Bellis perennis (English daisy)
Campanula carpatica (bellflower)
Chrysanthemum coccineum (painted daisy)
Dianthus barbatus (sweet William)
Dianthus deltoides (maiden pink)
Dianthus plumarius (grass pink)
Dicentra spectabilis (bleeding heart)
Digitalis purpurea (foxglove)
Heleborus niger (Christmas rose)
Hemerocallis (daylily)
Heuchera sanguinea (coral bells)
Iris (bearded iris)
Iris kaempferi (Japanese iris)
Limonium latifolium (statice, sea lavender)
Lupinus polyphyllus (lupine)
Monarda didyma (bee balm)
Paeonia (peony)
Papaver nudicaule (Iceland poppy)
Papaver orientale (Oriental poppy)
Pelargonium domesticum (Lady Washington geranium)
Penstemon (various) (beard tongue)
Phlox divaricata (sweet William phlox)
Phlox paniculata (summer phlox)
Phlox subulata (moss pink)
Platycodon grandiflorum (balloonflower)
Primula malacoides (fairy primrose)
Primula polyantha (polyanthus)
Rudbeckia hirta (coneflower)
Saxifraga (saxifrage)
Sedum spectabile
Senecio (cineraria)
Tulbaghia fragrans
Veronica (speedwell)
Viola odorata (sweet violet)

Salmon

Papaver orientale (Oriental poppy)

Orange

Althaea rosea (hollyhock)
Asclepias incarnata (swamp milkweed)
Asclepias tuberosa (butterfly weed)
Chrysanthemum morifolium (florists' chrysanthemum)
Dianthus (pink)
Erysimum asperum (Siberian wallflower)
Gazania hybrids
Geum chiloense (coccineum) (geum)
Helenium (Helen's flower)
Heliopsis (various) (orange sunflower)
Hemerocallis (various) (daylily)
Kniphofia (torch lily)
Linaria vulgaris (toadflax)
Papaver nudicaule (Iceland poppy)
Papaver orientale (Oriental poppy)
Penstemon (various) (beard tongue)
Phlox paniculata (summer phlox)
Primula polyantha (polyanthus)
Rudbeckia hirta (coneflower)
Strelitzia reginae (bird of paradise)
Viola cornuta (tufted viola)

Yellow

Achillea tomentosa (woolly yarrow)
Aconitum anthora (monkshood)
Althaea rosea (hollyhock)
Alyssum saxatile (alyssum or basket of gold)
Anthemis nobilis (chamomile)
Anthemis tinctoria (golden marguerite)
Aquilegia chrysantha (golden columbine)
Artemisia abrotanum (southernwood)
Caltha palustris (marsh marigold)
Centaurea gymnocarpa (dusty miller)
Chrysanthemum morifolium (florists' chrysanthemum)
Coreopsis grandiflora (tickseed)
Dianthus (pink)
Digitalis purpurea (foxglove)
Gaillardia grandiflora (blanket flower)
Gazania hybrids
Geum chiloense (coccineum) (geum)
Helenium (Helen's flower)
Helianthus decapetalus multiflorus (sunflower)
Heliopsis (various) (orange sunflower)
Hemerocallis (various) (daylily)
Hypericum (Saint-Johns-wort)
Kniphofia (torch lily)
Oenothera (various) (evening primrose)
Paeonia (various) (peony)
Papaver nudicaule (Iceland poppy)
Primula polyantha (polyanthus)
Rudbeckia hirta (coneflower)

Saxifraga (saxifrage)
Solidago (various) (goldenrod)
Viola cornuta (tufted viola)

Annuals
White

Ageratum houstonianum (floss flower)
Antirrhinum majus (snapdragon)
Arctotis stoechadifolia grandis (African daisy)
Begonia semperflorens (wax begonia)
Brachycome iberidifolia (Swan River daisy)
Browallia americana (browallia)
Calendula officinalis (calendula or pot marigold)
Callistephus chinensis (aster or China aster)
Campanula medium (Canterbury bell)
Catharanthus roseus (Vinca rosea) (Madagascar periwinkle)
Centaurea cyanus (bachelor's button, or cornflower)
Centaurea imperialis (royal sweet sultan)
Chrysanthemum
Clarkia amoena (farewell-to-spring)
Clarkia elegans (Clarkia)
Clarkia unguiculata (mountain garland)
Cleome spinosa (spider flower)
Cosmos bipannatus (cosmos)
Delphinium ajacis (larkspur)
Dianthus species (pinks)
Dimorphotheca sinuata (Cape marigold or African daisy)
Echium
Euphorbia marginata (snow-on-the-mountain)
Gomphrena globosa (globe-amaranth)
Gypsophila elegans (baby's breath)
Helichrysum bracteatum (strawflower)
Iberis amara (rocket candytuft)
Iberis umbellata (globe candytuft)
Impatiens balsamina (balsam)
Ipomea purpurea (morning glory)
Lathyrus odoratus (sweet pea, summer)
Limonium bonduellii (statice, sea lavender)
Lobelia erinus (lobelia)
Lobularia maritima (sweet alyssum)
Lupinus mutabilis (lupine)
Mathiola incana (stock)
Mirabilis jalapa (four-o'-clock)
Nemesia strumosa (nemesia)
Nicotiana alata
Nicotiana sanderae (flowering tobacco)
Nicotiana sylvestris
Nigella damascena (love-in-a-mist)
Oenothera biennis (evening primrose)
Papaver nudicaule (Iceland poppy)
Papaver rhoeas (Shirley poppy)
Petunia hybrids
Phlox drummondii (annual phlox)
Physalis alkekengi (Chinese lantern)
Portulaca grandiflora (rose moss)

Primula malacoides (fairy primrose)
Scabiosa atropurpurea (pincushion flower)
Schizanthus pinnatus (butterfly flower)
Senecio elegans (purple ragwort)
Tropaeolum majus (nasturtium)
Verbena hybrida (*hortensis*) (garden verbena)
Viola tricolor hortensis (pansy)
Zinnia angustifolia (Mexican zinnia)
Zinnia elegans (small-flowered zinnia)
Zinnia elegans (giant-flowered zinnia)

Blue

Ageratum houstonianum (flossflower)
Browallia americana (browallia)
Callistephus chinensis (aster or China aster)
Campanula medium (Canterbury bell)
Centaurea cyanus (bachelor's button or cornflower)
Convolvulus tricolor (dwarf morning glory)
Cosmos
Delphinium ajacis (larkspur)
Echium
Ipomoea purpurea (morning glory)
Limonium bonduellii (statice, sea lavender)
Linaria maroccana (baby snapdragon)
Lobelia erinus (lobelia)
Mathiola incana (stock)
Myosotis sylvatica (forget-me-not)
Nemesia strumosa (nemesia)
Nierembergia caerulea (blue cupflower)
Nigella damascena (love-in-a-mist)
Papaver rhoeas (Shirley poppy)
Salvia (sage)
Scabiosa atropurpurea (pincushion flower)
Trachymene caerulea (blue lace flower)
Verbena hybrids
Viola tricolor hortensis (pansy)
Zinnia elegans (giant-flowered zinnia)

Lavender

Callistephus chinensis (aster or China aster)
Centaurea cyanus (bachelor's button or cornflower)
Clarkia elegans (Clarkia)
Delphinium ajacis (larkspur)
Dianthus chinensis (China pink)
Limonium bonduellii (statice, sea lavender)
Lobularia maritima (sweet alyssum)
Zinnia elegans (small-flowered zinnia)

Violet

Antirrhinum majus (snapdragon)
Gomphrena globosa (globe-amaranth)
Ipomoea purpurea (morning glory)
Lobelia erinus (lobelia)
Trachymene caerulea (blue lace flower)
Zinnia elegans (giant-flowered zinnia)

Mauve

Impatiens
Schizanthus pinnatus (butterfly flower)

Lilac

Browallia speciosa major (browallia)
Cosmos
Iberis umbellata (globe candytuft)
Lathyrus odoratus (sweet pea, summer)
Lupinus (lupine)
Mathiola bicornus (night-scented stock)
Mathiola incana (stock)
Petunia hybrids
Phlox drummondii (annual phlox)

Purple

Antirrhinum majus (snapdragon)
Browallia americana (browallia)
Browallia speciosa major
Dianthus chinensis (China pink)
Echium
Impatiens
Ipomoea purpurea (morning glory)
Lathyrus odoratus (sweet pea, summer)
Linaria maroccana (baby snapdragon)
Lobularia maritima (sweet alyssum)
Lupinus (lupine)
Mathiola bicornus (night-scented stock)
Mathiola incana (stock)
Nemesia strumosa (nemesia)
Petunia hybrids
Phlox drummondii (annual phlox)
Salpiglossis sinuata (painted tongue)
Scabiosa atropurpurea (pincushion flower)
Schizanthus pinnatus (butterfly flower)
Senecio elegans (purple ragwort)
Verbena hybrids
Viola tricolor hortensis (pansy)
Zinnia elegans (giant-flowered zinnia)

Magenta

Impatiens

Wine

Centaurea cyanus (bachelor's button or cornflower)
Gaillardia pulchella (rose-ring Gaillardia)

Maroon

Coreopsis tinctoria (calliopsis)
Gaillardia pulchella (rose-ring Gaillardia)
Tropaeolum majus (nasturtium)
Zinnia angustifolia (Mexican zinnia)

Carmine

Delphinium ajacis (larkspur)

Scarlet

Linum grandiflorum 'Rubrum' (scarlet flax)
Salvia splendens (scarlet sage)
Verbena hybrida (*hortensis*) (garden verbena)
Zinnia elegans (small-flowered zinnia, giant-flowered zinnia)

Crimson

Amaranthus caudatus (love-lies-bleeding)
Gomphrenia globosa (globe-amaranth)
Linaria maroccana (baby snapdragon)
Mathiola incana (stock)
Nicotiana
Papaver rhoeas (Shirley poppy)
Portulaca grandiflora (rose moss)
Tropaeolum majus (nasturtium)

Red

Antirrhinum majus (snapdragon)
Brachycome iberidifolia (Swan River daisy)
Callistephus chinensis (aster or China aster)
Convolvulus
Helichrysum bracteatum (strawflower)
Impatiens balsamina (balsam)
Ipomoea purpurea (morning glory)
Mirabilis jalapa (four-o'clock)
Papaver glaucum (tulip poppy)
Primula malacoides (fairy primrose)
Salpiglossis sinuata (painted tongue)

Rose

Begonia semperflorens (wax begonia)
Centaurea moschata (sweet sultan)
Clarkia amoena (farewell-to-spring)
Clarkia elegans (Clarkia)
Cosmos bipannatus (cosmos)
Delphinium ajacis (larkspur)
Dianthus barbatus (sweet William)
Eschscholzia californica (California poppy)
Gypsophila elegans (baby's breath)
Iberis umbellata (globe candytuft)
Impatiens balsamina (balsam)
Lathyrus odoratus (sweet pea, summer)
Limonium bonduellii (statice, sea lavender)
Linum grandiflorum 'Rubrum' (scarlet flax)
Lobularia maritima (sweet alyssum)
Mathiola incana (stock)
Nemesia strumosa (nemesia)
Nigella damascena (love-in-a-mist)
Oenothera biennis (evening primrose)
Petunia hybrids
Phlox drummondii (annual phlox)
Polygonum orientale (princess feather)
Primula malacoides (fairy primrose)
Salvia splendens (scarlet sage)
Scabiosa atropurpurea (pincushion flower)
Schizanthus pinnatus (butterfly flower)
Senecio elegans (purple ragwort)
Viola tricolor hortensis (pansy)

Pink

Ageratum houstonianum (flossflower)
Antirrhinum majus (snapdragon)
Begonia semperflorens (wax begonia)

Callistephus chinensis (China aster)
Campanula (Canterbury bell)
Catharanthus roseus (Vinca rosea)
    (Madagascar periwinkle)
Celosia 'Plumosa' (plume cockscomb)
Centaurea cyanus (bachelor's button or cornflower)
Clarkia elegans (Clarkia)
Cleome spinosa (spider flower)
Cosmos bipinnatus (cosmos)
Cryophytum crystallinum (ice plant)
Delphinium ajacis (larkspur)
Dianthus chinensis (China pink)
Eschscholzia californica (California poppy)
Gypsophila elegans (baby's breath)
Helichrysum bracteatum (strawflower)
Iberis umbellata (globe candytuft)
Impatiens balsamina (balsam)
Ipomoea purpurea (morning glory)
Lathyrus odoratus (sweet pea, summer)
Linaria maroccana (baby snapdragon)
Lobelia erinus (lobelia)
Lupinus hartwegii (lupine, annual)
Mathiola incana (stock)
Mirabilis jalapa (four-o'-clock)
Myosotis sylvatica (forget-me-not)
Nemesia strumosa (nemesia)
Papaver rhoeas (Shirley poppy)
Petunia hybrids
Polygonum orientale (princess feather)
Primula malacoides (fairy primrose)
Salpiglossis sinuata (painted tongue)
Salvia splendens (scarlet sage)
Tropaeolum majus (nasturtium)
Verbena hybrida (*hortensis*) (garden verbena)

Salmon

Delphinium ajacis (larkspur)
Dimorphoteca sinuata (African daisy, Cape
    marigold)
Iberis umbellata (globe candytuft)
Papaver rhoeas (Shirley poppy)

Orange

Antirrhinum majus (snapdragon)
Calendula officinalis (calendula or pot marigold)
Chrysanthemum
Clarkia
Coreopsis tinctoria (calliopsis)
Dimorphoteca sinuata (African daisy, Cape
    marigold)
Eschscholzia californica (California poppy)
Gerbera jamesonii (Transvaal daisy)
Nemesia strumosa (nemesia)
Papaver rhoeas (Shirley poppy)
Portulaca grandiflora (rose moss)
Salpiglossis sinuata (painted tongue)
Tithonia rotundifolia (Mexican sunflower)

Viola tricolor hortensis (pansy)
Zinnia angustifolia (Mexican zinnia)
Zinnia elegans (small-flowered zinnia, giant-flowered
    zinnia)
Tagetes (marigold)

Bronze
Chrysanthemum

Gold

Calendula officinalis (calendula or pot marigold)
Celosia 'Plumosa' (plume cockscomb)
Eschscholzia californica (California poppy)
Gomphrena globosa (globe-amaranth)
Helianthus annuus (sunflower)
Tagetes (marigold)

Yellow

Antirrhinum majus (snapdragon)
Calendula officinalis (calendula or pot marigold)
Callistephus chinensis (aster or China aster)
Celosia 'Plumosa' (plume cockscomb)
Centaurea moschata (sweet sultan)
Chrysanthemum
Clarkia
Coreopsis tinctoria (calliopsis)
Cosmos sulphureus (yellow cosmos)
Dimorphoteca sinuata (African daisy, Cape
    marigold)
Eschscholzia californica (California poppy)
Gaillardia pulchella (rose-ring Gaillardia)
Gerbera jamesonii (Transvaal daisy)
Limonium sinuatum (statice, sea lavender)
Linaria maroccana (baby snapdragon)
Lupinus mutabilis (lupine)
Lupinus luteus (yellow lupine)
Mathiola incana (stock)
Mirabalis jalapa (four-o'-clock)
Nemesia strumosa (nemesia)
Oenothera biennis (evening primrose)
Portulaca grandiflora (rose moss)
Reseda odorata (mignonette)
Rudbeckia bicolor (coneflower)
Salpiglossis sinuata (painted tongue)
Tagetes (marigold)
Thunbergia alata (clockvine)
Tropaeolum majus (nasturtium)
Viola tricolor hortensis (pansy)
Zinnia angustifolia (Mexican zinnia)
Zinnia elegans (small-flowered zinnia)
Zinnia elegans (giant-flowered zinnia)

Bulbs
White

Acidanthera
Agapanthus (flower-of-the-Nile)
Anenome coronaria (poppy-flowered anemone)
Begonia (tuberous)

Calochortus (mariposa lily)
Camassia (camas)
Canna
Chionodoxa (glory of snow)
Colchicum autumnale (autumn crocus)
Crocus
Cyclamen (hardy)
Dahlia
Erythronium (dogtooth violet)
Freesia
Frittilaria
Galanthus
Gladiolus (gladiola)
Hemerocallis (daylily)
Hippeastrum (amaryllis)
Hyacinthus orientalis (common hyacinth)
Iris (bearded iris)
Iris tingitana (Dutch iris)
Lilium (lily)
Lycoris
Muscari (grape hyacinth)
Narcissus
Scilla hispanica (Spanish bluebell)
Sparaxis tricolor (wand flower)
Tulipa (tulip)
Watsonia
Zantedeschia (calla)
Zephyranthes (zephyr lily)

Blue

Agapanthus (flower-of-the-Nile)
Anenome coronaria (poppy-flowered anemone)
Calochortus (mariposa lily)
Camassia (camas)
Chionodoxa (glory of snow)
Crocus
Freesia
Hyacinthus orientalis (common hyacinth)
Iris (bearded iris)
Iris tingitana (Dutch iris)
Muscari (grape hyacinth)
Scilla hispanica (Spanish bluebell)
Sparaxis tricolor (wand flower)

Lavender

Anenome coronaria (poppy-flowered anemone)
Calochortus (mariposa lily)
Colchicum autumnale (autumn crocus)
Crocus
Dahlia
Erythronium (dogtooth violet)
Freesia
Gladiolus (gladiola)
Hyacinthus orientalis (common hyacinth)
Iris (bearded iris)
Iris kaempferi (Japanese iris)
Iris tingitana (Dutch iris)

Lilium (lily)
Muscari (grape hyacinth)
Sparaxis tricolor (wand flower)
Tulipa (tulip)

Violet, Purple

Agapanthus (flower-of-the-Nile)
Anemone coronaria (poppy-flowered anemone)
Calochortus (mariposa lily)
Colchicum autumnale (autumn crocus)
Crocus
Dahlia
Erythronium (dogtooth violet)
Freesia
Frittilaria
Gladiolus (gladiola)
Hyacinthus orientalis (common hyacinth)
Iris (bearded iris)
Iris kaempferi (Japanese iris)
Iris tingitana (Dutch iris)
Lilium (lily)
Muscari (grape hyacinth)
Scilla hispanica (Spanish bluebell)
Sparaxis tricolor (wand flower)

Red

Anemone coronaria (poppy-flowered anemone)
Begonia (tuberous)
Canna
Cyclamen (hardy)
Dahlia
Eremurus (desert candle)
Freesia
Frittilaria
Gladiolus (gladiola)
Hemerocallis (daylily)
Hyacinthus orientalis (common hyacinth)
Iris (bearded iris)
Iris kaempferi (Japanese iris)
Lilium (lily)
Lycoris radiata
Ranunculus asiaticus (turban buttercup)
Sparaxis tricolor (wand flower)
Tigrida (tiger flower)
Tulipa (tulip)
Watsonia
Zantedeschia (calla)
Zephryanthes (zephyr lily)

Pink

Amaryllis belladonna (belladonna lily)
Anenome coronoria (poppy-flowered anemone)
Begonia (tuberous)
Canna
Colchicum autumnale (autumn crocus)
Crocus
Cyclamen (hardy)
Dahlia

Erythronium (dogtooth violet)
Freesia
Gladiolus (gladiola)
Hemerocallis (daylily)
Hippeastrum (amaryllis)
Hyacinthus orientalis (common hyacinth)
Iris (bearded iris)
Iris kaempferi (Japanese iris)
Lilium (lily)
Lycoris squamigera
Ranunculus asiaticus (turban buttercup)
Scilla hispanica (Spanish bluebell)
Tigrida pavonia (tiger flower)
Tulipa (tulip)
Watsonia
Zantedeschia rehmanni (pink calla)
Zephyryathes (zephyr lily)

Orange

Begonia (tuberous)
Canna
Clivia miniata (Kaffir lily)
Dahlia
Freesia
Fritillaria
Gladiolus (gladiola)
Hemerocallis (daylily)
Hippeastrum (amaryllis)
Hyacinthus orientalis (common hyacinth)
Iris (bearded iris)
Iris tingitana (Dutch iris)
Lilium (lily)
Narcissus
Ranunculus asiaticus (turban buttercup)
Tigridia pavonia (tiger flower)
Tulipa (tulip)
Zantedeschia (calla)

Yellow

Begonia (tuberous)
Calochortus (mariposa lily)
Canna
Clivia miniata (Kaffir lily)
Crocus
Dahlia
Eranthis (winter aconite)
Eremurus (desert candle)
Erythronium (dogtooth violet)
Freesia
Frittilaria
Gladiolus (gladiola)
Hemerocallis (daylily)
Hyacinthus orientalis (common hyacinth)
Iris (bearded iris)
Iris tingitana (Dutch iris)
Lilium (lily)

Lycoris
Narcissus
Ranunculus asiaticus (turban buttercup)
Sparaxis tricolor (wand flower)
Sternbergia lutea
Tulipa (tulip)
Zantedeschia (calla)
Zantsdeschia ellottiana (golden calla)

Rock Garden Plants

White

Achillea (silver Alpine yarrow)
Arabis albida (wall rock cress)
Arabis alpina (mountain rock cress)
Arenaria grandiflora (showy sandwort)
Cerastium tomentosum (snow-in-summer)
Claytonia caroliniana (spring beauty)
Convallaria majalis (lily-of-the-valley)
Helleborus niger (Christmas rose)
Iberis sempervirens (evergreen candytuft)
Potentilla fruticosa (cinquefoil)
Saxifraga (saxifrage)
Sedum album (stonecrop)
Silene maritima (catchfly)

Blue

Ajuga reptans (carpet bugle)
Campanula carpatica (bellflower)
Centaurea montana (mountain bluet)
Gentiana acaulis (stemless gentian)
Iris cristata (crested iris)
Iris pumila (dwarf bearded iris)
Linum alpinum (Alpine flax)
Linum Lewisii (prairie flax)
Linum perenne (blue flax)
Lithodora diffusa
Myosotis sylvatica (forget-me-not)
Phlox divaricata (sweet William phlox)
Phlox subulata (moss pink)
Platycodon grandiflorum (balloonflower)
Plumbago (leadwort)
Veronica rupestris (creeping speedwell)

Lilac

Campanula carpatica (bellflower)
Campanula rotundifolia (harebell)
Iris cristata (crested iris)
Iris pumila (dwarf bearded iris)
Phlox divaricata (sweet William phlox)
Viola cornuta (tufted viola)

Purple

Anemone pulsatilla (pasque flower)
Aster alpinus (rock aster)
Aubrieta deltoidea (common aubrieta)
Platycodon grandiflorum (balloonflower)

Carmine

Dianthus deltoides (maiden pink)
Phlox stolonifera (creeping phlox)

Red

Aquilegia caerula (Colorado columbine)
Aquilegia canadensis (American columbine)
Epimedium rubrum
Hypericum repens (Saint-Johns-wort)
Sempervivum tectorum (houseleek)

Rose

Claytonia caroliniana (spring beauty)
Dianthus plumarius (grass pink)
Dicentra spectabilis (bleeding heart)
Helleborus niger (Christmas rose)
Heuchera sanguinea (coral bells)
Sedum stoloniferum (stonecrop)

Pink

Geranium grandifolium (cranesbill)
Gypsophila repens (creeping baby's breath)
Phlox subulata (moss pink)
Saxifraga (saxifrage)
Sedum album (stonecrop)
Sedum sieboldii

Yellow

Achillea tomentosa (woolly yarrow)
Alyssum saxatile (alyssum or basket of gold)
Alyssum saxatile compactum (dwarf goldentuft)
Alyssum argenteum (silver alyssum)
Aster alpinus (rock aster)
Draba olympica
Hypericum repens (Saint-Johns-wort)
Iris pumila (dwarf bearded iris)
Sedum acre (stonecrop)
Sedum sarmentosum
Sempervivum tectorum (houseleek)

By Common Name

Trees

Aleppo pine (*Pinus halepensis*)
Almond (*Prunus amygdalus*)
American arborvitae (*Thuja occidentalis*)
American ash (*Fraxinus americana*)
American beech (*Fagus grandifolia*)
American elm (*Ulmus americana*)
American hornbeam (*Carpinus caroliniana*)
American linden (*Tilia americana*)
Amur maple (*Acer ginnala*)
Anise magnolia (*Magnolia salicifolia*)
Arizona ash (*Fraxinus velutina*)
Arnold crab apple (*Malus arnoldiana*)
Arnold hawthorn (*Crataegus arnoldiana*)
Atlas cedar (*Cedrus atlantica*)
Australian tea tree (*Leptospermum laevigatum*)

Austrian black pine (*Pinus nigra*)
Austrian pine (*Pinus nigra*)
Bailey acacia (*Acacia baileyana*)
Balsam fir (*Abies balsamea*)
Big-leaf magnolia (*Magnolia macrophylla*)
Big-leaf maple (*Acer macrophyllum*)
Black alder (*Alnus glutinosa*)
Black cherry (*Prunus serotina*)
Black locust (*Robinia pseudoacacia*)
Blue gum (*Eucalyptus globulus*)
Box elder (*Acer negundo*)
Bristlecone pine (*Pinus aristata*)
Buttonwood (*Platanus occidentalis*)
California black oak (*Quercus kelloggii*)
California laurel (*Umbellularea californica*)
California live oak (*Quercus agrifolia*)
Camphor tree (*Cinnamomum camphora*)
Canary Island pine (*Pinus canariensis*)
Canoe birch (*Betula papyrifera*)
Carmine crab apple (*Malus atrosanguinea*)
Carolina hemlock (*Tsuga caroliniana*)
Carolina laurel cherry (*Prunus caroliniana*)
Carolina poplar (*Populus canadensis* 'Eugenei')
Catalina cherry (*Prunus lyonii*)
Cedar of Lebanon (*Cedrus libani*)
Chinese chestnut (*Castanea mollissima*)
Chinese elm (*Ulmus parvifolia*)
Chinese flame tree (*Koelrenteria henryi*)
Chinese juniper (*Juniperus chinensis*)
Chinese paper birch (*Betula albo-sinensis*)
Cider gum (*Eucalyptus gunnii*)
Cluster pine (*Pinus pinaster*)
Coast live oak (*Quercus agrifolia*)
Colorado spruce (*Picea pungens*)
Common alder (*Alnus incana*)
Common olive (*Olea europaea*)
Cork oak (*Quercus suber*)
Cornelian cherry (*Cornus mas*)
Crape myrtle (*Lagerstroemia indica*)
Cryptomeria (*Cryptomeria japonica*)
Cucumber tree (*Magnolia acuminata*)
David maple (*Acer davidii*)
Deodar cedar (*Cedrus deodara*)
Dogwood (*Cornus florida*)
Douglas fir (*Pseudotsuga taxifolia*)
Downy hawthorn (*Crataegus mollis*)
Eastern redbud (*Cercis canadensis*)
Eastern red cedar (*Juniperus virginiana*)
Eastern white pine (*Pinus strobus*)
English hawthorn (*Crataegus oxyacantha*)
English oak (*Quercus robur*)
English yew (*Taxus baccata*)
European ash (*Fraxinus excelsior*)
European beech (*Fagus sylvatica*)
European larch (*Larix decidua*)
European white birch (*Betula verrucosa* [*pendula*])
Evergreen magnolia (*Magnolia grandiflora*)

False cypress (*Chamaecyparis pisifera*)
Fern pine (*Podocarpus gracilior*)
Flowering almond (*Prunus triloba*)
Flowering ash (*Fraxinus ornus*)
Flowering dogwood (*Cornus florida*)
Formosan sweet gum (*Liquidasubar formosana*)
Fragrant snowball (*Styrax obassia*)
Franklinia (*Franklinia alatamaka*)
French pussy willow (*Salix caprea*)
Fringe tree (*Chionanthus virginica*)
Full-moon maple (*Acer japonicum*)
Giant arborvitae (*Thuja plicata*)
Gingko tree (*Gingko biloba*)
Glossy hawthorn (*Crataegus nitida*)
Goldenchain tree (*Laburnum watereri*)
Goldenrain tree (*Koelreuteria paniculata*)
Gray birch (*Betula populifolia*)
Green ash (*Fraxinus pennsylvanica lanceolata*)
Green wattle (*Acacia decurrens*)
Hackberry (*Celtis occidentalis*)
Hankow willow (*Salix matsudana*)
Hinoki cypress (*Chamaecyparis obtusa*)
Holly oak (*Quercus ilex*)
Honey locust (*Gleditsia triacanthos*)
Italian laurel fig (*Ficus retusa nitida*)
Italian stone pine (*Pinus pinea*)
Jack pine (*Pinus banksiana*)
Japanese black pine (*Pinus thunbergii*)
Japanese dogwood (*Cornus kousa*)
Japanese flowering cherry (*Prunus serrulata*)
Japanese flowering crab apple (*Malus floribunda*)
Japanese hemlock (*Tsuga diversifolia*)
Japanese maple (*Acer palmatum*)
Japanese pagoda tree (*Sophora japonica*)
Japanese red pine (*Pinus densiflora*)
Japanese snowball (*Styrax japonica*)
Japanese white pine (*Pinus parviflora*)
Japanese yew (*Taxus cuspidata*)
Japanese zelkova (*Zelkova serrata*)
Judas tree (*Cercis siliquastrum*)
Kangaroo thorn (*Acacia armata*)
Katsura tree (*Cercidiphyllum japonicum*)
Kobus magnolia (*Magnolia kobus*)
Korean fir (*Abies koreana*)
Korean stewartia (*Stewartia koreana*)
Lacebark pine (*Pinus bungeana*)
Large Chinese hawthorn (*Crataegus pinnatifida major*)
Laurel (*Lauris nobilis*)
Laurel oak (*Quercus laurifolia*)
Lavalle hawthorn (*Crataegus lavallei*)
Lily-of-the-valley clethra (*Clethra arborea*)
Little-leaf linden (*Tilia cordata*)
Loquat (*Eriobotrya japonica*)
Maidenhair tree (*Gingko biloba*)
Mountain ash (*Sorbus aucuparia*)
Mountain ebony (*Bauhinia variegata*)

Mountain maple (*Acer spicatum*)
Norway maple (*Acer platanoides*)
Norway spruce (*Picea abies*)
Ohio buckeye (*Aesculus glabra*)
Orchid tree (*Bauhinia blakeana*)
Oregon maple (*Acer macrophylla*)
Pacific dogwood (*Cornus nuttallii*)
Pecan (*Carya illinoinensis*)
Persimmon (*Diospyros virginiana*)
Pignut (*Carya glabra*)
Pine (*Pinus*)
Pineapple guava (*Feijoa sellowiana*)
Pin oak (*Quercus palustris*)
Plane tree (*Plantanus acerifolia*)
Plume albizzia (*Albizzia distachya*)
Ponderosa pine (*Pinus ponderosa*)
Red cap gum (*Eucalyptus erythocorys*)
Red cedar juniper (*Juniperus virginiana*)
Red fir (*Abies magnifica*)
Red gum (*Eucalyptus camaldulensis*)
Red horse chestnut (*Aesculus carnea*)
Red maple (*Acer rubrum*)
Red oak (*Quercus rubra*)
Red pine (*Pinus resinosa*)
River birch (*Betula nigra*)
Rocky Mountain juniper (*Juniperus scopulorum*)
Russian olive (*Elaeagnus angustifolia*)
Sargent cherry (*Prunus sargentii*)
Sargent crab apple (*Malus sargentii*)
Saucer magnolia (*Magnolia soulangeana*)
Sawara false cypress (*Chamaecypares pisifira*)
Scarlet oak (*Quercus coccinea*)
Scotch pine (*Pinus sylvestris*)
Shagbark hickory (*Carya ovata*)
Sharp-leaf jacaranda (*Jacaranda acutifolia*)
Shingle oak (*Quercus imbricaria*)
Siberian crab apple (*Malus baccata*)
Silk tree (*Albizzia julibrissin*)
Silver dollar gum (*Eucalyptus polyanthemos*)
Silver linden (*Tilia tomentosa*)
Single seed hawthorn (*Crataegus monogyna*)
Sitka spruce (*Picea sitchensis*)
Smoke tree (*Cotinus americanus*)
Sour cherry (*Prunus cerasus*)
Southern magnolia (*Magnolia grandiflora*)
Star magnolia (*Magnolia stellata*)
Sugar maple (*Acer saccharum*)
Sugar pine (*Pinus lambertiana*)
Sweet gum (*Liquidambar styraciflua*)
Sweet honey locust (*Gleditsia triacanthos*)
Swiss mountain pine (*Pinus mugo*)
Sycamore maple (*Acer tataricum*)
Sydney golden wattle (*Acacia longifolia floribunda*)
Tatarian dogwood (*Cornus alba*)
Tatarian maple (*Acer tataricum*)
Tree of heaven (*Ailanthus altissima*)
Trident maple (*Acer buergerianum*)

Tulip tree (*Liriodendron tulipifera*)
Veitch fir (*Abies veitchii*)
Vine maple (*Acer circinatum*)
Washington hawthorn (*Crataegus phaenopyrum*)
Water locust (*Gleditsia aquatica*)
Weeping acacia (*Acacia pendula*)
Weeping willow (*Salix babylonica*)
Western catalpa (*Catalpa speciosa*)
Western hemlock (*Tsuga heterophylla*)
White ash (*Fraxinous americana*)
White fir (*Abies concolor*)
White ironbark (*Eucalyptus leucoxylon* 'Rosea')
White mulberry (*Morus alba*)
White oak (*Quercus alba*)
White poplar (*Populus alba*)
White spruce (*Picea glauca*)
White willow (*Salix alba*)
Yate tree (*Eucalyptus cornuta*)
Yew pine (*Podocarpus macrophylla*)
Yulan magnolia (*Magnolia denudata*)

Shrubs

Abelia (*Abelia grandiflora*)
Alder buckthorn (*Rhamnus frangula*)
Alpine currant (*Ribes alpinum*)
American cranberry bush (*Viburnum trilobum*)
American elder (*Sambucus canadensis*)
Amur honeysuckle (*Lonicera maackii*)
Amur privet (*Ligustrum amurense*)
Andromeda (*Pieris floribunda*)
Arrowwood (*Viburnum dentatum*)
Athel tree (*Tamarix aphylla*)
Aucuba (*Aucuba japonica*)
Banks rose (*Rosa banksiae*)
Bearberry (*Arctostaphylos uva-ursi*)
Bearberry cotoneaster (*Cotoneaster dammeri*)
Beauty bush (*Kolkwitzia amabilis*)
Bellflower (*Enkianthus campanulatus*)
Black barberry (*Berberis gagnepainii*)
Black haw (*Viburnum prunifolium*)
Blue blossom (*Ceanothus thyrsiflorus*)
Bog rosemary (*Andromeda polifolia*)
Border forsythia (*Forsythia intermedia*)
Border privet (*Ligustrum obtusifolium*)
Bottlebrush (*Callistemon citrinus*)
Box honeysuckle (*Lonicera nitida*)
Bridal wreath spirea (*Spiraea vulgaris*)
Broadleaf euonymus (*Euonymus latifolius*)
Broom (*Cytisus hirsutum*)
Buttercup shrub (*Potentilla fruticosa*)
Butterfly bush (*Buddleia davidii*)
Buttonbush (*Cephalanthus occidentalis*)
Cabbage rose (*Rosa centifolia*)
California mock orange (*Carpenteria californica*)
California privet (*Ligustrum ovalifolium*)
Cape jasmine (*Gardenia jasminoides*)
Carolina jasmine (*Gelsemium sempervirens*)

Carolina rhododendron (*Rhododendron carolinianum*)
Chaste tree (*Vitex agnus-castus*)
Cherry elaeagnus (*Elaeagnus multiflorus*)
China rose (*Rosa chinensis*)
Chinese hibiscus (*Hibiscus rosa-sinensis*)
Chinese holly (*Ilex cornuta*)
Chinese photinia (*Photinia serrulata*)
Chinese lilac (*Syringa chinensis*)
Chinese witch hazel (*Hamamelis mollis*)
Cinquefoil (*Potentilla fruticosa*)
Common boxwood (*Buxus sempervirens*)
Common camellia (*Camellia japonica*)
Common juniper (*Juniperus communis*)
Common lilac (*Syringa vulgaris*)
Common privet (*Ligustrum vulgare*)
Common white jasmine (*Jasminum officinale*)
Cornelian cherry (*Cornus mas*)
Cranberry bush (*Viburnum trilobum*)
Cranberry cotoneaster (*Cotoneaster apiculata*)
Crape myrtle (*Lagerstroemia indica*)
Creeping juniper (*Juniperus horizontalis*)
Creeping mahonia (*Mahonia repens*)
Creeping willow (*Salix repens*)
Cut-leaf lilac (*Syringa laciniata*)
Damask rose (*Rosa damascena*)
David viburnum (*Viburnum davidii*)
Dense hypericum (*Hypericum densiflorum*)
Doublefile viburnum (*Viburnum tomentosum*)
Early deutzia (*Deutzia grandiflora*)
Early forsythia (*Forsythia ovata*)
English holly (*Ilex aquifolium*)
European cranberry bush (*Viburnum opulus*)
European red elder (*Sambucus racemosa*)
Evergreen euonymus (*Euonymus japonica*)
Father Hugo rose (*Rose hugonis*)
Flame azalea (*Azalea calendulaceum*)
Flowering currant (*Ribes sanguineum*)
Flowering quince (*Chaenomeles speciosa*)
Fountain buddleia (*Buddleia alternifolia*)
Fragrant daphne (*Daphne odora*)
Fragrant sarcocca (*Sarcococca ruscifolia*)
Fragrant snowball (*Viburnum carlcephalum*)
French pussy willow (*Salix caprea*)
French rose (*Rosa gallica*)
Fringe tree (*Chionanthus virginica*)
Garland spiraea (*Spiraea arguta*)
Glossy abelia (*Abelia grandiflora*)
Glossy privet (*Ligustrum lucidum*)
Hardy orange (*Poncirus trifoliata*)
Heather (*Calluna vulgaris*)
Heavenly bamboo (*Nandina domestica*)
Highbush blueberry (*Vaccinum corymbosum*)
Hills-of-snow (*Hydrangea arborescens* 'Grandiflora')
Himalayan cotoneaster (*Cotoneaster frigida*)
Hobblebush (*Viburnum alnifolium*)
Holly osmanthus (*Osmanthus heterophyllus*)

Hungarian lilac (*Syringa josikaea*)
Indian hawthorn (*Raphiolepis indica*)
Inkberry (*Ilex glabra*)
Inland ceanothus (*Ceanothus ovatus*)
Japanese andromeda (*Pieris japonica*)
Japanese aralia (*Fatsia japonica*)
Japanese barberry (*Berberis thunbergii*)
Japanese beauty-berry (*Callicarpa japonica*)
Japanese boxwood (*Buxus microphylla japonica*)
Japanese holly (*Ilex crenata*)
Japanese pittosporum (*Pittosporum tobira*)
Japanese privet (*Ligustrum japonicum*)
Japanese rose (*Rosa multiflora*)
Japanese skimmia (*Skimmia japonica*)
Japanese snowball (*Viburnum plicatum*)
Japanese snowflower (*Deutzia gracilis*)
Japanese viburnum (*Viburnum japonicum*)
Korean barberry (*Berberis koreana*)
Korean boxwood (*Buxus microphylla koreana*)
Korean white forsythia (*Abeliophyllum distichum*)
Large fothergilla (*Fothergilla major*)
Late lilac (*Syringa villosa*)
Lilac (*Syringa vularis*)
Littleleaf lilac (*Syringa microphylla*)
Locust (*Robinia pseudoacacia*)
Magellan barberry (*Berberis buxifolia*)
Magellan fuchsia (*Fuchsia magellanica*)
Mentor barberry (*Berberis mentorensis*)
Midwinter euonymus (*Euonymus bungeanus semi-persistes*)
Mountain andromeda (*Pieris floribunda*)
Mountain laurel (*Kalmia latifolia*)
Nannyberry (*Viburnum lentago*)
Natal plum (*Carissa grandiflora*)
New Jersey tea (*Ceanothus americanus*)
Oleander (*Nerium oleander*)
Oregon grape (*Mahonia aquifolium*)
Oriental viburnum (*Viburnum wrightii*)
Persian lilac (*Syringa persica*)
Periwinkle (*Vinca minor*)
Pfitzer juniper (*Juniperus chinensis* 'Pfitzeriana')
Pinkster flower (*Azalea nudiflorum*)
Red box cotoneaster (*Cotoneaster rotundifolia*)
Red chokeberry (*Aronia arbutifolia*)
Rhodora (*Rhododendron canadense*)
Rock spray (*Cotoneaster horizontalis*)
Rose acacia (*Robinia hispida*)
Rosebay rhododendron (*Rhododendron maxima*)
Rowan tree (*Sorbus ancuparia*)
Rugosa rose (*Rosa rugosa*)
Russian olive (*Elaeagnus angustifolia*)
Salal (*Gaultheria shallon*)
Sasanqua camellia (*Camellia sasanqua*)
Scarlet firethorn (*Pyracantha coccinea*)
Scentless mock orange (*Philadelphus grandiflora*)
Scotch broom (*Cytisus scoparius*)
Scotch rose (*Rosa spinosissima*)

Shadblow service berry (*Amelanchier canadensis*)
Sheep laurel (*Kalmia angustifolia*)
Shrub althaea (*Hibiscus syriacus*)
Shrubby Saint-Johns-wort (*Hypericum spathulatum*)
Siberian dogwood (*Cornus alba* 'Sibirica')
Siebold viburnum (*Viburnum sieboldii*)
Silverberry elaeagnus (*Elaeagnus pungens*)
Silverleaf cotoneaster (*Cotoneaster pannosa*)
Slender deutzia (*Deutzia gracilis*)
Small-leaf cotoneaster (*Cotoneaster microphylla*)
Smooth sumac (*Rhus glabra*)
Spanish jasmine (*Jasminum grandiflorum*)
Spicebush (*Lindera benzoin* [aestivale])
Spice viburnum (*Viburnum carlesii*)
Spreading cotoneaster (*Cotoneaster divaricata*)
Spring heather (*Erica carnea*)
Spring witch hazel (*Hamamelis vernalis*)
Strawberry bush (*Euonymus americanus*)
Strawberry tree (*Arbutus unedo*)
Surinam cherry (*Eugenia uniflora*)
Summer sweet (*Clethra alnifolia*)
Sweet bay (*Laurus nobilis*)
Sweet mock orange (*Philadelphus coronarius*)
Tatarian honeysuckle (*Lonicera tatarica*)
Tea rose (*Rosa odorata*)
Tender viburnum (*Viburnum dilatatum*)
Thunberg spiraea (*Spiraea thunbergii*)
Torch azalea (*Azalea calendulaceum*)
Veitch spiraea (*Spiraea veitchii*)
Veitch wintergreen (*Gaultheria veitchiana*)
Virginia rose (*Rosa virginiana*)
Warty barberry (*Berberis verruculosa*)
Wayfaring tree (*Viburnum lantana*)
Weeping forsythia (*Forsythia suspensa*)
Winged spindle tree (*Euonymus alata*)
Winterberry (*Ilex verticillata*)
Wintergreen barberry (*Berberis julianae*)
Wintergreen cotoneaster (*Cotoneaster conspicua*)
Winter honeysuckle (*Lonicera fragrantissima*)
Winter jasmine (*Jasminum nudiflorum*)

Perennials

Adam's needle (*Yucca filamentosa*)
Alyssum (*Alyssum saxatile*)
Astilbe (*Astilbe*)
Baby's breath (*Gypsophila paniculata*)
Balloonflower (*Platycodon grandiflorum*)
Basket of gold (*Alyssum saxatile*)
Bearded iris (*Iris*)
Beard tongue (*Penstemon*)
Bee balm (*Monarda didyma*)
Bellflower (*Campanula carpatica*)
Bishop's hat (*Epimedium grandiflorum*)
Blanket flower (*Gaillardia grandiflora*)
Bleeding heart (*Dicentra spectabilis*)
Blue flag (*Iris versicolor*)
Blue flax (*Linum perenne*)

Blue marguerite (*Felicia amelloides*)
Blue salvia (*Salvia patens*)
Bugle (Ajuga)
Bunchberry (*Cornus canadensis*)
Butterfly weed (*Asclepias tuberosa*)
Carpet bugle (*Ajuga reptans*)
Chamomile (*Anthemis nobilis*)
Chinese lantern (*Physalis alkekengi*)
Christmas rose (*Hilleborus niger*)
Cinquefoil (*Potentilla atrosanguinea*)
Common aubrieta (*Aubrieta deltoidea*)
Common periwinkle (*Vinca minor*)
Coneflower (*Rudbeckia hirta*)
Coral bells (*Heuchera sanguinea*)
Cranesbill (*Geranium grandiflorum*)
Creeping speedwell (*Veronica rupestris*)
Crested iris (*Iris cristata*)
Daylily (Hemerocallis)
Dusty miller (*Centaurea gymnocarpa*)
Dwarf basket of gold (*Alyssum saxatile compactum*)
Dwarf columbine (*Aquilegia alpina*)
English daisy (*Bellis perennis*)
Evening primrose (*Oenothera biennis*)
Evergreen candytuft (*Ibiris sempervirens*)
Everlasting pea (*Lathyrus grandiflorus*)
False dragonhead (*Physostegia virginiana*)
Florists' chrysanthemum (*Chrysanthemum morifolium*)
Forget-me-not (*Myosotis sylvatica*)
Four-o'-clock (*Mirabilis jalapa*)
Foxglove (*Digitalis purpurea*)
Fringed wormwood (*Artemisia frigida*)
Gas plant (*Dictamnus albus*)
Gayfeather (*Liatris pycnostachya*)
Geneva bugle (*Ajuga genevensis*)
Geum (*Geum chiloense*)
Giant reed (*Arundo donax*)
Globe thistle (*Echinops exaltatus*)
Golden columbine (*Aquilegia chrysantha*)
Golden marguerite (*Anthemis tinctoria*)
Goldenrod (Solidago)
Gold moss (*Sedum acre*)
Grass pink (*Dianthus plumarius*)
Grecian urn (*Acanthus mollis*)
Harebell (*Campanula rotundifolia*)
Heartleaf bergenia (*Bergenia cordifolia*)
Helen's flower (Helenium)
Heliotrope (*Heliotropium arborescens*)
Hollyhock (*Althaea rosea*)
Horsetail (*Equisetum hyemale*)
Houseleek (*Sempervivum tectorum*)
Indian paintbrush (*Lobelia cardinalis*)
Japanese anemone (*Anemone japonica*)
Japanese iris (*Iris kaempferi*)
Lady Washington geranium (*Pelargonium domesticum*)
Lily-of-the-valley (*Convallaria majalis*)

Loosestrife (Lythrum)
Lupine (*Lupinus polyphyllus*)
Maiden pink (*Dianthus deltoides*)
Marsh marigold (*Caltha palustris*)
Meadow sage (*Salvia paterns*)
Meadowsweet (*Spiraea alba*)
Michaelmas daisy (English aster)
Monkshood (*Aconitum anthora*)
Moss pink (*Phlox subulata*)
Mountain rock cress (*Arabis alpina*)
New England aster (*Aster novae-angliae*)
Orange sunflower (Heliopsis)
Oriental poppy (*Papaver orientale*)
Painted daisy (*Chrysanthemum coccineum*)
Painted daisy (Pyrethrum)
Pansy (*Viola tricolor hortensis*)
Pasque flower (*Anemone pulsatilla*)
Peony (Paeonia)
Perennial pea (*Lathyrus latifolius*)
Pincushion flower (*Scabiosa caucasica*)
Pitcher plant (*Sarracenia purpurea*)
Plantain lily (*Hosta plantaginea grandiflora*)
Poppy-flowered anemone (*Anemone coronaria*)
Prairie windflower (*Anemone pulsatilla*)
Primrose (Primula)
Roof houseleek (*Sempervivum tectorum*)
Rue anemone (*Anemonella thalictroides*)
Running sedum (*Sedum stoloniferum*)
Sand pink (*Dianthus armarius*)
Saint-Johns-wort (*Hypericum*)
Saxifrage (Saxifraga)
Sea lavender (*Limonium latifolium*)
Sea-pink (*Armeria maritima*)
Shasta daisy (*Chrysanthemum maximum*)
Siberian wallflower (*Erysimum asperum*)
Snow-in-summer (*Cerastium tomentosum*)
Solomon's seal (*Polygonatum multiflorum*)
Southernwood (*Artemisia abrotanum*)
Speedwell (Veronica)
Statice (*Limonium latifolium*)
Stock (*Mathiola incana*)
Stonecrop (Sedum)
Summer forget-me-not (*Anchusa capensis*)
Summer phlox (*Phlox paniculata*)
Sunflower (*Helianthus decapetalus multiflorus*)
Swamp milkweed (*Asclepias incarnata*)
Swamp rose mallow (*Hibiscus moschentos*)
Sweet rocket (*Hesperis matronalis*)
Sweet violet (*Viola odorata*)
Sweet William (*Dianthus barbatus*)
Sweet William phlox (*Phlox divaricata*)
Sweet woodruff (*Asperula odorata*)
Thrift (*Armeria maritima*)
Tickseed (*Coreopsis grandiflora*)
Toadflax (*Limaria vulgaris*)
Torch lily (Kniphofia)
True forget-me-not (*Myosotis scorpioides*)

Tufted viola (*Viola cornuta*)
Vesper iris (*Iris dichotoma*)
Virginia bluebell (*Mertensia virginica*)
Wall rock cress (*Arabis caucasica*)
Wax begonia (*Begonia semperflorens*)
Willow gentian (*Gentiana asclepiadea*)
Woodruff (Asperula)
Woolly yarrow (*Achillea tomentosa*)
Wormwood (*Artemesia albula*)
Yarrow (*Achillea ptarmica*)
Yellowflag (*Iris pseudacorus*)

Annuals

African daisy (*Arctotis stoechadifolia grandis*)
African daisy (*Dimorphotheca sinuata*)
African marigold (*Tagetes erecta*)
Annual lupine (*Lupinus hartwegii*)
Annual phlox (*Phlox drummondii*)
Aster (*Callistephus chinensis*)
Baby's breath (*Gypsophila elegans*)
Bachelor's button (*Centaurea cyanus*)
Balsam (*Impatiens balsamina*)
Basket flower (*Centaurea cyanus*)
Bells of Ireland (*Molucella laevis*)
Blue cup flower (*Nierembergia caerulea*)
Blue lace flower (*Trachymene caerulea*)
Browallia (*Browallia americana*)
Butterfly flower (*Schizanthus pinnatus*)
Calendula (*Calendula officinalis*)
California poppy (*Eschscholzia californica*)
Calliopsis (*Coreopsis tinctoria*)
Candytuft (Iberis)
Canterbury bell (*Campanula medium*)
Cape marigold (*Dimorphotheca sinuata*)
China aster (*Callistephus chinensis*)
China pink (*Dianthus chinensis*)
Chinese lantern (*Physalis alkekengi*)
Clarkia (*Clarkia elegans*)
Clockvine (*Thunbergia alata*)
Coleus (*Coleus blumei*)
Coneflower (*Rudbeckia bicolor*)
Cornflower (*Centaurea cyanus*)
Cosmos (*Cosmos bipinnatus*)
Evening primrose (*Oenothera biennis*)
Fairy primrose (*Primula malacoides*)
Farewell-to-spring (*Clarkia amoena*)
Floss flower (*Ageratum houstonianum*)
Flowering tobacco (*Nicotiana alata*)
Four-o'-clock (*Mirabilis jalapa*)
Forget-me-not (*Myosotis sylvatica*)
French marigold (*Tagetes patula*)
Garden nasturtium (*Tropaeolum majus*)
Garden verbena (*Verbena hybrida* [*hortensis*])
Giant-flowered zinnia (*Zinnia elegans*)
Globe-amaranth (*Gomphrena globosa*)
Globe candytuft (*Iberis umbellata*)
Ice plant (*Cryophytum crystallinum*)

Joseph's coat (*Amaranthus tricolor*)
Larkspur (*Delphinium ajacis*)
Lobelia (*Lobelia erinus*)
Love-in-a-mist (*Nigella damascena*)
Love-lies-bleeding (*Amaranthus caudatus*)
Madagascar periwinkle (*Catharanthus roseus*)
Mexican sunflower (*Tithonia rotundifolia*)
Mignonette (*Reseda odorata*)
Morning glory (*Ipomoea purpurea*)
Mountain garland (*Clarkia unguiculata*)
Nasturtium (*Tropaeolum majus*)
Nemesia (*Nemesia strumosa*)
Night-scented stock (*Mathiola bicornis*)
Painted tongue (*Salpiglossis sinuata*)
Pansy (*Viola tricolor hortensis*)
Petunia (Petunia)
Pincushion flower (*Scabiosa atropurpurea*)
Pink (Dianthus)
Plume cockscomb (*Celosia plumosa*)
Pot marigold (*Calendula officinalis*)
Princess feather (*Polygonum orientale*)
Purple ragwort (*Senecio elegans*)
Rocket candytuft (*Iberis amara*)
Rose moss (*Portulaca grandiflora*)
Rose-ring gaillardia (*Gaillardia pulchella*)
Royal sweet sultan (*Centaurea imperialis*)
Scarlet flax (*Linum grandiflorum* 'Rubrum')
Scarlet sage (*Salvia splendens*)
Sea lavender (*Limonium bonduellii*)
Shirley poppy (*Papaver rhoeas*)
Small-flowered zinnia (*Zinnia elegans*)
Snapdragon (*Antirrhinum majus*)
Snow-on-the-mountain (*Euphorbia marginata*)
Statice (*Limonium bonduellii*)
Stock (*Mathiola incana*)
Strawflower (*Helichrysum bracteatum*)
Summer forget-me-not (*Anchusa capensis*)
Sunflower (*Helianthus annuus*)
Swan River daisy (*Brachycome iberidifolia*)
Sweet alyssum (*Lobularia maritima*)
Sweet pea, winter (*Lathyrus odoratus*)
Sweet pea, summer (*Lathyrus odoratus*)
Sweet sultan (*Centaurea moschata*)
Sweet William (*Dianthus barbatus*)
Touch-me-not (*Impatiens balsamina*)
Transvaal daisy (*Gerbera jamesonii*)
Tulip poppy (*Papaver glaucum*)
Wax begonia (*Begonia semperflorens*)

Vines

American bittersweet (*Celastrus scandens*)
Blueberry climber (*Ampelopsis breviped-unculata*)
Burmese honeysuckle (*Lonicera hildebrandiana*)
Carolina jessamine (*Gelsemium sempervirens*)
Cat's-claw (*Doxantha unguis-cati*)
Chilean jasmine (*Mandevilla suaveolens*)
Climbing hydrangea (*Hydrangea petiolaris*)

Common allamanda (*Allamanda cathartica*)
Convolvulvus (*Ipomoea purpurea*)
Coral vine (*Antigonon leptopus*)
Creeping fig (*Ficus pumila* [*repens*])
Cross vine (Clystoma) (*Bignonia capreolata*)
Dutchman's-pipe (*Aristolochia durior*)
English ivy (*Hedera helix*)
Evergreen clematis (*Clematis armandi*)
Five-leaf akebia (*Akebia quinata*)
Glory grape (*Vitis coignetiae*)
Hall's honeysuckle (*Lonicera japonica* 'Halliana')
Horse brier (*Smilax rotundifolia*)
Japanese wisteria (*Wisteria floribunda*)
Kudzo vine (*Pueraria thunbergiana*)
Morning glory (*Ipomoea purpurea*)
Passion flower (*Passiflora caerulea*)
Plumbago (*Plumbago capensis*)
Porcelain ampelopsis (*Ampelopsis breviped-
    unculata*)
Rambler rose (Rosa)
Scarlet kadsura (*Kadsura japonica*)
Scarlet runner bean (*Phaseolus coccineus*)
Star jasmine (*Trachelospermum jasminoides*)
Sweet honeysuckle (*Lonicera caprifolium*)
Trumpet vine (*Bignonia capreolata*)
Virginia creeper (*Parthenocissus quinquefolia*)
White jasmine (*Jasminum officinale*)
Wintercreeper (*Euonymus fortunei*)
Winter jasmine (*Jasminum nudiflorum*)

Bulbs

Amaryllis (Hippeastrum)
Brodiaea (Brodiaea)
Buttercup (Ranunculus)
Butterfly lily (Hedychium)
Clivia (*Clivia miniata*)
Common calla (*Zantedeschia aethiopica*)
Crocus (*Crocus*)
Dark-eyed Gleditsia (*Acidanthera*)
Fawn lily (*Erythronium californicum*)
Glory lily (*Gloriosa rothschildiana*)
Glory of snow (Chionodoxa)
Grape hyacinth (Muscari)
Guernsey lily (*Nerine sarniensis*)
Guinea-hen flower (*Fritillaria meleagris*)
Hyacinth (*Hyacinthus*)
Jacobean lily (*Sprekelia formosissima*)
Lily (Lilium)
Lily-of-the-Nile (*Agapanthus africanus*)
Lily-of-the-valley (*Convallaria majalis*)
Mariposa lily (Calochortus)
Pineapple flower (*Eucomis comosa*)
Rainbow flower (Achimenes)
Shooting star (*Cyclamen neapolitanum*)
Snowdrop (Galanthus)
Snowflake (Leucojum)
Spring beauty (Claytonia)

Squill (Scilla)
Star-of-Bethlehem (*Ornithogalum umbellatum*)
Taro (*Colocasia esculenta*)
Tiger flower (*Tigridia pavonia*)
Tulip (Tulipa)
Wand flower (Sparaxis)
Winter aconite (Eranthis)

House Plants

African violet (*Saintpaulia ionantha*)
Amazon lily (*Eucharis grandiflora*)
Australian umbrella tree (*Schefflera actinophylla*)
Bamboo palm (*Chamaedorea elegans bella*)
Bellflower (Campanula)
Bird's-nest fern (*Asplenium nidus*)
Boston fern (*Nephrolepsis exaltata bostoniensis*)
Burro's tail (*Sedum morganianum*)
Camellia (Camellia)
Cape primrose (*Streptocarpus rexii*)
Cast-iron plant (*Aspidistra elatior*)
Century plant (*Agave americana*)
Ceriman (*Monstera deliciosa*)
Christmas cactus (*Zygocactus truncatus*)
Cinnamon orchid (*Lycaste aromatica*)
Common polypody (*Polypodium vulgare*)
Crown cactus (*Rebutia miniscula*)
Date palm (*Phoenix canariensis*)
Decorator plant (*Dracaena marginata*)
Dumb cane (*Dieffenbachia seguine*)
Easter cactus (*Schlumbergera gaertneri*)
Emerald fern (*Asparagus sprengeri*)
English ivy (*Hedera helix*)
False aralia (*Dizygotheca elegantissima*)
Fiddle-leaf fig (*Ficus lyrata*)
Fiddle-leaf philodendron (*Philodendron
    panduraeforme*)
Fishtail palm (*Caryota mitis*)
Flamingo flower (*Anthurium scherzerianum*)
Flowering maple (*Abutilon hybridum*)
Grape ivy (*Cissus rhombifolia*)
Hart's-tongue (*Phyllitis scolopendrium*)
Heartleaf philodendron (*Philodendron cordatum*)
Holly fern (Polystichum)
Ivy (*Hedera helix*)
Ivy-arum (*Scindapsus aureus*)
Jude plant (*Crassula argentea*)
Lady palm (*Rhapis excelsa*)
Lady's slipper (*Paphiopedilum*)
Lipstick vine (*Aeschynanthus lobbianum*)
Maidenhair fern (*Adiantum hispidulum*)
Mexican love vine (*Dipladenia amoena*)
Moth orchid (*Phalaenopsis amabilis*)
Norfolk Island pine (*Araucaria excelsa*)
Paradise palm (*Howea forsteriana*)
Peanut cactus (*Chamaecereus silvestri*)
Pickaback plant (*Tolmiea menziesii*)
Pothos (*Scindapsus aureus*)

Powder puff cactus (*Mammillaria bocasana*)
Rainbow cactus (*Echinocereus rigidissimus*)
Rubber plant (*Ficus elastica*)
Scarlet ball (*Notocactus haselbergii*)
Screw-pine plant (*Pandanus veitchii*)
Shrimp plant (*Beloperone guttata*)
Spanish shawl (*Schizocentron elegans*)
Spider-plant (*Chlorophytum elatum*)
Staghorn fern (*Platycerium bifurcatum*)
Star cactus (*Astrophytum ornatum*)

Strawberry geranium (*Saxifraga sarmentosa*)
Swiss-cheese plant (*Monstera deliciosa*)
Sword brake (*Pteris ensiformus*)
Sword fern (*Nephrolepis exaltata*)
Sword philodendron (*Philodendron hastatum*)
Syragus palm (*Cocos weddelliana*)
Wandering Jew (*Tradescantia fluminensis*)
Wax begonia (*Begonia semperflorens*)
Window palm (*Reinhardtia gracilis var. gracilior*)
Woolly torch (*Cephalocereus palmeri*)

Appendixes

State Agricultural Extension Services

Alabama	Alabama Polytechnic Institute, Auburn
Alaska	University of Alaska, College
Arizona	University of Arizona, Tucson
Arkansas	College of Agriculture, University of Arkansas, Fayetteville
California	College of Agriculture, University of California, Berkeley
Colorado	Colorado State University, Fort Collins
Connecticut	College of Agriculture, University of Connecticut, Storrs
	Connecticut Agricultural Experiment Station, New Haven
Delaware	School of Agriculture, University of Delaware, Newark
Florida	University of Florida, Gainesville
Georgia	College of Agriculture, University of Georgia, Athens
Hawaii	University of Hawaii, Honolulu
Idaho	University of Idaho, Moscow
Illinois	College of Agriculture, University of Illinois, Urbana
Indiana	Purdue University, Lafayette
Iowa	Iowa State College of Agriculture, Ames
Kansas	Kansas State College of Agriculture, Manhattan
Kentucky	College of Agriculture, University of Kentucky, Lexington
Louisiana	Agricultural College, Louisiana State University, Baton Rouge
Maine	College of Agriculture, University of Maine, Orono
Maryland	University of Maryland, College Park
Massachusetts	College of Agriculture, University of Massachusetts, Amherst
Michigan	College of Agriculture, Michigan State University, East Lansing
Minnesota	Institute of Agriculture, University of Minnesota, St. Paul
Mississippi	Mississippi State College, State College
Missouri	College of Agriculture, University of Missouri, Columbia
Montana	Montana State College, Bozeman
Nebraska	College of Agriculture, University of Nebraska, Lincoln
Nevada	College of Agriculture, University of Nevada, Reno
New Hampshire	University of New Hampshire, Durham
New Jersey	Rutgers University, New Brunswick
New Mexico	College of Agriculture, State College
New York	College of Agriculture, Cornell University, Ithaca
North Carolina	State College of Agriculture, University of North Carolina, Raleigh
North Dakota	State Agricultural College, Fargo
Ohio	College of Agriculture, Ohio State University, Columbus
Oklahoma	Oklahoma A. and M. College, Stillwater
Oregon	Oregon State College, Corvallis
Pennsylvania	Pennsylvania State University, University Park
Puerto Rico	University of Puerto Rico, Box 607, Rio Piedras
Rhode Island	University of Rhode Island, Kingston
South Carolina	Clemson Agricultural College, Clemson
Tennessee	College of Agriculture, University of Tennessee, Knoxville
Texas	Texas A. and M. College, College Station
Utah	College of Agriculture, Utah State University, Logan
Vermont	State Agricultural College, University of Vermont, Burlington
Virginia	Virginia Polytechnic Institute, Blacksburg
Washington	State College of Washington, Pullman
West Virginia	West Virginia University, Morgantown
Wisconsin	College of Agriculture, University of Wisconsin, Madison
Wyoming	College of Agriculture, University of Wyoming, Laramie

Gardens and Conservatories

Bellingrath Gardens
Mobile, Ala.

Armstrong Nurseries
Ontario, Calif.

Berkeley Rose Gardens
Berkeley, Calif.

Ferry Morse Seed Co.
Salinas, Calif.

Golden Gate Park Conservatory
San Francisco, Calif.

Henry E. Huntington Library Gardens
San Marino, Calif.

Melrose Iris Gardens
Modesto, Calif.

San Simeon
San Simeon, Calif.

Strybing Arboretum
San Francisco, Calif.

Sunset Magazine Gardens
Menlo Park, Calif.

Winterthur Museum & Gardens
Wilmington, Del.

Fairchild Gardens
Coconut Grove, Fla.

Florida Cypress Gardens
Winter Haven, Fla.

Dunaway Gardens
Newman, Ga.

George K. Ball Trial Grounds
West Chicago, Ill.

Humboldt Park
Chicago, Ill.

Lincoln Park Conservatory
Chicago, Ill.

Morton Arboretum
Lisle, Ill.

Jaenicke Gardens
Fort Wayne, Ind.

Shawnee Park
Louisville, Ky.

City Park
New Orleans, La.

Sherwood Gardens
Baltimore, Md.

Arnold Arboretum of Harvard
Jamaica Plains, Mass.

Gardens of Cranbrook
Bloomfield Hills, Mich.

Missouri Botanic Gardens
St. Louis, Mo.

St. Louis Conservatory
St. Louis, Mo.

Brooklyn Botanic Gardens
Brooklyn, N.Y.

The Cloisters
Fort Tryon Park, New York, N.Y.

The Colonial Garden
Elizabethtown, N.Y.

The Garden of the Museum of
Modern Art
New York, N.Y.

New York Botanical Gardens
Bronx, N.Y.

Sterling Forest Garden
Tuxedo, N.Y.

"Biltmore"
Asheville, N.C.

Daaes Arboretum
Newark, Ohio

Park of Roses
Columbus, Ohio

Hoyt Arboretum
Portland, Ore.

The Hershey Gardens
Hershey, Pa.

Longwood Gardens
Kennett Square, Pa.

Phipps Conservatory
Pittsburgh, Pa.

Magnolia Gardens
Charleston, S.C.

Fort Worth Botanic Gardens
Fort Worth, Tex.

The Gardens of Colonial Williamsburg
Williamsburg, Va.

Bishops Garden
Washington Cathedral, Washington,
D.C.

Dumbarton Oaks
Washington, D.C.

Ohme Gardens
Wenatchee, Wash.

Mitchell Gardens
Milwaukee, Wis.

Sources

The following is a list of suppliers where you can purchase plants. The list is by no means complete and although no endorsement is implied by listings here, I have dealt with the following companies through the years and found them to be reliable, and always willing to answer questions and give information about their plants.

PLANTS FOR THE GARDEN

Burgess Seed & Plant Co., Inc.
67 E. Battle Creek St.
Galesburg, Mich. 49053
Shrubs and trees; perennials, fruit trees, vegetables.

W. Atlee Burpee Co.
Philadelphia, Pa. 19132
Clinton, Iowa 52732
Riverside, Calif. 92502
Shrubs and trees; perennials and annuals, fruit trees, vegetables.

Henry Field Seed & Nursery Co.
Shenandoah, Iowa 91601
Shrubs and trees; vegetables, perennials.

Inter-State Nurseries
Hamburg, Iowa 51640
Shrubs and trees, perennials, vegetables.

Walter Marx Gardens
Boring, Oregon 97009
Perennials.

George W. Park Seed Co.
Greenwood, S.C. 29646
Perennials, annuals, trees and shrubs.

Stark Bros.
Louisiana, Mo. 63353
Trees and shrubs, roses, fruit trees.

Stern Nurseries
Geneva, N.Y. 14456
Trees and shrubs; perennials.

Wayside Gardens
Mentor, Ohio 44060
Shrubs and trees; perennials and annuals.

White Flower Farm
Litchfield, Conn. 06759
Perennials and annuals.

Bulbs, Corms, Tubers

P. DeJager & Sons, Inc.
188 Asbury St.
S. Hamilton, Mass. 01982

John Scheepers, Inc.
63 Wall St.
New York, N.Y. 10005

Roses

Armstrong Nurseries
Ontario, Calif. 91764

Jackson & Perkins Co.
Newark, N.Y. 14513
Medford, Oregon 97501

Star Roses
West Grove, Pa. 19390

Iris

Cooley Gardens
Silverton, Oregon 97381

Gilbert H. Wild & Sons
Sarcoxie, Miss. 64862

Indoor Plants

Alberts & Merkel Bros., Inc.
P.O. Box 537
Boynton Beach, Fla. 33435

Logees Greenhouses
55 North St.
Danielson, Conn. 06239

Merry Gardens
Camden, Maine 04843

Water Plants

Some water plants are available at local nurseries in early spring. The majority of them, however—water lilies and lotus in many varieties—are best ordered from suppliers specializing in these plants. These companies offer handsome color catalogs; write for them. It is the best way to select plants of your preference.

S. Scherer & Sons   *Water lilies.*
Waterside Rd.
Northport, N.Y. 11768

Michigan Bulb Co.   *Water lilies and supplies.*
Grand Rapids, Mich. 49502

Three Springs Fisheries   *Catalog available;*
120 Main Road   *excellent source for*
Lilypons, Md. 21717   *water lilies and supplies.*

William Tricker Inc.   *Catalog available; water*
Box 398   *lilies and other aquatic*
Saddle River, N. J. 07458 *plants. Supplies.*
or
Box 7845
Independence, Ohio 44131

Van Ness Water Gardens   *Catalog available; a*
2460 North Euclid Avenue   *fine supply of water lilies*
Upland, Calif. 91786   *and other aquatics.*
                           Supplies.

Julius Roehrs Co.
East Rutherford, N.J. 07073

Tinari Greenhouses
2325 Valley Rd.
Bethayres, Pa. 19006

Tropical Paradise Greenhouses
8825 W. 79th. St.
Overland Pk., Kans. 66200

Orchids

Hauserman Orchids
Box 363
Elmhurst, Ill. 60218

Margaret Ilgenfritz Orchids
Monroe, Mich. 48161

Jones & Scully, Inc.
2200 N.W. 33rd. Ave.
Miami, Fla. 33142

Gesneriads

Fischers Greenhouses
Linwood, N.J. 08221

Lyndon Lyon
14 Mutchler St.
Dolgeville, N.Y. 13329

POOLS, FOUNTAINS, ORNAMENTS, STATUARY

Many containers for pools are at local nurseries and garden centers. Mail order suppliers also furnish pools, fountains, and statuary. Write for catalogs.

Aldocraft Co.
210 Fifth Ave.
New York, N.Y. 10010

Aqualite Pool Co.   *Molded pools.*
430 Bedford St.
Whitman, Mass. 02382

Florentine Craftsmen, Inc.
654 First Ave.
New York, N.Y. 10016

Kenneth Lynch & Sons   *Excellent source for*
Wilton, Conn. 06897   *fountains and statuary of*
                           all kinds.

Rain Jet Corp.   *Fountain kits.*
301 S. Flower
Burbank, Calif. 91503

Tuscany Studios   *Statuary of all kinds.*
548 North Wells St.
Chicago, Ill. 60610

OUTDOOR LIGHT FIXTURES

Halo Lighting Division   Loran, Inc.
McGraw Edison Co.   P.O. Box 911
9301 West Bryn Mawr Ave.   Redlands, Calif. 92373
Rosemont, Ill. 60018

Lightolier Corp.   Shalda Lighting Products, Inc.
346 So. Claremont   P.O. Box 507
Jersey City, N.J.   Burbank, Calif. 91503

Plant Societies

These societies offer special information about specific plants; generally, they issue newsletters or bulletins that cannot be purchased at newsstands. The organizations will also answer your questions about your favorite plants. The following are national headquarters of these societies; most have local chapters in large cities.

African Violet Society of America, Inc.
Mrs. Robert Wright
P.O. Box 1326
Knoxville, Tenn.

American Begonia Society
Mrs. Margaret B. Taylor
111 Evelyn Drive
Anaheim, Calif.

American Camellia Society
Mr. Joseph H. Pyron
Box 465
Tifton, Ga.

American Daffodil Society
Mrs. Ernest J. Adams
1121 Twelfth Ave.
Huntington, W. Va.

American Dahlia Society
Mr. Edward B. Lloyd
10 Crestmont Rd.
Montclair, N.J.

American Fuchsia Society
California Academy of Science
Golden Gate Park
San Francisco, Calif.

American Gloxinia Society
Miss Diantha Brown
164–20 Highland Ave.
Jamaica, N.Y.

American Iris Society
Mr. Clifford W. Benson
Missouri Botanical Gardens
2237 Tower Grove Rd.
St. Louis, Mo.

American Orchid Society
Mr. Merle Reinikka
Botanical Museum of Harvard University
Cambridge, Mass.

Bromeliad Society Inc.
Miss Victoria Pallida
647 S. Saltair Ave.
Los Angeles, Calif.

Cactus & Succulent Society of America, Inc.
Mr. Scott Haselton
132 West Union St.
Pasadena, Calif.

Indoor Light Gardening Society of America, Inc.
Mrs. Fred D. Peden
4 Wildwood Rd.
Greenville, S.C.

Glossary

Annual—Plant that completes its life cycle in one season.

Biennial—Plant that requires two seasons to complete its life cycle; sometimes grown as an annual.

Broadcast—To scatter seeds rather than to sow them in rows.

Cambium—Layer of cells between bark and wood of some trees.

Chlorophyll—Green coloring matter of plants.

Coniferous—A tree that bears woody cones containing naked seeds.

Cutting—A piece—leaf, stem, or root—cut from a living plant for propagation use.

Damping-off—Decaying of stems of seedlings caused by fungi.

Deciduous—Plants that drop their leaves annually.

Dormant—The period when a plant makes no active visible growth.

Ecology—The study of the relationship between living organisms and their total environment.

Epiphyte—A plant growing on an elevated support, such as a tree.

Erosion—Washing away of sand or rock.

Flats—Shallow boxes used for young plants.

Forcing—A process of hastening the development of plants with heat.

Germination—The start of growth.

Grafting—A process by which one part of a plant is made to unite with another.

Habitat—The area where a plant is found growing wild.

Hardening-off—The process of reducing the amount of water and lowering temperature in order to toughen plants to withstand colder conditions.

Hardy—Frost-tolerant plant that can live over winter without protection.

Inorganic—Matter other than that of vegetable or animal origin.

Leaching—The loss of soluble fertilizers from the soil.

Mulch—A material spread on ground that covers soil to keep it moist or cool.

Organic—Relating to or derived from living organisms.

pH—A term that represents the hydrogen content by which scientists measure soil acidity and alkalinity.

Perennial—A plant that lives from year to year.

Pinching back—Taking off or plucking away the ends of shoots to encourage flower production.

Propagation—The process of increasing or multiplying plants.

Species—Plants possessing one or more distinctive characteristics common to all of them.

Stolon—A runner used to propagate a plant.

Subsoil—A stratum of earth lying directly beneath topsoil.

Succulent—Having leathery or watery tissue.

Sucker—Vegetative growth from the base of a plant.

Top-dressing—A process where soil or compost or fertilizer is used on the surface of the ground and cultivated in the top few inches.

Transplanting—The act of moving seedlings or mature plants from one place to another.

Books for Further Reading

LANDSCAPING AND PLANNING BOOKS

Eckbo, Garrett. *Art of Home Landscaping*. New York: McGraw-Hill, 1956.

Ireys, Alice R. *Plan and Plant Your Own Property*. New York: Barrows, 1967.

Ortloff, H. Stuart, and Henry B. Raymore. *The Book of Landscape Design*. New York: Barrows, 1959.

Pratt, Richard. *Ladies' Home Journal of Landscaping and Outdoor Living*. Philadelphia: Lippincott, 1963.

Stoffel, Robert J. *Do's and Don'ts of Home Landscaping*. New York: Hearthside Press, 1968.

White, J. E. Grant. *Designing a Garden Today*. New York: Abelard-Schuman, 1966.

Zion, Robert L. *Trees and Architecture in the Landscape*. New York: Litton Educational Publishing, Reinhold, 1969.

TREES AND SHRUBS

Bush-Brown, James. *Shrubs and Trees for the Home Landscape*. Philadelphia: Chilton Book Co., 1963.

Clark, Robert B. *Flowering Trees*. New York: Van Nostrand, 1963.

Dietz, Marjorie. *Concise Encyclopedia of Favorite Flowering Shrubs*. Garden City, N.Y.: Doubleday, 1963.

Perkins, Harold O. *Ornamental Trees for Home Grounds*. New York: Dutton, 1965.

Steffek, Edwin F. *Pruning Handbook*. New York: Van Nostrand, 1969.

Wyman, Donald. *Shrubs and Vines for American Gardens*. New York: Macmillan, 1970.

Wyman, Donald. *Trees for American Gardens*. New York: Macmillan, 1969.

Zucker, Isabel. *Flowering Shrubs*. New York: Van Nostrand, 1966.

GENERAL GARDENING BOOKS

Bush-Brown, James, and Louise Bush-Brown. *America's Garden Book*. New York: Scribner, 1958.

Dietz, Marjorie, ed. *Complete Illustrated Book of Garden Magic*. Chicago: Ferguson, Doubleday, 1969.

Editors of *American Home*. *American Home Garden Book*. New York: M. Evans & Co., Lippincott, 1963.

Editors. *Western Garden Book*. Menlo Park, Calif.: Lane Magazine & Book Co., 1969.

Rockwell, F. F., and Esther C. Grayson. *Rockwell's Complete Guide to Successful Gardening*. Garden City, N.Y.: Doubleday, 1965.

Seymour, E. *Wise Garden Encyclopedia*. New York: Grosset & Dunlap, 1970.

Snyder, Rachel. *Complete Book of Gardening*. New York: Van Nostrand, 1965.

Taylor, Norman. *Taylor's Encyclopedia of Gardening*. Boston: Houghton Mifflin, 1961.

REGIONAL BOOKS

Hume, Harold. *Gardening in the Lower South*. New York: Macmillan, 1954.

Schuler, Stanley. *Gardening in the East*. New York: Macmillan, 1969.

PERENNIALS AND ANNUALS

Cumming, Roderick W., and Robert E. Lee. *Contemporary Perennials*. New York: Macmillan, 1950.

Nehrling, Arno, and Irene Nehrling. *Picture Book of Perennials*. New York: Hearthside Press, 1964.

Rockwell, F. F., and Esther C. Grayson. *The Complete Book of Annuals*. Garden City, N.Y.: Doubleday, 1955.

Sunset Editorial Staff. *How to Grow and Use Annuals*. Menlo Park, Calif.: Lane Magazine & Book Co., 1967.

Wilson, Helen Van Pelt. *New Perennials Preferred*. New York: Barrows, 1961.

VINES AND GROUND COVERS, LAWNS

Brilmayer, Bernice. *All About Vines and Hanging Plants*. Garden City, N.Y.: Doubleday, 1962.

Carleton, Milton. *Your Lawn*. New York: Van Nostrand, 1959.

Foley, Daniel J. *Ground Covers*. Philadelphia: Chilton Book Co., 1961.

Howard, Frances. *Landscaping with Vines*. New York: Macmillan, 1959.

Schery, Robert W. *The Lawn Book*. New York: Macmillan, 1961.

Wyman, Donald. *Ground Cover Plants*. New York: Macmillan, 1956.

BULBS

Rockwell, F. F., and Esther C. Grayson. *Complete Book of Bulbs*. Garden City, N.Y.: Doubleday, 1953.

Wister, Gertrude S. *Hardy Garden Bulbs*. New York: Dutton, 1964.

LILIES

De Graff, Jan, and Edward Hyams. *Lilies*. New York: Funk & Wagnalls, 1968.

Rockwell, F. F., and Esther C. Grayson, with Jan de Graff. *The Complete Book of Lilies*. Garden City, N.Y.: Doubleday, 1961.

VEGETABLES AND FRUITS

Clarke, J. Harold. *Small Fruits for Your Garden*. Garden City, N.Y.: Doubleday, 1958.

Kraft, Ken, and Pat Kraft. *Fruits for the Home Garden*. New York: Morrow, 1969.

WATER GARDENING

Bartrum, John. *Water in the Garden*. London: W. C. John Gifford, Ltd. 1968.

Thomas, G. L. *Garden Pools, Water Lilies and Goldfish*. New York: Van Nostrand, 1958.

DISEASE AND PESTS

Pyenson, Louis. *Keep Your Garden Healthy*. New York: Dutton, 1964.

Westcott, Cynthia. *The Gardener's Bug Book*. Garden City, N.Y.: Doubleday, 1956.

PLANT PROPAGATION

Free, Montague. *Plant Propagation in Pictures*. Garden City, N.Y.: Doubleday, 1957.

Haring, Elds. *Complete Book of Growing Plants from Seeds*. New York: Hawthorn Books, 1968.

ORGANIC GARDENING

Hunter, Beatrice Trum. *Gardening Without Poisons*. Boston: Houghton Mifflin, 1964.

Staff of *Organic Garden Magazine. Encyclopedia of Organic Gardening*. Emmaus, Pa.: Rodale Books, 1969.

Tyler, Hamilton. *Organic Gardening Without Poisons*. New York: Van Nostrand Reinhold, 1970.

PATIO GARDENING

Brookes, John. *Room Outside*. New York: Viking Press, 1970.

Kramer, J. *Complete Book of Patio Gardening*. New York: Putnam, 1970.

Smith, Alice Upman. *Patios, Terraces, Decks and Roof Gardens*. New York: Hawthorn Books, 1970

CONTAINER GARDENING

Kramer, J. *Container Gardening: Indoors and Out*. Garden City, N.Y.: Doubleday, 1971.

Taloumis, George. *Outdoor Gardening in Pots and Boxes*. New York: Van Nostrand, 1962.

Teuscher, Henry. *Window-Box Gardening*. New York: Macmillan, 1956.

CITY GARDENING

Brett, William S., and J. E. Grant White. *Small City Gardens*. New York: Abelard-Schuman, 1967.

Truex, Philip. *The City Garden*. New York: Knopf, 1964.

GREENHOUSE GARDENING

Blake, Claire. *Greenhouse Gardening for Fun.* New York: Barrows, 1967.
Potter, Charles H. *Greenhouse, Place of Magic.* New York: Dutton, 1967.

INDOOR GARDENING

Crockett, James Underwood. *Foliage Plants for Indoor Gardens.* Garden City, N.Y.: Doubleday, 1967.

Kramer, J. *1000 House Plants and How to Grow Them.* New York: Barrows, 1969.
McDonald, Elvin. *The World Book of House Plants.* New York: World Publishing, 1963.

ORCHIDS

Hawkes, Alex D. *Orchids, Their Botany and Culture.* New York: Harper & Row, 1961.
Kramer, J. *Growing Orchids at Your Windows.* New York: Van Nostrand, 1963.

Index

Page numbers in **boldface** type refer to illustrations.

71 72 73 74 75 10 9 8 7 6 5 4 3 2 1